Preservation of Paper and Textiles of Historic and Artistic Value II

Preservation of Paper and Textiles of Historic and Artistic Value II

John C. Williams, EDITOR

Library of Congress

Based on a symposium sponsored
by the Cellulose, Paper and
Textile Division at the
178th Meeting of the
American Chemical Society,
Washington, D.C.,
September 10–12, 1979.

ADVANCES IN CHEMISTRY SERIES **193**

AMERICAN CHEMICAL SOCIETY
WASHINGTON, D. C.   1981

8/2/25

Library of Congress CIP Data

Preservation of paper and textiles of historic and artistic value II.
(Advances in chemistry series; 193)

Includes bibliographical references and index.

1. Books—Conservation and restoration—Congresses.
2. Paper—Preservation—Congresses. 3. Textile fabrics
—Conservation and restoration—Congresses.
I. Williams, John Covington, 1911–   . II. Ameri-
can Chemical Society. Cellulose, Paper, and Textile
Division. III. Series.

QD1.A355   no. 193   [Z701]   025.8'4   81–46
ISBN 0–8412–0553–1   ADCSAJ   1–355 1981

Advances in Chemistry Series

M. Joan Comstock, *Series Editor*

FOREWORD

ADVANCES IN CHEMISTRY SERIES was founded in 1949 by the American Chemical Society as an outlet for symposia and collections of data in special areas of topical interest that could not be accommodated in the Society's journals. It provides a medium for symposia that would otherwise be fragmented, their papers distributed among several journals or not published at all. Papers are reviewed critically according to ACS editorial standards and receive the careful attention and processing characteristic of ACS publications. Volumes in the ADVANCES IN CHEMISTRY SERIES maintain the integrity of the symposia on which they are based; however, verbatim reproductions of previously published papers are not accepted. Papers may include reports of research as well as reviews since symposia may embrace both types of presentation.

CONTENTS

Preface ix

PAPER

1. A National Preservation Effort: Hopes and Realities 3
   N. J. Shaffer

2. Archival Methods of Treatment for Library Documents 13
   P. Waters

3. Regional Conservation: A New England Example 25
   A. Russell

4. Paper Conservation in Spain 33
   J. P. McCleary

5. Permanence/Durability and Preservation Research at the Barrow
   Laboratory 45
   D. D. Roberson

6. Watermarks and What They Can Tell Us 57
   T. L. Gravell

7. Washing and Deacidifying Paper in the Same Operation 63
   L. C. Tang

8. The Effect of Magnesium Bicarbonate Solutions on Various Papers 87
   W. K. Wilson, R. A. Golding, R. H. McClaren, and J. L. Gear

9. Inhibition of Light Sensitivity of Papers Treated with Diethyl Zinc 109
   G. B. Kelly, Jr. and J. C. Williams

10. Yellowing of Modern Papers 119
    D. N.-S. Hon

11. Determination of Trace Elements in Paper by Energy Dispersive
    X-Ray Fluorescence 143
    V. F. Hanson

12. The Crystallinity of Cellulosic Fibers: Dependence on History and
    Influence on Properties 169
    R. H. Atalla

13. The Application of Several Empirical Equations to Describe the
    Change of Properties of Paper on Accelerated Aging 177
    G. D. Mendenhall, G. B. Kelly, and J. C. Williams

14. A Kinetic Study of the Influence of Acidity on the Accelerated
    Aging of Paper 189
    J. S. Arney and A. H. Chapdelaine

15. The Effect of Humectant and Wet Strength Resin on the Folding
Endurance of Alkalized Paper 205
J. C. Williams

16. The Effects of Varying Relative Humidity Conditions on the
Folding Endurance of Aged Paper Samples 217
A. C. Sclawy

17. Methods for Enhancing Ultraviolet and Radiation Grafting of
Monomers to Cellulose and Derivatives to Improve Properties of
Value to Conservation 223
N. P. Davis, J. L. Garnett, M. A. Long, G. Major, and K. J. Nicol

18. The Impact of Increasing Paper Consumption and Resource
Limitations on Alkaline Papermaking 241
R. W. Hagemeyer

TEXTILES

19. Textile Conservation for Period Room Settings in Museums and
Historic Houses 253
M. Fikioris

20. Color Conservation Problems of an Early Twentieth Century
Historic Dress 275
E. D. Adams Wilson

21. Dye Analysis of a Group of Late Intermediate Period Textiles
from Ica, Peru 291
M. E. Geiss-Mooney and H. L. Needles

22. Protection of Light-Sensitive Blue Wool Fabric with Cellulose
Acetate Films Containing Ultraviolet Stabilizers 301
T. L. Vigo and N. E. Wyatt

23. Reinforcing Degraded Textiles: Some New Approaches to the
Application of Consolidants 315
J. K. Hutchins, S. P. Hersh, P. A. Tucker, D. M. McElwain,
and N. Kerr

24. Assessing the Effects of Pesticidal Chemicals on Historic Textiles .. 333
S. M. Spivak, J. Worth, and F. E. Wood

Index 345

PREFACE

Conservators work in an interesting field of art and science interwoven, repairing the havoc created in artifacts by time, by molds, by insects, by polluted atmospheres, and by people. Some of their most difficult problems are those that were created by conservators of earlier times who used irreversible techniques, overly strong adhesives, and aggressive bleaches.

Symposia, such as the one reported in this volume, give scientists and conservators the opportunity to meet and communicate. Scientists need to be educated in the problems facing conservators. Conservators should learn where science can assist and where it cannot. The problems of conservation can be quite difficult and may take years to solve or may be unsolvable. The permanence of paper dropped abysmally, starting around 1850. The reasons for this drop were researched for one hundred years before the answers were found. Another several years passed before it was demonstrated that sized permanent paper could indeed be made on the paper machine. Permanent paper can actually be manufactured more economically than the impermanent variety. There is less attack on the machinery of the plant, and the plant effluent is cleaner. Yet papermakers continue to produce the inferior product. Our libraries and archives must still accept short-lived acid paper to add to their already overflowing collections of brittle books.

The problem of mass vapor-phase methods for the deacidification of books or textiles has received a great deal of attention in the last few years. Such treatments are best applied to current books in which the paper is still strong. Rebuilding strength into textiles or books by a vapor-phase treatment is eminently desirable. Both problems are discussed in this volume. When solved, the processes will probably be carried out in special plants by chemists rather than by conservators.

On the other hand, there are many operations in conservation, used by conservators, that have been studied by chemists for years, such as bleaching, washing, and adhering. The correct procedures should be presented to conservators in relatively nontechnical language. There is a need for a text written along these lines.

Conversely, conservators have information of value to scientists working in the field of permanence. William Wilson, one of the contributors to this volume, points out that:

Conservators have at their disposal a large body of practical information, some of which has been written down, but is fragmented and not always easy to find.

If this information were written down by a committee in the form of recommended procedures, under the umbrella of ASTM, a giant step in effective communciation should occur.

Scientists who are working, or planning to work, on long-term stability of materials should visit museums, archives and libraries, and invite comments and observations of personnel responsible for maintaining the viability of collections. This represents a gold mine of information that has been largely overlooked.

The desirable communication between conservators and scientists has occurred in our two symposia and in the two volumes which have resulted. Hopefully, the meetings and collaboration will continue.

My thanks to Mr. Norman Shaffer of the Preservation Office of the Library of Congress for his encouragement and support of this project.

JOHN C. WILLIAMS
Library of Congress
Washington, DC
January, 1980.

PAPER

A National Preservation Effort

Hopes and Realities

NORMAN J. SHAFFER

Preservation Office, Library of Congress, 10 First Street, SE, TJB G-1008, Washington, DC 20540

The size and complexity of preservation problems facing research libraries call for institutional cooperation. In the 1960s, specific needs of a national preservation effort were identified and these needs have remained the bases of discussions up to the present time. Initially, there was an assumption that most of the identified needs would be met and solved at the national level by a centralized agency— most frequently mentioned was the Library of Congress. What, in effect, has developed is a national preservation effort on the part of the Library of Congress that provides both direct and indirect services to the library, archive, and preservation communities. Research and fabrication developments carried out at the Library have contributed to the national effort and will continue to do so in the future, but local and regional planning and cooperation are essential, if a national program is to be realized.

A ny discussion of a national preservation program for library materials must review the documents, concepts, and events that mold our present thinking. Such a program is nebulous in the broad sense, but specific in its component parts. This is attributable partly to the relatively short time the idea of a national preservation program has been a subject of serious discussion and partly to the varied constituencies involved and interested in the preservation of such materials. Librarians, scientists, and conservators relate to such a program in different ways and tend to consider most important those facets of the program most germane to their interests and skills.

While research libraries have a variety of formats and materials requiring preservation, the major and immediate problem is the poor quality of paper upon which much library material has been printed for at least the last 125 years. My purpose is not to recount the successes of paper technology that have brought us to our present plight, but to consider what has been proposed and what is being done to save our written records within a national framework. I shall examine: how this concern came to national library attention; what configurations have been suggested for a national preservation program; and what progress has been made in realizing such an effort.

During the past 125 years, there has been no conspiracy of silence on the poor quality of paper. Most of the protests and calls for change have taken a prospective approach in that publishers, papermakers, and even Congress have been called upon to improve the quality of paper or, at the least, provide for special library editions of selected publications that would be printed on high quality and long-lasting paper. Justin Winsor, associated with the Boston Public Library during the 1860s and 1870s and Librarian of Harvard from 1877–1897, tried to persuade the Boston newspaper publishers to print special editions of their papers on long-lasting stock for library collections. He met with no success (1). The Librarian of Congress, John Russell Young, in his "Annual Report" of 1898 called to the attention of Congress the "questionable quality of the paper upon which so much of the Library material is printed." He went on to note that collections of papers from earlier eras were in excellent condition while modern papers, printed only a few years earlier, already were beginning to show signs of deterioration. He recommended that the copyright law be amended to require that items granted copyright protection be printed on paper of a fixed quality (2). Congress has taken no action on that recommendation to date, although the use of the copyright law to require that a limited number of copies of publications be printed on long-lasting paper is still suggested from time to time. Printing and publishing technology and economics argue against such a solution.

While individuals able to attract national attention continued to speak to the paper problem, a collective voice was still to be heard. Seeking an improvement in newsprint, the American Library Association (ALA) formed a Committee on the Deterioration of Newsprint Paper in 1911 (3). The committee worked with the American Newspaper Publishers' Association in surveying publishers concerning the possibility of special library editions. Some positive responses were received, but when the ALA committee surveyed libraries, they found most were interested only in permanent files of local papers. The committee concluded that special newspaper editions were possible, if libraries were willing to pay for such editions. Perhaps as a result of the consciousness raising of this committee, some all-rag editions did appear in later years. Notable among these was the *New York Times,* which printed an edition of 150–200 copies on all-rag paper from 1927 to 1953; the *Chicago Tribune* printed such an edition from 1928 to 1940; and the *London Times* was available in a rag edition from 1917 until the beginning of World War II.

While librarians had the physical evidence of paper deterioration before them everyday, there was no lack of scientific study of the paper problem. Verner Clapp points out that at least 479 investigative reports and articles relating to paper deterioration were produced between 1885 and 1963 (*4*). If the evidence was available confirming that library materials were deteriorating and would continue to do so at a rapid rate until a better quality paper was used, why were there not more collective protests and actions? Clapp concludes, correctly I believe, that it was a combination of economics, chemical knowledge, and communication (*4*).

The link between the scientific investigation of paper deterioration and the library community was forged in 1957 when the Council on Library Resources began funding research at the William J. Barrow Research Laboratory in Richmond, Virginia. Barrow's revelations concerning the relationship between paper acidity and paper deterioration as well as the possibility of extending the life of acid paper by storing it at cooler temperatures than are normally available in libraries were responsible, at least in part, for the research library community's first substantial proposal for collective action to save deteriorating materials.

The Association of Research Libraries (ARL), which is the collective voice of United States and Canadian research libraries, was alarmed by the findings of the Barrow studies, which concluded that the majority of books printed during the first half of the 20th century would be unusable by the beginning of the next century. Stirred to action, the ARL formed a Committee on the Preservation of Research Library Material in 1960. Assisted by a grant from the Council on Library Resources in 1962, the committee charged one of its members, Gordon Williams, with the task of analyzing the situation and formulating possible solutions. The results of Williams' effort, "The Preservation of Deteriorating Books; An Examination of the Problem with Recommendations for Solutions," was completed in 1964 and adopted by the ARL in January 1965 (*5*). The report's boldness and simplicity have established it as a first source to consult when seeking background on a national preservation program for library materials. During the early deliberations of the committee, the general feeling was that microreproduction was the only solution to preserving the intellectual content of many deteriorating materials. Pointing out that the physical book has many advantages over a microfilm copy and drawing upon the data developed by Barrow concerning the extension of a book's life through cold storage, Gordon Williams dismisses the production of a microform copy of all deteriorating materials as economically unfeasible. Williams calls for the creation of a federally supported central agency that would insure the physical preservation of one copy of every deteriorating book in research libraries for as long as possible. Specifically, the central agency would:

1. undertake the centralized preservation of deteriorating records deposited by libraries;
2. coordinate its own preservation program with local programs of individual libraries to assure that all significant records are preserved while avoiding unwitting duplication;
3. assure the ready availability of microform or full size photocopies of deteriorating materials to all libraries;
4. itself preserve in the interest of textual preservation, economy, and the ready availability of copies, all microform masters made at its expense or deposited by others, and coordinate the preservation of microform masters made by other agencies (5).

This report recognizes the fact that such a central agency would be dependent upon donations from cooperating libraries and that most libraries would not part with "rare books" or materials of great local or institutional interest.

The rare books problem has been a red herring when evaluating the feasibility of a national preservation collection. Because libraries provide better care and protection for rare materials, these works are in less danger of disappearing than the volumes in the general stack areas. The ARL committee's primary concern was and is with the great mass of publications of the last and this century, not the exceptional volume that has been elevated to the status of a "rare book."

The Gordon Williams report led to a joint ARL–LC meeting in December 1965, which resulted in a commitment on the part of the Library of Congress to establish a national preservation program that specifically would include a research laboratory. In 1967, the Library began developing a comprehensive preservation program with the appointment of Frazer G. Poole to head the effort.

It is doubtful that the concept of a "national preservation program" had the same meaning for all parties present at that December 1965 meeting. Obviously, the Williams report brought library preservation concerns to the national level and the report did provide a blueprint. Because of past library community successes in receiving support from the Federal government in coordinating and, more importantly, in funding identified national needs, there was some expectation that events might develop rather rapidly along the lines of ARL report.

On the other hand, in 1967 the Library of Congress had neither a unified nor broad-based preservation program and was in no position to head a national program in either a direct or advisory capacity. The first order of business was to develop the Library's program to care for and conserve the national collections (i.e., the Library's collections). Over the next several years, considerable reorganization and staff growth took place at the Library. True to its commitment, the Library established a research and testing laboratory in 1971 with the assistance of a $70,000 grant from the Council on Library Resources. In the following year, the research program began exploring some of the long-standing problems of paper and book preservation. During the early 1970s, the Library's preservation effort was organized into five offices working under the direction of the Preservation Office. These offices responded to the Library's needs as follows:

1. the Binding Office managed and monitored the Library of Congress commercial binding and rebinding program;
2. the Collections Maintenance Office shifted, moved, and cleaned the collections as necessary;
3. the Preservation Microfilming Office identified and prepared for microfilming those volumes in the general collections found to be deteriorated badly, but worth saving primarily for their informational rather than bibliographical or intrinsic value;
4. the Preservation Research and Testing Office carried out research on long-standing preservation problems and conducted the Library's quality control program on materials being ordered to house and treat the collections; and,
5. the Restoration Office conserved or restored those Library materials warranting such treatment.

The present composition of the Preservation Office differs slightly from the above description in that a recent Library reorganization transferred the functions and personnel of the Collections Maintenance Office to another division. In 1977, a National Preservation Program Office was added to the Preservation Office organizational structure. In addition to those functions directly under the control of the Preservation Office, the Library, beginning in fiscal year 1968, presented a budget that grouped items relating to preservation under a single heading.

With this growth and reorganization, had the Library developed a national preservation program? Yes and no. Yes, in that the Library was coping with the preservation problems of its own collections that belong to the nation. The research and testing carried out in the Preservation Research and Testing Office were accruing to the benefit of all libraries and archives interested in the preservation of their collections. The Library had not developed a national preservation program in the sense that no plans were afoot for a great central repository to accept the last copies of deteriorating titles held by the research library community. The lack of progress in this area no doubt led to some disappointments.

The recent library community experience with centralized cataloging as carried out by the Library might have raised expectations as to what could be done in a relatively short period of time. Centralized cataloging is the concept that recognizes duplicate cataloging as wasteful and holds that a book should be cataloged only once and the catalog data distributed to those libraries acquiring the same book. The Library began meeting this need in a modest way in the early 1900s with the sale of its printed catalog cards. Centralized cataloging began to reach its potential in 1966 when Title II C of the Higher Education Act directed the Library to acquire and catalog "all library materials currently published throughout the world which are of value to scholarship" (6). Various surveys conducted since that time find the Library is meeting about 80% of the research library cataloging information needs.

There is an obvious parallel between cataloging a book once and preserving a book once, but no enabling or directing legislation has yet come about directing the Library to assemble, control bibliographically, and service a national preservation collection. When the Williams report was issued, it was contended generally that libraries would be unwilling to surrender volumes to a national collection. This contention may have been correct at that time, but the situation in the mid 1960s was quite different from that of today. The 1960s and early 1970s were a time of great library building activity and of growing budgets for library materials. The concept of "the bottomless pit" was still very much in vogue in research libraries. The optimism of the 1960s has evaporated in the glare of today's tight budgets, soaring materials costs, and a substantial curtailment of library building. Given these conditions, some collective preservation storage of lesser used materials probably would be welcomed by the research library community.

As the Library of Congress program developed, preservation activities in several research libraries began to grow. The continuing concern of the research library community was evinced by a second ARL report authored by Warren J. Haas in 1972. In "Preparation of Detailed Specifications for a National System for the Preservation of Library Materials," (7) Mr. Haas addressed the problem of library preservation from the vantage point of a library administrator—he was the Director of Columbia University Libraries at the time the report was prepared. Mr. Haas seeks a synthesis of what we can do with what we now know. The state of research and training are summarized briefly and practical recommendations are made concerning basic needs in these fields. Haas notes in the report that an informal survey of research libraries revealed that fewer than twenty libraries in this country were anxious for preservation actions on a massive scale in the near future. Preservation obviously did not have the same appeal as catalog copy. Differing somewhat from the earlier approach outlined by Gordon Williams, Haas calls for both more preservation programs in individual liberties and collective action in the form of a coordinated national preservation collection. The recommendation is made that those libraries most concerned with preservation problems should form a "preservation consortium," and attack those areas of greatest concern. Haas feels that it is "unrealistic to assume that a new and separate national collection devoted exclusively to preservation purposes will be established in the near future. . . . This assumes an institutional altruism that seems overly optimistic" (7). In the face of this assumption, the report calls for a coordinated system of collections that would be designated as parts of a national collection. Libraries holding parts of this collection would agree to store the books under certain minimal conditions and would control the use of these volumes— they would not be available for interlibrary loan.

In December of 1976, the Library of Congress responded to growing preservation concerns by convening a two-day meeting in Washington to discuss a national program. Approximately fifty persons working in the area of preservation or interested in the problem attended.

While the Washington conference broke little new ground, it did serve as an occasion to review developments that had occurred over the previous two decades and to focus on those accumulated preservation needs requiring urgent attention (8). The first day began with a review of the Library of Congress preservation program and then turned to specific aspects of a national preservation program.

Appropriately, Gordon Williams, author of the previously mentioned ARL report on the deterioration of research collections, was the first speaker from outside the Library of Congress. Because of his long interest in preservation and his position as director of the Center for Research Libraries—a cooperative effort to store, acquire, and service lesser used materials that is supported by libraries across the nation—his remarks are of particular interest. Addressing the question as to why so little has been done on a national scale in the light of the evidence developed by the Barrow Laboratory that provided understandable data pointing to a grim future for the majority of library collections, Williams surmised that while research libraries hold thousands of deteriorating volumes, these works fall in the little-used category and have not presented a major inconvenience for patrons. Consequently, library administrators have not been pressured to insure usability of such materials (8). Williams reviewed the economics of a national preservation collection and countered the contention that libraries would be unwilling to give up their collections to a national center. He pointed out that the Center for Research Libraries is a central depository for lesser used and esoteric research materials that have been donated by research libraries.

Other talks on the first day reviewed the state of micrographics technology and how this technology might be applied to format conversion in a national preservation collection. Papers followed on bibliographic support for a national program, and the need for continuing scientific research to solve short- and long-term problems. Dr. Robert Feller, in his paper on the need for scientific support, made a point about basic research and the time lag before results are realized, a time lag of which those of us involved in developing solutions are only too aware. He states, "We don't always know how fast we're going, or even whether we're looking in the right places for the answers" (8). Because library and archive preservation problems have been the subject of little scientific research until recently, we have a great deal of ground cover to develop even tentative answers to pressing preservation questions. Of particular note in the remaining talks delivered on the first day was a presentation by Mr. Paul Banks concerning the training of conservators.

The second day was given over to free-ranging discussions concerning the points raised on the first day. In summary, the Washington Conference identified as preservation needs of greatest priority the concept of a national preservation collection, the continuing need for scientific research, the training of conservators, and the education of library administrators.

Not necessarily as a result of this conference, but following the event, the Library of Congress appointed a National Preservation Program Officer in July 1977. The function of this office is to work with the various Preservation Office heads to develop the advisory and direct services that the Preservation Office can provide. The office also represents the Preservation Office in cooperative preservation projects such as the United States Newspaper Project and will explore theoretical and practical long-term managerial approaches and solutions to national library preservation problems.

Recently, the *Library Journal* began a series of articles on various aspects of preservation that was prefaced with an introduction making the point that what is evolving is a nationwide rather than a national preservation program (9). Instead of a monolithic approach to solving preservation problems in research libraries, institutional, regional, and State programs are forming a mosaic of preservation efforts.

The Library of Congress national preservation program provides both direct and indirect services to the library, archival, and preservation community. Direct services are performed in that members of the Preservation Office respond to invitations to speak on various aspects of preservation, conduct workshops for outside groups, and participate in formal academic conservation and preservation courses. In addition, some limited collection survey work is done and consultations on library and fire disasters are a frequent contribution. The Preservation Office gradually has become a national reference service on preservation problems and responds to all inquiries that are within the office's area of expertise.

The indirect services provided by the Preservation Office may be the greater contribution in the long run. The research and testing conducted by the Research Laboratory have contributed significantly to preservation/conservation knowledge and techniques. After careful materials testing and experimentation with design, some fabrications developed in the Preservation Office have been made available by commercial firms to the public at large.

In the near future, the Preservation Office will be issuing a newsletter entitled, *The National Preservation Report*. The Preservation Office does this in response to a long-felt need and will attempt to provide news of preservation activities to the librarian, archivist, conservator, and scientist.

Much remains to be done in addressing the large problem of saving our research collections. At the Library of Congress, we will concentrate on making better known those services and contributions that we can provide. We cannot carry the responsibility of a national program on our own; we must look to the archival and research library community for commitments and support in realizing some of the long-standing goals of a national program. The Library's role will be to encourage, assist when possible, and coordinate institutional, state, and regional efforts.

Literature Cited

1. Grove, Lee E. "Paper Deterioration—An Old Story," *Coll. Res. Libr.* **1964**, 25, 366–367.
2. U. S. Lib. Cong. "Annual Report," Government Printing Office, Washington, DC, **1898**, 45–46.
3. Grove, L. E. "Paper Deterioration—An Old Story," *Coll. Res. Libr.* **1964**, 25, 370–371.
4. Clapp, V. W. "The Study of Permanent/Durable Book-Paper, 1115–1970," *Restaurator Supplement No. 3*, **1972**, 23.
5. Williams, G. "The Preservation of Deteriorating Books; An Examination of the Problem with Recommendations for a Solution," presented at the *65th Meet. Assoc. Res. Libr., Washington, DC, Jan. 1965*, 10–42.
6. Goodrum, C. A. "The Library of Congress;" Praeger: New York, 1974; p. 211.
7. Haas, W. J. "Preparation of Detailed Specifications for a National System for the Preservation of Library Materials," *U.S. Dept. Health, Educ., Welfare* **1976**, p. 20, No. 0-8004.
8. U.S. Library of Congress document presented at the *Proc. Plan. Conf. Nat. Preserv. Progr. held at Libr. Cong., Washington, DC, Dec. 1976*, pp. 29, 65.
9. Darling, Pamela W. "Towards a Nationwide Preservation Program," *Library Journal* **1979**, (May), 1012.

RECEIVED December 4, 1979.

Archival Methods of Treatment for Library Documents

PETER WATERS

Preservation Office, Library of Congress, Washington, DC 20540

Preserving the great and growing collection of the Library of Congress is a Herculean task. There are numerous techniques available, including silking, lamination, encapsulation, boxing, deacidification, and cold storage. Decisions must be made, often in the face of incomplete evidence, on which treatment(s) to use. What will most extend the life of an artifact? What will the next conservator have to undo that we have done? Every generation of restorers has left problems and created damage that have plagued succeeding generations. Our generation's legacy to the future may be better because of better training for conservators, and the effective and growing collaboration between practicing conservators and conservation scientists. We advocate a conservative approach to conservation. Where we cannot restore completely, we often can stop degradation effectively, hoping thereby to transmit the work to our successors unimpaired and receptive to more advanced techniques that may develop in the future.

As a practicing conservator with over twenty-five years experience in book and paper conservation, I view with approbation the increasing number of young people who are choosing this profession. My colleagues and I welcome the opportunity to train them in the important task of preserving our artistic, literary, and scientific heritage. I find the work and interest of conservation scientists extremely helpful.

At the Library of Congress the responsibility for making decisions on the treatment of important, or not so important, documents is a heavy one—decisions on when and how to treat, or when not to treat, or on when to store and how to store. How are we best to use limited resources of trained personnel and often inadequate budgets? How do we best establish priorities with the custodians of the collections? These are decisions that all conservation staffs are facing.

At the Library of Congress current estimates indicate that for materials presently identified as rare, with permanent research value, complete conservation will require about twelve thousand five hundred man years of work. Other parts of the collections are in equally serious condition (1). However, archival conservation in a library setting diminishes the role of restoration of individual artifacts in favor of carefully selected actions more immediately directed toward the greatest possible prolongation of useful life—hence our philosophy and practice of "phased" preservation. In practice, useful life may be projected as a thousand years or more for some items, or as little as fifty years for others. Thus, in the broadest sense, conservation comprises methods of buying time, of putting off that inevitable day when organic materials are reduced to dust.

Environmental controls and stabilizing treatments can, of course, slow down decay rates, but the rate will be dependent on the condition of the untreated artifact as well as its original makeup and its inherent ability to withstand use, abuse, and unfavorable environmental conditions.

All materials do not age at the same rate. This fact is important for all of us to appreciate—our scientist colleagues, when designing mass preservation treatments, and the conservators, who are charged with responsibility for recommending and carrying out treatments and housing procedures that need to be specific for each category of library and archive material, in keeping with curatorial and/or institutional policy. Any institution's management policy toward preservation is perhaps the most important element in any effort to arrest decay and preserve the kinds of collections that future generations will wish to enjoy and use for research. Without firm direction or a firm preservation philosophy, precious resources may be wasted, as when too much effort is spent on treating small numbers of individual items at the expense of important large bodies of collections for which preservation measures need to be devised.

In addition to a well defined philosophy, library and archive preservation requires very long range planning. What form might a library or archive repository take in fifty to one hundred years time? Will those patterns have to change? Will growth rates permit a rational, orderly preservation effort, or will they be so large as to stultify efforts to produce meaningful programs?

If we are to come to grips with our present preservation problems, massive efforts must be made to reduce the size of collections on a selective basis, to limit growth rates by stricter evaluations, and above all, to define, plan for, and accept realistic lifespans of usefulness on materials to be retained in original format. Policies based on the assumption that all materials must be retained indefinitely will ultimately result in sizable parts of those collections becoming unsalvageable because preservation resources have been spread too thin.

This problem of controlling future growth is one of the greatest challenges in this field. Whether or not this generation is capable of facing up to it remains to be seen. Either we face up to it now or convey to the next generation an inheritance greatly diminished by our failure to make the hard choices.

The state of the art for the conservation of large collections of items can be expressed at the Library of Congress in two words: "phased preservation." This entails better housing for collections, better protection for individual items by use of alkaline folders or mats and boxes, or polyester film folders and encapsulations, and better surveying to establish needs for future treatment. Necessary treatments may then be given orders of priority and scheduled for execution in phases over an appropriate period of time.

We must have an appreciation for the problems of our curator colleagues and work in collaboration with them. We hope they in turn will be concerned for and become knowledgeable in matters of preservation. It is not necessary for either curator or conservator to become a scientist, but understanding the concepts, methods, and language of science will help them both not only to work with scientists but also to know how to ask the right kind of questions or define with precision the particular problems they may wish them to investigate. The more precise the definition of the problem, the more likelihood there is that the questions will lead to answers that can be relevant to actual conservation practice.

The library and archive community has been awaiting anxiously the development of viable systems of mass deacidification, hoping that they could be a major breakthrough in conservation. Strengthening systems also have great appeal to those who believe there may be a miracle cure-all down the road. I am afraid, however, that a great number of librarians may be in for a disappointment. Viable systems certainly are needed and a few may be close to realization, especially for papers of reasonable physical strength, but I am not convinced that brittle material ever can be endowed with a long life expectancy. It is well known that there are millions of items in this state now, let alone those that will be reduced to brittleness if they remain in their present environment.

Since Washington summers are known for high temperature and humidity levels, it might be said that the collections at the Library of Congress have suffered from a natural accelerated aging process. The majority of nineteenth and twentieth century books and unbound items that are brittle in the Library of Congress, and no doubt other collections, became so prior to the gradual installation of general air conditioning, completed in the late 1960s. Since then, the rate of deterioration of all materials is believed to have been slowed.

Thus, the desire for mass deacidification treatment systems must be coupled with the recognition that reduction of temperatures and humidity levels is an equally important and perhaps more effective way of slowing down the rate of deterioration for sensitive material. Just as we have selected areas in libraries for rare book rooms and special storage areas, a modern library should, in my opinion, plan to have large areas for cold storage, not necessarily for general collections, but for collections that are dormant, in low use, but valuable. Many far-sighted librarians, especially Gordon Williams, have recommended such an approach, but curiously little has been done to make it a reality (2). It would be advantageous if library planners and architects could become more sensitive to factors affecting preservation of collections.

Relationships of Historic Technology to Longevity of Paper

The early western papers produced by the scholar printers, such as Jenson in Venice, in the late fifteenth and early sixteenth centuries in many cases have survived in pristine condition. Some of the factors in the longevity of these papers include the high crystallinity of the cellulose molecules in the fibers produced from retted flax and the use of wooden stampers for beating the fibers, which leads to great strength retention and good fibrillation with maximum opacity and density. In the course of their production, these papers apparently absorbed alkaline salts and magnesium and calcium carbonates, probably from natural stream water and the liming of pulps.

Some of these early papers were sized, at least one Italian paper mill, in Pesche, being known to have used a size made from scrapings of parchment skins (split skeepskins) called "fleshings." The adhesive action of the gelatin would have caused a substantial amount of calcium carbonate to be locked around the fibers. Other beneficial features of the manufacture of these papers were that they had no fillers, were sun-bleached, and had few metallic impurities to hasten serious oxidation.

After the invention of the Hollander beater in the late 1600s, metallic impurities (copper and iron) got into the paper pulp by contact with the metal rotary grinders. This type of beater is blamed also for the accelerated decline of quality in papers because its particular beating action shortened the fibers. Another production change reduced the amounts of alkaline earth carbonates present: new forms of gelatin, made from sinew and muscle, did not possess the natural alkalinity of the byproduct of the parchment maker.

One can see evidence throughout fifteenth and sixteenth centuries works of the suspicion that binders had for the new material called paper. Because binders were used to handling vellum-section books, it is perhaps not surprising to see vellum guards used to support the sewing threads in paper-sectioned books. Bookbinders who had produced what we would now call a kind of archival binding, without adhesive in its construction, began to use adhesives in response to increased demand and production. The very strong structures comprising the spines of books gradually began to be reinforced with whole wheat flour paste, later to give way to bookbinding gelatin glues, which have had a disastrous effect on bindings and paper ever since. As reliance on these adhesives grew, the strong sewing structures of earlier centuries unfortunately were retired gradually.

Unbound Materials

As unbound paper materials became damaged and worn by use or weakened by the deterioration resulting from "improved" methods of manufacture, they have been given restorative treatments representing the entire gamut of binder's know-how. For two or three hundred years now, water-soluble adhesives have been used throughout Europe and this country in the strengthening, mending, lining, or mounting of manuscripts, maps and documents, and records of all sorts. Adhesives have ranged over the years from the traditional parchment size to starch and gelatin; gelatin, glycerin, and alum; or numerous variations of these, right down to present-day synthetic formulations.

The water used in adhesives for restoration may have been impure. Cooking pots may have been made of copper, as was the traditional binder's glue pot, or iron. The resulting presence of significant amounts of metallic impurities has contributed to deterioration of the papers through oxidation, in turn leading to high acidity levels and a breakdown of the cellulose chains. The signs of contaminated pastes are usually brown brush marks, overall browning, brittleness, and so-called foxing marks. With these adhesives, restoration of manuscripts was carried out with a selection of papers according to need: matching, if possible, for inserts; thin and strong for edging; transparent for overlays. Goldbeater's skin was also used. Large maps long have been mounted on woven fabrics of linen or cotton.

By the mid nineteenth century, as the weakened condition of the collections of paper materials in major European and American libraries and archives began to attract increased concern, new strengthening methods were developed (3). The most significant of these was silking— the application of a silk gauze to both sides of a document. The process seems to have been adopted first at the National Archives of France, where it is said to have been in use as early as the 1860s (4). It subsequently appeared almost simultaneously in the United States, where a patent was granted in 1896 to Francis W. R. Emery of Taunton, Massachusetts, for a special process using silk or paper and paraffin, and in Italy where silking came into use first in the Vatican Library (5, 6). The famous St. Gall Conference convened in 1898 by Father Franz Ehrle, Prefect of the Vatican Library, to consider manuscript restoration problems and announce the successful development there of a silking technique, was one of the most significant events in the history of archival preservation in the western world (7). While no American is recorded attending the meeting, its proceedings profoundly influenced the choice of restoration techniques practiced in succeeding decades in such institutions as the Library of Congress, whose William Berwick (d. 1920) attained and taught a real mastery of the silking technique (8, 9).

Silking has been used, with variations, in this country and in Europe until recent times. However, it began to fall into disfavor in many sectors in the 1930s as the research efforts of the National Bureau of Standards and of William J. Barrow publicized the qualities of cellulose acetate as the preferred material for the lamination of documents (10, 11). Equipment for cellulose acetate/tissue lamination according to the Barrow system was installed in the Library of Congress Branch of the G.P.O. in 1947 and 1950, receiving heavy use until about 1971, but silking continued to be carried out through the late 1960s.

It may be interesting to note that William Barrow, who opposed silking because of its "limited life expectancy of twenty to thirty years" found that lamination with cellulose acetate was not archival unless the documents were first bathed in alkaline solutions, leaving an alkaline reserve in the paper (12). Why, I wonder, did he not use the same rationale for silking? It appears that all silking was applied without prior deacidification or alkaline washing of manuscripts; that concept was a product of our more scientific age. If those procedures had been carried out, it is possible that the silking technique with high quality fabric might have equalled or surpassed the quality of any current method of lamination. Visually, it is superior to cellulose acetate lamination, and its reversibility is far greater.

In the Library of Congress collections one can find good and bad examples of the two systems, silking and cellulose acetate lamination. One can only conclude, therefore, that in addition to adequate treatment of the papers before lamination, the craftsman's manipulative techniques of application, (and, with silking, pressing and drying) are fundamental to truly archival protection.

In 1973, the Library of Congress Preservation Office initiated the use of polyester film encapsulation as a technique for the conservation of maps, manuscripts, posters, and carefully selected works of art on paper.

This procedure was intended particularly for those paper artifacts that are fragile and brittle. The main reason for this development was the growing body of evidence documenting the continuing (or even increased) degradation associated with the use of adhesives and impregnants. Library holdings of permanent archival or research value urgently needed a type of physical protection that would not contribute to chemical instability or permanently affect their visible appearance in any way and that was instantly reversible. Since that time, polyester film encapsulation now has replaced almost entirely lamination and other support techniques relying on adhesives in this library (13).

The conservation profession (as differentiated from restoration) is still relatively young, not more than about fifty years old. The four major graduate programs in this country for conservation of art and historic artifacts have had considerable success in training conservators to respond to the needs of individual works of art, with paper and objects conservation recently moving up to a place of equal importance with paintings. Even so, despite the learning opportunities of internships, there are still not enough experienced practicing conservators who are able to deal with the large issues in conservation. Furthermore, as long as available training continues to be weighted toward the treatment of single rare artifacts, I am afraid that not very many students will be interested enough to specialize in the conservation of library and archival materials, for which a different point of view is needed. It can be very satisfying, of course, to pull out all the stops in treatment of a single item of great value. Recognition by administrators of libraries and archives of the desperate preservation needs of their collections may lead to more training programs with this specialization. When that happens, and I hope it will, let us not forget that a creative, imaginative approach to problems often develops best when it follows on a mastery of craftsmanship obtainable only by years of practical experience.

Conservation differs from restoration in its greater concern for the structural and artistic integrity of both single items and large collections. Throughout past centuries, restoration has often led to unnecessary and, to later generations at least, undesirable alterations in the historic character of artifacts. Restoration of books and of unbound material was, and often is, an almost totally subjective matter; valuable items have been mistreated, deterioration accelerated, and historical documentation on the original condition of an artifact neither recorded nor preserved. This has been particularly apparent in restoration and rebinding in Europe and America in the past two hundred years. In libraries and archives, prints, drawings, and other works of art on paper, manuscripts and cartographic material have been treated not by specialists with respect for individual problems but by binders of varying degrees of manual skill and often very little sensitivity. Only in the past thirty to forty years has this situation gradually improved. In the United States, a greater sophistication reflects many factors: the leadership of the first conservators and conservation scientists of the Fogg Museum of Harvard University, beginning with George L. Stout and Rutherford J. Gettens; a tremendous growth of interest in art history, in studio arts and crafts, and the historic preservation movement; the dedication of the small band of American art on paper conservators and their dissemination of knowledge of oriental paper techniques; and by the international involvement of binders, restorers, conservators, and scientists in the rescue operations for thousands of rare books and documents damaged in the flood in Florence in 1966.

It now can be said that the need for a more scientific approach by conservators has been recognized and that the specialty of library and archival conservation is perceived increasingly as being on the level of painting and museum artifact conservation in value and complexity. The goal that some of us have been striving for since the mid 1960s has come within our reach.

Of course, a purely scientific approach to conservation problems can be unbalanced too. A good conservator's choice of a specific course of treatment should take into account a variety of considerations based on a very liberal background training. He should have considerable knowledge of how previous treatments on related material have succeeded or failed and of the art historical significance of items involved. In formulating decisions, the conservator should know how to extract relevant information from such diverse sources as provenance data, testing procedures, and scientific literature. Last but not least, he should have achieved an advanced level in master craftsmanship so that mind, eye, hand, and heart can coordinate fully, each attribute informing the others in proper balance. Such individuals are very scarce as yet, but treatment decisions by persons with less extensive background can be inappropriate and sometimes damaging.

Professional paper conservators, as a group, try to discourage all "do-it-yourself" or universal treatments by amateurs. Such a position may seem negative and unhelpful to private owners or to custodians responsible for serving materials to readers. Nevertheless, we cannot condone, for instance, the use of pressure-sensitive tapes for mending anything but expendable material: few are safe for use on paper artifacts, without potential for reaction of the adhesive with the chemical components of the paper artifact, and most will skin the surface of the sheet if removed. Since conservators often spend a high proportion of their time attempting to correct previous restoration procedures or arrest the resulting degradation, they try to work closely with curators in sound planning and budgeting for professional treatment, especially for collections of permanent research value.

Temptation to do-it-yourself, however, is always present; library materials needing repair grow more numerous every day, and at the same time the market offers increasing numbers of tempting proprietary products that are advertised as being of archival quality—as indeed some are. The list includes dry mounting film and tissues, heatset tissues, pressure-sensitive tapes, rag boards (which may be made from cotton and/or wood fiber), storage containers, and nonaqueous deacidification solutions.

Although mending materials are not among them, there are in fact some good, useful products on the market. The intelligent collector or custodian should shop around, ask hard questions, try to avoid being misled, and insist on being supplied with data supporting advertising claims of "archival quality." When in doubt, one should check further with conservation authorities, especially those with experience in independent materials testing, to develop a sound basis on which to defend particular choices.

A hypothetical case history may be useful at this point to demonstrate how a paper conservator comes to a decision on a course of treatment. Let us imagine a lithograph by an important twentieth century artist, printed on poor paper that has become brittle. There are a few stains, the nature of which may or may not be susceptible to nondestructive identification. Analysis of the fiber is made by microscopy and a surface pH reading taken, which confirms a high acidic level and accounts for the embrittlement. The conservator is convinced that the acidity should be neutralized and an alkaline reserve left in the paper substrate to protect it and slow down its rate of deterioration. However, he knows also that these treatments may change the character of both paper support and medium. This is a typical dilemma. Usually, a conservator will decide that the artistic intention is the primary element to conserve. In our hypothetical example, no deacidification is carried out. Attempts may be made to remove or reduce the stains locally in non-design areas. General use of a bleaching solution, a questionable procedure under most circumstances because of the difficulty of its complete removal from the paper, may be considered justifiable because of special circumstances. On the other hand, the paper may be left as it is or it may be washed in quality water to reduce acidity.

Such procedures would be considered to be appropriate, though not necessarily adequate, by most professional conservators. They look forward to a time when all aspects of the preservation needs of an item can be satisfied by safe treatments. So far, conservation scientists have not been able to help with answers for some very serious problems; no research to date, for example, has provided guidelines as to how to prevent slight color changes in paper or media resulting from the application of alkaline solutions to arrest decay of the paper support.

As a consequence of the absence, to date, of scientific assistance with this difficult question, many nineteenth and twentieth century works of art on poor paper are not being deacidified.

Now let us consider the added problems in another hypothetical case history of a color print produced over one hundred years ago. How can the conservator know what changes may have occurred already in the colored design layer? The term "original condition" is used often in art conservation. Is this its condition as the conservator sees it now, as he can prove it to have been earlier, or as he imagines it to have been when first produced? Was any change the result of natural causes or of some earlier treatment? If there is reasonable evidence that natural color changes may have occurred, would treatment slow down these changes, stabilize and return altered colors to original condition, or alter completely their stability, causing dramatic changes in the future? Here again, the conservator is not yet supported by sufficient scientific research. He needs data to demonstrate how treatments designed to arrest degradation in paper supports will affect ultimately any pH-sensitive pigments, dyes, and inks that artists use, and what possible interactions between support and media may be expected. Similar questions exist with regard to unaltered retention of the image in manuscript materials.

Deacidification: How and When to Use It

Deacidification is one of the most controversial subjects presently confronting paper and book conservators. Certain facts are well established: much research into paper deterioration leaves no question of the benefits of reducing or removing harmful acidity by the use of alkaline earth carbonate solutions, particularly when treatment leaves at least one percent alkaline salt in the paper. Paper permanence definitely is improved by deacidification and this is not part of the controversy. What is controversial is its use in the face of unpredictable reactions to alkaline treatments. It is possible that pH-sensitive inks, dyes, and pigments and/or paper characteristics may undergo change in visual effects, and for this reason it can happen that, of two conservators consulted for the same material, one might recommend for and one against such a treatment. Furthermore, there might be enough rationale for each recommendation that both might be considered valid. In the final analysis, however, it must be the value of the treatment as conservation that settles the question. Avoiding a treatment is not necessarily sound conservation sense. Using a treatment on the basis that it is the best we can do in the light of current thinking can be equally unsound. We must hope, therefore, that we can encourage conservation scientists to look into the problem for us, but since it can be virtually impossible to limit examples to a narrow field of testing, it will be a particularly difficult undertaking.

Literature Cited

1. "A National Preservation Program," presented at *Conf. Libr. Congr. Preserv. Off., Washington, D.C., 1976.*
2. *Ibid.*
3. Marwick, Claire S., M.A. Thesis, The American Univ., Washington, D.C., 1964.
4. *Ibid.*, p. 161.
5. Francis W. R. Emery U.S. Patent 561 503, 1896.
6. Nicholson, E. W. B. "Report to the Curators of the Bodleian Library on the Conference held at St. Gallen, Sept. 30 and Oct. 1, 1898, upon the preservation and repair of old manuscripts," unpublished data.
7. *Ibid.*
8. Marwick, Claire S., M.A. Thesis, The American Univ., Washington, D.C., 1964.
9. Berwick, William. "The Repairing and Binding of Archives," *Am. Hist. Assoc. Annual Report*, pp. 154–161.
10. Wilson, William K., Forshee, B. W. "Preservation of Documents by Lamination"; Natl. Bur. Stand. Monogr. 5, Washington, D.C., 1959.
11. Poole, Frazer G. 'William James Barrow," *Libr. Conserv.* 1978.
12. Barrow, William J. "Deacidification and Lamination of Deteriorated Documents, 1938–1963, *Am. Arch.* **1965**, *28*(2), 285.
13. "Polyester Film Encapsulation"; U.S. Libr. Congr. Preserv. Off.: Washington, D.C., 1980.

RECEIVED December 4, 1979.

Regional Conservation

A New England Example

ANN RUSSELL

New England Document Conservation Center, Abbot Hall, School Street, Andover, MA 01810

The New England Document Conservation Center was founded in 1973, to serve as a shared conservation resource, eliminating wasteful duplication of equipment and making available on a regional basis the very scarce skills of professionally trained paper conservators. Although the concept of regional conservation centers has been recognized widely as the most promising solution to the nation's massive conservation problem, only a few centers have been established successfully. Serious financial challenges are implied in the mandate of a center to support itself by serving a relatively impoverished clientele. This chapter outlines the problems of running a conservation center including the pressures of marketing, pricing, estimating, staffing, and the element of unpredictability every time a book is disbound or a document immersed in water. Using NEDCC's experience, this chapter assesses the conditions necessary for establishing a conservation center.

One of the tribulations of the New England Document Conservation Center is that very few people can remember our name. This was driven home to us earlier this summer when a client sent us a number of prints for treatment, and addressed her package: "Paper Conservation Center, North Andover, Massachusetts." We received a call from someone at the town dump who said a package of prints, which appeared to be for us, had been delivered to their paper recycling program. It was fortunate that some employee noticed this was the first time they had ever received trash by registered mail.

0065-2393/81/0193-0025$05.00/0

History

The New England Document Conservation Center, or NEDCC, was founded six years ago by the New England Library Board, with the help of start-up funds from the Council on Library Resources. The purpose was to provide paper conservation services to libraries, historical organizations, and public records offices that could not afford in-house laboratories. The idea was that a shared resource could eliminate wasteful duplication of equipment and make available on a regional basis the skills of professional paper conservators. It was expected that after a start-up period, the Center would be self-supporting through fees for its services.

Today our governing authority is the New England Library Board, which is made up of the state libraries of the six New England states. The Board still provides operating grants to the Center, amounting to $30,000 or 10% of the annual budget. This subsidy helps to insure the continuity of the Center and to underwrite educational services of benefit to the nonprofit organizations we serve.

Activities

NEDCC is located in Abbot Hall on the campus of Phillips Academy in Andover, Massachusetts. It is the only regional center in the country specifically oriented to conservation of library and archival materials as opposed to museum collections. Having begun life in the basement of the Merrimack Valley Textile Museum, we are pleased that we now have windows on all four sides. We have a large, spacious paper conservation laboratory, and specialized equipment such as our Israeli-made leaf caster. This is used to fill losses in book pages or documents and to reinforce crumbled edges.

We have a bookbindery, in which we try, whenever possible, to preserve the original bindings of books. Books that must be rebound usually are done in leather. Our binders use methods of sewing that are nondamaging to the book block, such as sewing on tapes or raised cords; when possible, sewing is done through the original holes. Only permanent, durable materials are employed. In general, strengthening the books is more important than producing an exact facsimile.

Our newest facility is a preservation microfilm unit, which was funded by a grant from the National Historical Publications and Records Commission. We specialize in filming of hard-to-film materials, such as manuscripts, glass plate negatives, and other materials that, because of their fragile condition, are not suitable for high speed handling by commercial service bureaus.

Our mobile vacuum fumigator can be used on the premises of an institution that faces a mold or insect problem. It also can be pressed into service during a library disaster if wet books begin to develop mold or mildew. The Center offers free disaster assistance to any library or nonprofit institution in the region that suffers a fire or flood, and we can rush a staff member to the scene to supervise recovery operations. Once we were called about a disaster of a new and different kind. A public library in southern Massachusetts had a skunk in its stacks. After trying to lure it out with cat food, the Assistant Librarian pushed it down the stairs with a broom, at which point the skunk sprayed the genealogy section. In this case, no one from our staff offered to rush to the scene.

NEDCC also provides on-site consultation to individual institutions, including surveys of storage facilities and collection evaluations. We help institutions evaluate their conservation needs and establish long-range conservation programs that can be carried out over a period of years to stretch the available dollars. Helping libraries to select materials for conservation on the basis of a rational plan is one of the most important services we provide. In general, we recommend that an institution invest first in improving environmental conditions and storing materials in acid-free folders and boxes.

Professional conservation is labor intensive by nature. It requires highly skilled staff and takes a lot of time. Thorough examination must proceed treatment. Every step must be done by hand and should be documented thoroughly. A photographic record must be kept. Even in a nonprofit, regional center, conservation cannot be performed cheaply. In general, our services are appropriate for rare materials but not for the mass of research collections.

Because the Center does work for several hundred different institutions, we must be able to handle a wide range of materials: manuscripts, vellum documents, maps, posters, architectural drawings, photographs, and books in all conditions.

Although we like to think we can perform almost any treatment that involves paper, there are some jobs we can't or won't do. For example, we were once approached by a man who had a large number of cancelled stock certificates. He had the idea that if he could find a paper conservator to fill in the holes, he could turn them in for cash. Although it is unusual for us to turn down work, this was one job we passed by.

NEDCC always has viewed itself as a prototype, and has hoped that other centers would spring up to serve other regions of the country. Although the concept of regional conservation has been recognized widely by the conservation profession, and by cultural organizations, as the most promising solution to the nation's massive conservation problem, only a few centers have been established successfully. Of these, only NEDCC specializes in treatment of library and archival materials.

Regional centers have faced a number of challenges: financial problems, lack of management expertise, lack of professionally trained conservation staff, and conflicts with host institutions. The greatest challenge in my view is the mandate for regional centers to be financially self-supporting. Is self-sufficiency a realistic expectation? This is a proposition that has not yet been tested fully.

Every aspect of NEDCC's operation is influenced by the fact that we must run like a business to meet the payroll and pay the rent.

Pricing

Demand for our services is inhibited by the cost, which is often higher than the value of the book or document. Prices are based on the number of hours of labor required to complete the treatment of the item. Quality conservation cannot be done quickly, and it is difficult to perform professional conservation at prices low enough to stimulate heavy use. If we could slash our hourly rate in half, we might be swamped with work, but necessity dictates that we charge rates that realistically reflect the costs of providing the service. As it is, our prices are somewhat lower than those of a private conservator or commercial concern, but they are still prohibitively high for many of the institutions that would like to bring work to us.

Estimating

The success of our pricing structure depends on the ability of our conservators to estimate accurately the cost of each job. When an object is brought to the Center, the Senior Conservator or Book Conservator examines it thoroughly, writes a condition report and treatment proposal, and calculates the amount of time involved in each step of the work to prepare a cost estimate. This is extremely difficult to do, because the treatment of no two objects is ever the same. Two photographs that appear to be in similar condition may be mounted on backings with different adhesives, one of which comes off easily in water, and one which will not come off in any known solvent. Bound materials are especially tricky to estimate. It is impossible to judge the condition of the spine until the book has been pulled apart. But we cannot pull apart a client's book until he gives the go-ahead to do the work. We recently pulled apart a book that we had agreed to treat at a relatively low price and found that every section was guarded with a pressure sensitive tape, which had bonded to the paper like cement. If a job takes longer than estimated, we have no means for making up our loss. Our Senior Conservator is fond of saying that there are no bonanzas in conservation, only disasters.

Staffing

Lack of availability of trained conservation staff has been a perennial tribulation for the Center. The number of professional paper conservators in the country is woefully limited, and most of these are well situated in institutions that value them highly. The list of paper conservators certified by the American Institute for Conservation numbers fewer than forty, and of these, there are only a handful whose expertise is in library conservation. In hiring staff, we are in competition with subsidized institutions, such as museums and large research libraries, which can offer higher salaries, leisurely working conditions, and lucrative moonlighting opportunities. It took more than one year for NEDCC to recruit a new Senior Conservator to head our laboratory, and nine months to find an appropriate Book Conservator.

Other Tribulations

The bigger the job is, the longer the period of time between when we begin work and when we receive the check. The business we are in is so specialized that there are no dependable sources of supplies. Mulberry paper, used for lining documents and prints, is made by hand in Japan, and the quality, delivery time, and price fluctuate wildly. The leather we use for binding books comes from England, and must be ordered sight unseen. Some of our clients know very little about professional conservation and have unrealistic expectations. For example, a new client might be disappointed if, following extensive treatment, a document does not look "as good as new."

Though we are able to treat the very rare items in our clients' collections, which warrant expensive restoration, there is need for low cost alternatives and mass treatment techniques for less rare materials. The technology is simply not available to meet this need. Conservators have no insurance should they ruin a valuable object. No insurance company can provide malpractice insurance for conservators at less than exorbitant cost. While trained conservators do examine an object thoroughly prior to treatment and then proceed with great caution, it is hardly comforting to know that this type of insurance protection is not available.

Outlook for the Future

A few weeks after I took the job as Director of NEDCC, a Board meeting was held, and I reported on all the pressures I was experiencing: no cash to meet the payroll, little work to keep the staff busy, no progress in our effort to hire a Senior Conservator. And one of the Board members responded cheerfully, "No one said it was going to be easy." Running a regional conservation center will never be easy. On the other hand, today, less than a year later, I feel that NEDCC is strong and viable. We have been virtually self-supporting for the past six months, and we have many reasons for optimism about our future.

We have been highly fortunate in recruiting new conservation staff of the highest caliber. Our new Senior Conservator, Mary Todd Glaser, brings to the Center an international reputation as a conservator of art on paper. She was trained at New York University and formerly served as Secretary of American Institute for Conservation and as Chairman of the Board of Examiners for the Certification of Paper Conservators. Her presence at the Center enables us to become more active in the area of fine arts conservation.

Our book conservation program now has been placed under the direction of Sherelyn Ogden, who came to us from Newberry Library, where she worked for five years. A new photographic conservator, Gary Albright, joined our staff in January, 1980, upon completion of a National Endowment for the Arts funded internship with Jose Orraca at Winterthur.

New expertise in fine arts, together with increased confidence of administrators in the Center has increased the Center's workload to record levels. However, success brings its own tribulations: our loyal clients, who were used to prompt service, are now encountering delays of several months.

Our Board has been highly supportive of the Center during the difficult period from which we are now emerging, and, at least for the time being, is providing grant funding to support the Center's disaster assistance program and educational work. Our Advisory Committee, which represents the various clients groups we serve, also has provided a great deal of encouragement and has helped to provide the Center with work and promote our activities in all six of the New England states. At one Advisory Committee meeting, a librarian from Rhode Island remarked that the existence of NEDCC makes New England the envy of archivists and librarians in all other regions of the country. This kind of goodwill toward the Center makes the whole struggle seem worth the effort.

What Others Can Learn from NEDCC's Experiences

Some conclusions may be drawn about the conditions necessary for the successful founding of a center. Financial support from a board or from members is needed on a continuing basis, not just during a start-up

period, so that a center will never have to be totally self-supporting. Top
caliber conservation staff to head the laboratory is a prerequisite and this
commodity is in extremely short supply. The goodwill and commitment
of clients is needed, as is management expertise on the part of administrative staff.

Conclusion

Today, building on the original ideas, dedication, and hard work of
Rockwell Potter, Walter Brahm, George Cunha, and the others who
created NEDCC, the present staff under the direction of Ann Russell,
Mary Todd Glaser, Sherelyn Ogden, and Andrew Raymond, are trying to
solve many of the vexing administrative and management problems. We
have learned much during our own relatively short times at the Center
and from the experiences of those who preceded us in the management
and technical direction of the facility. We are committed to doing our
best to help preserve the printed and written records and works of art
that are part of our heritage.

RECEIVED October 23, 1979.

Paper Conservation in Spain

JOHN P. McCLEARY

National Center for the Restoration of Books and Documents,
Serrano 115, Madrid 6, Spain

*Paper conservation, as known today, is new to Spain. Until
a few years ago, custodians of the nation's records on paper
and parchment could only despair at the deterioration taking place. The restorers—craftsmen, in reality—scarcely
were trained to tackle the broad problem. The pleas and
warnings of those who wanted something done went un-
heeded. Here and there individual authorities sought
professional help from abroad, but results proved minimal.
In 1969, a dramatic change took place. Conservation was
raised from the empirical to the scientific level. The breakthrough: a law that provided for a centralized agency to
restore the nation's archival and library materials, determine
the causes of deterioration, and train personnel to carry out
these tasks.*

Nearly six and one half centuries ago, in A.D. 1338, Pedro IV, king
of several dominions in eastern Spain, issued a royal decree relating
to the manufacturing of paper, an industry started by the Moors in A.D.
1150 in Xatvia (now Jatvia). It seems that when the Christians conquered
the Moors, the paper industry changed hands. Over a period of time
their product, which was quite permanent and durable, became rather
shoddy. In essence, the enlightened king decreed that the Christian
manufacturers of Xatvia had to abide by and adhere to Arabian practices;
those who did not would be handed severe penalties (*1*). King Pedro IV,
who fortunately had interest as well as authority, no doubt contributed
to the preservation of Spain's historical documents.

Returning to more recent times, the story of paper conservation in
Spain would be incomplete without the mention of a handful of people
who saw the urgent need for measures that would prevent or attenuate

0065-2393/81/0193-0033$05.00/0
© 1981 American Chemical Society

the ever-increasing deterioration of the nation's bibliographic and documental riches. Most in this select group were archivists and librarians closest to the problem, some were professionals in other fields, some were simply bibliophiles. They lived at different times and acted largely independently of each other, not as a group. Once in a while, individuals of prominence would either write on the subject for journals or speak before prestigious forums. The reception was usually enthusiastic; all agreed the problem was critical, that something should be done. But within a short time the matter always was shelved. Where there was interest, there was insufficient authority; where there was authority, the interest was short-lived.

The Precursors

One of the first to sound the warning was Dr. Rico y Sinobas, a university professor and physicist, who deplored the short life of books published during his time, the nineteenth century. Prior to his death in 1898 he prophesied, with uncanny accuracy, that the lack of scientific methods and disregard for the practical arts in the manufacture of paper in Spain would make the twentieth century witness to "the pulverized corner of archives and the stacks of bookshops and libraries where slow combustion is taking place in the leaves of books; the custodians, believing that the volumes are well protected because so many watch over them, can do nothing useful to stop the process" (2).

During the first quarter of the twentieth century, there were efforts to establish workshops in various archives and libraries through individual enterprise. One such endeavor was made by the Central Library in Barcelona, which sent selected technicians to the Vatican Library in Rome for training. Later, a small restoration laboratory was started in the Central Library, which, for the time, was one of the most advanced in the country (3). It remained active for some thirty-five years; the operation ceased when its personnel were transferred to other duties. During the same era, the National Library in Madrid established a career field never heard of before: Paper Restorer. The position was filled by a self-taught mender of engravings, documents, and maps, who on retirement was not replaced.

Dr. Amalio Gimeno, another scientist, was probably one of the first to discuss the physical and chemical causes of book deterioration. In 1932, during a presentation before the Spanish Academy of Exact, Physical, and Natural Sciences that he called "Pathology of the Book," he listed the factors that caused deterioration as dust, humidity, excessive temperature, fireplaces, and gaslights (4). Also, he accused the paper industry of planting the seed of destruction in their products and cited a study made in 1924 by the Central School of Industrial Engineers on machine versus handmade paper. In this study, which had been requested by a ministry of the government, he concluded that neither the machinery nor the process used in the manufacturing of paper was to blame for an inferior product; at fault were the nature of the fiber, the sizing, the fillers. The industrial engineers recommended that the government set standards to avoid such dangers. The report, according to Dr. Gimeno, "fell into a void."

During the Civil War, 1936–1939, the destruction of Spain's cultural riches was widespread; books and documents were a frequent target. Their usual fate was the torch; the insufficiently kindled are being restored today. There was scant progress in the field of conservation after the Civil War or in the subsequent period of neutrality during World War II. Nevertheless, during this time the Central Library in Barcelona pluckily announced to all archives and libraries that its restoration laboratory offered the following services: book washing, sizing, mending of paper attacked by strong inks, disinfection of books and documents, binding, especially in parchment, pressing of parchment, and, in general, whatever was related to conservation of books and documents (5).

The techniques used by the Central Library were relatively sophisticated for the time; local librarians were given short indoctrination courses in those techniques and learned how to make simple repairs on books. However, in the majority of Spain's libraries, bookbinders, if they were available, doubled as restorers; in archives, people did paste-and-paper repairs in addition to regular duties. No one, not even at the Central Library, was available to confront the broader problems of deterioration facing the custodians of the nation's records on paper and parchment.

In 1949, a member of the Pontifical University in Comillas conducted a survey of facilities dedicated to the pathology of the book (6). The conclusion was simple enough: Spain had no center capable of studying the discipline comprehensively. The report mentioned the many good intentions, only partially realized, of a dedicated few to establish such a capability; it recommended strongly an entity of established prestige such as the Central Library or the National Library to initiate and sponsor a national center. Nothing came of the idea.

Probably no one person did more to educate the Spanish public, many archivists and librarians included, on paper conservation than Professor Alfonso Gallo, founder of the Institute of Pathology of the Book in Rome. The opportunity came in 1951 during a congress in Madrid of Spain's National Association of Librarians, Archivists, and Archeologists (7). For the occasion, Professor Gallo brought specimens and other materials from his museum on the pathology of the book for display at the National Library. He spoke on the physical, chemical, and biological causes of damage to library materials with particular enthusiasm because, at the time, the sponsor of his visit to Madrid, Spain's Superior Council of Scientific Investigations, hoped to establish a laboratory modeled after the institute in Rome. Again, despite all good intentions, the project did not materialize.

When Professor Gallo was in Madrid, a person who attended the professor's lectures, saw the exhibitions, and left with an indelible impression, was a young archivist named Dr. Sánchez Belda (8). A perceptive and tenacious man, he was to climb quickly through the ranks of his chosen profession. In 1956, when he was named director of the National Historical Archives in Madrid, he chose two members of the Auxiliary Corps of Archivists, Librarians, and Archaeologists, an organization of civil servants who have no professional university degrees, for training at the Institute of Pathology of the Book. His idea was to establish a modest laboratory in the National Historical Archives as a nucleus for a future central facility. The neophyte conservators completed one year of training and set up a facility based on the procedures and techniques used in Italy. However, the project was destined to an ephemeral life. The budding center lasted for only four years. Thanks to a bureaucratic policy that job descriptions had to match assignments, the two conservators were transferred. Thus, the idea of a national facility was shelved, but only temporarily.

National Law on Conservation

In 1938, Dr. Sánchez Belda was promoted from Director of the National Historical Archives to the Director General of Archives and Libraries, a position with political influence, under the Minister of Education and Science. Now there was not only interest but, perhaps more important, authority together in the same person. One of his first chores was to draft legislation that would implement his project of a few years before. In a matter of months after Dr. Belda took office, the Spanish chief of state signed a decree dated September 15, 1969, that established the National Center for the Restoration of Books and Documents under the Director General of Archives and Libraries (9).

The mission of the Center as specified in the decree is simple and straightforward. The Center was directed to:

1. Restore the deteriorated items that belong to the documental and bibliographic patrimony of the nation.
2. Study, on a scientific basis, what causes the destruction of graphic materials, and what constitutes proper conservation measures to establish standards for the construction and installation of archives and libraries.
3. Study the measures and procedures required to carry out its mission.

4. Train technicians who can carry out adequately the tasks assigned to them.

5. Keep the General Directorate of Archives and Libraries informed of the problems that arise in the conservation and security of bibliographic and documental material.

No one could ask for better terms of reference to carry out a conservation mission: scientific examination, restoration, preservation, training.

A complementary order to the above decree was signed in May, 1972, that: i) named the Center advisor to the Director General of Archives and Libraries, ii) gave the Center technical supervision over any restoration workshops that might be installed in libraries or archives under authority of said Director General, iii) authorized the Center to establish the guidelines and instructions for said workshops relating to the systems, methods, and procedures to be used in restoration (*10*).

In June 1973, the Center held a roundtable discussion with Spain's key archivists, librarians, and scientists to establish a program to fulfill its additional national mission. It was agreed that restoration workshops would be installed in the principal archives and libraries of the nation, and that assistance would be given to others that already had workshops (*11*).

The National Center for the Restoration of Books and Documents

Looking back on the Center's very short history, its progress has been remarkable. Sharing space with the National Historical Archives, it started with six young people selected from the restoration community. Most were graduates of the state-run School of Arts and Crafts and had been restoring oil paintings or archeological artifacts. Only one had training in paper restoration: a stint at the Boston Museum of Fine Arts. One was a bookbinder. They literally taught each other; some added to the Center's store of knowledge by visiting centers in Europe. Nearly all materials and equipment were purchased abroad; practically none existed in Spain. Thus people, knowledge, materials, and equipment were combined. Then, a chemist joined the fledgling organization; the empirical method of restoration found itself aided and led by science. Paper conservation in the modern sense of the word was underway.

Ten years later, the Center's staff totals forty-five people: eight are in administration, four in maintenance and security, seven are scientific staff, twenty-six are restorers. There are ten additional people in the field: four restorers at the National Library, two at the General Administration Archives in Alcalá de Henares, one with the Archives of the Royal Chancellery in Valladolid, one with the Royal Archives of Simancas, one at the Archives of the Kingdom in Valencia, and one with the Archives of the Indies in Seville. The last four archives have workshops with some equipment in place, some on the way. They will, in time, count with additional personnel. If future plans materialize, the same four and, perhaps, others will become regional centers with direction from Madrid.

The Center's central organization in Madrid is composed of the following: Director, Chief of the Technical Department; in the latter are the Control Room, the Chemistry, Physics, and Biology Laboratories, and seven workshops: Book Restoration, Prints and Drawings, Manuscripts, Lamination, Leafcasting, Parchment, and Seals. The training mission is the direct responsibility of the Director.

To give the reader an idea of the Center's organizational duties and how paper conservation is practiced today, a brief description follows. Since space and time do not permit a detailed account of restoration techniques, the gaps will be obvious. The reader, therefore, is invited to contact the Center for any additional information.

Director. The Director is a professional woman archivist who reports to the Director General of Archives and Libraries. She is responsible for the supervision of the Center in all respects: scientific, technical, administrative, and training. Coincidentally, she has a second and correlated responsibility: Director, National Center for Microfilm.

Chief, Technical Department. The present chief holds the rank of professor of paper conservation, polytechnic level. He is responsible for the establishment and maintenance of restoration standards and techniques used by the Center and field workshops.

Control Room. Here all artifacts, including those requiring fumigation, are registered. As much data or historical and bibliographic information as possible is obtained before treatment and is recorded on a registration card that is slipped into a plastic jacket along with photographs taken by the Center's photo laboratory. The jacket stays with the artifact during restoration and each section records on individual cards the work done. On completion of the work, final photographs are taken to complete the before-and-after record that joins the other data for permanent filing in the Control Room.

Chemistry, Physics, and Biology Laboratories. As a rule, before any artifact is subjected to treatment, the chemistry laboratory determines the causes of any alterations or deterioration. The nature and structure of the artifact, its pigments and inks, are identified to avoid negative reactions to prescribed treatment. Fixatives are recommended if required; these may be cellulose acetate dissolved in acetone, soluble nylon, or acrylic resin sprays. Once stains are identified, several possible solvents are selected. For deacidification, either magnesium bicarbonate or barium hydroxide usually is recommended, depending on whether an aqueous or nonaqueous solution is called for. Bleaching is discouraged, but when necessary, hypochlorites are used with suitable antichlors.

The chemist's chore does not end here. The restorer has an open door to the laboratory at any time during the restoration process. If required, the chemist goes directly to the workbench for any questions or problems that may arise.

The basic mission of the Physics and Biology Laboratories is to test paper treated with products used in the restoration process. Physics is in an air-conditioned room, maintained at 60% relative humidity at 21°C, equipped with machines for testing folding endurance, tensile, and burst strength of paper. Biology runs tests, primarily with culture media, to determine the susceptibility of the treated paper to attack by micro-organisms; these are identified and a determination is made on how to avoid or eradicate them. Aging chambers are available for tests made by the laboratories.

Within a short time, a paper laboratory will be added to the existing three facilities. Its task will include the identification and composition of fibers and constituents in paper artifacts; the main job will be the refinement and preparation of pulp for the mechanical repair of paper, not only in the Center but in the field.

Book Restoration Shop. Most of the work done in this shop by five restorers is on books from the sixteenth to eighteenth centuries, although incunabula are common. Many are codices of the eleventh century, some are of tenth century vintage.

If a book is to be rebound or repaired, a sound block is not touched, that is, no resewing is done. Exceptions to this rule would be books that must be taken apart for chemical treatment, or books that must be repaired in a leaf caster because of extensive damage, for example, by insects. In such cases, if a leather binding of rare or historical value is salvageable, it is removed carefully for later use. Samples of the book's components are saved; notations are made of details that will permit duplication of the original craftwork. Additional photographs are taken if necessary.

Since the book restorers do not treat or repair paper, the Manuscript Shop receives the loose pages. In the meantime, the book restorers prepare the materials needed for rebinding; this includes the repair of original boards or the construction of new ones. Metal parts are repaired and missing ones are duplicated. If the old leather binding is to be reused, the sides and the spine are separated into three pieces, cleaned, dressed, and the edges are pared. Later, they are pasted onto a full leather binding of matching color covering the resewn textblock. If the old binding cannot be used but is of rare value, a two-compartment box is made for it and the newly bound book.

Prints and Drawings Shop. There are five restorers here: three are very capable watercolorists, one works in oils, one is an expert drafts-man. This shop also restores maps, broadsides, miniatures, and fans.

No other shop has such a variety of artifacts and such a myriad of challenging restoration problems.

The first step in the restoration process is dry cleaning with soft erasers. Old mounts or supports, usually highly acidic, are removed. Immersion in water is prescribed for removal of discoloration in the more stable forms of art on paper: etchings, prints, engravings, and some drawings. For specific stains that cannot be removed with water or other solvents, bleaching agents are applied locally. Deacidification by total immersion is preferred; a spray is used when this is not possible.

Tears are repaired with Japanese tissue, missing areas are filled in with paper similar to the artifact. Repair paper of specific caliper and tone is made in the leaf caster. Adhesives vary: methyl cellulose, wheat paste, or a mixture of polyvinyl alcohol with rice paste. The mixture is most useful because it permits use of a warm tacking iron to hasten the drying process. Where missing areas have been patched, the restorer reconstructs only those lines and colors that are already discernable, lest the work be called an attempt at falsification.

Manuscripts Shop. Four restorers devote their time to the restoration of what amounts to single leaves of paper or one folded to make a double leaf; the majority of artifacts are from the era prior to the mid eighteenth century. Setting aside the damage done by man, most of the deterioration encountered is caused by fungoid and insect attack; in the case of manuscripts, the damage from the acid in iron-gall inks is particularly serious.

Mechanical cleaning is the first step in the restoration process. Stains are removed only if the text is impossible to read. Bleaching agents seldom are used. Deacidification, if called for, is a standard procedure.

For the most part, repairs are done in the traditional manner. In the case of a rare document, an effort is made to use repair paper of the same era. Fortunately, there is usually a supply on hand, thanks to forays to the Madrid flea market where old documents can be found for a reasonable price. Paper made in the leaf caster also is used for repairs, particularly if tonal qualities are sought. Small holes are filled with paper fibers mixed with methyl cellulose.

Lamination Shop. This shop has four restorers who keep an Arbee machine in constant use, laminating material that does not lend itself to other methods of repair. Polyethylene film and Japanese tissue are used to make a sandwich for the damaged artifact in a process that uses application of heat, then pressure with metal rollers, to complete the cycle.

Apart from the normal lamination process, the Center has developed a technique that is used extensively for repairing missing areas of artifacts. First, a half-sandwich is made: a tissue on the bottom, the poly-

ethylene film next, then the artifact (deacidified if required) on top.
Repair paper covers the missing area of the artifact plus a bit of overlap.
The half-sandwich is placed between a Teflon carrier and slipped into
the machine's heated platens. When the lamination cycle ends, the
artifact, film, tissue, and repair paper are bonded together except for the
overlap of the repair patch. This is trimmed with a scalpel; a hot tacking
iron assures a clean union. A polyethylene film is placed on the unlami-
nated side of the artifact, a tissue next, then into the machine for the
final step. The process is rapid and an incalculable amount of time is
saved in mending tears, holes, and missing areas.

In addition to the Center's laminator, there is a similar model at the
National Library, and one at the General Administration Archives.
Eventually, all field restoration workshops will have lamination machines.

Leaf Casting Shop. The principle of leaf casting or mechanical
repair of paper is quite simple: paper fibers are suspended in a chamber
filled with water. The bottom of the chamber has a grid that supports
the document undergoing repair. When the water is sucked down, the
fibers stay in the missing areas of the document.

In cooperation with a Spanish industrial firm, Vicente Viñas of the
Center developed a leaf caster, the Vinyector, which uses a pump and
an electromagnetic-compressed air system to direct the flow of water into
a chamber where pulp slurry is added. The water is then sucked down
into a tank, forming a repair on the artifact as described above. This
cycle takes about one minute to complete.

The machine is an ecologist's dream because instead of draining
several liters of water after each repair, the water in an enclosed tank,
capacity 130 L, is used over and over again. The water can be filtered
by passing it through blotting paper.

Four auxiliary tanks can be coupled to and operated from the
Vinyector's control panel. The tanks can hold solutions for deacidification,
bleaching, or rinsing. This system, designed for small workshops with a
few technicians, is obviously a slow one; for this reason the Center uses
only the basic leaf caster. An additional feature of the machine, again
for small workshops, is that its chamber can be sealed hermetically and
used for fumigation with, for example, commercial mixtures of ethylene
oxide and carbon dioxide.

There are three operators in this shop running two leaf casters with
another machine on standby. There are two leaf casters at the restoration
workshop of the General Administration Archives, one at the Royal
Archives of Simancas, one at the Archives of the Royal Chancellery in
Valladolid, one projected for the Archives of the Indies, and another
projected for the Archives of the Kingdom in Valencia. The leaf caster
will be standard equipment for all workshops; the projected figure,
counting those in place, will be about twelve machines.

Parchment Shop. There are five restorers in this shop. Parchment documents and book covers to be restored get a mechanical surface cleaning with soft erasers then harder ones, if required, to remove dirt and grime. Hard, embrittled, and dry artifacts have their inks and pigments fixed with an acrylic resin spray or with a fine brush dipped in paraloid before immersion in a bath of ethanol and water (70% and 30%, respectively).

The parchment is lifted out when it feels pliable to the touch (this can take from several hours to a few days) and is blotted to remove excess solution; fresh blotters and press comes next. After a day or two, the parchment is removed; in most cases it has reached a stable state.

In very stubborn cases, another treatment is used. Inks and pigments are fixed and the artifact is immersed in a bath of polyethylene glycol (PEG 400). An entire codex can be placed in two or three large plastic tubs and kept there until the parchment is soft and pliable. This procedure can take days or weeks. The parchment is removed and blotted and pressed in the same manner as the treatment in ethanol and water. If the parchment becomes translucent while in the bath, the phenomenon will disappear with the blotting and pressing process.

Since the parchment has been treated with a hygroscopic (but chemically stable) substance it must be kept away from excessive humidity and temperature to avoid microbiological attack.

Seals Shop. There is a great wealth and variety of seals belonging to the medieval documentation of Spain. Fortunately, these individual pieces of art have survived the ravages of time in a better manner than the documents to which they are appended or applied. Those seals that do require attention are mended with pins and beeswax, but the majority of work done is for exhibitions and to have reproductions available for academic research. Seals of great rarity or historical value are reproduced as they enter the Center, or impressions are made in the field and later cast in this shop. Generally, molds of originals are made of synthetic rubber and casts of resin. One craftsman runs this shop.

Training. One of the principal missions of the Center is to train people to restore and conserve the documental and bibliographic riches of the nation as prescribed in the decree of 1969. Restorers are trained at the Center in a school that requires three years of intensive study and practice. The instructors are personnel of the Center, members of the Professional Corps of Archivists, Librarians, and Archaeologists, and professors of local universities. The first year is divided equally between theoretical and practical courses, the second is practical, the third year is for practical specialization. There are also concentrated, one-year courses primarily for Latin American students, although many from other parts of Europe have attended. Most of those who take these courses have a background of experience in restoration or are practicing archivists and librarians.

Conclusion

Its progress notwithstanding, paper conservation in Spain has just begun. There is much to do but at the moment, unfortunately, the resources available will not stretch that far. The legislation that pulled the many loose strands together was a good start. But the problem is overwhelming when one considers the immensity of the book and archival inventory that needs immediate attention. This does not count the records, written or printed on paper of poor quality, that find their way into the national collection. The situation is aggravated by the countless nonstate entities—institutions, municipalities, monasteries, convents, private organizations—that seek and are given help.

In the meantime, there is a long line of books and records awaiting treatment at the Center and its field workshops. The input has to be controlled because of limited facilities. More space is needed, to be filled by more technicians, more material, and equipment; to do this more funds are needed. But in a country with serious economic problems, the Center's priorities are not considered of immediate urgency.

The Center is trying to overcome these obstacles by diverting its resources to areas where the most good can be done: more rapid and economical methods of restoration, and expansion of restoration facilities in the major archives and libraries of the nation.

Meanwhile, other programs must wait. Whether or not they are ever realized, they do constitute a national need: construction of suitable buildings for poorly housed archives and libraries, or, at least, improvement of present facilities; climate control, a priority requirement, in view of the intolerable levels of environmental pollution in Spain's urban centers; a national program for custodians of books and documents that alerts them to the conservation problems they face and what action can be taken within budgetary limitations; a movement to stimulate the manufacture of a permanent type of paper; an expanded microfilm program as part of a cooperatively organized national preservation program; and an expanded research program for the many conservation problems that exist today in the peninsula, the Balearic Island, the Canary Islands, and the Spanish enclaves in North Africa.

Literature Cited

1. "Cuna del Papel Europeo en la Jatvia Arábiga"; Cronista de Jatvia: Valencia, 1961.
2. Rico y Sinobas, M. "El Arte del Libro en España"; Editorial Escelicer, S. L.: Madrid, 1941; pp. 491–493.
3. Library of Catalonia, personal communication, February 1979.
4. Gimeno, A. "La Patología del Libro," Discourse at the Academia de Ciencias Exactas, Físicas, y Naturales, Madrid, 1932.
5. Zamorano, A. "Laboratorio de Restauración de Libros de la Biblioteca Central," in *Anuario de la Biblioteca Central* **1941**.

6. Bustamante, J. M. "Nota Sobre la Patología del Libro," in *Biblioteconomía* 1949, IV.
7. Bustamante, J. M. "Patología del Libro," in *Razón y Fe* March, **1951.**
8. Conversation with Dr. Sánchez Belda, Director, National Historical Archives, Madrid, February 3, 1980.
9. "Decreto 1930/1969 de 24 de Julio," in *Boletín Oficial del Estado* Sept. 15, **1969.**
10. "Orden Ministerial Complementaria de 18 de Mayo de 1972," in *Boletín Oficial del Estado* May 31, **1972.**
11. "Centro Nacional de Restauración de Libros y Documentos," CNRLD pamphlet, 1976.

RECEIVED October 23, 1979.

Permanence/Durability and Preservation Research at the Barrow Laboratory

DAVID D. ROBERSON

James River Paper Co., P.O. Box 2218, Richmond, VA 23217

The work of William J. Barrow and his laboratory spanned more than forty years. His methods made acetate lamination of deteriorated documents practical and useful. He did much to spread the understanding that acidity is the major cause of paper deterioration, and his deacidification processes are in wide use. Commercial production of permanent/durable paper was begun in 1959 and eight such papers were available in 1973. An average activation energy of 25.3 kcal/mol was determined for the loss of folding endurance and tear resistance. 1470 book papers from the period 1507–1949 were studied. Moist accelerated aging is faster than dry oven aging but not necessarily more like natural aging. A bulk morpholine treatment process for bound books raises the pH of acid papers and prolongs their useful life by a factor of 4–5. The Barrow Laboratory closed in 1977.

William James Barrow's long involvement in preservation began in 1932. His first restoration work was done at the Virginia State Library using methods he had learned at the Library of Congress. While working at the Mariners Museum in Newport News in the late 1930s, he developed the first practical roller laminator for the lamination of weakened and disintegrating documents with cellulose acetate film. A major improvement on this process was the addition of strong long fiber tissue to the laminate. This strengthened the document without sacrificing legibility. The acetate so filled the tissue and document surface that there was very little light scattering and the added layers were quite transparent.

0065-2393/81/0193-0045$05.00/0

Barrow wondered about the deteriorative processes that made lamination necessary. There was no reason to suppose that degradation was stopped by lamination. He concluded that the acidic nature of the paper itself was the primary cause of the degradation and then began to look for ways to combat the problem. By the end of 1945, he had developed his deacidification process in which solutions of calcium hydroxide and calcium and/or magnesium bicarbonate are used to neutralize acidity and leave within the paper an alkaline material to combat acidity from future degradation and pollution.

It was now possible to greatly reduce paper's deterioration rate and to restore integrity and strength to those already damaged (1). Barrow's equipment and techniques for doing this have been acquired by more than thirty institutions, worldwide.

He observed early that the papers most in need of lamination were those made after 1875. In 1957, a testing program was begun on five hundred books published in the first half of the twentieth century (2). Most of them were in poor condition, primarily because of the use of alum–rosin sizing in their manufacture. Acidic air pollution is harmful and some of the early wood pulps may have been very poor, not because of any innate deficiency in the raw material, but because of poor control of the pulping process and poor washing. But among the papers tested, neither of these factors was as damaging as the introduction of acidity at the time of paper manufacture.

Long Life Papers

However, there were abundant examples of much older papers that were still in very good condition and the question naturally arose as to the possibility of producing a long-lasting paper at moderate cost with modern methods. Barrow first defined this objective in a quantitative way based on examination of nineteen book papers then in general use and papers from seven books printed between 1534 and 1722 (3). Tentative strength specifications were set at 300 MIT folds at 0.5 kg tension and 60 g Elmendorf tear resistance, both measured in the weaker direction. These values were comparable with those found in the old rag papers and clearly attainable in the modern chemical wood papers. A requirement for strength retention after heat aging was set to permit a maximum acceptable deterioration rate slightly greater than those exhibited by the obviously stable old papers. At this rate, the paper under normal conditions would last three hundred years. This prediction of useful life from the testing of samples aged in an oven was based on work begun in Sweden and further developed by the National Bureau of Standards. Barrow's working assumption was that seventy-two hours at 100°C is equivalent to twenty-five years at normal temperatures.

The two parts of these performance specifications are reflected in the term "permanent/durable" that began to be used to identify such papers. Durability is the level of physical strength and flexibility necessary to withstand extensive use and handling. Permanence indicates a degree of chemical stability that permits only very slow deterioration.

With the advice of A. L. Rothschild and others, a series of experiments was begun in the Herty Foundation laboratories that culminated, in December 1959, in the production, on commercial equipment, of a paper meeting the tentative specifications. This was done at the Standard Paper Manufacturing Company in Richmond, Virginia. The pulps were all chemical wood; the sizing was alkyl ketene dimer, which is compatible with mild alkalinity; and calcium carbonate was added to maintain alkalinity (*3*).

The same approach was soon thereafter applied, at the request of the American Library Association, to library catalog cards. The new nonacid cards made from chemical wood pulps were able to outlast the acidic ones made previously from rag, in spite of rag's potential for higher initial strength. Barrow's proposed specifications for a minimum cold extraction pH of 6.0 and a minimum diagonal folding endurance of 800 are now incorporated in the American National Standards Z 85.1 (*4*).

In 1961, the Council on Library Resources, under the presidency of Verner W. Clapp, provided a grant for the establishment of the W. J. Barrow Research Laboratory in the Virginia Historical Society Building. This facility afforded space and equipment that were not available in the cramped quarters of the restoration shop.

Another study undertaken with the sponsorship of the ALA Library Technology Project involved the study of damage to books in library handling and circulation, and the development of test equipment to duplicate that damage so that bookbinding specifications could be written in terms of probable performance rather than in the restrictive terms of materials and methods of manufacture (*5*).

Effect of Temperature

One project that continued throughout the life of the new laboratory was called "Effect of Temperature." For this study, five production runs of paper were made in two different mills producing a total of thirteen papers. Seven of these have been tested extensively as were three commercial papers.

Matched sets of folding endurance and tear resistance test specimens were prepared from each paper to be aged at several temperatures. Aging was done in forced circulation ovens that were supplied with air having a dewpoint of 53°F. At intervals, sets of test specimens were removed from the oven and tested to monitor the deterioration process.

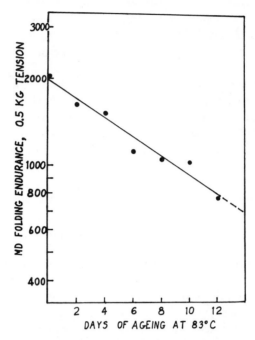

Figure 1.   Machine direction folding endurance deterioration of an acid book paper upon heat aging

The data was plotted against time of aging on semilog coordinates and the best straight line was fitted to it by the least squares regression method (Figure 1). This is the mathematical model for a first-order reaction and experience indicates that it is the best general model for paper deterioration. The slope of this line, called the rate constant (k), is a measure of the reaction rate. Comparing rate constants obtained at different temperatures for the same paper, it was found that on average, for each 15°C increase in aging temperature, the rate of deterioration is multiplied by a factor of 4.8. In the course of this study, more than two hundred rate plots have been done for temperatures ranging from 125°C to 38°C.

If a straight line results when the logs of the rate constants for several temperatures are plotted against the inverse of their respective absolute temperatures, the Arrhenius relation may be applied and the activation energy for the process, which is represented by the slope of the line, is independent of temperature. Arrhenius plots for the deterioration of paper are usually linear (Figure 2). It has been suggested that the activation energy calculated in this way is an average for several simultaneous chemical and physical processes. It is interesting that similar values may be calculated on the basis of folding endurance or tear resistance deterioration in either the machine or cross direction.

In any case, the linearity of the relation permits extrapolation to normal temperatures to obtain an estimate of natural aging rate. The full process of testing an adequate number of samples at several intervals for each of several temperatures is very time consuming but such an extrapolation is the most legitimate way to predict useful life of a paper.

Permanence evaluation or comparisons based on aging at one elevated temperature assume that the same increase in temperature will produce the same increase in deterioration rate for all papers. This is a questionable assumption for materials as varied as papers. If it were true, Arrhenius lines for all papers would be parallel. Comparison of such lines for the loss of machine direction folding endurance in ten different papers shows that nine of them have similar, though not all equal, slopes (Figure 3). The tenth is so very different that its validity may be questioned though there are no apparent grounds for discarding it. Even among the nine lines with similar slopes there are some that cross. When two lines cross, it means that the papers represented do not have the same relative stability at room temperature that they have at some elevated temperature.

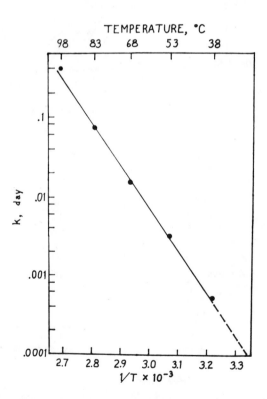

Figure 2.   Effect of temperature on deterioration rate

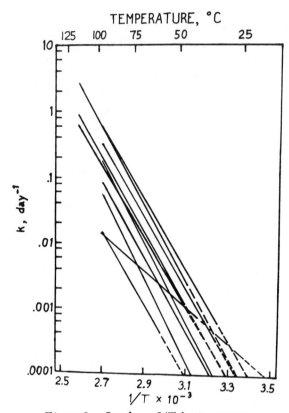

Figure 3.   Log k vs. 1/T for ten papers

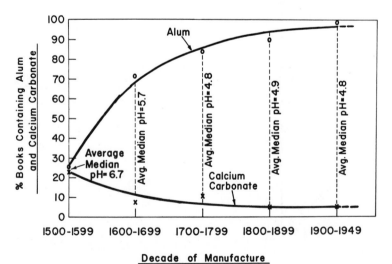

Figure 4.   Presence of alum and calcium carbonate in book papers, 1500–
1949 (8)

Activation energies calculated from these lines show in a quantitative way the differences in their slopes. The thirty-six values calculated in this study (excluding the very odd results obtained on the paper mentioned earlier) averaged 25.3 kcal/mol and 72% of them were within 2 kcal/mol of that value. That value translates into a natural aging equivalency of 68 years of natural aging for three days at 100°C, which is higher than the 25 years Barrow used in his earlier work, the 28 years reported by van Royen, and the 18.5 and 20.5 years calculated from the data produced by Wilson and Rasch and it is considerably lower than the 306 years calculated from the 30 kcal/mol activation energy suggested by Browning and Wink. As a practical matter, single temperature accelerated aging tests will continue, but it is important that their limitations be understood.

Polyvinyl acetate emulsions for manual application in the production of adhesive bound books were examined for stability. It was found, among other things, that plasticized homopolymers had poor or moderate stability, while copolymer types showed very high stability. The addition of calcium carbonate and calcium acetate could improve the lasting qualities of unstable materials but had little effect on the very stable ones. The addition of these buffering agents made the adhesive less acid and less damaging to papers (6).

Barrow's examination of papers from books printed during the first half of the twentieth century was extended backward in time to the beginning of the sixteenth century. A great deal of papermaking history is recorded in the papers from the 1470 old books that were tested (7, 8). The increasing use of alum during the period is apparent as is a concurrent decline in the presence of carbonate (Figure 4). The rapid increase in the use of rosin size in the nineteenth century can be seen (Figure 5). A general decline in the present strength of papers began in those made around 1670, which is approximately the time, according to some authorities, the Hollander beater was being developed (Figure 6). The advent and increasing use of chemical and groundwood pulps during the last half of the nineteenth century may be detected by fiber analysis, but there is no obvious evidence of these developments in the strength properties of papers from that period.

Test Methods

It had been suggested that accelerated aging in ovens supplied with ambient air is "unnatural" in that the moisture content of paper under such conditions is much lower than in papers under normal conditions and that the validity of heat aging would be increased by controlling the relative humidity of the aging environment at some level comparable with natural conditions. At the Barrow Laboratory, papers have been aged at a variety of humidities and temperatures in three different kinds

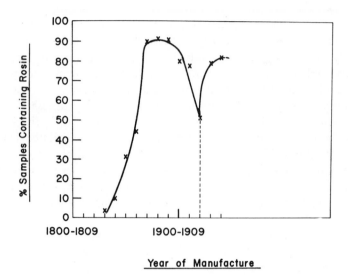

Figure 5.   Rosin in book paper, 1800–1949 (8)

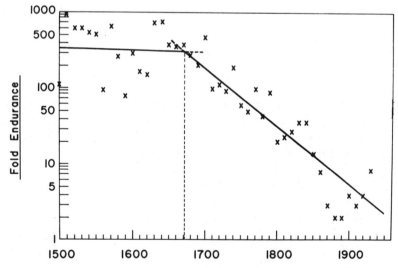

Figure 6.   Folding endurance of book papers, 1507–1949 (8)

of apparatus. It was demonstrated at the Barrow Laboratory, as at other laboratories, that deterioration is faster at higher relative humidity but there is apparently not yet any strong evidence that deterioration under moist conditions is any different from deterioration under dry conditions or that it is any more like natural aging. If the only certain advantage of moist aging is that it is faster, then it is hardly worth the additional cost and trouble as a routine test method. Comparison of papers aged by different methods might give useful clues to the degradation mechanisms but this has not been explored thoroughly.

About ten years after the publication of Barrow's tentative specifications, a survey was undertaken to develop and authenticate revised specifications for permanent/durable book paper. The resulting new specifications called for higher levels of initial strength and lower rates of deterioration, but of the thirty-two papers tested, eight satisfied all requirements, whereas there was only one a decade earlier (*9, 10*). The minimum pH was raised from 6.5 to 7.5. This one relatively simple test would permit the elimination of some papers from consideration without any need for more complicated evaluation methods.

The MIT folding endurance test has been used frequently because it measures an important paper property that is very sensitive to heat aging, but it can be time consuming and the results rather variable (*9*). It is not unusual for the highest value in a group of test results to be four or more times as great as the lowest value. One reason for this is the variable nature of paper and the fact that the actual test area is small. Use of a weight rather than the spring scale to keep tension on the sample did not reduce the coefficient of variation in 100 tests, neither did the use of the blower. However, both of these tended to increase the test result.

The folding edges on the MIT machine are supposed to have a radius of curvature of 0.015 ± 0.001 inch. It is important that these tolerances be observed strictly and, if practical, they should be reduced. Tests showed that folding heads at the edges of these tolerances will produce, on average, an 8% change in the mean result.

Because of the variation in folding endurance results, it is necessary that many tests be run on a paper to produce a reliable mean. At the Barrow Laboratory, fifty tests were standard. This takes time, but a rate plot based on a few tests per point is of doubtful value. There is a need for an improved folding endurance tester or an entirely new instrument for reliably and conveniently measuring flex fatigue.

There has been some interest in thermal analysis methods for permanence evaluation. An attempt was made to correlate various features of differential scanning calorimetry thermograms for a group of papers with their stability under oven aging. In some cases, the correlation coefficient was encouragingly high but the standard error of estimate showed that the relation was no more useful for predicting permanence than was pH.

Ever since the beginning of deacidification, the desirability of methods that do not require taking a book apart has been apparent. Barrow tried to deacidify with ammonia but the effect did not last. In 1963, he was working on a process in which the pages of a bound book

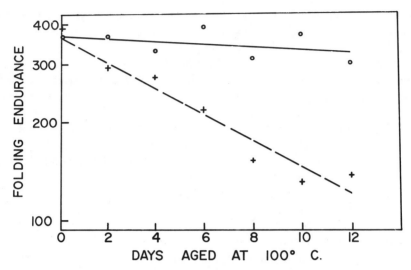

Figure 7. Change in aging rate attributable to morpholine–water vapor treatment of an acid paper: (○), treated, (+) untreated (12)

were sprayed with a water–alcohol solution of magnesium bicarbonate (*11*). The amount of water involved was not enough to cause swelling of the paper, which would damage the binding.

A much more recent development is the morpholine process in which fifty books per hour are treated in an evacuated chamber with morpholine–water vapor (*12*). In its present form, it was effective on 95% of the papers treated, prolonging their life on average by a factor of 4–5 (Figure 7). Though it does not leave a titratable alkaline reserve in the paper, acid papers treated in this manner aged in the presence of 5 ppm SO_2 at 75°C and 60% relative humidity deteriorate more slowly than if untreated. Recent tests of twenty treated books at the Library of Congress show that their pH has not declined in two years. The equipment for the process was set up in the Virginia State Library where 35,000 books were treated in the first seven months of operation.

The usefulness of accelerated aging and other tests to evaluate permanence is reduced greatly by lack of information as to how they relate to natural aging. Very long term natural aging programs have been proposed before, and some abortive attempts have been made, but there is still a need for a paper archives in which thoroughly tested papers can be kept indefinitely and continuity can be assured for a testing program following the process of natural deterioration.

William J. Barrow died in 1967 and was succeeded as director of the laboratory by Dr. Robert N. DuPuis. Dr. Bernard Forestier Walker served from 1971 until 1977 and the author was acting director when the laboratory closed in the summer of 1977.

Literature Cited

1. Barrow, William J. "Manuscripts and Documents: Their Deterioration and Restoration"; University of Virginia Press: Charlottesville, VA, 1955; p. 86.
2. Barrow, W. J. "Deterioration of Book Stock, Causes and Remedies"; Church, R. W., Ed.; The Virginia State Library: Richmond, 1959; p. 70.
3. Barrow, W. J. "The Manufacture and Testing of Durable Book Papers"; Church, R. W., Ed.; The Virginia State Library: Richmond, 1960; p. 64.
4. Barrow, W. J. "Permanence and Durability of Library Catalog Cards"; Library Technology Project, American Library Association: Chicago, 1961; p. 40.
5. Library Technology Project "Development of Performance Standards for Bindings Used in Libraries, Phase II"; American Library Association: Chicago, 1966; p. 53.
6. Barrow, W. J. "Polyvinyl Acetate (PVA) Adhesives for Use in Library Bookbinding"; W. J. Barrow Research Laboratory: Richmond, 1965; p. 66.
7. Barrow, W. J. "Strength and Other Characteristics of Book Papers 1800-1899"; W. J. Barrow Research Laboratory: Richmond, 1967; p. 116.
8. W. J. Barrow Research Laboratory "Physical and Chemical Properties of Book Papers, 1507-1949"; W. J. Barrow Research Laboratory, Inc.: Richmond, 1974; p. 48.
9. Roberson, David D. "Revised Specifications for Uncoated Permanent/Durable Book Paper"; ERIC Document Reproduction Service: Arlington, VA, 1975; p. 126.
10. W. J. Barrow Research Laboratory *American Archivist* **1975**, *38*(3), 405.
11. Barrow, W. J. "Spray Deacidification"; W. J. Barrow Research Laboratory: Richmond, 1964; p. 62.
12. Williams, John C., Ed. "Preservation of Paper and Textiles of Historic and Artistic Value," *Adv. Chem. Ser.* **1977**, *164.*

RECEIVED November 27, 1979.

Watermarks and What They Can Tell Us

T. L. GRAVELL

305 Mansion Road, Wilmington, DE 19804

A watermark, when reproduced accurately, can give a possible date of composition and place of origin for the document on which it appears. Such information often will prove or disprove the authenticity of maps, prints, books, or manuscripts. Accurate copies of watermarks can be made in roomlight by exposing Dylux 503 to visible light and developing it with ultraviolet light.

The first researchers of early handmade paper relied on tracings to reproduce the various watermarks for study, a method that could produce only approximate copies no matter how much care was exercised. In 1960, beta-radiography came into use and for the first time, accurate watermark reproductions were available for study. The beta plate, while producing good prints, was very expensive. Although the time required to make a print has been reduced to an hour or less, in some cases, the cost is still so high that the plate is out of the reach of most researchers. With the use of a photosensitive paper known as Dylux 503 good, clear, and accurate reproductions can be had at a very low cost.

Briefly, the process involves placing the watermarked paper and the Dylux 503 in very close contact and exposing the sheets to visible light, such as that of a super diazo fluorescent tube, for one to five minutes at a time. A blue daylight fluorescent tube will work; however, the time of exposure will be longer. Since the watermark creates a thinness in handmade paper, the visible light will pass through this thinness with greater intensity and thus nullify the yellow dye coating on the Dylux 503 sheet. The exposure time varies with the contents and thickness of each sheet. After exposure, the sheets are separated and the exposed Dylux is passed under a long-wave ultraviolet light. This ultraviolet irradiation causes the unaffected coating to turn a bright blue, thus forming an exact copy of the watermark (*see* Figures 1–4). Some care

0065-2393/81/0193-0057$05.00/0
© 1981 American Chemical Society

*Figure 1. A Thomas Amies, Dave Mill watermark on wove paper, ca.
1811*

must be used in handling Dylux 503, for while room light permits safe
handling for up to five or ten minutes without this special paper losing
effectiveness, sunlight will, in a very few minutes, cause it to lose its
ability to react. The rapidity of making prints, the low cost, and the
ability to be used in room light, which is a definite safety feature in
handling manuscripts, make Dylux 503 a very useful tool in reproducing
the watermarks of early handmade paper.

*Figure 2. Post Horn by John Bick-
ing, Chester County, Pennsylvania,
on laid paper, ca. 1792*

*Figure 3. Eagle and crossed flags of Henry Hudson, East Hartford,
Connecticut, on laid paper, ca. 1830*

Watermarks in early paper can be both very helpful and very disappointing. They can help by telling by whom and where the paper
was made and are disappointing in that they cannot give us the exact
date of when a document was composed originally. Two surveys have
been made using eighteenth and nineteenth century documents from
four libraries: The Morris Library of the University of Delaware,
Eleutherian Mills Historical Library, Library of the Historical Society
of Delaware, and the Henry Francis du Pont Winterthur Museum. All

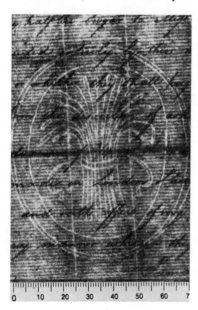

*Figure 4. Sheaf of wheat by John
Matthews, Delaware County, Pennsylvania, on laid paper, ca. 1800*

of the documents counted contained dated watermarks and an original date of use. The first survey was made in 1974 using over one hundred pieces and the second was done in 1977 with over two hundred items. The first survey showed that 96.1% of the dates of use, and the second showed that 98.8% of the dates of use, were within nine years of the date shown in the watermark. Records are being kept so future surveys can be made as additional dated watermarks are found. While only seven dated watermarks between the years 1596 and 1681 were found in the collection of the Folger Shakespeare Library, all had been used within a six-year period. Unfortunately, the French-dated watermarks of this same era (eighteenth and nineteenth centuries) cannot be used. The edict of 1739 that set forth the terms under which French paper could be made had one section so worded that French papermakers believed that French paper was to be watermarked with the date 1742. Therefore, all French paper carried this date for a number of years. I have seen only one letter watermarked 1742, which was signed by Voltaire, and dated 1742; the item is in the John Boyd Thacher Autograph collection at the Library of Congress. Other manuscripts with the 1742 watermark date have been found with dates of use from twenty-eight to seventy-one years later.

There are a number of ways in which watermarks can help with a date; for instance, if the paper has a dated watermark, you know that it could not have been used before that date. A prompt book in the Folger Shakespeare Library has a written date of 1784 while the pages are watermarked 1799, which in turn indicates the contents were copied from an earlier work. Dated watermarked paper, when in printed books, is a great help in establishing the date of publication. For example, a volume of John Gay's *Fables,* the title page of which shows the published date of 1793, is on paper watermarked "W Balston–1810." It would seem that the original plate was used over again perhaps to cut costs or the book is a pirated edition. In the period before there was any means of mechanical copying, all such work was done by hand and there are a number of these copied letters, deeds, indentures, land surveys, and maps filed as originals in our archives. There is a letter dated Valley Forge, 1778, and signed Geo. Washington that is on paper watermarked "Smith & Alnutt– 1815." Washington died in 1799. In Henry Toulis's book *History of Romish Treasons* (Folger Shakespeare Library copy), published in London during 1671, there is a description of how a letter, reportedly written by James 6th of Scotland, was proved a forgery by the "mark in the paper." Restrikes from original plates often are found. Charles Blasko-witz's map Bay of Narragansett dated 1777 can be found on paper dated "J Whatman–1794." A political satire cartoon by Thomas Tegg with a written date of 1812 has been seen on paper dated 1823 by the watermark.

Watermarks also can help with a date by associating one watermark with another. During the 1600s, when watermarks stood for both the size and quality of paper, papermakers used the pot as a symbol for ordinary quality paper 12 × 15 inches and a Cardinal's hat, pillars, or a Crozier horn for the same size paper, but of a better quality. A document that had the watermark of a Cardinal's hat and the initials E.L.P. was undated; however, the watermark of a pot with the same initials (E.L.P.) was known to be on a letter dated 1651. Since the same papermaker no doubt made both sheets, it seemed safe to assume that the undated document also had originated in the 1650s. Later, another manuscript was found with the watermark of a Cardinal's hat initialed E.L.P. and was dated 1658.

There is another type of watermark that is often a help and that is a mark left in the paper by the stitches that joined the endless wire screen used on the early paper machines. These marks are in the form of a series of short dashs or a ropelike line of marks across the sheet. Since papermaking machinery did not come into being until after 1804, 1804 is the earliest such marks could appear in paper. These stitch marks can give only a starting point, so they must be treated with caution. The endless belt that created them remained in use for a number of years, so such marks could have a long life. At the Henry Francis du Pont Winterthur Museum, there are two manuscripts so marked. On one, #77X349, dated 1831, the stitch marks appear very uniform, as though they had been sewn by a machine; the second, #77X290, dated 1841, has stitches that are uneven in both size and placement, which would seem to indicate they were handsewn and pre-dated the 1831 type. While on the subject of machine-made paper, it might be well to mention the dandy roll and the watermarks it produced. The dandy roll is said to have come about because of a dislike of the machine-made wove paper, many customers wanted the older laid type of paper. The dandy roll was invented and patented by the Englishmen John and Christopher Phipps in 1825 and the first rolls for sale were made by John Marshall Co. of England in 1826. The Marshall Co. was purchased in 1969 by W. Green Son & Waite Ltd. The roll was shaped as a cylinder made of a wire screen stretched over wooden ribs. The horizontal wires of the screen made the laid line effect and the wooden ribs that ran at 90° to the horizontal wires created the chain lines. The paper pulp on the endless screen of the machine was carried under the dandy roll, which then made the impression in the paper. The first dandy rolls were unwatermarked, but in 1839, William Joyson, an English papermaker, sewed the first watermark on the roll at his mill in Kent. The American-made dandy rolls were not watermarked until 1847; this date means little, as English-made dandy rolls were in use in this country from the first.

Knowledge of when and where a papermill was located is as important for dating as are the watermarks. There is a map of lower Delaware, hand drawn and dated 1702, which is on paper with a Gilpin watermark. The Gilpin mill on the Brandywine did not start operations until 1787; thus, the map could not have been drawn on this paper in 1702. Another such instance is a Saur Bible, printed in 1762 (and bound at Efrata, Lancaster County, Pennsylvania) on paper with the watermarks of "WP" and the "Arms of Virginia," watermarks used by William Parks of Williamsburg, Virginia. William Parks died at sea in 1750 on a trip to England and his mill was sold in 1752. There are no records to show that the mill operated beyond that date. It seems unlikely that any supply of paper made by Parks lasted for ten or twelve years, perhaps Saur (he was also a papermaker) or Conrad Schutz, who had worked for Parks, purchased the molds and brought them to Pennsylvania for use in his own mill.

In conclusion, watermarks very often tell us what a document is by telling us what it isn't.

RECEIVED October 23, 1979.

Washing and Deacidifying Paper in the Same Operation

LUCIA C. TANG

Preservation Office, Library of Congress, Washington, D.C. 20540

Use of a chemical feeder allows the conservator to wash paper with deionized water containing added calcium ions, wash and deacidify simultaneously, or to directly deacidify paper. Examples of these processes are given in which varying ratios of alkali were fed to deionized water. The resultant alkaline reserves produced in two types of papers are shown.

The washing and deacidification of paper to improve its permanence has been an object of investigation for many years, and a number of methods of accomplishing this have been suggested. Numerous reports on aqueous, nonaqueous, and vapor phase deacidification procedures have appeared in the literature. Barrow (1) has published on the use of divalent alkaline earth bicarbonates dissolved in water. These compounds not only neutralize acidity, they also leave an alkaline residue or buffer in the paper that protects it from acid atmospheres that it may encounter or acid generated by oxidation. Barrow (1) immersed the paper in the solution and gave it a long soak or marination.

For years, conservators have been concerned about the water used for washing paper artifacts. Although deionized water and distilled water are employed extensively in washing paper artifacts, tap waters have found wide application as well. Unfortunately, very purified water, such as distilled or deionized waters, have been found to shorten the life of some papers (2), probably through removal of calcium ion. Tap water also has certain drawbacks. It usually contains chlorine, which acts to oxidize cellulose, and traces of iron and copper compounds, which may act as oxidation catalysts for paper stored under humid conditions. Tang and Jones (2) concluded that water used for washing paper artifacts should be free from chlorine and iron and copper compounds, all of which accelerate the deterioration of cellulose, and suggested that the preferred washing process use distilled or deionized water made acceptable by passing it through a column of calcium carbonate chips.

To improve the washing techniques even further is the purpose of this investigation. Washing and deacidifying paper in the same operation will be discussed. This process achieves improved control of both washing and deacidifying by the use of a chemical feeder. A change in flow rate of the chemical feeder, which brings in the alkaline component, directly affects the washing and deacidification efficiency. The results of this study, hopefully, will point out to conservators how to select the amount of alkaline solution giving the greatest enhancement of washing, and also the method of adding enough of the alkaline solution to deacidify and create an alkaline reserve in the paper. This is done by adjusting the alkaline solution flow to the flow rate of the deionized or distilled water.

Experimental

Experimental System. A diagram illustrating the operation of the chemical feeder technique used for this investigation is shown in Figure 1. The deionized water was purified by passing tap water through a cation exchange cartridge (Universal cartridge, No. 1506-20, Cole Parmer Instrument Company) and a second cation exchange cartridge (Research cartridges, No. 1506-30, Cole Parmer Instrument Company) to remove

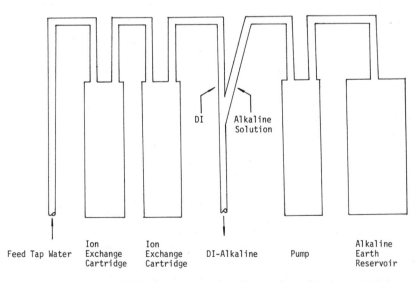

Figure 1.   Deionized–alkaline system by chemical feeder process; DI is deionized water; alkaline earth is a divalent compound, i.e., Ca^{+2} or Mg^{+2}.

all metal ions. The calcium hydroxide was obtained from Fisher Scientific Company and was U.S.P. grade. The alkaline solution for the alkaline earth reservoir was prepared from a saturated calcium hydroxide solution. Two types of pumps were chosen for the chemical feeder process. A bellows metering pump was selected for a low flow rate of alkaline solution, from 2.3 mL/min to 5.6 mL/min. A Monostat peristaltic pump, Varistatic solid state model, was used for the flow ranges of 8.9–100 mL/min. The pumps delivered the alkaline solution to the deionized water system at the appropriate rate. The deionized–alkaline water was a mixture of deionized water (DI) and alkaline solution (Ca^{+2} or Mg^{+2}). The flow rate of the deionized water was kept at a constant value in the ranges of 436–451 mL/min, while the alkaline earth flow rate was chosen to give desired concentrations for washing and for deacidification.

Sample Preparation. Two papers were selected. One was Champion Foldur Kraft, a bleached southern kraft paper, containing rosin size and fillers, from a single roll of known composition. The other paper was newsprint that had already been cut into sheets when received by the laboratory. The newsprint was analyzed as follows: 80% groundwood and 20% unbleached sulfite.

The five different types of DI–Ca water used for the experimental washing and deacidification of these papers are listed in Tables I and II. Ten 8″ × 10″ pieces of each paper were used for each washing. Papers were prewet with 1:1 solution of denatured alcohol and distilled water, then were put immediately into the wash water. The washing procedure consisted of immersing the sample in the test water and leaving it there for a predetermined amount of time, either one or three hours. The paper was held between diamond-shape, open-mesh rubber matting for support, and these "sandwiches" were stacked in a polypropylene tray; the DI–Ca water entered the tray from one side through a tube and overflowed the tray at the opposite side. The sheets were at all times surrounded by moving water. The DI–Ca water flowed through the stack of paper at the appropriate flow rate (*see* Tables I and II).

For each paper, both Foldur Kraft and newsprint, there were ten sample sets and one unwashed set, which was used as a control. The air dried samples were subjected to accelerated aging in humid (90°C/50% relative humidity) and dry (100°C) circulating air ovens for one, two, three, and five weeks. At regular seven-day intervals one sheet from each sample set was removed and tested.

Table I. Water Analyses from Chemical Feeder Process

Method	Rate of $Ca(OH)_2$ (mL/min)	Rate of DI (mL/min)	ppm Ca in DI–Ca Water	pH	Conductivity (micromhos)
A	2.3	450.7	9.2	9.9	33.5
B	5.6	452.7	11.4	10.4	106.0
C	8.9	446.3	15.4	10.7	175.0
D	23.4	457.6	36.4	10.8	442.0
E	100.0	436.0	112.8	11.9	1500.0

Table II.   Calcium Content in Paper from Chemical Feeder Process

Method	ppm Ca in DI–Ca Water	Washing Duration (Hours)	Ca Content (ppm) Newsprint	Foldur Kraft
Unwashed	0.0	0	1178 ± 190	610 ± 12
A	9.2	1	2077 ± 376	1922 ± 311
		3	2716 ± 285	1865 ± 417
B	11.4	1	2820 ± 553	1972 ± 129
		3	3269 ± 437	2046 ± 922
C	15.4	1	3109 ± 233	2090 ± 394
		3	3360 ± 380	2186 ± 399
D	36.4	1	9813 ± 942	4493 ± 210
		3	9788 ± 369	5737 ± 999
E	112.8	1	9790 ± 154	4306 ± 77
		3	9459 ± 51	4829 ± 402

Analytical Methods. CONDUCTIVITY MEASUREMENTS.   Conductivity was measured on ElectroMark Analyzer Model #4402. Triplicate readings were taken on each of the DI–Ca waters.

ATOMIC ABSORPTION SPECTROSCOPY.   A titanium punch was used to cut 2.8-mm-diameter samples from the papers for calcium analysis. A Perkin–Elmer Model AD-2 Electronic Ultramicrobalance was used for the accurate weighing of the paper samples. Calcium content in the DI–Ca waters and the papers was determined using a Varian Techtron AA-6 Spectrophotometer, with a Model 90 Carbon Rod Atomizer and Potentiometer A-25 Recorder (3). The solid samples (paper samples) were introduced into the graphite cup atomizer with tweezers. The standard solutions and DI–Ca waters were inserted into the cup atomizer by means of 5-μL Oxford pipet.

BRIGHTNESS MEASUREMENTS.   Brightness was measured according to TAPPI T452m-58 using the Photovolt Model 670 Meter. Brightness was measured at ten different places on both sides of the sheets, then the readings were averaged.

FOLDING ENDURANCE MEASUREMENTS.   The MIT folding endurance test was run at 1/2 kg load in the machine direction, according to TAPPI T511-su-69.

pH MEASUREMENTS.   pH was run according to the procedure of Kelly (4), Pulp pH Procedure. A Fisher Accumet Model 320 pH Meter was used in the measurements.

ACIDITY AND ALKALINE RESERVE MEASUREMENTS.   Acidity was titrated directly with standard NaOH solution to determine total acid content.

Alkaline reserve was measured by acidifying to pH 3, boiling to remove CO_2, cooling, and back titration with standard NaOH solution to pH 7 (4).

Results and Discussions

The Deionized Water–Alkaline System.   The DI–Ca water analyses from the chemical feeder process are shown in Table I. As the amount of calcium ions in the deionized water was increased, the conductivity values became higher. The amounts of calcium in the DI–Ca water can be measured by conductivity. The pH of the deionized water was 6.3. The pH of saturated calcium hydroxide solution is 12.3. Addition of 9.2 ppm Ca as $Ca(OH)_2$ in the deionized water raised the pH to 9.9. The level of the pH increased with additional amounts of calcium ions in the DI water. The measurement and adjustment of the calcium solution flow was essential, both for washing and for the deacidification efficiency.

Table II shows the calcium content in paper from the chemical feeder process. With the addition of 9.2 ppm Ca in DI water, the treated newsprint paper's calcium content doubled in comparison with the control. The treated Foldur Kraft paper contained three times more calcium than did the unwashed paper. The more calcium that was added in the DI water, the higher the amounts of calcium absorbed in the papers during the washing and deacidification process. However, the absorption of calcium in the paper reached a saturation point. This is the reason why newsprint and Foldur Kraft papers that are treated with 36.4 ppm Ca in the DI–Ca water imbibed the same amount of calcium as the papers washed with 112.8 ppm Ca in the DI–Ca water.

Folding Endurance.   The folding endurance of paper is one of its useful and important properties and the test has been employed for years in specifying and controlling paper quality. The change in folding endurance gives a sensitive measure of the deterioration of paper with age. Folding endurance data can be displayed readily. A plot of the logarithm of folding endurance vs. time of aging in dry or humid ovens yields a linear relationship (5, 6, 7, 8). The decrease in folding endurance may thus be modeled as a first-order reaction. Life expectancy was taken as the number of days of artificial aging a paper could tolerate before folding endurance dropped to one fold. This was determined by extrapolating the straight line to intersect the abscissa.

Projected life of the control (unwashed) has been divided into projected life of the DI–Ca water washed paper to give a ratio expressing the value of treatment. Generally, washing by the chemical feeder process increased the initial folding endurance. The projected life or slope of the folding endurance indicated an increase in the longevity from two to twelve times among two papers after washings in the chemical feeder process (*see* Tables III and IV; and Figures 2–3). Dry and humid oven aged papers that were washed with 9.2 or 11.4 ppm Ca in DI waters substantially increased in fold retention over the unwashed

Table III. Folding Endurance of Foldur

100°C Dry Oven Accelerated Aging

Method	ppm Ca in DI–Ca Water	Treatment (h)	Folding Endurance at ½ kg	
			0 days	7 days
O	0.0	unwashed	1128 ± 167	306 ± 80
A	9.2	1	1514 ± 236	1143 ± 334
		3	1695 ± 152	1188 ± 206
B	11.4	1	1642 ± 435	1145 ± 228
		3	1480 ± 281	1125 ± 203
C	15.4	1	1476 ± 281	1043 ± 79
		3	1621 ± 254	1035 ± 216
D	36.4	1	1303 ± 122	1157 ± 273
		3	1324 ± 214	1062 ± 155
E	112.8	1	1425 ± 140	956 ± 131
		3	1358 ± 208	1072 ± 139

50% Relative Humidity 90°C Humid Oven Accelerated Aging

Method	ppm Ca in DI–Ca Water	Treatment (h)	0 days	7 days
O	0.0	unwashed	1128 ± 167	128 ± 42
A	9.2	1	1514 ± 236	695 ± 136
		3	1695 ± 152	1024 ± 243
B	11.4	1	1642 ± 435	1052 ± 188
		3	1400 ± 281	984 ± 176
C	15.4	1	1476 ± 281	1036 ± 146
		3	1621 ± 254	1085 ± 216
D	36.4	1	1303 ± 122	999 ± 133
		3	1324 ± 214	1101 ± 81
E	112.8	1	1425 ± 140	962 ± 180
		3	1358 ± 208	1076 ± 112

Kraft Paper After Chemical Feeder Process

100°C Dry Oven Accelerated Aging

Folding Endurance at ½ kg			*Predicted Life, Days in Oven*	*Treatment Index*
14 days	*21 days*	*35 days*		
15 ± 6	3 ± 2	0	24.4	1.0
801 ± 124	657 ± 124	97 ± 36	99.5	4.1
1200 ± 345	786 ± 120	319 ± 68	162.4	6.7
862 ± 116	741 ± 203	336 ± 80	169.7	7.0
874 ± 89	705 ± 112	391 ± 71	194.8	8.0
1129 ± 262	719 ± 178	374 ± 93	192.8	7.9
1015 ± 151	783 ± 145	403 ± 60	198.1	8.1
923 ± 88	741 ± 112	558 ± 80	284.9	11.7
870 ± 90	785 ± 79	552 ± 57	294.4	12.1
954 ± 269	830 ± 122	562 ± 122	299.7	12.3
890 ± 125	712 ± 144	529 ± 111	267.0	10.9

50% Relative Humidity 90°C Humid Oven Accelerated Aging

12 ± 4	3 ± 1	0	23.9	1.0
372 ± 83	97 ± 54	4 ± 2	46.3	1.94
689 ± 151	250 ± 50	31 ± 21	67.1	2.81
872 ± 173	467 ± 159	60 ± 26	82.9	3.5
856 ± 180	298 ± 47	136 ± 39	105.4	4.4
698 ± 88	389 ± 81	108 ± 25	98.6	4.1
889 ± 323	619 ± 119	161 ± 55	117.5	4.9
734 ± 119	573 ± 111	186 ± 78	133.3	5.6
750 ± 198	680 ± 106	172 ± 36	129.1	5.4
866 ± 141	509 ± 77	138 ± 26	113.2	4.7
827 ± 82	689 ± 110	214 ± 82	142.7	6.0

Table IV.   Folding Endurance of Newsprint

100°C Dry Oven Accelerated Aging

Method	ppm Ca in DI–Ca Water	Treatment (h)	Folding Endurance at ½ kg	
			0 days	7 days
O	0.0	unwashed	129 ± 57	25 ± 9
A	9.2	1 3	120 ± 69 185 ± 31	66 ± 39 84 ± 42
B	11.4	1 3	143 ± 42 110 ± 28	87 ± 30 79 ± 18
C	15.4	1 3	236 ± 64 102 ± 52	98 ± 23 74 ± 15
D	36.4	1 3	152 ± 34 175 ± 47	69 ± 17 64 ± 18
E	112.8	1 3	167 ± 41 133 ± 24	99 ± 25 122 ± 53

50% Relative Humidity 90°C Humid Oven Accelerated Aging

O	0.0	unwashed	129 ± 57	12 ± 3
A	9.2	1 3	120 ± 69 185 ± 31	66 ± 19 55 ± 14
B	11.4	1 3	143 ± 42 110 ± 28	74 ± 16 89 ± 39
C	15.4	1 3	236 ± 64 102 ± 52	82 ± 14 95 ± 18
D	36.4	1 3	152 ± 40 175 ± 47	69 ± 12 84 ± 26
E	112.8	1 3	167 ± 41 133 ± 24	61 ± 27 73 ± 20

Paper After Chemical Feeder Process

100°C Dry Oven Accelerated Aging

Folding Endurance at ½ kg			*Predicted Life, Days in Oven*	*Treatment Index*
14 days	*21 days*	*35 days*		
7 ± 2	3 ± 1	0	26	1.0
23 ± 14	15 ± 4	4 ± 1	47.5	1.8
63 ± 18	30 ± 16	8 ± 1	59.9	2.3
77 ± 27	39 ± 14	24 ± 10	93.5	3.6
75 ± 25	30 ± 12	14 ± 4	77.1	3.0
38 ± 16	56 ± 20	20 ± 5	80.8	3.1
84 ± 26	69 ± 27	19 ± 10	106.7	4.1
84 ± 35	27 ± 9	35 ± 14	109.9	4.2
49 ± 19	65 ± 33	42 ± 17	147.0	5.7
61 ± 26	59 ± 16	28 ± 9	102.6	3.9
98 ± 36	51 ± 23	37 ± 15	124.2	4.8

50% Relative Humidity 90°C Humid Oven Accelerated Aging

2 ± 0.5	0	0	16.0	1.0
22 ± 11	9 ± 3	1 ± 0.4	36.8	2.3
24 ± 12	16 ± 11	3 ± 1	44.6	2.8
70 ± 23	45 ± 13	13 ± 6	77.0	4.8
63 ± 24	66 ± 16	16 ± 5	92.7	5.8
75 ± 23	28 ± 18	20 ± 8	75.5	4.7
61 ± 19	64 ± 19	29 ± 14	131.2	8.2
47 ± 24	65 ± 17	24 ± 7	106.2	6.6
89 ± 37	66 ± 19	34 ± 6	119.0	7.4
58 ± 20	56 ± 14	34 ± 10	126.4	7.9
75 ± 26	69 ± 25	29 ± 7	128.2	8.0

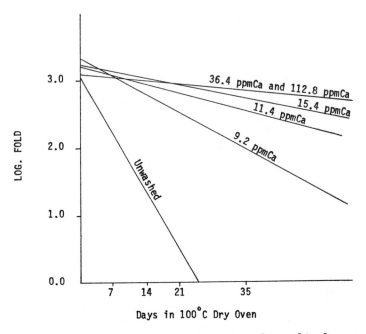

Figure 2. *Foldur Kraft paper washed for 1 h in chemical feeder process*

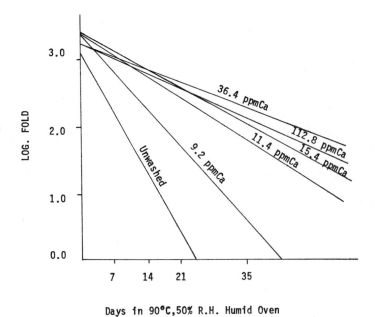

Figure 3. *Foldur Kraft paper washed for 1 h in chemical feeder process*

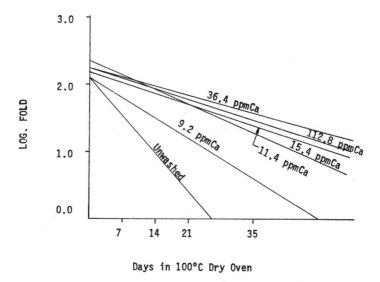

Figure 4. Newsprint paper washed for 1 h in chemical feeder process

papers (*see* Figures 2–5). However, papers treated with 36.4 or 112.8 ppm Ca in DI water exhibited a much lower increase in folding endurance than did the papers that were washed with 9.2 or 11.4 ppm Ca in DI water. Surprisingly, papers deacidified with 112.8 ppm Ca in DI water

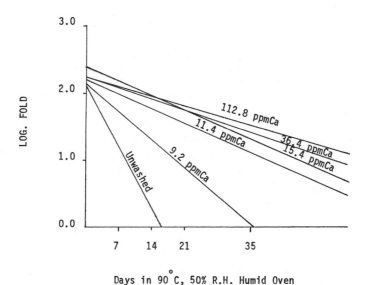

Figure 5. Newsprint paper washed for 1 h in chemical feeder process

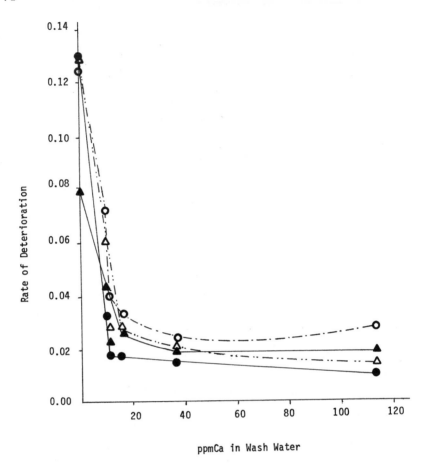

Figure 6.   The effect of calcium content on rate of deterioration of papers;
rate of deterioration is taken from the slope of the log folding endurance
vs. time of aging curve; (●) FK dry, (○) FK humid, (▲) NP dry, (△) NP
humid

gave the same or less improvement in the folding endurance than the
papers that were treated with 36.4 ppm Ca in DI water. Figure 6
shows the effect of calcium content on the rate of deterioration of paper.
Untreated paper deteriorates very quickly. The most efficient treatment
for slowing down the deterioration of paper is 11.4 ppm Ca in DI water.
Once the solute absorption in the papers reaches a saturated point, the
effective treatments do not depend on the concentration. In all washings
in the chemical feeder process, the three hours washing gave a slight
improvement in paper permanence over the one hour washing (*see* Tables
III and IV). However, for most purposes, the improvement at three
hours hardly justifies the additional time required.

Brightness. Tables V and VI show the effect of the treatments on brightness in both dry and humid oven aging. Foldur Kraft samples remain the same in initial brightness values after various treatments in the chemical feeder process. However, all treated newsprint samples dropped in initial brightness. The degree of loss in initial brightness for treated newsprint samples depended on the amounts of calcium fed in DI water. After dry and humid aging, all washed Foldur Kraft and newsprint samples were improved in brightness retention in comparison with the unwashed samples. The improvement in brightness retention did not depend on solute concentration in this experiment.

Table V.   Aging Tests on Washed Paper, Effect on Brightness, Foldur Kraft Paper

100°C Dry Oven Accelerated Aging

Method	ppm Ca in DI–Ca Water	Treat-ment (h)	Brightness (units)				
			0 days	7 days	14 days	21 days	35 days
O	0.0	unwashed	75.0	68.8	64.5	61.4	57.8
A	9.2	1	75.1	72.0	70.3	69.9	67.1
		3	75.4	72.3	70.8	70.5	68.4
B	11.4	1	75.0	71.9	71.0	70.2	68.4
		3	75.0	71.9	71.3	70.4	68.6
C	15.4	1	74.6	71.7	70.1	70.0	68.8
		3	74.8	72.1	71.3	70.5	68.7
D	36.4	1	75.2	72.4	71.3	70.7	69.2
		3	75.3	72.4	71.8	70.6	69.0
E	112.8	1	74.1	72.3	71.0	70.5	68.7
		3	75.0	72.5	71.6	70.8	69.4

50% Relative Humidity 90°C Humid Oven Accelerated Aging

Method	ppm Ca in DI–Ca Water	Treat-ment (h)	0 days	7 days	14 days	21 days	35 days
O	0.0	unwashed	75.0	65.5	62.8	56.3	50.6
A	9.2	1	75.1	70.0	67.5	65.0	60.8
		3	75.4	70.0	67.9	65.4	60.8
B	11.4	1	75.0	69.7	68.0	65.8	60.7
		3	75.0	69.9	67.9	64.0	60.4
C	15.4	1	74.6	69.3	67.4	64.2	59.7
		3	74.8	69.0	67.7	65.4	61.3
D	36.4	1	75.2	69.9	68.3	65.7	61.9
		3	75.3	70.3	68.2	65.6	61.7
E	112.8	1	74.1	70.1	67.4	65.1	60.9
		3	75.0	69.7	67.8	66.2	61.7

Table VI.   Aging Tests on Washed Paper, Effect on Brightness, Newsprint Paper

100°C Dry Oven Accelerated Aging

Method	ppm Ca in DI–Ca Water	Treatment (h)	Brightness (units)				
			0 days	*7 days*	*14 days*	*21 days*	*35 days*
O	0.0	unwashed	52.4	44.5	39.4	36.0	31.1
A	9.2	1	50.6	45.4	42.5	40.1	35.6
		3	50.5	45.7	42.6	41.0	36.4
B	11.4	1	47.7	44.0	42.1	40.4	36.5
		3	46.7	44.3	42.6	41.3	37.3
C	15.4	1	45.6	43.5	42.3	40.6	37.1
		3	46.5	43.0	41.5	40.4	37.1
D	36.4	1	45.1	41.9	41.3	39.3	37.2
		3	44.7	42.7	41.0	38.8	37.4
E	112.8	1	43.5	42.7	39.5	39.0	37.0
		3	43.2	42.4	41.5	38.8	36.7

50% Relative Humidity 90°C Humid Oven Accelerated Aging

Method	ppm Ca in DI–Ca Water	Treatment (h)	Brightness (units)				
O	0.0	unwashed	52.4	37.4	33.1	29.6	27.0
A	9.2	1	50.6	44.5	40.8	37.3	32.5
		3	50.5	45.3	41.9	38.3	32.9
B	11.4	1	47.7	44.6	41.6	38.9	34.4
		3	46.7	45.0	42.0	40.1	35.7
C	15.4	1	46.5	43.7	40.9	38.9	35.8
		3	46.5	43.6	41.1	39.0	35.4
D	36.4	1	45.1	41.9	40.4	37.8	34.4
		3	44.7	42.0	40.4	38.7	35.1
E	112.8	1	43.5	42.2	39.9	37.8	34.8
		3	43.2	42.3	39.4	38.0	34.4

pH of Treated Papers. The pH values in the DI–Ca waters are shown in Table I. The effect on the pH of the newsprint and Foldur Kraft papers after the chemical feeder process in the dry and humid ovens is shown in Tables VII and VIII, and Figures 7 and 8. The unwashed samples had a pH 4.8–5.1. After air drying for several hours, the washed papers varied from pH 6.5 to pH 9.1. The amount of calcium that was fed into the DI water played an important role in the pH values of the washed and deacidified sheets. Results indicate that the treated papers above pH 6.5 generally have a very slow rate of degradation and that unwashed samples below pH 5.1 progressively degrade more rapidly (*see* Figures 2–6). Treated papers exhibited a gradual decline in pH after thirty-five days accelerated aging. After dry and humid oven aging, the papers that had been treated in the chemical feeder process remained at a pH above 7, this is, therefore, a true deacidification process. The papers that had only been washed remained below pH 7, so this cannot be considered as deacidification but only as washing. A calcium content of the DI–Ca water of 9–15 ppm is the proper concentration for washing the paper. The chemical feeder system can be used to put this amount

Table VII. Aging Tests on Washed Paper, Effect on pH, Foldur Kraft Paper

100°C Dry Oven Accelerated Aging

Method	ppm Ca in DI–Ca Water	Treatment (h)	pH				
			0 days	7 days	14 days	21 days	35 days
O	0.0	unwashed	4.95	5.1	5.1	5.15	4.95
A	9.0	1	6.4	6.1	6.0	6.0	5.6
		3	6.9	6.4	6.3	6.25	5.95
B	11.4	1	7.5	6.65	6.65	6.4	6.3
		3	7.2	6.7	6.6	6.5	6.2
C	15.4	1	7.1	7.3	7.1	6.9	6.55
		3	7.4	7.05	6.95	6.7	6.4
D	36.4	1	8.5	8.15	7.5	7.6	7.4
		3	8.5	8.15	7.5	7.7	7.3
E	112.8	1	8.65	8.5	8.5	8.4	8.2
		3	9.1	8.6	8.6	8.55	8.45

50% Relative Humidity 90°C Humid Oven Accelerated Aging

O	0.0	unwashed	4.95	5.1	5.15	5.1	4.85
A	9.2	1	6.4	5.9	5.75	5.6	5.4
		3	6.9	6.25	6.1	5.95	5.75
B	11.4	1	7.5	6.7	6.45	6.3	5.95
		3	7.2	6.6	6.25	5.95	5.85
C	15.4	1	7.1	7.0	6.6	6.35	6.2
		3	7.4	6.8	6.5	6.25	6.05
D	36.4	1	8.5	7.8	7.6	7.5	7.0
		3	8.5	8.2	7.7	7.3	7.2
E	112.8	1	8.65	8.7	8.6	8.3	8.4
		3	9.1	8.85	8.7	8.55	8.4

Table VIII.   Aging Tests on Washed Paper, Effect on pH, Newsprint Paper

100°C Dry Oven Accelerated Aging

Method	ppm Ca in DI–Ca Water	Treat- ment (h)	0 days	7 days	14 days	21 days	35 days
O	0.0	unwashed	4.82	4.8	4.6	4.55	4.2
A	9.2	1	6.5	5.6	5.35	5.25	4.95
		3	6.7	6.3	5.7	5.55	5.1
B	11.4	1	7.9	7.0	6.5	5.8	5.4
		3	8.05	7.35	7.0	6.6	6.05
C	15.4	1	8.15	8.0	7.2	6.95	6.7
		3	8.25	7.6	7.65	7.45	7.25
D	36.4	1	8.5	7.65	7.5	7.6	7.15
		3	8.6	7.7	7.75	7.8	7.4
E	112.8	1	8.85	7.85	7.95	7.95	7.8
		3	8.65	8.2	8.1	8.2	7.8

50% Relative Humidity 90°C Humid Oven Accelerated Aging

Method	ppm Ca in DI–Ca Water	Treat- ment (h)	0 days	7 days	14 days	21 days	35 days
O	0.0	unwashed	4.82	4.5	4.35	4.25	3.95
A	9.2	1	6.5	5.6	5.35	5.05	4.85
		3	6.7	6.05	5.6	5.2	5.0
B	11.4	1	7.9	6.75	6.15	5.8	5.8
		3	8.05	7.15	6.95	6.7	6.3
C	15.4	1	8.15	7.8	7.15	7.05	6.9
		3	8.25	7.85	7.75	7.45	7.3
D	36.4	1	8.5	7.45	7.6	7.5	7.05
		3	8.6	7.8	7.95	7.95	7.4
E	112.8	1	8.85	8.45	8.1	8.15	8.0
		3	8.65	8.45	8.15	8.2	7.85

into the DI water for the washing process. When the calcium content of the DI–Ca water is brought above 20 ppm by the chemical feeder, the paper is deacidified as well as washed. After dry and humid oven accelerated aging, the 36.4- or 112.8-ppm-Ca–DI water deacidified papers showed no significant changes in pH values. This is indicative of a stabilized paper.

Alkaline Reserve. The alkaline reserve served to protect paper from acidity, either from a polluted environment or from the paper structure itself. It is very important that the treatment leave an adequate alkaline reserve in the paper to prevent it from becoming acid again. Papers washed with the 9.2-ppm-Ca–DI water did not have an alkaline reserve but did have a reduced acidity content. Tables IX and X show the chemical feeder process producing alkalinity in washed papers that remained during and after accelerated aging. Although newsprint and Foldur Kraft papers washed with 11.4- or 15.4-ppm-Ca–DI water have a small alkaline reserve, this alkaline reserve had been consumed, leaving the cellulose in an acid condition in the subsequent artificial aging. Newsprint papers treated with 112.8-ppm-Ca–DI water contained 1.3%

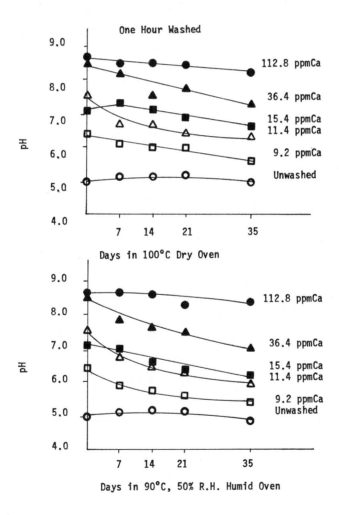

Figure 7.   Effect on pH of Foldur Kraft paper after chemical feeder process

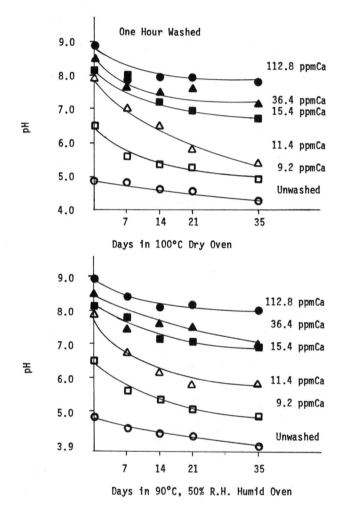

Figure 8.   Effect on pH of newsprint paper after chemical feeder process

CaCO₃; however, Foldur Kraft papers deacidified with the same amount of DI–Ca water contained only 0.35% CaCO₃. Alkaline reserves in the paper depended on the pick up of the paper, its absorbency, and the solute concentration. After humid oven aging, newsprint and Foldur Kraft papers treated with 36.4- and 112.8-ppm-Ca–DI water showed retention of their alkaline reserve. Thus, an adequate deposition of calcium carbonate during the chemical feeder process gave sufficient protection and indicated paper permanence. There was no powdering on the paper surface. The results indicate that the papers washed with 9.2-ppm-Ca–DI water were well washed; the papers washed with 11.4- or 15.4-ppm-Ca–DI water were given both washing and partial deacidification; and the papers treated with 36.4- or 112.8-ppm-Ca–DI water received a complete deacidification treatment plus an adequate alkaline reserve.

Conclusion

It had been found earlier that paper washed in distilled or deionized water containing no calcium ions is less stable than paper that had been treated. It has now been shown that regulated addition of alkaline earth compounds with the chemical feeder allows utilization of deionized or distilled water to give superior results in washing paper artifacts. It is considered that use of the chemical feeder will make a significant change in the design of washing or washing and deacidification equipment. In this chapter, a peristaltic or bellows metering pump was used as a chemical feeder to adjust the DI water–alkaline ratio by varying the flow rate of the alkaline solution. Superior washing was accomplished with the 9-ppm-Ca-level deionized water created by the metering pump. For washing and deacidification, 14–20 ppm Ca was added to deionized water by the chemical feeder process. The third application is complete deacidification with production of an adequate alkaline reserve in the paper. This is done by adding 36–112 ppm Ca in the deionized or distilled water by the chemical feeder. A washing time of one hour appears adequate; longer times give only slightly better results. In summary, the DI–alkaline system using the chemical feeder provides an extremely high degree of flexibility, allowing easy washing and deacidification of paper by the conservator.

Acknowledgments

I wish to thank Dr. John C. Williams, Research Officer, and Mr. Peter Waters, Restoration Officer, for the support, guidance, and assistance given for this study.

Table IX. Aging Tests on Washed Paper,

100°C Dry Oven Accelerated Aging

Method	ppm Ca in DI–Ca Water	Treatment (h)	0 days		7 days	
			Acidity (meq/kg)	Alkaline Reserve (%CaCO$_3$)	Acidity (meq/kg)	Alkaline Reserve (%CaCO$_3$)
O	0.0	unwashed	25		22.5	
A	9.2	1 3	2.7 2.6		5.4 8.6	
B	11.4	1 3		0.05 0.06	2.7 3.0	
C	15.4	1 3		0.04 0.08		0.03 0.13
D	36.4	1 3		0.27 0.27		0.14 0.15
E	112.8	1 3		0.35 0.36		0.31 0.25

50% Relative Humidity 90°C Humid Oven Accelerated Aging

Method	ppm Ca in DI–Ca Water	Treatment (h)	Acidity (meq/kg)	Alkaline Reserve (%CaCO$_3$)	Acidity (meq/kg)	Alkaline Reserve (%CaCO$_3$)
O	0.0	unwashed	25		22.5	
A	9.2	1 3	2.7 2.6		12.5 9.1	
B	11.4	1 3		0.05 0.06	3.0 2.6	
C	15.4	1 3		0.04 0.08	0.9 0.0	
D	36.4	1 3		0.27 0.27		0.10 0.14
E	112.8	1 3		0.35 0.36		0.33 0.30

Effect on Alkalinity of Foldur Kraft Paper

100°C Dry Oven Accelerated Aging

14 days		21 days		35 days	
Acidity (meq/kg)	*Alkaline Reserve (%CaCO₃)*	*Acidity (meq/kg)*	*Alkaline Reserve (%CaCO₃)*	*Acidity (meq/kg)*	*Alkaline Reserve (%CaCO₃)*
22.5		22.5		27.5	
10.8		11.1		15.6	
8.7		7.9		10.2	
2.9		10.1		6.7	
2.7		5.1		4.3	
0.6		1.1		3.7	
	0.03	1.0		3.1	
	0.09		0.07		0.03
	0.11		0.07		0.06
	0.29		0.34		0.24
	0.25		0.30		0.26

50% Relative Humidity 90°C Humid Oven Accelerated Aging

14 days		21 days		35 days	
22.5		22.5		30.0	
12.8		14.6		17.7	
8.8		10.2		13.3	
7.8		13.0		8.9	
6.1		7.9		8.9	
1.6		4.4		6.8	
2.9		5.6		5.9	
	0.08		0.07		0.06
	0.06		0.09		0.06
	0.28		0.25		0.24
	0.26		0.21		0.22

Table X. Aging Tests on Washed Paper,
100°C Dry Oven Accelerated Aging

Method	ppm Ca in DI–Ca Water	Treat-ment (h)	0 days Acidity (meq/kg)	0 days Alkaline Reserve (%CaCO₃)	7 days Acidity (meq/kg)	7 days Alkaline Reserve (%CaCO₃)
O	0.0	un-washed	53.0		56.7	
A	9.2	1 3	5.5 4.0		26.6 8.75	
B	11.4	1 3		0.18 0.28		0.054 0.16
C	15.4	1 3		0.39 0.50		0.47 0.31
D	36.4	1 3		0.69 0.78		0.60 0.67
E	112.8	1 3		1.37 1.37		1.27 1.29

50% Relative Humidity 90°C Humid Oven Accelerated Aging

Method	ppm Ca in DI–Ca Water	Treat-ment (h)	0 days Acidity (meq/kg)	0 days Alkaline Reserve (%CaCO₃)	7 days Acidity (meq/kg)	7 days Alkaline Reserve (%CaCO₃)
O	0.0	un-washed	53.0		80.0	
A	9.2	1 3	5.5 4.0		26.9 13.6	
B	11.4	1 3		0.18 0.28	3.3	0.14
C	15.4	1 3		0.39 0.50		0.25 0.44
D	36.4	1 3		0.69 0.70		0.63 0.67
E	112.8	1 3		1.37 1.37		1.34 1.39

Effect on Alkalinity of Newsprint Paper

100°C Dry Oven Accelerated Aging

14 days		21 days		35 days	
Acidity (meq/kg)	Alkaline Reserve (%CaCO₃)	Acidity (meq/kg)	Alkaline Reserve (%CaCO₃)	Acidity (meq/kg)	Alkaline Reserve (%CaCO₃)
66.7		76.7		100.0	
33.0		44.4		73.3	
29.4		40.0		54.0	
10.5		26.3		45.5	
0.0		5.6		25.0	
	0.22		0.15	5.5	0.22
	0.28		0.31		
	0.54		0.50		0.62
	0.58		0.61		0.50
	1.28		1.22		1.20
	1.10		1.47		1.08

50% Relative Humidity 90°C Humid Oven Accelerated Aging

Acidity (meq/kg)	Alkaline Reserve (%CaCO₃)	Acidity (meq/kg)	Alkaline Reserve (%CaCO₃)	Acidity (meq/kg)	Alkaline Reserve (%CaCO₃)
90.0		96.7		123.3	
36.8		55.6		61.1	
32.6		40.8		56.0	
15.7		28.6		52.9	
0.0		2.2		11.9	
	0.22		0.22	2.25	
	0.40		0.34		0.24
	0.58		0.50		0.44
	0.63		0.67		0.56
	1.40		1.35		1.24
	1.30		1.40		1.17

Literature Cited

1. Barrow, W. J. "Permanence/Durability of the Book III—Spray Deacidification"; W. J. Barrow Research Laboratory: Richmond, VA, 1964; p. 12.
2. Tang, L. C.; Jones, N. M. *J. Am. Inst. Conserv.* **1979**, *18*(2), 61–81.
3. Tang, L. C. *J. Am. Inst. Conserv.* **1978**, *17*(2), 19.
4. Kelly, G. B. *Arch. Bibl. Belgique* **1974**, *12*, 91–105.
5. Barrow, W. J. "Permanence/Durability of the Book II—Test Data of Naturally Aged Papers"; W. J. Barrow Research Laboratory: Richmond, VA, 1963.
6. Wilson, W. K.; Harvey, J. L.; Mandel, J.; Worksman, T. *Tappi* **1955**, *38*(9), 543.
7. Church, R. W., Ed. "The Manufacture and Testing of Durable Book Papers"; Virginia State Library: Richmond, VA, 1960.
8. Browning, B. L.; Wink, W. A. *Tappi* **1968**, *51*(4), 156–163.

RECEIVED October 23, 1979.

8

The Effect of Magnesium Bicarbonate Solutions on Various Papers

WILLIAM K. WILSON, RUTH A. GOLDING, R. H. McCLAREN, and JAMES L. GEAR

GSA, National Archives and Records Service, Preservation Services Division, Washington, DC 20408

As part of a long-range program on a study of the effects of various deacidification procedures on paper, the effects of $Mg(HCO_3)_2$ on the physical and chemical properties of several old papers, some multicolored maps, and handsheets made from a bleached hardwood kraft were studied. Reflectance usually increased with deacidification. Tear and tensile energy absorption also improved, and these properties are important to the handling properties of papers. The sizing of the papers studied was destroyed by deacidification in $Mg(HCO_3)_2$. It was shown that deacidification did not remove aluminum from the carboxyl groups in laboratory handsheets. The stability toward accelerated aging at 90°C in closed cells of various handsheets led to inconclusive results.

This chapter describes some work on the effect of magnesium bicarbonate solutions on several old papers, some maps, and some handsheets made in the laboratory especially for this study. Also included are some data on the interaction of metals with cellulose, as the metal on the carboxyl groups is thought to be of importance in the stability of paper (*1–6*). This is part of an extensive study of deacidification that is being carried out by the Research Laboratory of the Preservation Services Division of National Archives and Records Service.

Several investigators have studied the effects of deacidification on paper. Flieder (*7*) evaluated several deacidification procedures using breaking length, fold, burst, tear, reflectance, opacity, pH, copper number, and ash as criteria of change. Accelerated aging for 72 h at 105°C and for 4 h at 87°C and 60% relative humidity was employed as measures of comparative stability before and after various treatments. She favored the Barrow two-stage process (8) or treatment with borax (9). Hey is firmly opposed to the use of borax as a deacidification agent (10).

Santucci has done some interesting work on deacidification (11, 12) as well as accelerated aging (13). He prefers an unsaturated solution of magnesium bicarbonate, a saturated solution of magnesium carbonate, or tap water. As he points out, the latter two do not provide an appreciable alkaline reserve. For nonaqueous deacidification, he suggests the use of Smith's magnesium methoxide spray (14). Santucci stresses that one should start with a paper of known and reproducible characteristics, as the use of commercial papers of unknown composition has caused much confusion. He also discusses moist and dry accelerated aging, and describes a procedure for aging paper in closed cells (13). The latter is more degradative than when the same temperature and relative humidity are employed at atmospheric pressure.

The pioneering work on deacidification was done over forty years ago by Schierholz (15) and by Barrow (8), who applied Schierholz's patent in the development of his two-step process of calcium hydroxide followed by calcium bicarbonate. Many other approaches have been devised since that time, including the use of magnesium bicarbonate introduced at National Archives and Records Service (NARS) by Gear (16). In addition, some of the articles that discuss various deacidification procedures have been authored by Kelly (17, 18), Werner (19), Williams (20), Smith (21, 22, 23), and Walker (24).

A subject that has received considerable attention over the years is the effect of metals on the stability of cellulose. Sihtola (1, 2, 3) showed that metals on the carboxyls influenced the extent of yellowing during accelerated aging. Data developed by Parks (4, 5, 6) on accelerated aging of handsheets indicate that the metal on the carboxyls greatly influences stability. Hudson (25) and Lanwell (26) observed that certain metals in paper catalyzed the oxidation of SO_2 to SO_3. Thus, the exposure of paper to SO_2 can be much more serious than at first glance. Spinner (27, 28) has studied the effect of iron and copper salts on the yellowing of paper. Williams (29) studied the performance of copper as an oxidation catalyst in accelerated aging, and was able to show that a small amount of sodium carbonate arrested the degradation. Back (30) showed that certain metals induced dimensional stability in fiber building board, apparently due to crosslinking. A similar reaction has been found to occur in paper (4).

Magnesium bicarbonate solutions for deacidification usually are prepared from basic magnesium carbonate by passing CO_2 gas through a slurry of the carbonate in water. However, it has been found that magnesium hydroxide is a much more convenient source of magnesium (31, 32). The hydroxide dissolves readily in water through which CO_2 is bubbled. It has a definite chemical composition, in contrast to the basic carbonate, so a solution of definite strength may be prepared with no need for analysis. Solutions up to about 0.2M have been prepared. As has been noted by others (*11*), the pH of the solution is no indication of strength and the more concentrated solutions have a tendency to precipitate.

The ranges of pH values in which solutions of magnesium bicarbonate are stable have been measured and are listed in Table I (*32*). These data show that the pH of a solution of magnesium bicarbonate depends on the concentration of salt in solution and on the concentration of CO_2. If care is taken to preserve the CO_2 content of a solution, no trouble should be encountered with precipitation.

There is no "standard consensus concentration" of magnesium bicarbonate solution for deacidification of paper. Some conservators prefer a high concentration to assure an adequate alkaline reserve. Others object to the "chalky feel" of papers so treated. A concentration of 0.05M was used in this study unless otherwise indicated.

The pH range of magnesium bicarbonate solutions is quite broad, and extends from about 6.4 to about 9.5. As the chemistry of the deacidification process probably depends, to some extent, on the pH of the solution, this, plus the uncertainty of the composition of commercial paper samples, may explain some of the differences in results from one laboratory to another. One also must remember that about twenty possible chemical modifications of the anhydroglucose ring in cellulose may be written down.

In connection with a program at the National Bureau of Standards, sponsored by National Archives and Records Service (*33*), on the development of specifications for permanent record papers, some handsheets were made from a pulp in which the carboxyls were covered with aluminum. Just before the sheet was formed, some calcium carbonate was added to the headbox. Thus, the cellulose had aluminum on the carboxyls, a characteristic of instability, and the paper had a calcium carbonate filler, a characteristic of stability.

Although these handsheets were stable toward dry aging at 90°C, they were unstable toward accelerated aging at 90°C and 50% relative humidity. However, they were more stable than aluminum-exchanged handsheets without calcium carbonate filler.

This poses a question concerning deacidification. If a deacidification procedure does not remove aluminum from the cellulose carboxyls, will the paper have the stability that one would expect from a paper with an alkaline filler? In an attempt to answer this question, a series of handsheets was made from a hardwood kraft pulp. This pulp was selected because: (a) it had a carboxyl content of 5.75 mmol/100 g pulp, which is similar to that of some old papers; (b) it was easy to beat in a laboratory beater; and (c) the physical properties of the handsheets were in the "old

Table I. Range of pH Values in Which Solutions of Magnesium
Dioxide, and the Latter Was Then Removed by

Strength of bicarbonate solution, (M)

pH values

at saturation with CO_2
at first opalescence[a]
at heavy opalescence
at considerable precipitation
after several hours, bubbling with no precipitation

pH range from CO_2 saturation

to opalescence
to maximum pH without precipitation[b]

[a] "Milkiness" attributable to appearance of fine particles of precipitate.
[b] No precipitation occurred in these solutions after several hours bubbling.

paper" range. Before making handsheets, the pulp was treated to provide
the desired metal on the carboxyls.

In reviewing the literature on the effect of deacidification on paper,
three important factors emerge: (a) it is desirable to work with papers
that are reproducible, well characterized, and similar in properties, both
chemical and physical, to old papers; (b) much more work needs to be
done on the interaction of metals with the carboxyls in cellulose; and (c)
a standard procedure for accelerated aging that includes some moisture in
the aging atmosphere is desperately needed.

Experimental

Preparation of Solutions of Magnesium Bicarbonate. Magnesium
bicarbonate solutions were prepared as needed by bubbling CO_2 from a
tank of compressed gas through a fritted glass diffuser into a volumetric
flask containing a suspension of magnesium hydroxide in distilled water
(32). When solution was complete, water was added to the mark and the
flask agitated to effect thorough mixing.

Methods of Analysis and Testing. The organic material extracted
from paper by water and by magnesium bicarbonate solutions was oxidized with an excess of potassium dichromate in about $10M$ sulfuric acid
solution at about 125°C. Specimens were extracted with 20 mL water or
magnesium bicarbonate solution, rinsed with 15 mL water, and 5mL of
$0.5N$ $K_2Cr_2O_7$ was added to the combined extract and rinsings. The addition of 50 mL of concentrated sulfuric acid, slowly and with stirring,
raised the temperature through heat of dilution to about 115°C. The solutions were heated on a hot plate, and removed when the temperature
reached 125°C. The excess dichromate was determined by electrometric
titration (calomel, platinum) with ferrous ammonium sulfate solution
($1N$ in $1N$ H_2SO_4). The oxidation step is similar to that outlined in a
TAPPI standard for determination of alkali solubility (34).

Bicarbonate Are Stable. Solutions Were Saturated with Carbon
Bubbling Oxygen Through the Solution (*32*)

0.15	0.10	0.05	0.04	0.035	0.025
6.98	6.9(	6.68	6.61	6.53	6.40
8.50	8.56	9.18	—[b]	—[b]	—[b]
8.57	8.56	9.19	—	—	—
8.52	8.54	8.98	—	—	—
—	—	—	9.37	9.53	9.53
1.52	1.66	2.50	—	—	—
—	—	—	2.76	3.00	3.13

[a] Although no precipitation occurred during the experiment, precipitation occurred in each solution after standing overnight.

Preparation of Solutions of Magnesium Bicarbonate for Deacidification of Documents

The theoretical factor for total oxidation of glucose is 7.5 mg of glucose per meq of dichromate. For total oxidation of cellulose, the factor is 6.75 mg cellulose per meq of cellulose. As indicated in TAPPI T 235, the actual oxidation is not quite theoretical and is given as 6.85 mg cellulose per meq of dichromate. Pentosans and paper sizing materials give different oxidation factors.

A TAPPI method for pH was used (*35*), care being taken to prevent any of the paper from touching the electrodes during the measurement process (*36*).

Stiffness (*37*), folding endurance (*38*), Sheffield smoothness (*39*), porosity (*40*), and internal tearing resistance (*41*) were determined by appropriate TAPPI methods.

Reflectance was determined with a commercial UV/visible recording spectrophotometer with integrating sphere, using a vitrolite standard calibrated by the National Bureau of Standards. The value at 457 nm was taken arbitrarily as the reflectance. This is similar, but not equivalent to, TAPPI brightness (*42*).

Sizing values were determined using a fluorescent dye described by van den Akker et al. (*43*).

Qualitative examination of papers for glue was performed according to TAPPI T 417 (*44*).

Metals in pulps and papers were determined after wet-ashing with nitric acid by atomic absorption techniques using a commercial instrument. Tensile properties (load at break, elongation at break, energy to break) were determined using a commercial recording load-elongation machine (*45*).

Deacidification was carried out in covered enameled trays, after which the papers were suspended from a line and allowed to air-dry without pressing.

Samples Used for Evaluation. The following samples of old papers were obtained from the NARS Document Restoration Laboratory and the origins of some of them are unknown:

1. U.S. District Court Book, Montgomery, Alabama, Executive Docket, May, 1839–December, 1860.
2. Economy linen ledger.
3. Ruled ledger.
4. Customers journal, Frederiksted 1788–1789.
5. Christiansted weigh book, 1771.
6. Old paper, bad condition.
7. Ruled ledger.
8. Old paper.
9. Plain old paper.
10. St. Croix journal.

Preparation of the pulp (beating) for papermaking was performed according to TAPPI recommendations (46). Water from a reverse osmosis unit was used as the beating medium. Handsheets were prepared with the standard British handsheet machine, again using reverse osmosis water (47).

A wood pulp, designated as Pulp F, was used in some of the experiments. It contained (manufacturer's data) about 85% α-cellulose and 15% hemicelluloses. The carboxyl content was about 2.5 mmols/100 g pulp.

A hardwood kraft pulp was used for handsheets. This had a carboxyl content of about 5.75 mmols/100 g pulp.

Seven maps were included in this study. Six of them were U.S. Department of Interior, Geological Survey maps of areas of North Carolina identified below. A Civil War map, Lab No. 7, was included in the study.

U.S. Geological

Lab No.	Date	Survey No.	Area
1	1950	N3500-W7815/15	Coharie
2	1944	N3515-W7815/15	Four Oaks
3	1914	N3515-W7730/15	Kinston
4	1959	N3445-W7830/15	Roseboro
5	1959	N3445-W7845/15	Saint Pauls
6	1957	N3500-W7745/15	Seven Springs

Results and Discussion

In this section, data are presented on the effects of deacidification on: (a) oxidizable material extracted from some old papers; (b) changes in physical properties of these old papers; and (c) changes in physical properties of several multicolored maps. The results of some experiments on the interaction of metal ions with a hardwood kraft pulp are given, and discussed in relation to deacidification and probable stability. A series of handsheets made from a hardwood kraft pulp, after treatment of the pulp with various metal ions, were studied in relation to the effects of deacidification on the removal of aluminum and on stability before and after deacidification. In this chapter, deacidification is defined as treating paper with a solution of magnesium bicarbonate, which leaves an alkaline buffer in the paper.

Tap water is defined in this chapter as the water that is supplied in the Washington, DC area. The composition varies, mostly by season. Tap water composition may vary greatly among geographical areas.

Oxidizable Material. To check the laboratory procedure for oxidation of organic material extracted from old papers, weighed amounts of glucose, a filter paper, and a papermaking pulp (Pulp F) were oxidized; the data are given in Table II. Pulp F is slightly out of line, but this can be explained on the basis of its substantial pentosans content, which requires a slightly different factor in milligrams of pulp oxidized per milliequivalents of dichromate.

Table II. **Oxidation of Carbohydrate Materials with Potassium Dichromate in Sulfuric Acid at 125°C**

Glucose (% oxidation)	Filter Paper (% oxidation)	Pulp F (% oxidation)
100	99	102
101	96	103
99	100	104
100	100	102
99	99	104
99	99	103

Data on the amounts of material extracted from some old papers and Pulp F are given in Table III. As these extractions were made under typical deacidification conditions, one cannot claim great precision, but a very interesting situation emerges when the data in each category are summed up. It appears that water and $Mg(HCO_3)_2$ extract similar amounts of oxidizable material, but appreciably larger amounts of material are removed by water followed by $Mg(HCO_3)_2$. The extracts were not filtered, so no distinction is made between soluble matter and particulate matter.

Assuming that these data are typical of old papers that might be deacidified, the amount of material that may be removed during the deacidification process is not substantial.

Data on the effect of pH and concentration of $Mg(HCO_3)_2$ solutions on the amount of oxidizable material extracted from papers are given in Table IV. The changes are not pronounced or very significant, but it appears that the amount of material extracted increases with concentration and with pH. From this standpoint only, assuming that these samples are representative, there need be little concern about the pH or the concentration of $Mg(HCO_3)_2$ deacidification solutions.

Table III.   Oxidizable Material Extracted from Old Papers and Pulp F by Distilled Water, By Distilled Water Followed by 0.05M Mg(HCO₃)₂, and by Magnesium Carbonate Alone

	Treatment (amount removed (%))		
Sample Number	*Water Only*	*Water Followed by 0.05 M Mg(HCO₃)₂*	*0.05M Mg(HCO₃)₂ Only*
1	1.3	3.2	1.5
2	1.5	2.0	1.4
3	3.8	3.6	3.4
4	1.3	3.0	1.2
5	3.0	3.0	3.2
6	2.4	2.3	2.0
7	1.1	3.8	1.2
8	1.4	1.4	1.6
9	1.4	2.4	1.8
10	2.8	3.4	2.3
Pulp F	0.05	0.07	0.04
$\sum$ [a]	20.0	28.1	19.6

[a] Ignoring pulp F.

Data on the amount of oxidizable material extracted with distilled water and with tap water are given in Table V. From the summations of the values, it is obvious that the differences are negligible.

Table IV.   Effect of pH and Concentration of Magnesium Bicarbonate Solutions on Amount of Oxidizable Material Extracted from Papers

	Concentration of Mg(HCO₃)₂ (M)	
pH	*0.05 (amount extracted %)*	*0.15 (amount extracted %)*
Sample 1		
6.80	1.1	—
6.90	—	1.4
7.82	1.1	—
8.26	—	2.0
8.94	1.8	—
Sample 3		
6.60	2.9	—
6.64	2.9	—
6.90	—	3.5
7.86	2.9	—
8.26	—	3.8
8.80	3.7	—
8.94	3.6	—

Table V. Comparison of the Amount of Oxidizable Material Extracted with Distilled Water and With Tap Water

	Oxidizable Material Extracted with Water	
Sample Number	Distilled (amount, %)	Tap (amount, %)
1	1.1	1.0
2	1.5	1.2
3	2.6	2.8
4	1.2	1.3
5	2.4	2.8
6	2.2	2.0
7	1.2	0.9
8	1.4	1.3
9	1.5	1.2
10	2.2	2.4
Σ	17.3	16.9

Table VI provides data on the oxidizable material extracted from paper No. 3 with water followed by magnesium bicarbonate as a function of time. For this particular paper, the amount of oxidizable material extracted reaches a maximum in about twenty minutes.

Data on the effect of temperature on the extraction of oxidizable material from paper No. 3 are given in Table VII. There is some uncertainty between 3°C and 10°C, and the differences probably represent experimental error. From 10°C to 44°C, the trend is unmistakable. The increased extraction at 44°C could be attributable, at least in part, to an increase in pH through loss of CO_2 (*see* Table IV). In any event, the temperature coefficient of extraction is not great enough to cause concern during deacidification.

Effect of Water and of Magnesium Bicarbonate on pH of Old Papers. Data on the effect of soaking in water and/or magnesium bicarbonate for

Table VI. Oxidizable Material Extracted from Paper No. 3, as a Function of Time, with Distilled Water Followed Immediately with 0.05M $Mg(HCO_3)_2$

Time of Extraction (min)		Amount Extracted (%)		
H_2O	$Mg(HCO_3)_2$	H_2O	$Mg(HCO_3)_2$	Total
1	1	1.8	0.6	2.4
5	5	1.6	0.9	2.5
10	10	2.3	0.8	3.1
20	20	2.6	0.9	3.5
20	20	2.7	0.9	3.6
30	30	2.9	0.8	3.7
60	60	3.1	0.7	3.8
60	60	3.0	0.7	3.7

Table VII. Effect of Temperature on the Extraction of
Oxidizable Material from Paper No. 3

Amount Extracted by

Tem- perature (°C)	H_2O, Only (%)	$Mg(HCO_3)_2$, Only (%)	H_2O (%) $+$	$Mg(HCO_3)_2$ (%) $=$	Total (%)
3	2.4	3.6	2.6	0.9	3.5
10	3.0	3.4	2.4	0.7	3.1
24	3.1	4.1	3.0	0.8	3.8
44	3.9	5.0	3.8	0.6	4.4

30 min on pH are given in Table VIII. As might be expected, soaking in water increases the pH. This already has been noted by Santucci (11). Although a range of pH values would be expected from a group of papers treated with magnesium bicarbonate, it is surprising that the range is almost one pH unit. The pH values for the papers treated with magnesium bicarbonate alone are higher, except in one case, than the papers treated with water and then magnesium bicarbonate. Apparently, the papers already wet with water do not take up as much magnesium bicarbonate. Washing with distilled water tends to remove stabilizing metals (1, 2, 3, 48, 49, 50), and should be followed with deacidification.

Data on the effect of time of soaking in water followed by soaking in 0.05M $Mg(HCO_3)_2$ on the pH of paper No. 3 are given in Table IX. It appears that even one minute of soaking in magnesium bicarbonate provides considerable buffering, although this would need to be substantiated by measurement of alkaline reserve. A short soaking time could be an advantage where inks were somewhat sensitive to water, but resistant enough to withstand a water solution for a short time.

Table VIII. Effect of Soaking in Water and/or Magnesium
Bicarbonate for 30 Minutes Each on the pH
of Several Old Papers

pH After Following Treatments

Sample Number	None	H_2O	$Mg(HCO_3)_2$	H_2O Followed by $Mg(HCO_3)_2$
1	6.74	6.70	10.05	9.71
2	4.67	5.52	8.34	8.29
3	4.33	4.70	9.32	9.14
4	6.74	6.70	10.05	9.71
5	4.49	5.42	9.15	8.87
6	4.66	5.35	9.06	9.14
7	5.35	5.75	8.91	8.76
8	6.06	6.43	9.84	9.72
9	5.14	5.62	9.45	9.12
10	4.69	5.48	10.28	10.21

Table IX. Effect of Various Times of Soaking in Water Followed by Magnesium Bicarbonate on the pH of Paper No. 3

Time in (min)		
H_2O	$Mg(HCO_3)_2$	pH
0	0	4.33
1	1	8.64
5	5	8.74
10	10	9.05
20	20	9.16
30	30	9.22
60	60	9.44

Effect of Water and of Magnesium Bicarbonate on Sizing of Old Papers. Data on sizing values of old papers and of some other papers as a comparison, before and after treatments with water and/or magnesium bicarbonate, are given in Table X. In this test, a dye that becomes fluorescent when wet is sprinkled over the paper specimen, which is then floated on water. The endpoint is determined visually, using a fluorescence black light as a source of exciting irradiation. It is obvious that either water or magnesium bicarbonate reduces the sizing values substantially. The sizing values for papers No. 4 and No. 8 are so low that

Table X. Sizing Values of Old Papers and Some Other Papers[a]

Sample Number	Glue	None	Water	$Mg(HCO_3)_2$	Water Followed by $Mg(HCO_3)_2$
				Treatment	
1	no	955	220	351	67
2	yes	810	341	133	85
3	no	66	46	9	6
4	yes	7	15	3	7
5	yes	105	18	4	5
6	yes	71	13	5	8
7	yes	405	216	217	210
·8	no	4	6	7	8
9	yes	198	61	58	73
10	yes	103	25	8	4
Pulp F		0.8	0.6	0.6	
Paper towel		< 1	< 1		
Tablet		> 1800			
Memo pad		> 1800			

[a] After soaking for 30 min in water, soaking 30 min in $Mg(HCO_3)_2$, or soaking 30 min in water followed by 30 min in $Mg(HCO_3)_2$. Sizing value given in seconds.

changes after treatments are meaningless. It is interesting that the sizing value of paper No. 1 is so high, as it contains no glue, although some other sizing material may be present.

Effect of Water and of Magnesium Bicarbonate on Physical Properties. Data on several physical properties of old papers before and after treatment with water or magnesium bicarbonate are given in Table XI. The tearing strength usually increases after treatment with water or

Table XI. Tearing Strength, Folding Endurance, Smoothness and Stiffness Data on Old Papers after Soaking in Water or in 0.05M Mg(HCO₃)₂

Sample Number	Treatment	Tear (g)	Fold (double folds 500 g tension)	Smoothness (Sheffield units)	Stiffness (Taber units)
1	none	93	1	276	32
	H_2O	111	7	297	33
	$Mg(HCO_3)_2$	130	13	305	30
2	none	64	1	116	10
	H_2O	86	1	133	6
	$Mg(HCO_3)_2$	79	1	138	6
3	none	90	49	346	14
	H_2O	119	100	392	19
	$Mg(HCO_3)_2$	113	140	391	22
4	none	101	660	378	11
	H_2O	116	430	387	6
	$Mg(HCO_3)_2$	138	110	387	12
5	none	200	520	384	7
	H_2O	134	230	386	7
	$Mg(HCO_3)_2$	146	230	386	10
6	none	72	3	380	5
	H_2O	127	11	374	6
	$Mg(HCO_3)_2$	138	6	374	7
7	none	82	43	107	9
	H_2O	126	130	172	11
	$Mg(HCO_3)_2$	99	130	173	8
9	none	106	130	396	12
	H_2O	125	180	396	16
	$Mg(HCO_3)_2$	131	130	404	16
10	none	158	6	388	6
	H_2O	92	11	384	10
	$Mg(HCO_3)_2$	85	8	387	10

Table XII. Tensile Properties of Old Papers after Soaking in Water or in 0.05M Mg(HCO₃)₂

Sample Number	Treatment	Load at Break (N/m)	Elongation at Break $(\%)$	Tensile Energy Absorption (J/m^2)
1	none	7990	1.1	66
	H_2O	7310	2.1	102
	$Mg(HCO_3)_2$	6770	2.0	96
2	none	3560	0.6	15
	H_2O	3840	1.0	24
	$Mg(HCO_3)_2$	4070	0.9	26
3	none	4120	1.6	51
	H_2O	3640	2.8	79
	$Mg(HCO_3)_2$	3830	3.1	94
4	none	3550	3.1	84
	H_2O	3480	3.7	95
	$Mg(HCO_3)_2$	3290	3.1	78
5	none	3650	1.7	45
	H_2O	2740	2.0	41
	$Mg(HCO_3)_2$	3300	2.3	54
7 Sheet A	none	4920	1.4	50
	H_2O	4880	2.2	85
	$Mg(HCO_3)_2$	4930	2.2	72
7 Sheet B	none	4160	1.0	31
	H_2O	4010	1.7	52
	$Mg(HCO_3)_2$	4300	1.7	57

$Mg(HCO_3)_2$, although No. 5 and No. 10 are exceptions. The increase in tearing strength after treatment is not too surprising, as the tensile energy absorption (Table XII) usually increases after treatment. The folding endurance does not show any particular pattern, as some papers increase and some decrease in folding endurance after treatment. Neither smoothness nor stiffness show any particulart trend, and the changes do not appear to be significant.

Data on the tensile properties of old papers before and after treatment with water or $0.05M$ $Mg(HCO_3)_2$ are given in Table XII. The changes in tensile strength are not significant to the document restorer. The changes in elongations to break and tensile energy absorption (TEA) are quite pronounced and are significant to the restorer. The increases in elongation and, therefore, as the tensile does not change much, the TEA, mean that the capacity of the paper to do work and absorb energy before rupturing has increased with a deacidification treatment.

Table XIII. Effect of Water Followed by 0.05M Mg(HCO$_3$)$_2$ on the Reflectance at 457 nm of Old Papers

| Sample Number | Reflectance after Treatment with | | | Change after Treatment | | |
	None	H$_2$O	Mg(HCO$_3$)$_2$	None to H$_2$O	H$_2$O to Mg(HCO$_3$)$_2$	Total
1	43.2	46.2	51.2	3.0	5.0	8.0
2	49.7	52.5	54.2	2.8	1.7	4.5
3	52.8	58.0	59.0	5.2	1.0	6.2
4	56.8	61.7	61.6	4.9	−0.1	4.8
5	39.6	44.9	45.3	5.3	0.4	5.7
6	31.9	31.0	45.7	−0.9	14.7	13.8
7	61.1	60.9	61.8	−0.2	0.9	0.7
8	58.3	64.3	64.3	6.0	0.0	6.0
9	59.2	63.3	63.1	4.1	−0.2	3.9
10	26.2	29.6	28.7	3.4	−0.9	2.5

As most of these papers are handsheets, the variation in properties from sheet to sheet is substantial. This is shown by the data on the two sheets of paper No. 7. Specimens were taken from one sheet only in determining the effect of various treatments on old papers.

Table XIV. Effect of Deacidification with Magnesium Bicarbonate Maps and a

Map Number	Date	Treatment	Fold, MIT, 1 kg tension (double folds)	Tear (g)
1	1950	none	46	123
		Mg(HCO$_3$)$_2$	66	134
2	1944	none	120	131
		Mg(HCO$_3$)$_2$	140	152
3	1914	none	82	157
		Mg(HCO$_3$)$_2$	91	178
4	1959	none	54	136
		Mg(HCO$_3$)$_2$	160	168
5	1959	none	120	147
		Mg(HCO$_3$)$_2$	180	163
6	1957	none	96	154
		Mg(HCO$_3$)$_2$	93	155
7	1862	none	2	96
		Mg(HCO$_3$)$_2$	2	99

Effect of Water and of Magnesium Bicarbonate on Reflectance of Old Papers. Data on the reflectance of old papers after soaking in water for 30 min and then in 0.05M Mg(HCO$_3$)$_2$ for 30 min are presented in Table XIII. Soaking in water usually increases the reflectance substantially. Further treatment with magnesium bicarbonate did not produce a dramatic increase in reflectance except in paper No. 1. Assuming that these data are representative, this provides the order of magnitude of whitening one may expect from deacidification with magnesium bicarbonate.

To obtain these data it was necessary to measure the reflectance of the same area before and after treatment. The samples were so non-uniform that measuring specimens at random and calculating the average was of little value.

Deacidification of Maps. Data on the effect of deacidification on several U.S. Geological Survey Maps and a Civil War Map are given in Table XIV. The folding endurance improved except in the last two maps. Although the statistical significance of the increases are questionable except for No. 4, all of the five maps increase in fold. All of the tearing strength values increase substantially except two. Nothing is outstanding about the stiffness values. Smoothness decreases except in two cases. This is to be expected, and it is unimportant.

for Thirty Minutes on the Properties of Six U.S. Geological Survey Civil War Map

Stiffness (Taber units)	Smoothness (Sheffield units)	pH	Sizing (s)	Reflectance (%)
9	93	6.0	160	80.9
14	26	8.5	23	79.2
12	102	6.1	170	82.6
14	262	8.4	17	78.9
17	106	6.3	240	67.3
14	246	7.7	40–60	68.6
12	109	6.4	210–290	74.8
13	253	8.4	25–110	74.2
7	114	6.1	190	78.1
15	254	8.0	25–85	76.2
3	111	6.2	150–280	78.2
18	231	8.1	12–40	76.2
3	275	5.6	9	51.4
3	278	8.1	2	51.4

Table XV. Effect of Deacidification with Magnesium Carbonate
for Thirty Minutes on the Tensile Properties of Six U.S.
Geological Survey Maps and a Civil War Map

Map Number	Date	Treatment	Load at Break (N/m)	Elongation at Break (%)	Tensile Energy Absorption (J/m²)
1	1950	none	5810	2.4	90
		$Mg(HCO_3)_2$	5430	3.1	113
2	1944	none	6675	2.3	105
		$Mg(HCO_3)_2$	5695	2.7	104
3	1914	none	5330	2.0	71
		$Mg(HCO_3)_2$	4715	2.6	86
4	1959	none	5735	1.9	73
		$Mg(HCO_3)_2$	5120	2.4	78
5	1959	none	6525	2.0	89
		$Mg(HCO_3)_2$	6520	3.4	146
6	1957	none	4635	1.9	60
		$Mg(HCO_3)_2$	4635	2.3	71
7	1862	none	1655	1.7	19
		$Mg(HCO_3)_2$	1320	2.1	20

The pH values of the maps before deacidification are surprisingly
high. This is in keeping with the data developed by Smith (51) who
studied the effect of deacidification on maps. The pH values after
deacidification are not nearly as high as the pH values of the old papers
after deacidification. These maps apparently contain a buffer that was
built in during manufacture.

The sizing of the maps is destroyed by soaking in magnesium bicarbonate. Reflectance does not change appreciably.

Data on the effect of deacidification on the tensile properties of the
maps are given in Table XV. From the variability of the data it is
questionable if the decreases in tensile strength are significant, although
all of the differences represent decreases. With the exception of maps
No. 1 and No. 5, the same is true for elongation. Although most of the
changes in tensile energy absorption are increases, map No. 5 is the only
one that shows a significant increase.

Interactions of Cellulose with Metal Ions. Interactions of metal ions
with cellulose and the influence of metals on the carboxyls on stability
was discussed in the introduction. Some metals are held much more
tenaciously than others, but research workers do not always agree
concerning the relative order. Our concern in this chapter is with inter-

actions of calcium, magnesium, and aluminum with cellulose, especially under deacidification conditions. As an atomic absorption unit was available, it was feasible to determine the small amounts of metal attached to the carboxyls after destruction of the cellulose by digestion with nitric acid.

The bleached hardwood kraft mentioned in the introduction was soaked in a solution of aluminum sulfate and washed thoroughly with water. This "aluminum pulp" was soaked in three concentrations of magnesium acetate for time periods up to sixty minutes, washed, wet-ashed with nitric acid, and analyzed for magnesium and aluminum. The data are given in Table XVI. It does not appear that any aluminum is removed by magnesium acetate. The pick-up of magnesium appears to be a function of time and of magnesium concentration.

Table XVI.   Exchange of Aluminum Pulp[a] with Mg[++] Solutions (Mg(CH$_3$COO)$_2$)[a]

Concentration of Mg[++] Solution (mmol/L)	0.104		0.208		0.417	
Metals in Pulp	*Mg*	*Al*	*Mg*	*Al*	*Mg*	*Al*
Time of Pulp in Mg[++] Solution (min)						
0	0.000	0.020	0.000	0.020	0.000	0.024
2	0.003	0.021	0.005	0.024	0.013	0.023
4	0.004	0.023	0.006	0.024	0.015	0.023
6	0.003	0.024	0.005	0.024	0.015	0.022
8	0.004	0.026	0.006	0.027	0.017	0.021
10	0.003	0.024	0.009	0.024	0.014	0.021
20	0.004	0.023	0.005	0.023	0.017	0.024
60	0.002	0.021	0.006	0.023	0.018	0.022

[a] Metals in pulp were determined by wet-ashing followed by atomic absorption. Data given as mmol/g.
[b] Bleached hardwood kraft soaked in a solution of aluminum acetate. Presumably, carboxyls are in Al salt form.

The exact formation of salts with cellulosic carboxyls has never been resolved. The carboxyl content of the hardwood kraft pulp is about 0.0575 mmol/gram of pulp. If one adds up the meq of metals that have been sorbed by g cellulose, the milliequivalents of metals exceeds the milliequivalents of carboxlys. If one assumes that 1 mmol of metal reacts with 1 meq of carboxyl, then there is a surplus of carboxyls. It would appear that the reaction of metals with carboxyls is nonstoichiometric. Using aluminum sulfate as an example, the product of the

Table XVII. Analysis of Handsheets for Metals[a]

| Treatment of Handsheets | Metals Content of Paper (mmol/g pulp) | | |
	Al	Ca	Mg
None—untreated pulp	0.000	0.018	0.005
Deacidified	0.000	0.005	0.195
None—untreated pulp	0.000	0.018	0.005
Calcium	0.000	0.022	0.006
Calcium-deacidified	0.000	0.004	0.166
None—untreated pulp	0.000	0.018	0.005
Aluminum	0.052	0.013	0.004
Aluminum-deacidified	0.041	0.008	0.241

[a] Carboxyl content of pulp = 0.0575 mmol/g.

reaction with a cellulose carboxyl might be $O{=}\overset{\mid}{C}{-}O{-}AlSO_4$. This could be checked by analyzing for sulfur, although the method would need to be very sensitive.

In order to translate this into the real world of papermaking, and of deacidification, handsheets were made under controlled conditions from the hardwood kraft pulp. The pulp was first treated with calcium acetate solution to cover the carboxyls with calcium. Some of this pulp was then treated with $Al_2(SO_4)_3$ solution. Handsheets were then made from the original pulp, from the calcium pulp, and from the aluminum pulp. Some of these handsheets were deacidified. The metals contents of these handsheets were then determined and the data are given in Table XVII.

It is obvious the magnesium bicarbonate takes out some of the aluminum, but aluminum is removed very incompletely from these handsheets.

Some of these handsheets were then aged at 90°C in a closed cell system devised by Gear and MacClaren (unpublished work). The data were not conclusive, and it will be necessary to repeat the work under rigidly controlled conditions. This work is in progress. It is anticipated that the interaction of metals with cellulose and the performance of some of the products of these interactions with respect to deacidification and to stability toward accelerated aging will be the subject of a subsequent report.

Conclusions

1. Up to about 4% of oxidizable material, based on the weight of the paper, was removed from old papers by water and/or $0.05M$ $Mg(HCO_3)_2$ solution. The temperature coefficient of solubility and the magnesium bicar-

bonate concentration coefficient of solubility were real, but not of sufficient magnitude to be of concern to the document restorer. The same is true with respect to the pH of magnesium bicarbonate solutions.

2. Reflectance of old papers usually increased after deacidification.

3. Tear and tensile energy absorption usually increased, and these properties are important to the handling properties of paper.

4. The sizing of the old papers was destroyed by treatment with magnesium bicarbonate.

5. Deacidification improved the tearing strength and, to a lesser extent, the folding endurance and tensile energy absorption, of a group of U.S. Geological Survey maps. Reflectance was unaffected. Sizing essentially was destroyed.

6. The pH values of the maps before deacidification were in the neutral range, and treatment with magnesium bicarbonate did not result in high pH values—8.5 was the maximum.

7. Neither magnesium acetate nor magnesium bicarbonate was able to remove aluminum from a hardwood kraft pulp in which the aluminum presumably was attached to the carboxyls.

8. Experiments performed under very carefully controlled conditions will be required to define the true nature of deacidification.

Literature Cited

1. Sihtola, H.; Sumiala, R. "The Influence of Cations on the Yellowing of Monocarboxycellulose," *Papper Trae* **1963**, *45*(2), 43–48.
2. Virkola, N. E.; Hentola, Y.; Sihtola, H. "Carboxyl Groups and Cations as Factors Affecting the Yellowing of Cellulose, 3rd Communication," *Papper Trae* **1958**, *40*, 627–631, 634.
3. Sihtola, H.; Virkola, N. E. "Influence of Chlorine Dioxide on the Yellowing of Cellulose, 4th Communication," *Papper Trae* **1959**, *41*, 35–41.
4. Parks, E. J.; Hebert, R. L. "Accelerated Aging of Laboratory Handsheets: Changes in Acidity, Fiber Strength, and Wet Strength," NBS Report 10627, NITS, COM 75-10164, Dec. 1971.
5. Parks, E. J.; Hebert, R. L. "Accelerated Aging of Laboratory Handsheets: Retention of Folding Endurance, Internal Tear, Bursting Strength, and Tensile Strength," NBS Report 10628, NTIS, COM 75-10165, Dec. 1971.
6. Parks, E. J.; Hebert, R. L. "Accelerated Aging of Laboratory Handsheets: Reflectance, Moisture Regain, Sonic Modulus, and DTA," NBS Report 10687, NTIS, COM 75-10162, Feb. 1972.
7. Flieder, Françoise. "La Désacidification des Papiers," *Bull. Miscellanea in Memorium Paul Coremans* **1975**, 151–169.
8. Barrow, W. J.; Sproull, R. C. "Permanence in Book Papers," *Science* **1959**, *129*(Apr.), 1075.

9. Pravilova, T. A.; Instrubtsina, T. V. "Preservation of Paper Documents by the Buffering Method," in "Preservation of Documents and Papers," Flyate, D. M., Ed., Academy of Sciences of the USSR Laboratory for the Preservation and Restoration of Documents, Israel Program for Scientific Translations: Jerusalem, 1968; 72.

10. Hey, Margaret. "Kitchen Chemistry: The Reasons Why Not," in *The Abbey Newsletter* Oct. 1977, No. 11, 1.

11. Santucci, L. "Paper Deacidification Procedures and Their Effects," Les Techniques De Laboratoire Dans L'Etude Des Manuscripts, *Colloq. Int. C. N. R. S.*, 1972, 548.

12. Santucci, L.; Ventura, G.; Zappalà-Plossi, Maria Grazia "An Evaluation of Some Non-aqueous Deacidification Methods for Paper Documents," Archives Et Bibliotheques De Belgique, Brussels, Special No. 12, **1974,** 131–156.

13. Santucci, L.; Zappalà-Plossi, Maria Grazia "Invecchiamento Della Carta in Tubo Chiuso, Problemi Di Conservazione, Part II"; Compositori: Bologna, 1973; p. 501–512.

14. Smith, Richard Daniel U.S. Patent 3 676 182, 1972.

15. Schierholz, O. J. U.S. Patent 2 033 452, 1936.

16. Gear, J. L. "Lamination After 30 Years: Record and Prospect," *American Archivist* **1965,** *28,* 293.

17. Kelly, G. B., Jr. "Practical Aspects of Deacidification," Archives Et Bibliothèque De Belgique, Brussels, Special No. 12, **1974,** 91.

18. Kelly, G. B., Jr.; Tang, Lucia C.; Krasnow, Marta K. in "Preservation of Paper and Textiles of Historic and Artistic Value," *Adv. Chem. Ser.* **1977,** *164,* 62.

19. Werner, A. E. A. "Methods of Deacidifying Paper," *J. Soc. Archivists* **1969,** *3,* 491.

20. Williams, J. "Chemistry of the Deacidification of Paper," *Bull. Am. Group-IIC* **1971,** *12*(Oct.), 16.

21. Smith, R. D. "Paper Deacidification: A Preliminary Report," *Libr. Q.* **1966,** *36*(Oct.), 273.

22. Smith, R. D. "New Approaches to Preservation," *Libr. Q.* **1970,** *40*(Jan.), 139.

23. Smith, R. D. in "Preservation of Paper and Textiles of Historic and Artistic Value," *Adv. Chem. Ser.* **1977,** *164,* 149.

24. Walker, B. F. in "Preservation of Paper and Textiles of Historic and Artistic Value," *Adv. Chem. Ser.* **1977,** *164,* 72.

25. Hudson, F. L.; Milner, W. D. "The Permanence of Paper: The Use of Radioactive Sulfur to Study the Pick-up of Sulfur Dioxide by Paper," *Pap. Technol.* **1961,** *2,* 155–161.

26. Langwell, W. H. "The Permanence of Paper," *Br. Pap. Board Makers' Assoc., Inc., Tech. Sect.* **1952,** *29,* 21–28.

27. Spinner, I. H.; MacKinnon, M. H.; Lilley, J. W. "The Effects of Iron and Copper on the Brightness and Brightness Reversion of Oxidized Cellulose," *Pulp Pap. Mag. Can.* **1966,** *67,* T114–118.

28. Spinner, I. H. "Brightness Reversion: A Critical Review with Suggestions for Further Research," *Tappi* **1962,** *45,* 495–514.

29. Williams, J. C.; Fowler, C. S.; Lyon, M. S.; Merrill, T. L. in "Preservation of Paper and Textiles of Historic and Artistic Value," *Adv. Chem. Ser.* **1977,** *164,* 37.

30. Back, E. L. "Thermal Auto-Crosslinking in Cellulose Material," *Pulp Pap. Mag. Can.* **1967,** *68,* T165–171.

31. Wilson, W. K.; McKiel, Mary C.; Gear, J. L.; MacClaren, R. H. "Preparation of Solutions of Magnesium Bicarbonate for Deacidification," *Am. Archivist* **1978,** *41,* 67–70.

32. Wilson, W. K.; McKiel, Mary C.; Gear, J. L.; MacClaren, R. H. "Preparation of Solutions of Magnesium Bicarbonate for Deacidification," in National Archives and Records Service Conservation Technology Publication, Table 8.

33. Parks, E. J.; Wilson, W. K. National Bureau of Standards, unpublished data.

34. TAPPI method T 235 Alkali Solubility of Pulp (TAPPI methods are issued by the Technical Association of the Pulp and Paper Industry, One Dunwoody Park, Atlanta, GA 19103).

35. TAPPI method T 509, Hydrogen Ion Concentration (pH) of Paper Extracts—Cold Extraction Method.

36. Parks, E. J.; Hebert, R. L. "A Source of Error in Paper Extract pH Determinations: Contact between Paper and Reference Electrodes," NBSIR 75-915, NTIS No. PB 249-775.

37. TAPPI method T 451, Flexural Properties of Paper (Clark Stiffness).

38. TAPPI method T 511, Folding Endurance of Paper (MIT Tester).

39. TAPPI Useful Method UM 518 Smoothness of Paper (Sheffield).

40. TAPPI Useful Method UM 524 Porosity of Paper by Resistance to Air Flow.

41. TAPPI method T 414, Internal Tearing Resistance of Paper.

42. TAPPI method T 452, Brightness of Paper and Paperboard.

43. van den Akker, J. A.; Nolan, Philip; Dreshfield, A. C.; Heller, H. F. "The Fluorescence Size Test: An Improved Method and a New Instrument for Measuring the Water Resistance of Paper," *Pap. Trade J.* **1939,** *103*(Nov. 23, 33), TAPPI Section, 279.

44. TAPPI method T 417 OS-68, Proteinaceous Nitrogenous Materials in Paper (Qualitative).

45. TAPPI method T 404, Tensile Breaking Strength of Paper and Paperboard.

46. TAPPI Method T 200 Laboratory Processing of Pulp (Beater Method).

47. TAPPI Method T 205 Forming Handsheets for Physical Tests of Pulp.

48. Wilson, W. K.; Forshee, B. W. "Degradation of Cellulose Acetate Films," *SPE J.* **1959,** *15,* 146.

49. AIC Newsletter, *Inst. Conserv. Hist. Artistic Works* **1978,** (Aug.).

50. AIC Newsletter, *Am. Inst. Conserv. Hist. Artistic Works* **1979,** (Feb.).

51. Smith, R. D. "Maps, Their Deterioration and Preservation," *Special Libraries* **1972,** *63*(Feb.), 59.

RECEIVED November 30, 1979.

Inhibition of Light Sensitivity of Papers Treated with Diethyl Zinc

GEORGE B. KELLY, JR. and JOHN C. WILLIAMS

Preservation Office, Library of Congress, Washington, DC 20540

The degradative effect of UV light on paper is well known. In the presence of zinc oxide and high humidity, the effect is increased significantly. Since the original diethyl zinc paper deacidification process left zinc oxide as an alkaline reserve, ways to inhibit accelerated degradation were sought. The presence of 0.05% iodide in the paper is sufficient to inhibit completely the accelerated degradation with little effect on brightness. Also effective is modifying the diethyl zinc process to leave zinc carbonate rather than zinc oxide as the alkaline reserve. Books treated by the modified process do not show increased light sensitivity but show photodegradation rates similar to or slightly less than those of untreated books.

In the vapor phase process of deacidification with diethyl zinc currently under development by the Library of Congress (*1, 2, 3*), the treated paper generally has contained 2%–4% zinc oxide in addition to the zinc salts of the acids originally present. The zinc oxide acts as an alkaline reserve to protect the paper from future contact with acid environments or internal acids generated by oxidation of the paper constituents. Although the treatment is very effective and greatly prolongs the life of the paper, some degradation can occur by other routes such as photodegradation.

Egerton (*4*) has shown that the presence of zinc oxide, as well as certain other substances, can increase significantly the "tendering" or photodegradation of textiles by UV light when exposed in the presence of high humidity. No increase was shown in dry air.

Table I.

Untreated

Paper	pH	Acidity Meq/kg	Bright-ness	Thick-ness (in.)	Folding Endurance, MIT 1/2 kg load	
					MD	CD
JCPA-60 Offset[a]	5.9	12	77	0.0041	696 ± 165	472 ± 167
Foldur Kraft[b]	4.9	24	75	0.0061	1510 ± 200	1306 ± 320
Newsprint[c]	5.2	40	51	0.0038	147 ± 23	23 ± 17
Mead Bond[d]	5.6	20	86	0.0048	250 ± 92	277 ± 91
Whatman #1[e]	6.1	2	82	0.007	33 ± 3	20 ± 3
Superior Off-set Book[f]	5.9	12	75	0.0035	1596 ± 258	968 ± 118

[a] U.S. Government Printing Office Stock #16929 = 30% softwood kraft, 70% hardwood kraft, 13% clay filler.
[b] Champion Paper Company = 90% softwood bleached kraft, 10% hardwood bleached kraft, 8% filler.
[c] U.S. Government Printing Office = 20% softwood bleached sulfite, 80% groundwood.

The function of the zinc oxide was shown to be that of a catalyst in the photochemical oxidation of water to hydrogen peroxide, which then attacked the textile fibers to increase the degradation. If this mechanism also could be applied to paper, as it almost surely could, it would constitute an undesirable limitation on the effectiveness of the diethyl zinc process as a stabilizer for paper. Although the extent of the damage from this source undoubtedly would be small because of the infrequent exposure to UV light at high humidity, it was felt that the degree of damage must be investigated and, if possible, methods devised to inhibit the accelerated degradation attributable to the zinc oxide.

This chapter covers the effect of light from a GE sunlamp (high in UV light) on papers containing zinc oxide under moist (60% relative humidity) and dry (8% relative humidity) conditions in comparison with the effects on untreated controls, the effects of iodide as a negative catalyst, and the effect of converting the zinc oxide to zinc carbonate before exposure to avoid the catalytic photochemical reaction.

Experimental

A series of papers containing varying amounts of zinc oxide was selected from among those that had been treated with diethyl zinc in the development of the treatment process. The properties of these papers before and after treatment are shown in Table I. All papers were conditioned by TAPPI Method T-402 before testing. Samples of the treated papers and the untreated controls were exposed for 88 h to the light of

Properties of Papers

Treated with DEZ

pH	ZnO (%)	Brightness	Folding Endurance, 1/2 kg load	
			MD	CD
7.6	3.7	76	670 ± 155	518 ± 136
7.7	3.7	74	1479 ± 298	1092 ± 151
7.8	5.1	49	135 ± 59	32 ± 12
7.5	2.4	84	250 ± 60	132 ± 46
7.3	2.2	82	31 ± 3	22 ± 8
7.6	2.6	75	1491 ± 339	1002 ± 121

[d] Mead Corporation = 33.3% refined rag, 33.3% bleached kraft, 33.4% bleached sulfite.
[e] W. R. Balston Company, England = filter paper.
[f] Allied Paper Company = 5% bleached hardwood kraft, 95% bleached softwood kraft, 25% filler.

a GE sunlamp, type 275RS in a Sunlighter II apparatus (from Test Lab Apparatus Company, Amherst, New Jersey). The spectral distribution of the radiant energy from the lamp is shown in Table II. Conditions in the Sunlighter II measured 60°C and 8% relative humidity. After exposure, the papers were conditioned (TAPPI T-402) and tested for machine direction (MD) folding endurance by TAPPI Method T-511. The results are shown in Table III.

Samples of the treated papers and the corresponding controls were exposed for 88 h to the sunlamp at a distance of 24 cm in a Blue M Powermatic 60, Fluid Flo Oven at 60°C and 60% relative humidity, conditioned after exposure, and tested for folding endurance as above. The results are also shown in Table III.

Samples of the treated papers were exposed briefly to a low concentration of hydrogen iodide (about 2% by volume) in a polyethylene chamber with forced circulation by a small muffin fan. The papers were aerated several hours in the draught of a hood following the exposure to hydrogen iodide. Iodide content of the papers was determined by macerating a 2.5-g sample of the paper in 200 mL of water in a Waring blender, filtering the pulp, washing, and diluting the filtrate to 500 mL. Iodide was determined on 25-mL aliquots of the filtrate by acidifying with 15 mL of $4N$ H_2SO_4, adding 3 drops of 3% ammonium molybdate, 7 mL of 1% starch solution, and 10 mL of 3% H_2O_2. The solution was mixed and allowed to stand for 1 min, then the color was matched against a standard developed simultaneously, containing known amounts of iodide. The iodide contents of the papers are shown also in Table III.

The iodide-treated paper samples were exposed for 88 h at 60°C and 60% relative humidity to the sunlamp and compared with the similarly exposed controls containing zinc oxide but no iodide. After exposure, the samples were conditioned and tested for MD fold endurance, with the results shown in Table III.

Table II. Spectral Distribution of Radiant Energy GE
Sunlamp, Type 275RS, 2500 Lumens Output

Wavelength (Å)		Principle Lines	Radiant Energy (watts)
2600	2700	2652	0.004
2700	2800	—	—
2800	2900	2804	0.05
2900	3000	2967	0.13
3000	3100	3022	0.34
3100	3200	3131	0.88
3200	3300	—	0.07
3300	3400	3341	0.16
3400	3500	—	0.05
3500	3600	—	0.09
3600	3700	3654	2.51
3700	3800	—	0.09
3800	4000	—	0.16
4000	4100	4047	0.72
4100	4300	—	0.09
4300	4400	—	1.48
4400	5400	—	0.30
5400	5500	5461	1.73
5500	5700	—	0.15
5700	5800	5780	1.73
5800	7600	—	4.13

Table III. Effect of Zinc Oxide on Paper in Presence of UV

MIT Fold Endurance, 1/2 kg load, MD

	Controls, No ZnO Present	
Light Exposure (h)	0	88
Papers	Exposed at 8% Relative Humidity, 60°C	
JCPA60	696 ± 165	336 ± 74
Foldur Kraft	1510 ± 300	1201 ± 175
Newsprint	147 ± 23	33 ± 15
	Exposed at 60% Relative Humidity, 60°C	
JCPA60	696 ± 165	240 ± 59
Foldur Kraft	1510 ± 300	411 ± 65
Newsprint	147 ± 23	11 ± 3
Mead Bond	250 ± 92	96 ± 33
Whatman #1	33 ± 3	18 ± 3
Superior Offset Book	1599 ± 258	878 ± 138

Finally, the diethyl zinc deacidification process described in a previous publication (3) was modified as follows: After the diethyl zinc exposure was complete for a 400 book charge to the chamber, the operating pressure in the chamber was raised from 30 mm to 200 mm by admitting carbon dioxide. The excess diethyl zinc was destroyed by admitting 3 gal of methanol to the chamber. When tests of the gas in the chamber showed no diethyl zinc vapor to be present (after about 1 h), 3 gal of water was admitted to the chamber. The fan was turned on to circulate the moist carbon dioxide and the pressure was increased to 600 mm by the addition of more carbon dioxide. Circulation in the chamber was continued for 24 h, at which point the fan was shut off and the chamber evacuated. The chamber was repressured with air to atmospheric pressure and the books were removed. Seven books were selected at random (Table IV) and several pages were removed from the same signature in each book from which control pages had been removed before the treatment. The treated pages and the corresponding controls were exposed to the sunlamp at 60°C and 60% relative humidity for 88 h as described above. The treated pages and controls were tested for MD folding endurance after conditioning for 24 h. The results are shown in Table V.

Results and Discussion

The six papers selected for the investigation of increased light sensitivity with zinc oxide covered the range of zinc oxide contents usually found in the diethyl zinc treatments: 2.2%–5.1% zinc oxide. Most of the

Light and Humidity, and the Protective Effect of Iodide (I⁻)

MIT Fold Endurance, 1/2 kg load, MD

| Treated, ZnO Present | | I^- Present | I^- Content |
| No I^- Present | | 88 | (% by weight) |
0	88		
Exposed at 8% Relative Humidity, 60°C			
670 ± 155	603 ± 139	—	—
1479 ± 298	1419 ± 355	—	—
135 ± 59	58 ± 16	—	—
Exposed at 60% Relative Humidity, 60°C			
645 ± 77	74 ± 40	390 ± 150	0.08
1381 ± 212	82 ± 25	465 ± 171	0.15
135 ± 59	1.8 ± 0.6	22 ± 8	0.43
250 ± 60	60 ± 37	180 ± 56	0.05
31 ± 3	6.6 ± 1.2	29 ± 5	0.32
1491 ± 339	603 ± 173	1283 ± 248	0.16

Table IV.   Books Selected for Light Exposure Tests after Modified Diethyl Zinc Treatment[a]

Book Number	Description
1713	Organization and Procedures Survey of the Interstate Commerce Commission, abridged edition; Booz, Allen, and Hamilton: 1960
1794	Oklahoma Statutes Annotated, Title II, Cities and Towns 551— end; West Publishing Company: 1951
1833	Complete Guide to Two-Year Colleges and Four-Year Specialized Schools and Programs, James Cass and Max Birnbaum; Harper and Row: 1969
1855	Practice for the Armed Forces Tests, David Turner; Arco: 1965
1915	Table of Natural Logarithms for Arguments Between 0 and 5 to 16 Decimal Places, NBS Applied Mathematics Series 31; U.S. Government Printing Office: 1953
1979	Federal Reporter, Volume 489F, Second, U.S. Court of Appeals, Court of Claims, Court of Customs and Patents; West Publishing Company: 1974
2054	American Men of Science, 10th Edition, The Physical and Biological Sciences S–Z; Jacques Callell Press: 1961

[a] Alkaline reserve converted to zinc carbonate by exposure to moist carbon dioxide immediately after diethyl zinc treatment.

treatments had given zinc oxide contents near the lower end of this range, but the higher levels were included to emphasize any detrimental effects. All of the papers selected were from single rolls of paper to insure minimum variation of properties from sheet to sheet.

Table V.   Effect of Light and Humidity[a] on Book Papers Impregnated with Zinc Carbonate

	Folding Endurance	
Book Number	Control	Impregnated with Zinc Carbonate[b]
1713	1839 ± 451	1880 ± 543
1794	13.5 ± 4.5	20.3 ± 4.8
1833	12.4 ± 6.3	17.7 ± 9.7
1855	25 ± 8.6	40 ± 25
1915	1 ± 0	3 ± 0.5
1979	28 ± 20	28 ± 15
2054	6 ± 3	5 ± 2

[a] 88 h at 60% relative humidity and 9 1/2 inches from sunlamp.
[b] $1.97 \pm 0.24\%$ $ZnCO_3$ based on conditioned weight of paper.

The diethyl zinc treatments did not change the folding endurance or brightness of the papers to any significant degree (Table I). When the papers were exposed to UV light at low relative humidity (8%), significan losses in folding endurance resulted for both the treated samples and the controls. However, in no case did the treated papers containing zinc oxide show greater loss in folding endurance than the untreated controls. Therefore, at low relative humidity there is no accelerated degradation from the presence of zinc oxide. This is in full agreement with the results of Egerton (4) on cotton textiles.

At high (60%) relative humidity, the treated papers showed accelreated degradation as evidenced by the much greater loss in folding endurance of the papers containing zinc oxide as compared with the untreated controls after 88 h exposure to the sunlamp (Table III). This also is in agreement with Egerton's results on textiles (4). However, in view of the intense UV irradiation of the papers in this test, the accelerated decomposition is surprisingly modest, with the zinc-oxide containing papers averaging about 38% of the folding endurance of the controls after both were exposed. Nevertheless, the presence of any accelerated degradation is undesirable, and this led to attempts to overcome the catalytic effect of the zinc oxide.

Since iodide had been used as a negative catalyst by Minor and Sanyer (5) in the oxygen bleaching process to protect the cellulose from degradation, the treated sheets containing zinc oxide were impregnated with small amounts of iodide by a brief exposure to hydrogen iodide, resulting in iodide contents of 0.05%–0.43% in the papers. Even the smallest amount of iodide, 0.05%, proved adequate in protecting the sheets containing zinc oxide from accelerated degradation under the sunlamp at high humidity. In fact, most of the iodide-containing sheets retained more of the original folding endurance than the untreated controls (Table VI). Therefore, the iodide functioned as a negative catalyst to protect the cellulose from the accelerated degradation caused by the zinc oxide. The larger amounts of iodide gave slightly better retention of fold (Table VI), but caused irregular staining of the papers above about 0.1% iodide content. This appears to be associated with additives in the paper, as no stains occurred with the Whatman filter paper despite the rather high iodide content.

While the iodide treatment was successful in overcoming the UV light sensitivity at high humidity, hydrogen iodide is corrosive and its use in the large vacuum chamber could cause maintenance problems in prolonged use. Therefore, the conversion of zinc oxide to zine carbonate was investigated as a possible means of eliminating the catalytic effect.

When diethyl zinc reacts with a hydroxyl group such as those in cellulose, it forms an ethylzincoxycellulose group, $C_2H_5ZnO—R$. When

Table VI.   Retention of Fold, Percentage in Papers with
Zinc Oxide Exposed to Light and Humidity

Papers	Unheated Control	With ZnO	With ZnO and Iodide
Exposed at 8% Relative Humidity, 60°C			
JCPA60	48.2	90.0	
Foldur Kraft	79.5	95.9	
Newsprint	22.4	42.9	
Exposed at 60% Relative Humidity, 60°C			
JCPA60	34.5	11.5	60.4
Foldur Kraft	27.2	5.9	33.6
Newsprint	7.5	1.3	16.9
Mead Bond	38.4	24.0	72.0
Whatman #1	54.5	21.3	93.5
Superior Offset Book	61.1	40.4	86.0

this group is exposed to air after the treatment, it hydrolyzes from the moisture in the air to yield ethane and zinc oxide, and the cellulose hydroxyl group is reformed. It was hoped that hydrolysis in the presence of carbon dioxide would cause the zinc to go directly to the carbonate rather than the oxide.

The conversion to carbonate was tried with a 400-book treatment run in which the excess diethyl zinc was destroyed with alcohol after partially backfilling the chamber with carbon dioxide. After adding water to hydrolyze the zinc cellulosate compound, the backfilling with carbon dioxide was continued to nearly atmospheric pressure to force the damp carbon dioxide into the books. At the same time, the atmosphere in the chamber was circulated with a fan for 24 h to insure good contact. After such treatment, paper samples from the books showed effervescence when immersed in dilute acid, indicating the presence of carbonate. Samples of paper from books previously treated with diethyl zinc (where the carbon dioxide was not used) showed no such effervescence.

Books selected at random from the 400-book run (Table IV) showed no difference in folding endurance between pages that had undergone the treatment and the untreated control pages that had been removed from the same signature before the diethyl zinc treatment when both sets were exposed to the light from the sunlamp at high humidity for 88 h (Table V). (In comparing treatments on books it is important to confine comparisons to paper from single signatures, as the signatures within any given book frequently are taken from several batches of paper and may have widely differing properties from signature to signature.)

Since there was no significant difference in the loss in folding endurance between the controls with no zinc carbonate and the treated papers containing about 2% zinc carbonate when exposed to light and humidity, it is obvious that no accelerated degradation results from the zinc carbonate.

With this demonstration that zinc carbonate does not catalyze the photodegradation of paper in the presence of UV light and high humidity, we feel that the diethyl zinc process, as modified by the final carbon dioxide exposure, is now commercially feasible.

Future Work

The improved aging characteristics noted with the iodide present indicate that it may be functioning as an antioxidant for the paper as well as a means of inhibiting the production of hydrogen peroxide. Therefore, the introduction of antioxidants into the paper by vapor phase techniques will be investigated as a possible means of further improvement of the expected life of the treated paper.

Literature Cited

1. Williams, J. C.; Kelly, G. B., Jr. *Bulletin, American Institute for Conservation* 1974, *14*, 69–77.
2. Williams, J. C.; Kelly, G. B., Jr. U. S. Patent 3 969 549, 1976.
3. Kelly, G. B., Jr.; Williams, J. C. "Mass Deacidification with Diethyl Zinc, Large Scale Trials," *Sixth Annual Meeting of American Institute for Conservation of Historic and Artistic Work, Fort Worth, Texas, June 1–4, 1978.*
4. Egerton, G. S. "The Role of Hydrogen Peroxide in the Photochemical Degradation of Cotton Sensitized by Vat Dyes and Some Metallic Oxides," in *J. Text. Inst.* 1948, (Sept.), T305–T318.
5. Minor, J. L.; Sanyer, N. "Carbohydrate Stabilization with Iodide in Oxygen Bleaching of Kraft Pulps," in *TAPPI* 1974, *57*, 109–112.

RECEIVED October 23, 1979.

Yellowing of Modern Papers

DAVID N.-S. HON

Department of Forest Products, Virginia Polytechnic Institute and State University, Blacksburg, VA 24061

Paper in its applications must satisfy a number of criteria, and of these, permanence and durability are the most important ones. Unfortunately, modern papers produced from wood pulps contain a high quantity of vulnerable cellulose and hemicellulose that have been oxidized during the pulping processes. They are relatively unstable toward light, heat, moisture, air, and other environmental factors. In addition, because of the shortage and high cost of raw materials, modern "high-yield" papers contain oxidized cellulose and hemicellulose; they also incorporate a considerable amount of lignin and extraneous material from wood, which further impairs the paper quality—permanence and durability. In this chapter, discoloration or yellowing of modern papers as a consequence of the oxidative reactions of cellulose, hemicellulose, and lignin as well as color stabilization is reviewed. Suggestions for further research in color stabilization are made.

Four of the most significant developments in the progress of mankind are attributed to the Chinese: the magnetic compass, gunpowder, printing, and paper (1). The invention of paper by T'sai Lun, a member of the Imperial Guard and Privy Councillor, was announced to the Hai Emperor of China in A.D. 105 (2). It was a unique event. At that time, the Chinese macerated fibers from rice stalks, flax, hemp, and bark in water and drained the suspension on a mold covered with silk cloth. The fiber mats were removed and dried in the sun to form paper. This uniqueness is attested to by its slow communication to other parts of the world: five hundred years to reach Korea and Japan; six hundred years to Samarkand and the Arab world; and one thousand years to Europe,

0065-2393/81/0193-0119$05.75/0

and even later to America in 1690 (3). During that period, rags of cotton, flax, jute, and hemp comprised the sole source of raw materials used in paper manufacture.

Since the advent of papermaking, the use of rags or bast fibers grew rapidly prior to 1800, creating a shortage of papermaking raw materials. It has been reported that at that period, even linen shrouds from exhumed corpses were sold for papermaking (4). In 1719, Rene de Reaumur, a brilliant French scientist, suggested that paper could be made from the fibers of plants without using rags or linen. However, it took until 1764 for a German clergyman, Dr. Jacob Scäffer, to make paper experimentally with a wide variety of plant materials and to demonstrate that these vegetable fibers could be a substitute for rags, yet no interest was apparently aroused at that time. At the beginning of the nineteenth century, with the use of paper and printing press increasing rapidly, the demand for paper outstripped the production of the handmade paper and mass production techniques were called for. In 1840, Scäffer's idea was picked up by a German bookbinder named Christian Völter. He developed a wood grinder to produce goundwood pulp in 1844 and patented it in 1847. This was the beginning of mechanical pulp production. This development rapidly increased the production of newsprint, although the pulp was poor in quality, especially in strength and durability, being inferior to present-day mechanical pulp. In 1851, two Englishmen, Hugh Burgess and Charles Watt, produced pulp from willow shavings boiled in a solution of lye, making the first soda pulp from wood. This was the beginning of chemical pulp production. The advantages of chemical wood pulp over mechanical pulps were soon appreciated. Following this invention, the sulfite process was invented by an American chemist, Benjamin Tilgman, in 1867; the sulfate (kraft) process was invented in 1889 by a German chemist, Carl Dahl of Danzig. From this we can realize that within only a few years, a revolutionary change had taken place in the pulp and paper world.

Now, about one hundred years has elapsed. The fundamental pulping and papermaking principles still remain the basics of today's modern papermaking. Advances in engineering and technology have made it possible to produce increasingly larger tonnages and a vast variety of paper products by very cost-effective methods. Today world consumption of paper amounts to about 150 million tons annually, of which 94%–95% is produced from wood, and the remainder mainly from other vegetable fibers. Ironically, the historical event seems to be repeated today; under the severe constraints of pollution control and energy conservation, we are experiencing the shortage of fiber raw materials. The result of this is the production of high-yield fibers that retain high amounts of lignin (or even extractives) in the pulp fibers. And the new development in this area is the appearance of thermomechanical pulps that obtain pulp yields as high as 100%. It should be borne in mind that when dealing with high-yield pulps, the number of fibers in certain amounts of raw material is fixed and cannot be increased in the pulping process. Yield, therefore, has a different meaning in pulping than in ordinary chemical processes. Differences in yield mean only that the fibers of the higher yield pulps contain more lignin and hemicellulose.

In summary, modern pulping processes may be considered to be chiefly mechanical, mechanochemical (semichemical), and chemical processes. The classification in terms of pulp yield is depicted in Figure 1.

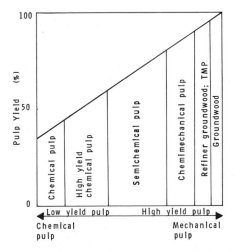

Figure 1. Modern pulping process vs. pulp yield

Modern papers, which were invented after the revolutionary changes of one hundred years ago, have serious problems—either in permanence or in durability. Most paper produced from wood fibers does not show the permanence of rag papers and discoloration is more critical than in rag papers. It has been noted that modern writing papers and books tend to have a much shorter life expectancy than those manufactured one hundred years ago (*4–9*). In essence, the increased use of wood fibers, the use of chemical additives (especially those promoting increased acidity), and environmental conditions have been given to account for these results. The literature dealing with these topics is now very large; it would not be wise to attempt an extensive review here in addition to those that already exist (*6, 10–19*). It is my intention in this chapter to consider the discoloration of modern papers, and the inhibition or the control of discoloration.

Chemical Consituents of Modern Papers

As we know, from earliest times up to the present days, the substances used as vehicles for writing have been numerous. The papers of one hundred years ago were basically made from rags of cotton and linters. The principal chemical constituent of these sources is cellulose, a polymeric carbohydrate composed of long linear chains of β-linked anhydroglucopyranose. The chains in cellulose are composed of as many as ten thousand glucose units (degree of polymerization). The composition of wood fibers is quite different from that of cotton, as can be seen from Table I. The chemical constituents of modern papers are compli-

Table I. Chemical Constituents of Wood and Cotton

	Wood		
	Softwood (coniferous)	*Hardwood (deciduous)*	*Cotton*
Cellulose (%)	43	43	93–96
Hemicellulose (%)	~ 28	~ 38	1–2
Lignin (%)	23–33	16–25	0
Extractives (%)	5–8	2–4	3–4 [a]
Ash (%)	~ 1	~ 1	~ 1

[a] Mainly fats and waxes.

cated. They usually are comprised of cellulose, hemicellulose, lignin, and extractives as those present in wood. In addition, for most of the papers, fillers, sizing agents, and other additives are added to improve paper properties. For comparison, the chemical composition of wood and unbleached pulp fibers are given in Table II. Low-yield chemical pulps usually contain high amounts of cellulose and hemicellulose. Hemicellulose is an amorphous, polymeric carbohydrate having a slightly branched structure. The degree of polymerization is only about two hundred to five hundred sugar units per molecule. In addition to cellulose and hemicellulose, the high-yield chemical pulps also contain lignin, which is a three-dimensional, highly crosslinked, amorphous polymer that is

Table II. Chemical Constituents of Wood and Pulp Fibers

	Wood	*Unbleached Pulp Fibers*
Cellulose (%)	43	80–90
Hemicellulose (%)	25–35	10–20
Lignin (%)	20–30	1–3
Extractives (%)	3–8	0
Ash (%)	~ 1	0

partly aromatic in nature; it contains methoxyl groups, aliphatic and phenolic hydroxyl groups, and various types of ether linkages. In mechanical pulps, for example, groundwood, refiner groundwood, and thermomechanical pulps, most of the lignin and extractives (if not all) are retained in the cellulose fibers.

The retention of lignin is evidently an important feature of high-yield pulping. Native lignin is of hydrophobic nature and the way in which it is combined with the hemicelluloses makes the whole lignin–hemicellulose compound quite inaccessible to water and prevents it from swelling. Therefore, high lignin content can be expected to affect the paper properties considerably by making the fibers stiff, by decreasing the bonding activity of the fiber surface, and by inhibiting swelling.

Hemicellulose, besides improving yield, was desirable in pulp for the production of strong papers. The presence of hemicellulose in the pulp reduces the time and power required to soften and fibrillate fiber during beating operations. The hemicelluloses, because of their amorphous nature (compared with a high degree of crystallinity of cellulose), low molecular weight, and presence of hydroxyl groups in the molecule, have a great affinity for water. The hydrophilic nature of the hemicellulose leads to two results—the ability to absorb water, which renders the fiber more plastically deformable, that is, plasticizing effect; and the capacity of promoting interfiber bonding when the water is removed by drying. Hemicelluloses have been shown to contribute greatly to tensile and bursting strength and to folding endurance of the pulp sheet.

Though paper is largely fibrous in character, an important part is often played by other materials added during manufacture (20). Fine particles of mineral fillers such as china clay (kaolin), titanium dioxide, calcium carbonate, and talc (magnesium silicate), as well as various types of pigments and sizing agents, are used to improve the properties of the final paper. Fillers are added to fill the voids between the fibers in printing paper so as to smooth its surface. Fillers improve printing not only because they result in increased smoothness, but also because they make the paper surface less hydrophilic and, thus, more receptive to the usual oil printing inks. They also improve the opacity and brightness of the paper. Rosin sizing usually forms a water-repellent deposit around the fibers, and so prevents writing ink from spreading on the paper.

Color in Pulps

In general, color problems encountered in pulps arise either from color already present in wood, or from chemical changes that take place during the grinding, cooking, refining, and bleaching processes. Based on the literature, much of the color in wood pulps can be attributed to residual lignin and lignin derivatives as well as to the presence of other coloring matters such as quinones, flavones, and condensed tannins (21). It has been reported that the brightness of lab-prepared refiner mechanical pulp related well to wood brightness and absorption coefficient. The latter was related linearly to the lignin content (22). The graying and red–brown discolorations of wood resulting from exposure to sunlight in open air are related to photolytic degradation of wood components and related oxidation (23). Alkaline pulps are generally much darker than other pulps, and this may be attributable to the presence of more highly condensed and unsaturated lignin and phenolic materials. However, the nature of the chromophoric systems involved, and the mechanism of their formation, require more research. The color of high-yield pulps, including mechanical pulps, is much more dependent on the wood species than that of low-yield pulps, because a greater portion of the lignin and extractives remain. A survey of the chromophoric groups in paper recently has been made available (21).

General Principles of Pulp Bleaching

The objective of bleaching is to produce a white pulp of stable color obtained at reasonable cost and a minimum deleterious effect on the physical and chemical properties of the pulp. Inasmuch as the major chromophoric substances in wood pulps are derived from the lignin substrate, it must be chemically changed to colorless configurations in a stable form, or it must be oxidized, reduced, or hydrolyzed, rendering it soluble in aqueous solutions and so removable from the pulp. The two major methods of bleaching are based on these principles (23, 24).

1. Lignin Preserving or Lignin Bleaching Method. This is applied to mechanical and semichemical pulps. During this treatment, lignin chromophores are being destroyed without considerable removal of lignin. This usually is done by one stage of bleaching with hydrosulfite (dithionite) or peroxide, or two-stage combinations of them.

2. Lignin Removing Method. This is for chemical and semichemical pulps. During this process, most of the lignin is dissolved and removed from the pulp fibers. The removal of lignin improves the brightness and the paper properties of semichemical and high-yield chemical pulp fibers. For economic and qualitative reasons, this usually is done in several stages, consisting of sequential chlorination and alkaline extraction.

Discoloration or Yellowing Reaction

Although pulp may be bleached to various brightness levels by oxidation or reduction, all bleached pulps diminish in brightness with age. Normally, the pulp develops a yellow color. It is believed that color reversion can be a consequence of the oxidation of nearly every constituent of pulp and paper, namely cellulose, hemicellulose, lignin, extractives, impurities such as metal ions, and paper additives such as rosin, alum, glue and starch. The factors contributing to the color reversion are, by and large: air (oxygen), moisture, light, and atmospheric pollutants of industrial origin, either alone or in various combinations. Of these many environmental factors, sunlight may be singled out as the most important contributor to discoloration of modern papers, whereas other elements may function as promoters to accelerate the photoinduced yellowing reaction. Therefore, this paper will only review the light-induced yellowing reaction. It is hoped that an understanding of the photoinduced yellowing mechanisms will provide an essential background for a scientific review of the current status of photochemistry of modern papers.

Effect of Light on Discoloration of Modern Papers

The first law of photochemistry, named the Grotthus–Drapper Principle, states that for a photochemical reaction to occur, the first event must be the absorption of light by some component of the system. The second law of photochemistry, named the Stark–Einstein Principle, states that a molecule can only absorb one quantum of radiation. The absorbed energy in the resultant excited molecule may be dissipated by either photophysical or photochemical processes. It is the latter of these that eventually changes the chemical and mechanical properties of the substance (26, 27). Thus, the reactions based on the absorption of radiation by the chemical components of modern papers are of prime importance in discoloration.

Although pure cellulose is not a good light absorber, it does absorb light strongly below 200 nm with indications of some absorption between 200 nm and 300 nm, and a tail of absorption extending to 400 nm (28). This may be attributable to the introduction of adventitious impurities or oxidation of the polymer during processing. The main light-absorbing species are believed to be acetal, carbonyl, carboxyl groups, and metallic impurities (28, 29, 30, 31). Because of the structural similarity, the UV absorption characteristics of hemicellulose should resemble those of cellulose. Lignin shows a sharp increase in light absorption just below 400 nm, which continues to increase gradually to a high absorption at 200 nm with a distinct peak at 280 nm (32). Extractives and other chemical additives, such as rosin, usually have the ability to absorb light between 300 nm and 440 nm (33). As a consequence, it is quite obvious that most of the components in modern papers are capable of absorbing visible and UV light to undergo photochemical reactions that ultimately lead to discoloration and degradation reactions. However, the rates of

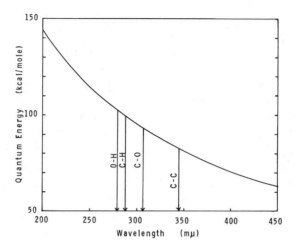

*Figure 2.   Bond dissociation energies of chemical bonds in paper con-
stituents in relation to light energy quanta*

discoloration vary enormously with the chromophoric system in modern
paper. From a chemical point of view, it is not surprising that all organic
chemical constituents of modern paper are susceptible to degradation by
terrestrial sunlight, since there is no problem regarding the availability
of energy in the near UV region (*34*). In fact, the quantum energies
associated with light in this region of the spectrum are sufficient to break

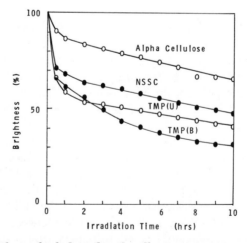

*Figure 3.   Ultraviolet-light-induced yellowing of various pulps.   Keys:
NSSC, neutral sulfite semichemical pulp; TMP(U), unbleached thermomechanical pulp; TMP(B), bleached thermomechanical pulp.*

the chemical bonds in the chemical constituents of modern papers (*35, 36*). The energies of light quanta and the bond energies of various bonds in chemical constituents are shown in Figure 2. The indication of yellowing of different modern papers is shown in Figure 3 (*37*). It is obvious that the brightness of lignin-containing pulp fibers is reduced at a rather faster rate than pure paper. Similar results were observed in 1935 by Richter (*38*). He noticed yellowing of all types of papers that had been exposed to 100 h of sunlight. Following this, similar observations were also reported by Kohler (*39*) and Lewis et al. (*40, 41*), and recently reported by Gellerstedt et al. (*42*) for mechanical pulp. It is accepted generally that photooxidative discoloration follows the usual mechanism for the oxidation of polymers; that is, a chain process initiated by free radicals that are formed after the absorption of a quantum of UV light.

MODERN PAPER ——LIGHT——→ [MODERN PAPER]*

[MODERN PAPER]* ——————→ [FREE RADICAL INTERMEDIATES]

[FREE RADICAL INTERMEDIATES] ——————→ SECONDARY REACTION

SECONDARY REACTION ——————→ YELLOWING PRODUCTS

Figure 4.   Direct photoinduced discoloration of modern paper

In general, it is possible to distinguish two kinds of reactions leading to discoloration of modern paper. These are designated as direct- and photosensitizer-induced discoloration. The general mechanistic schemes for these reactions are shown in Figures 4 and 5.

SENSITIZER ——LIGHT——→ [SENSITIZER]*

[SENSITIZER]* + MODERN PAPER ——————→ SENSITIZER + [MODERN PAPER]*

[MODERN PAPER]* ——————→ [FREE RADICAL INTERMEDIATES]

[FREE RADICAL INTERMEDIATES] ——————→ SECONDARY REACTION

SECONDARY REACTION ——————→ YELLOWING PRODUCTS

Figure 5.   Photosensitized discoloration of modern paper

Cellulose.   It has been known for about one hundred years that sunlight degrades cellulose (*43*), and much work has been done on the photochemistry of cellulose (*35, 43–50*).

The photochemical effects of solar irradiation on cellulose products have been ascribed to a complex set of reactions in which both the absorption of light and the presence of oxygen, moisture, and impurities are involved (*35, 51*). Solar radiation usually is defined as an electromagnetic radiation with an energy distribution extending to wavelengths below 200 nm (52). However, almost all the radiation of wavelengths less than 286 nm is absorbed in the earth's atmosphere because of a layer of ozone that exists at high altitudes, and the presence of oxygen, carbon dioxide, and water vapor (52, 53, 54). Although the UV portion of solar radiation from 286 nm to 400 nm that reaches the surface of the earth constitutes only about 5% of the total irradiation from the sun (55), it is capable of direct photolysis of cellulosic materials and especially the cleavage of glycosidic bonds, causing a decrease in strength (56–60) and the degree of polymerization (61–66), and an increase in alkali solubility (56, 67, 68), and copper number (69–73). The photochemical reaction of cellulose is accompanied by the formation of peroxide when oxygen is present (66, 68, 74). The formation of hydroperoxides in cellulose molecules has two important consequences. First, the subsequent thermal stability of the polymer will be reduced appreciably because hydroperoxides are thermally unstable. Second, the resistance of the polymer to light will be impaired because hydroperoxides are decomposed readily by light to yield free radicals that, in turn, can cleave polymer backbones and promote further oxidation. The consequences of this latter reaction will probably lead to the formation of carbonyl, including lactone, and carboxyl groups that contribute to the discoloration reaction—yellowing and browning (66). Many other factors, such as moisture, oxygen, metal ions, and atmospheric pollutants, also will exert an influence on the photochemistry of cellulose (35). These latter degradation processes may not necessarily be by direct photolysis, but could arise from the photosensitizing effect. The moisture content in cellulose is an important factor contributing to the acceleration of free radical formation, which leads to the degradation and yellowing when cellulose is exposed to sunlight (75). Moisture is also known to have accelerated the rate of aging (76–81). However, diffused sunlight and light in the yellow or red region appear to have very little action. Some bleaching action of sunlight also has been reported by Herzberz (82); and Edge and McKenzie (83) have found both yellowing and bleaching effects. It was recognized that degradation and discoloration of cellulose was only a surface effect rather than a bulk reaction (84, 85) because sunlight can only penetrate into paper or woody materials less than 0.02 cm (86, 87).

An increased degradation effect has been observed with an increase in the temperature at which cellulose was irradiated. Spirora and Flyate (88) observed that changes caused by UV radiation are about the same as those caused by thermal aging. Desai (89) reports that the wet strength of papers exposed to UV increases as does that of heat-treated pulp. Launer and Wilson (33), using irradiation at wavelengths of 330 nm to 440 nm, found that papers made of cotton and wood fibers with practically no lignin yellowed when irradiated in air without temperature control. However, when the sheet temperature was controlled to 30°C, bleaching took place (*61*). No evidence of a temperature coefficient of yellowing was noticeable with the far UV region in the temperature range of 10° to 30°C. It appears that light effects should be studied in the absence of heat effects.

In modern papers, it is expected that contaminants or substances such as dyes, various kinds of sizing agents, and some chemicals are present. These agents, by and large, have the ability to absorb light and then transfer the energy to cellulose to accelerate degradation or oxidation through photosensitizing pathways. It has been suggested that the yellowing of paper may result from the destruction of ultramarine or other blue color used in the manufacture of paper (*90*) or from the oxidation of fats, waxes, resins, etc., present in papers (*91,92*), or from the sensitizing effect of glue or gelatin sizes present in the papers (*93*). It has been found that rosin-sized papers exhibited rapid yellowing by light (*94,95, 96,97*). Metal ions were found to accelerate degradation and yellowing by forming metal complexes with cellulose to enhance light absorption (*98*), or by catalytic reactions (*71,98–103*). The acid present in the paper also seems to be the most harmful chemical in causing the yellowing of modern papers (*91*).

Hemicellulose. It is considered that photodegradation of hemicellulose is identical to that of cellulose (*104*). It has been reported that oxygen accelerates the photochemical reaction of hemicelluloses, including xylan and glucomanan (*105*). The photolytic rupture of the molecular chain of hemicellulose is brought about either at the end of the molecule or in the middle of the chain (*106*). Yasuda et al. (*107*) recognized that hemicellulose after photoirradiation would yield monosaccharides followed by transformation into the colored materials. Rollinson (*108*), Roudier et al. (*109,110*), and Giertz (*111*) found that the colored substances formed in pulp yellowing are water soluble and related to the oxidative degradation of hemicellulose. Yellowing of pulps through the oxidation of hemicellulose also has been verified by many researchers (*112,113,114*), and it has been recognized that carbonyl groups on the hemicellulose are probably responsible for yellowing (*76*).

Lignin. The constitutional model of lignin (*115*) gives a broad picture of the reactive groups available in native lignin. These consist of ethers of various types, primary and secondary hydroxyl groups, carbonyl groups, carboxyl and ester functions, ethylene groups. Furthermore, sulfur-containing groups such as thiols and sulfonic acids may be introduced as a consequence of kraft or acid sulfite pulping. Since lignin is a phenylpropanoid polymer, there also exist a number of aromatic and phenolic sites and activated aliphatic locations capable of participating in discoloration reactions. Obviously, the complexity of the structure of components as well as reactions hinder the studying of potential chromophoric groups in lignin.

Many reports reveal that photochemical oxidation is the major reaction in the degradation of lignin (116–124). The phenolic groups in lignin molecules are associated closely with its oxidation to colored quinonoid products. Phenoxy radicals are generated readily from free phenolic groups by the action of light, and the phenoxy radicals are the major intermediates that are transformed into colored end products (116–124). From the yellowing patterns of esterified and alkylated newspaper and wood, Leary (124) concluded that the yellowing of lignin components normally begins with the oxidation of the phenolic structural units of lignin. He suggested that the phenolic groups are first oxidized by hydrogen atoms transferred to a neighboring excited molecule or free radicals. This leads to the formation of phenoxy radicals, which are then demethylated and oxidized to colored quinonoid structures. This mechanism has been substantiated by means of ESR studies by Hon (123). Studying lignin model compounds, Luner (116) suggested that quinones originate through a free radical through oxygen attacking lignin in the α-position of the aliphatic side chain of phenylpropane units containing phenolic hydroxy groups. The sidechain is split off, thereby fragmenting the molecule. Successively, p-quinonoid degradation products are obtained.

When lignin is irradiated with light of wavelengths shorter than 350 nm, an adverse effect on the molecule has been recognized in terms of color build-up, or the formation of chromophoric groups, especially o-quinone. This adverse effect was accelerated by the presence of oxygen. However, no such effect was observed when the sample was irradiated with light longer than 350 nm, yet a photobleaching effect was recognized using wavelengths such as 400 nm or longer (123). It also has been reported that yellowing was accompanied by a progressive disappearance of a chromophore with λ_{max} of 348 nm. The IR spectral changes associated with the disappearance of this 348-nm chromophore show that it has a carbonyl absorption at 1640–1660 cm^{-1} (125). Lin and Kringstad (126) stated that lignin building units bearing saturated sidechains are insensitive to light of 300 nm–390 nm and, hence, that the major components of lignin presumably are not involved in the yellowing process. However, lignin model compounds containing α-carbonyl groups absorb light of 300 nm–390 nm and form colored products. The authors concluded that α-carbonyl groups play a major role in the yellowing of lignin. The function of α-carbonyl groups as photosensitizers in promoting photoyellowing has been substantiated by Brunow and Eriksson (120), and by Hon (123). Kringstad and Lin (118) proposed that α-carbonyl groups can, after excitation to a triplet state, abstract hydrogen from a phenol.

A phenoxy radical and a benzyl alcohol radical were formed. The phenoxy radical can react further to form yellow products, while the benzyl alcohol radical is assumed to reoxidize to a carbonyl structure by reaction with oxygen. In this way, the α-carbonyl compound functions as a photosensitizer when irradiated in the presence of air and a phenolic compound. Also, the photochemical cleavage of benzylic aryl ether linkages, which contribute to the discoloration reaction of lignin, has been observed by Gierer and Lin (117) and by Hon (123). Continuing on their study, Brunow and Sivonen (121) revealed that oxygen present in the photoirradiated system quenched the excited carbonyl species and the phenol was dehydrogenated by excited oxygen. They concluded that yellowing of lignin is limited by the excited carbonyl groups, which in turn lead to the formation of excited oxygen molecules. This oxygen reacts with phenolic groups to produce phenoxy radicals, which lead to the formation of yellow products.

The photochemical reaction of lignin also has been studied in detail by Hon (123). Several facts have been elicited. They are: (a) phenoxy radicals were produced readily from free phenolic hydroxy groups by the action of light; (b) carbon–carbon bonds adjacent to α-carbonyl groups were photodissociated via the Norrish Type I reaction; (c) the Norrish Type I reaction did not occur effectively in those compounds with ether bonds adjacent to α-carbonyl groups—photodissociation took place at the ether bonds; (d) compounds bearing benzyl alcohol groups are not susceptible to photodissociation except when photosensitizers are present; and (e) α-carbonyl groups functioned as photosensitizers in the photodegradation of lignin.

Gellerstedt and Pettersson (121) suggested that conjugated double bonds in lignin are susceptible to light-induced oxidation, yielding carbonyl structures that participate in the discoloration reaction.

High-Yield Pulps. High-yield pulps composed of cellulose, hemicellulose, and lignin are more susceptible to discoloration by light than low-yield chemical pulps. This is indicated clearly by Figure 3 as well as reported by many investigators (10, 85, 127, 128, 129). Wilson and Harvey (130) found that when irradiating sheets while controlling sheet temperature, a greater yellowing was obtained with sheets of high lignin content. The yellowing of newspaper sheets was caused by light over the wavelength range of 3550 Å to 4000 Å, whereas bleaching effects also have been reported for groundwood by using visible light (124, 131–135).

Color or Brightness Reversion

Color or brightness reversion of papers is the loss of brightness through the discoloration or yellowing that occurs during storage; it is accelerated by exposure to light, heat, chemicals, and high humidities.

Brightness reversion is one of the serious problems for paper industries, restorers, paper conservators, and librarians, because the brightness of neither unbleached nor bleached pulp is permanent, and the causes and prevention of reversion still are not known entirely.

Brightness reversion or yellowing has been attributed in the past to nearly every constituent of pulp and paper. A considerable amount of work has been published in recent years on the influence of various pulp constituents on brightness reversion. Yet, the mechanism of the color reversion is of a complex nature, and the various pulp constituents can either contribute directly or react with each other.

At the First International Bleaching Conference at Appleton, Wisconsin, in 1955, in the final panel discussion on bleaching problems, fourteen theories were put forward to account for brightness reversion. They are listed here for reference purposes: (a) residual lignin; (b) furfural; (c) reductone formation from carbohydrates; (d) residue resin; (e) poor washing; (f) pH; (g) metallic catalysts; (h) metallic resinates; (i) diffusion; (j) carbonyl groups; (k) water impurities; (l) microorganisms; (m) low bleach residual; and (n) UV radiation.

Brightness reversion occurs in bleached chemical pulps that are practically freed of lignin and extractives. It is quite apparent that this undesirable effect must be attributed largely to the chemical structure alteration of carbohydrates during pulping process, especially in the bleaching stages. Essentially, the extent to which pure cellulose is responsible for brightness reversion is hard to establish because of the difficulty in preparation of a perfect cellulose. However, glucose is known to contribute to discoloration upon aging (136).

It has been proposed that over-oxidation of carbohydrates contributed to color reversion (76, 77, 137, 138, 139, 140). Carbonyl groups, including aldehyde carbonyl, carboxyl groups, and low molecular weight fractions containing these groups, contribute to brightness reversion (141). Reducing end groups do not appear to be involved in color reversion (142). The color instability of cellulose and hemicellulose is attributable to the presence of carbonyl and carboxyl groups (113, 143–149). Experimental data have shown that carbonyl and carboxyl groups at carbon atoms 2 and 3 are of importance. One investigation indicated that carbonyl groups are responsible for about half the color reversion of cautiously bleached pulp (150). It also has been established that uronosidic carbonyl groups have a detrimental effect on the color stability (151). Sjostrom and Erikksson (143) reported that the influence of carbonyl groups is magnified greatly by the presence of carboxyl groups. However, Rapson et al. (144) claimed that carbonyl groups are responsible for color reversion; carboxyl groups are not important at all.

In a study of aging of bleached pulps, Kleinert and Marraccini (152) reported that moisture was found to promote not only peroxide formation, but, to some extent, also brightness reversion, particularly in the absence of air. In addition, it is accepted generally that color reversion is accelerated during air aging at elevated temperatures through thermal oxidation. Chadeyeron (*147*) and Giertz and McPherson (*113*) indicated that the condensation of carbonyl groups during bleaching was the main cause of heat reversion. Rapson and Hakim (*143*) proposed that heat reversion can be reduced greatly if carbonyl is oxidized to carbonyl or reduced to hydroxyl.

In his excellent review paper, Spinner has summarized the factors causing brightness reversion (*10*). They are adapted as follows:

1. Aldehyde groups on carbon atoms 2 and 3 of the anhydroglucose unit cause reversion.
2. Carboxyl groups on carbon atoms 2 and 3 of the anhydroglucose unit cause reversion. In the acid form and at an aging temperature of $105°C$, the carboxyl groups contribute much less (roughly about a tenth) to reversion than an equivalent number of carbonyl groups. Ion exchange of hydrogen for sodium ions causes the reversion, while replacement by calcium decreases reversion.
3. Primary hydroxyl groups in carbon atoms 2 and 3 of the anhydroglucose unit do not cause reversion, even when this oxycellulose is hydrolyzed with HCl.
4. Aldehyde or hemiacetal end groups (C_1) of the anhydroglucose chain do not cause reversion.
5. The degree of polymerization does not have any effect on the extent of reversion.
6. Keto groups in carbon atoms 2 and/or 3 of the anhydroglucose unit cause reversion, but whether reversion is attributable to C_2 or C_3 or both types of ketone has not been settled.

Color reversion becomes a significant problem for the lignin-containing, high-yield pulp paper. Loras (*153*) reported that yellowing increased with the chlorine number of unbleached pulps and showed some correlation between yellowing and residual lignin. Howard and Histed (*154*) suggested that the major cause of brightness reversion is attributable to the chlorinated lignin residue left in pulps at the termination of bleaching.

Lignin-containing, high-yield pulps turn yellow when exposed to light. As described earlier, lignin is a phenolic compound with a strong absorption of UV light. The consequence of light absorption results in a radical reaction mechanism in which oxygen takes a part. This leads to demethoxylation, cleavage of aliphatic sidechain, and the formation of semiquinones and quinoid configuration. Details of this reaction have been described in a previous section, and a recent review paper on chromophoric groups in wood and pulps is available (*21*).

The effect on color reversion by traces of heavy metal ions has been reported (*129, 155, 156, 157, 158*). The presence of ferric and cupric ions greatly decreases the brightness stability, although some metal ions, including magnesium and manganese, seem to improve brightness. Metal salts are known to affect the rates and products of several reactions of cellulose itself. In some instances, they accelerate the autooxidation and photooxidation of wood pulps (31, 98, 159, 160). In addition to affecting the aging of cellulose, metal salts may cause color forming reactions with other pulp constituents. Alder and Haggarth (156) showed that iron reacted with the noncellulosic components of unbleached sulfite pulp. Upon aging, the pulp reddened.

Other minor pulp constituents, the resins or extractives, also have pronounced bearing on brightness reversion (161–165). In removing the resin in a bleached sulfite pulp by extracting with alcohol, Tongren found that the reversion rate was reduced (162). Giertz (163) lowered the reversion of bleached sulfite pulps to about one-third of their original value by alcohol–benzene extraction. Aalto (164) found that an ether extraction of a sulfite pulp prevented reversion to some extent. It should be borne in mind that not all resin components cause reversion, but when resin does, the resultant reversion appears to be approximately linear with the resin content.

Color Stabilization

In the preceding sections, discoloration and brightness reversion were discussed. Chemical constituents in modern papers exhibit a wide range of susceptibilities to oxidation that can be explained in part by differences in structures. Stabilization of color against thermal and photooxidation can be enhanced by modification of the polymer structure to eliminate the more reactive sites or chromophoric functional groups and to introduce groups that contribute to color stabilization.

Rapson and Hakim (144) have given a review of the color reversion problem and have shown that color reversion can be reduced if carbonyl was oxidized to carboxyl with chlorine dioxide, or reduced to hydroxyl with sodium borohydride. Luner (165) had success in raising brightness of cold soda pulp from white birch with sodium borohydride. Some investigators believed that carbonyl groups were also elements contributing to color reversion. Croon et al. (167) reported that the transformation of the carbonyl groups in the pulp to the hydrogen form by a sulfur dioxide treatment usually increases brightness stability in a moist atmosphere, and decreases it under dry conditions.

Earlier discussion of lignin chromophores has indicated that the free hydroxyl group is a reactive center in the reaction taking place when lignin is degraded by light. As a consequence, it is possible that by blocking phenolic hydroxyl groups, for example, by etherification or esterification (124, 168), lignin may be protected completely against photochemical discoloration. Singh (*169*) has shown that blocking of reactive hydroxyl groups by benzoyl chloride in groundwood pulp is accompanied by an increase in the brightness and the brightness stability of the pulp. However, he indicated that the attempt to develop this benzolation bleaching process was unsuccessful because of the large excess of benzoyl chloride required. Acetylation, diazomethane methylation, and borohydride reduction of groundwood would increase the brightness to a certain extent (*124, 168, 170, 171*). Callow and Speakman (*172*) investigated the color stability of jute fiber and observed that acetylated and methylated jutes were lighter in color than the untreated fiber. Nakamura et al. (*173*) and Gierer (*174*) suggested that the acetylation involved the phenolic, para-hydroxy benzyl alcohol, and other alcoholic groups in the lignin. Lin and his co-workers (*117, 118*) claimed that the stabilizing effect of methylation, benzolation, and acetylation on high-yield pulps is not exclusively by the blocking of phenolic hydroxyls in lignin, but also by the blocking of aliphatic hydroxyls in polysaccharides. Loras (*175*) reported that color stability against light was improved appreciably by acetylation of unbleached pulp and pulp bleached with peroxide or dithionite before acetylation. The decrease in brightness by heat treatment also was reduced by acetylation of unbleached and bleached pulp. Krinstad (*127*) suggested the possible use of different types of antioxidants to retard the yellowing or degradation of high-yield pulps on exposure to light. He showed that some derivatives of benzophenone and the sodium salts of citric, ascorbic, and thiodipropionic acids have some retarding effects. Reineck and Lewis (*176*) tested the ability of a series of antioxidants to reduce yellowing of groundwood when exposed to light. Only three substances were found that showed retarding effects. These were dimethyldehydroresorcinol, *o*-aminophenol, and an UV sensitizer of undescribed nature. However, the pulp developed color when impregnated with the first two compounds.

Conclusion

From the preceding discussion, it is obvious that discoloration or yellowing of modern papers is a complex set of reactions depending upon the historical background of the materials, methods of fiber and paper production, and the conditions of their usage and storage.

"Pure" cellulose and hemicellulose should be unaffected by exposure to natural sunlight. It generally is believed that it is the presence of impurities in the commercial cellulose, introduced during pulping processing or autooxidation, that results in light absorption by the polymer and that may initiate photochemical reaction. The major chromophoric groups are believed to be carbonyl and carboxyl groups, hydroperoxides, and metallic impurities. Lignin is sensitive to sunlight. The α-carbonyl groups, conjugated double bonds, quinonoid structures, and phenolic hydroxyl groups in lignin are the vulnerable functional groups that absorb harmful incident radiation leading to photochemical reactions. The photoinduced discoloration of modern paper is enhanced further by the presence of paper additives and impurities as well as the presence of moisture, heat, and oxygen.

To effectively prevent photoinduced discoloration of modern paper, one must consider the environment in which it may be stored, exhibited, or used, and the causes of its yellowing. In view of the photochemistry involved, some form of photostabilization of modern paper is essential if adequate protection against the detrimental effects of solar irradiation is to be achieved.

Principally, the photostabilization of modern paper involves the retardation or elimination of the various photophysical and photochemical processes that take place during photoinduced discoloration. This goal may be accomplished by the following three stabilizing systems.

1. *Physical Modification of Modern Paper.* This system relies on the presence of stabilizers for its stabilizing action. The stabilizers are of four general types (*177, 178, 179*): UV screeners, UV absorbers, quenching compounds, and free radical scavengers. By strict definition, in this case, UV screens are materials that are interposed as a shield between the modern paper and the radiation source. They function by reflecting the damaging incident light, thereby limiting its penetration into the bulk of the paper. Ultraviolet absorbers function by absorbing and dissipating UV irradiation that would otherwise initiate discoloration of modern paper. Quenching compounds function by dissipating the excited energy from modern paper. Free radical scavengers act as a trapping means to catch the free radicals generated in the modern paper before they stabilize themselves as colored end products.

2. *Chemical Modification of Modern Paper.* Chemical modification encompasses both the purification of modern paper and the alteration of chromophoric configurations of the chemical constituents in paper to produce the desired photostability.

   Impurities that enhance the photo-induced reaction can be foreign materials incorporated during processing (such as metallic impurities), or they can be an integral part of paper components (such as carbonyl or carboxyl groups). Consequently, elimination or reduction in the amount of impurities, either foreign or as part of paper components, is a practical approach to stabilization. Furthermore, elimination of chromophoric systems in the paper components by introducing new functional groups that are insensitive or less sensitive to light is essential. Benzolation, methylation, acetylation, and sodium borohydride reduction demonstrate such improvement, yet most of these processes are too expensive to be practical. Development of new processes that are economically feasible is required.

3. *Combination of Physical and Chemical Modification of Modern Paper.* The photostabilization of modern paper can be further improved by combination of the above-mentioned two systems. The addition of stabilizers to chemically modified modern paper can avoid further photo-induced reactions through the incomplete elimination of the chromophoric moiety in the paper.

Literature Cited

1. Mitchell, J., Ed. "The Random House Encyclopedia"; Random House: New York, 1977; p. 1440.
2. "Papermaking: Art and Craft"; Library of Congress: Washington, D.C., 1968; p. 9.
3. Hunter, D. "Papermaking in Pioneer America"; Univ. of Pennsylvania Press: Philadelphia, 1952.
4. Haylock, E. W. "Paper: Its Making, Merchanting and Usage": The Natl. Assoc. of Paper Merchants: London, 1974; p. 8.
5. Malin, H. M., Jr. *Chemistry* 1979, *52*, 17.
6. Barrow, W. J.; Sproull, R. C. *Science* 1959, *129*, 1075.
7. Church, R. W., Ed. "Deterioration of Book Stock, Cause and Remedies"; Virginia State Library, 1959.
8. Church, R. W., Ed. "The Manufacture and Testing of Durable Book Papers"; Virginia State Library, 1960.
9. Stuhrke, R. A. In "The Development of Permanent Paper," *Adv. Chem. Ser.* 1977, *164*, 24.
10. Spinner, I. H. *Tappi* 1962, *45*, 495.
11. Stubchen-Kirchner, H. *Österr. Chem.-Zt.* 1962, *63*, 319.
12. Neimo, L. *Paperi Ja Puu* 1964, *46*, 7.
13. Byrne, J.; Weiner, J. "Permanence"; Bibliographic Series No. 213; Institute of Paper Chemistry: Appleton, WI, 1964.
14. Louden, L. "Paper Conservation and Restoration"; Bibliographic Series No. 284; Institute of Paper Chemistry: Appleton, WI, 1978.
15. Poole, F. G. *Am. Archivist* 1977, *40*, 163.
16. Browning, B. L.; Wink, W. A. *Tappi* 1968, *51*, 156.
17. Gray, G. G. *Tappi* 1969, *52*, 325.
18. Luner, P. *Tappi* 1969, *52*, 796.
19. Williams, J. C., Ed. "Preservation of Paper and Textiles of Historic and Artistic Value," *Adv. Chem. Ser.* 1977, *164*.
20. Britt, K. W., Ed. "Handbook of Pulp and Paper Technology," 2nd ed.; Van Nostrand Reinhold: New York, 1970; Chap. 8.
21. Hon, D. N.-S.; Glasser, W. *Polym.-Plast. Technol. Eng.* 1979, *12*, 159.
22. Wilcox, M. D. *Sven. Papperstidn.* 1975, *78*, 22.
23. Kleinert, T. N. *Holzforsch. Holzverwert.* 1970, *22*, 21.
24. Rydholm, S. A. "Pulping Process"; Interscience: New York, 1965; p. 839.
25. Rapson, W. H., Ed. "The Bleaching of Pulp," Tappi Monograph Series No. 27; Tappi: New York, 1963; p. 8.
26. Ranby, B.; Rabek, J. F. "Photodegradation, Photooxidation and Photostabilization of Polymers"; John Wiley & Sons: New York, 1975; p. 6.
27. Calvert, J. G.; Pitts, J. N., Jr. "Photochemistry"; John Wiley & Sons: New York, 1966; p. 19.

28. Hon, N.-S. *J. Polym. Sci., Polym. Chem. Ed.* **1975,** *13,* 1347.
29. Beelik, A.; Hamilton, J. K. *Papier* **1959,** *13,* 77.
30. Beelik, A.; Hamilton, J. K. *J. Org. Chem.* **1961,** *26,* 5074.
31. Hon, N.-S. *J. Polym. Sci., Polym. Chem. Ed.* **1975,** *13,* 1933.
32. Goldschmid, O. "Lignins"; Sarkanen, K. V.; Ludwig, C. H., Eds.; Wiley–Interscience: New York, 1971; Chap. 6, pp. 241–266.
33. Launer, H. F.; Wilson, W. K. *J. Res. Natl. Bur. Stand.* **1943,** *30,* 55.
34. Stowe, B. S.; Fornes, R. E.; Gilbert, R. D. *Polym.-Plast. Technol. Eng.* **1974,** *3,* 159.
35. Hon, N.-S. *J. Polym. Sci., Polym. Chem. Ed.* **1976,** *14,* 2497.
36. Hon, N.-S. *J. Macromol. Sci.–Chem.* **1976,** *A 10,* 1175.
37. Hon, D. N.-S., unpublished data.
38. Richter, G. A. *Ind. Eng. Chem.* **1935,** *27,* 177.
39. Kohler, S. *Tek. Tidsk.* **1935,** *7,* 49.
40. Lewis, H. F.; Reineck, E. A.; Fronmuller, D. *Tech. Assoc. Paper Ser.* **1945,** *28,* 157.
41. Lewis, H. F.; Reineck, E. A.; Fronmuller, D. *Paper Trade J.* **1945,** *121*(8), 44.
42. Gellerstedt, G.; Kringstad, K.; Lindfors, E. L. "Singlet Oxygen"; Ranby, B.; Rabek, J. F., Eds.; John Wiley & Sons: New York, 1978; p. 302.
43. Witz, G. *Bull. Soc. (Rouen)* **1883,** *11,* 188.
44. Appleby, D. K. *Amer. Dyest. Rep.* **1949,** *38,* 148, 189.
45. Robinson, H. M.; Reeves, W. A. *Amer. Dyest. Rep.* **1961,** *50,* 17.
46. Phillips, G. O. *Adv. Carbohydr. Chem.* **1963,** *18,* 9.
47. Phillips, G. O.; Arthur, J. C., Jr. *Text. Res. J.* **1964,** *34*(497), 572.
48. Desai, R. L. *Pulp Pap. Mag. Can.* **1968,** T332.
49. Baugh, P. J.; Phillips, G. O. "Cellulose and Cellulose Derivatives"; Bikales, N. M.; Segal, L., Eds.; Interscience: New York, 1971; Vol. 5, p. 1047.
50. Yoshimoto, T. *Mokuzai Gakkaishi* **1972,** *18,* 49.
51. Kathpalia, Y. P. *Indian Pulp Pap.* **1961,** *15,* 442.
52. Stoker, H. S.; Seager, S. L.; Capener, R. L. "From Source to Use Energy"; Scott, Foresman and Co.: Glenview, IL, 1975; p. 48.
53. Koller, L. R. "Ultraviolet Radiation," 2nd ed.; John Wiley & Sons: New York, 1965; Chap. 4.
54. Nobel, P. S. "Introduction to Biophysical Plant Physiology"; W. H. Freeman and Co.: San Francisco, 1974; p. 172.
55. Hirt, R. C.; Searle, N. Z. *Appl. Polym. Symp.* **1967,** *4,* 61.
56. Sadov, F. I.; Artemova, V. S. *Tekst. Promst.* **1967,** *7,* 22.
57. Egerton, G. S. *J. Soc. Dyers Colour.* **1967,** *63,* 161.
58. Egerton, G. S. *De Tex.* **1952,** *11,* 28.
59. Henk, H. J. *Melliand Textilber.* **1952,** *33,* 488.
60. Kato, H. *Kami Pa Gikyoshi* **1962,** *16,* 835.
61. Launer, H. F.; Wilson, W. K. *J. Am. Chem. Soc.* **1949,** *71,* 958.
62. Race, E. J. *J. Soc. Dyers Colour.* **1949,** *65,* 56.
63. Stillings, R. A.; Van Nostrand, R. J. *J. Am. Chem. Soc.* **1944,** *66,* 753.
64. Flynn, J. H.; Wilson, W. K.; Morrow, W. L. *J. Res. Natl. Bur. Stand.* **1958,** *60,* 229.
65. Kauffman, H. *Melliand Textilber* **1916,** *7,* 617.
66. Hon, D. N.-S. *J. Polym. Sci., Polym. Chem. Ed.* **1979,** *17,* 441.
67. Padmanabhan, T. S. A. *Cellul. Res. Symp. (New Delhi)* **1958,** *1,* 19.
68. Kujirai, C. *Sen'i Gakkaishi* **1966,** *22*(20), 84.
69. Lewis, H. F. *Pap. Trade J.* **1932,** *95*(21), 29.
70. Barr, G.; Hatfield, I. H. *J. Text. Inst.* **1927,** *18,* 490T.
71. Barr, G.; Hatfield, I. H. Dep. Sci. Ind. Res. 2nd Rept. Fabrics Coordinating Res. Comm. **1930,** 95–112.
72. Oguri, S. *J. Soc. Chem. Ind. Japan* **1934,** *37,* 201.
73. Buccar, M. de. *Papeterie* **1961,** *63,* 49.

74. Kleinert, T. N.; Sieber, F. *Holzforschung* **1955**, *9*, 15.
75. Hon, N.-S. *J. Polym. Sci., Polym. Chem. Ed.* **1975**, *13*, 955.
76. Tongren, J. C. *Pap. Trade J.* **1938**, *107*(8), 34.
77. Richter, G. A.; Wells, F. L. *Tappi* **1956**, *39*, 603.
78. Egerton, G. S.; Attle, E.; Rathor, M. A. *Nature* **1962**, *194*, 968.
79. Yabrora, R. R. *Bum. Promst.* **1957**, *32*, 15.
80. Orr, R. S.; Weiss, L. C.; Humphreys, G. C.; Mares, T.; Grant, J. N. *Text. Res. J.* **1954**, *24*, 399.
81. Shitola, H. *Pap. Timber (Finland)* **1963**, *45*, 71.
82. Herzberg, W. *Wochenbl. Papierfabr.* **1925**, *56*, 35.
83. Edge, S. R. H.; McKenzie, H. M. *Proc. Tech. Sect. Pap. Makers' Assoc. G. B. Irel.* **1937**, *17*(2), 437.
84. Desai, R. L.; Shields, J. A. *J. Colloid Interface Sci.* **1969**, *31*, 585.
85. Hon, N.-S. *J. Polym. Sci., Polym. Chem. Ed.* **1975**, *13*, 2641.
86. Hon, D. N.-S.; Ifju, G. *Wood Sci.* **1978**, *11*, 118.
87. MacClaren, R. H.; Wells, F. L.; Rosequist, J. V.; Ingerick, D. F. *Tappi* **1962**, *45*, 789.
88. Spirova, L. V.; Flyate, D. M. *Nauchn. Tr. Leningr. Akad.* **1968**, *113*, 6.
89. Desai, R. L. *Bi-mon. Res. Notes, Can. For. Dep.* **1968**, *24*, 25.
90. Schoeller, V. *Wochenbl. Papierfabr.* **1912**, *43*, 3222, 3408, 3489, 3673, 3963, 4148, 4336.
91. Aribert, M.; Bouvier, B. *Papeterie* **1920**, *42*, 338, 386.
92. Colpe, D. *Papiergeschichte* **1968**, *18*, 53.
93. Hitchins, A. B. *Paper* **1918**, *22*, 11.
94. Klemm, P. "Klimsch's Jahrbuch"; Leipzig Griben's Verlag Frankfurt, West Germany, **1901**; p. 32.
95. Klason, P. *Sven. Kem. Tidskr.* **1912**, *4*, 86.
96. Zschokke, B. *Wichenbl. Papierfabr.* **1913**, *44*, 2976, 3165.
97. Aribert, M.; Bouvier, F. M. *Papeterie* **1920**, *42*, 338, 386.
98. Hon, N.-S. *J. Appl. Polym. Sci.* **1975**, *19*, 2789.
99. Beelik, A.; Hamilton, J. K. *J. Org. Chem.* **1961**, *26*, 5074.
100. Puyster, B. de. *Color Trade J.* **1923**, *13*, 23.
101. Wultsch, F.; Limontschew, W.; Schindler, G. *Papier* **1963**, *17*, 326.
102. Henk, H. J. *Melliand Textilber.* **1938**, *19*, 730.
103. Williams, J. C.; Fowler, C. S.; Lyon, M. S.; Merrill, T. L. In "Metallic Catalysts in the Oxidative Degradation of Paper," *Adv. Chem. Ser.* **1977**, *164*, 37.
104. Yoshimoto, T. *Mokuzai Gakkaishi* **1972**, *18*, 49.
105. Yamagishi, T.; Yoshimoto, T.; Minami, K. *Mokuzai Gakkaishi* **1970**, *16*, 87.
106. Peng, J. Y.; Minami, K.; Yoshimoto, T. *Mokuzai Gakkaishi* **1967**, *13*, 155.
107. Yasuda, S.; Nagaoka, M.; Hanzawa, J. *Res. Bull. Coll. Exp. For., Hokkaido Univ.* **1974**, *31*, 1.
108. Rollinson, S. M. *Tappi* **1955**, *38*, 625.
109. Roudier, A.; Saulquin-Bisson, A. *Atip.* **1959**, *3*, 109.
110. Roudier, A.; Sauret, G. *Atip.* **1959**, *4*, 187.
111. Giertz, H. W. *Sven. Papperstidn.* **1945**, *48*, 317.
112. Monzie, P.; Monzie, D.; Raoux, H. *Atip.* **1959**, *32*.
113. Giertz, H. W.; McPherson, J. *Sven. Papperstidn.* **1956**, *59*, 93.
114. Centola, G. *Ind. Papet.* **1951**, *5*, 111.
115. Sarkanen, K. V.; Ludwig, C. H. "Lignins"; Wiley–Interscience: New York, 1971; p. 1.
116. Luner, P. *Tappi* **1960**, *43*, 819.
117. Gierer, J.; Lin, S. Y. *Sven. Papperstidn.* **1972**, *75*, 233.
118. Krinstad, K. P.; Lin, S. Y. *Tappi* **1970**, *53*, 2296.
119. Lin, S. Y.; Krinstad, K. P. *Nor. Skogind.* **1971**, *9*, 252.
120. Brunow, G.; Eriksson, B. *Acta Chem. Scand.* **1971**, *25*, 2779.
121. Brunow, G.; Sivonen, M. *Pap. Puu* **1975**, *57*, 215.

122. Gellerstedt, G.; Pettersson, E.-L. *Acta Chem. Scand.* **1975,** *B 29,* 1005.
123. Hon, N.-S. Ph.D. Dissertation, Virginia Polytechnic Institute & State Univ., Blacksburg, 1977.
124. Leary, G. J. *Tappi* **1968,** *51,* 257.
125. Leary, G. *Austr. Corros. Eng.* **1970,** *14,* 9.
126. Lin, S. Y.; Kringstad, K. P. *Tappi* **1970,** *53,* 658.
127. Kringstad, K. P. *Tappi* **1969,** *52,* 1070.
128. Kringstad, K. P. *Papier* **1973,** *27,* 462.
129. Imsgard, F.; Falkehag, I.; Kringstad, K. P. *Tappi* **1971,** *54,* 10.
130. Wilson, W. K.; Harvey, J. L. *Tappi* **1953,** *36,* 459.
131. Leary, G. J. *Tappi* **1967,** *50,* 17.
132. Nolan, P.; Van den Akker, J. A.; Wink, W. A. *Pap. Trade J.* **1945,** *121*(11), 33.
133. Van den Akker, J. A.; Lewis, H. F.; Jones, G. W.; Buchanan, M. A. *Tappi* **1949,** *32,* 187.
134. Sandermann, W.; Schlumbom, F. *Holz Roh- Werkst.* **1962,** *20,* 245.
135. Claesson, S.; Olson, E.; Wennerblom, A. *Sven. Papperstidn.* **1968,** *71,* 335.
136. Roudier, A.; Saulquin-Bisson, A. *Atip.* **1959,** 109.
137. Centola, G. *Ind. Papet.* **1951,** 5, 111.
138. Swartz, J. N. *Conv. Pulp Pap. Mag. Can.* **1946,** *47,* 203.
139. Prelinger, H. *Pap. Trade J.* **1938,** *107*(11), 81.
140. Rollinson, S. M. *Tappi* **1955,** *38,* 625.
141. Rapson, W. H.; Corbi, J. C. *Pulp Pap. Mag. Can.* **1964,** *65,* T-459.
142. Rapson, W. H., Ed. "The Bleaching of Pulp," Monograph No. 27; Tappi: New York, 1963; p. 283.
143. Sjostrom, E.; Errikson, E. *Tappi* **1968,** *51,* 16.
144. Rapson, W. H.; Hakim, K. A. *Pulp Pap. Mag. Can.* **1957,** *58,* 151.
145. Rapson, W. H.; Anderson, C. B.; King, G. F. *Tappi* **1958,** *41,* 442.
146. Jappe, N. A.; Kaustinen, O. A. *Tappi* **1959,** *42,* 206.
147. Chadeyron, L. *Ind. Papet.* **1954,** *1,* 21.
148. Jullander, I.; Brune, K. *Acta Chem. Scand.* **1957,** *11,* 570.
149. Rapson, W. H. *Tappi* **1956,** *39,* 284.
150. Jullander, I.; Brune, K. *Sven. Papperstidn.* **1959,** *62,* 728.
151. Rapson, W. H.; Corbi, J. C., presented at the *First Can. Wood Chem. Symp. Toronto, Canada, Sept. 1963.*
152. Kleinert, T. N.; Marraccini, L. M. *Sven. Papperstidn.* **1963,** *66,* 189.
153. Loras, V. *Nor. Skogind.* **1953,** 9, 160.
154. Howard, E. J.; Histed, J. A. *Tappi* **1964,** *47,* 653.
155. Talwar, K. K.; McDonnell, L. F. *South. Pulp Pap. Manuf.* **1955,** *18,* 44, 97.
156. Adler, E.; Haggroth, S. *Sven. Papperstidn.* **1950,** *53,* 287.
157. Czepiel, T. P. *Tappi* **1960,** *43,* 289.
158. Wultsch, V. F.; Limontschew, W.; Schindler, G. *Papier* **1963,** *17,* 326.
159. Keller, E. L.; Simmonds, F. A. *Pap. Trade J.* **1942,** *115*(14), 98.
160. Casciani, F.; Storin, G. K. *Tech. Assoc. Pap.* **1942,** *25,* 489.
161. Bergman, J.; Hartler, N.; Stockman, L. *Sven. Papperstidn.* **1963,** *66,* 547.
162. Tongren, J. C. *Pap. Trade J.* **1938,** *107,* 76.
163. Giertz, H. W. *Sven. Papperstidn.* **1945,** *48,* 317.
164. Aalto, E. O. *Pap. Puu* **1954,** *36,* 71.
165. Rapson, W. H.; Anderson, C. B. *Pulp Pap. Mag. Can.* **1960,** *61,* T-495.
166. Luner, P. *Tappi* **1960,** *43,* 819.
167. Croon, I.; Dillen, S.; Olsson, J. E. *Sven. Papperstidn.* **1966,** *69,* 139.
168. Andrews, D. H.; Des Rasier, P. *Pulp Pap. Mag. Can.* **1966,** *67,* T-119.
169. Singh, R. P. *Tappi* **1966,** *49,* 281.
170. Manchester, D. F.; McKinney, J. W.; Pataky, A. A. *Sven. Papperstidn.* **1960,** *63,* 699.
171. Peill, P. L. D. *Nature* **1946,** *158,* 554.

172. Callow, H. J.; Speakman, J. B. *J. Soc. Dyers Colour.* **1959,** *65,* 758.
173. Nakamura, Y. *Ind. Eng. Chem.* **1957,** *49,* 1388.
174. Gierer, J. *Acta Chem. Scand.* **1954,** *8,* 1319.
175. Loras, V. *Pulp Pap. Mag. Can.* **1968,** *69,* 57.
176. Reineck, E. A.; Lewis, H. F. *Pap. Trade J.* **1945,** *121* (21), 27.
177. Trozzolo, A. M. "Polymer Stabilization"; Hawkins, W. L., Ed.; Wiley–Interscience: New York, 1972; pp. 159–213.
178. McKellar, J. F.; Allen, N. S. "Photochemistry of Man-Made Polymers"; Applied Science: London, 1979; pp. 199–255.
179. Ranby, B.; Rabek, J. F. "Photodegradation, Photooxidation, and Photo-stabilization of Polymers"; John Wiley & Sons: New York, 1975; pp. 362–411.

RECEIVED October 23, 1979.

Determination of Trace Elements in Paper by Energy Dispersive X-Ray Fluorescence

VICTOR F. HANSON

The Henry Francis du Pont Winterthur Museum, Winterthur, DE 19735

Detection of up to thirty trace elements present in paper, documents, prints, and watercolor paintings from x-ray fluorescence spectra demonstrates possibilities for determining which elements are present in the original paper, which were added by the papermaker, which were suspended or dissolved in the processing water, which were picked up from the processing equipment, which were added by the user of the paper, and on which side of two-sided printings (such as currency) do the various elements reside. Element densities in $\mu g/cm^2$ were determined in a group of American and European papers made between 1637 and 1900. Comparable data are also reported for modern paper in the form of United States currency, which was found to contain high concentrations of fugitive lead, barium, chromium, and iron, except for three issues of $1 bills made with experimental lead-free inks in 1969.

The Henry Francis du Pont Winterthur Museum, which has two hundred period rooms and display areas of American furniture and furnishings on a beautiful 960-acre, park-like estate, dedicated the Louise Crowinshield Research Wing in 1969. A research and analytical laboratory, it was to provide facilities and techniques to determine the chemical composition of the thousands of objects in the Collection.

Such compositional information was desired to: Provide the curator with a badly needed sixth sense to detect fake art objects, which were appearing on the market at an alarming rate. Assist the art conservators in selecting the most appropriate materials and methods to restore and repair objects in the Collection. Assist art historians to establish more accurately the maker, time, and place where the objects were made.

0065-2393/81/0193-0143$06.50/0

Advise the owner of alterations, repairs, and maintenance procedures that had been employed by prior owners.

The energy dispersive x-ray fluorescence spectrometer, which had been developed recently as a qualitative analysis instrument, showed promise of meeting the goals of the new laboratory (1). Its unique features, which earned it the name, "The Curator's Dream Instrument," are: The measurements require neither sampling nor alteration of the object in any way. Systems for obtaining quantitative analysis data are now operational (1). Concentrations of up to thirty elements above chlorine (Z = 17) can now be printed out simultaneously. Techniques have been developed that minimize errors caused by sample size, shape, position, overlapping spectral peaks, matrix effects, and baseline compensation. Interpretative procedures have been established that recognize the shallow depth of penetration of the excitation radiation (2).

Analytical Equipment

The components assembled at Winterthur in 1970 to make up the energy dispersive x-ray fluorescence analyzer system employed in this study of trace elements in paper, documents, prints, and watercolor paintings were: Kevex Series 3000P cryogenic system and detector (sample "viewing diameter," 15 mm; detector resolution, 170 eV at 5.9 keV

Table I. Computer Factors Employed in This Chapter

ELEMENT	CHANNEL	FACTOR	EXPONENT	CORR CHAN	CORR FACTOR
ANTIMONY..	331.00000	.03300	1.00000	32.00000	.00000
ARSENIC...	134.00000	.00400	1.00000	16.00000	-1.10000
BARIUM....	403.00000	.05500	1.00000	33.00000	.00000
BISMUTH..	165.00000	.01000	1.00000	16.00000	-.50000
CADMIUM...	291.00000	.06400	1.00000	34.00000	-.38000
CALCIUM...	46.00000	.03650	1.00000	33.00000	-.80000
CERIUM....	433.00000	.01000	1.00000	32.00000	-.90000
CESIUM....	387.00000	.01000	1.00000	32.00000	-.50000
CHROMIUM..	68.00000	.06500	1.00000	31.00000	-.60000
COBALT....	88.00000	.04800	1.00000	35.00000	-.82000
COPPER....	102.00000	.01800	1.00000	12.00000	-1.10000
GALLIUM...	115.00000	.00100	1.00000	.00000	.00000
MOLYBDENUM	216.00000	.00835	1.00000	.00000	.00000
IRON......	81.00000	.06000	1.00000	35.00000	-.70000
LANTHANUM.	419.00000	.20000	1.00000	3.00000	-1.00000
LEAD......	161.00000	.02200	1.00000	22.00000	-2.00000
MANGANESE.	76.00000	.17000	1.00000	31.00000	-1.00000
MERCURY...	150.00000	.01680	1.00000	2.00000	-.20000
NICKEL....	95.00000	.02260	1.00000	35.00000	-.70000
POTASSIUM.	42.00000	.00560	1.00000	33.00000	-.60000
RUBIDIUM..	169.00000	.00450	1.00000	16.00000	-.06000
SELENIUM..	142.00000	.00100	1.00000	.00000	.00000
SILVER....	280.00000	.03000	1.00000	34.00000	-.87000
STRONTIUM.	179.00000	.00450	1.00000	.00000	.00000
TIN.......	316.00000	.05100	1.00000	32.00000	-1.10000
TITANIUM..	58.00000	.00250	1.00000	33.00000	-1.50000
VANADIUM..	64.00000	.00100	1.00000	26.00000	-.02000
YTTRIUM...	189.00000	.00370	1.00000	16.00000	-.09000
ZINC......	110.00000	.01100	1.00000	12.00000	-1.00000
ZIRCONIUM.	199.00000	.00200	1.00000	.00000	.00000
XX72......	72.00000	.00000	1.00000	.00000	.00000
XX........	338.00000	.00000	1.00000	.00000	.00000
XX53......	53.00000	.00000	1.00000	.00000	.00000
XX........	295.00000	.00000	1.00000	.00000	.00000
XX86.....	86.00000	.00000	1.00000	.00000	.00000

Table II.   Summary of Analyses of Two Brass Candlesticks

A.L. #	863.1	863.2	848A.1	848A.2	848A.3
SEQ. #	#B1770	#B1771	#B1678	#B1679	#B1680
TEST DATE	113,1979	113,1979	81,1979	81,1979	81,1979
TEST TIME	8:59	9:5	13:7	13:10	13:17
ACCESSION #	NONE	NONE	66.1341	66.1341	66.1341
OWNER	CHLNGSWRTH	CHLNGSWRTH	WINTERTHUR	WINTERTHUR	WINTERTHUR
OBJECT	CANDLESTIC	CANDLESTIC	CANDLESTIC	CANDLESTIC	CANDLESTIC
DESC'N	K	K	K	K	K
PART	SHAFT	BASE	BASE OBV.	SHAFT	SHAFT'
MAKER	?	?	/	/	/
DATE	MODERN?	MODERN?	/	/	/
PROV'NCE	ENG./HOL.	ENG./HOL.	/	/	/
ELEMENT	WEIGHT %	WEIGHT %	WEIGHT %	WEIGHT %	WEIGHT %

	ELEMENT	WEIGHT %	WEIGHT %	WEIGHT %	WEIGHT %	WEIGHT %
1	ANTIMONY..	.21333	.27787	.09960	.03798	.04383
2	ARSENIC...	.00000	.00000	.00000	.00000	.00000
3	BISMUTH...	.00202	.00128	.00010	.00006	.00009
4	CADMIUM...	.01713	.00000	.00665	.00445	.00000
5	COBALT....	.00000	.00000	.00000	.00000	.00000
6	COPPER....	72.23442	78.48419	79.23920	72.45422	72.12579
7	GOLD......	.05796	.05493	.01045	.01349	.04126
8	IRON......	1.12368	1.66412	.73116	.37141	.46412
9	LEAD......	6.27668	2.76741	1.52377	1.07124	1.12311
10	MANGANESE.	.00000	.00000	.00000	.00000	.00000
11	MERCURY...	.00000	.00000	.00000	.00000	.00000
12	NICKEL....	.00000	.00000	.00000	.00000	.00000
13	SILVER....	.06756	.06840	.06910	.08845	.08984
14	TIN.......	2.95118	2.26054	.79557	.28914	.30190
15	ZINC......	17.05605	14.42125	17.52440	25.66956	25.81006
17	XXQ.......	.00000	.00000	.00000	.00000	.00000
18	XXR.......	.00000	.00000	.00000	.00000	.00000
19	XXS.......	.00000	.00000	.00000	.00000	.00000
20	XXT.......	.00000	.00000	.00000	.00000	.00000

at half peak); Kevex Energy Calibrator Model 4000P (range control, 5–100 keV; zero suppression, 0–100 keV); Packard 960 analog–digital convertor (This unit was modified by the addition of a selector switch and resistor networks to bias out signals beyond the ranges designated in Table V. This modification provided a continuous spectrum from the three excitation sources over 0–40 keV and eliminated most of the source backscatter, thereby improving the signal to noise ratio (Figure 1).); Packard 901 computer memory (two 512 pulse count storage memories; pulse count capacity, 10^6 per channel); Packard 960A system control (preset counts, 1–10^5; preset time, 1–10^5 s); Packard 970 tape/type control (This system interfaces memory with various read-out systems.); Hewlett Packard 4004B X–Y point plotter; Tektronix 602 display scope; Hewlett Packard computer system installed in 1977 (21 MX computer, Model 9885S disk drive, Model 9885M disk drive, Model 2762A line printer, Model 2644A terminal).

The computer program was developed by P. H. Gaither of Winterthur's Scientific Advisory Committee. Table I shows the normalizing and baseline correction factors employed in the computer program.

The present equipment provides a typed read-out of concentrations of fifteen elements in metallic objects (Table II) and up to thirty elements in nonmetallic objects such as glass/ceramics (Table III) and paper (Table IV) within fifteen minutes, with accuracies well within the needs of the museum staff.

Table III. Summary of Analyses of Five Glass Objects, Concentrations in Parts per 10,000 (pp10k)

A.L. #	8 16	890.1	890.2	892.8	894.21.1
SEQ. #	#G1123	#G1197	#G1198	#G1206	#G1235
TEST DATE	130,1979	177,1979	177,1979	180,1979	183,1979
TEST TIME	12:16	10:47	11:17	14:42	10:34
ACCESSION #	NONE	NONE	NONE	NONE	NONE
OWNER	J GOTJEN	NATL PARK	N PARK SER	QUINCY	PMA
OBJECT	PURPLE ENG	GREEN GLAS	GREEN GLAS	BOTTLE LIP	GREEN GLAS
DESC'N	RAVED SMAL	S WINE BOT	S MUG	FRAGMENT	S SHERD
PART	BOTTOM	SIDE	SIDE	SIDE	SIDE
MAKER	AMELUNG?	WISTAR	WISTAR	GERMANTOWN	HILLTOWN
DATE	C 1785?	1740-1760	1740-1760	1752-1754	1755-80
PROV'NCE	MARYLAND?	NJ	NJ	BRAINTREE	BUCKS CO
ELEMENT	pp10k	pp10k	pp10k	pp10k	pp10k

	ELEMENT					
1	ANTIMONY..	1.18650	.00000	.02300	.15410	.13110
2	ARSENIC...	.48202	.00000	.60368	.00000	97.08563
3	BARIUM....	38.26275	48.61050	41.80952	16.73101	21.18600
4	BISMUTH...	1.43560	.67397	.52546	.49400	41.35313
5	CADMIUM...	.00160	.00740	.00690	.00980	.00690
6	CALCIUM...	1495.0012	2652.9800	2279.6767	1419.9953	330.65979
7	CERIUM....	.08650	.19790	.25410	.15350	.11710
8	CESIUM....	.38190	.51800	.80120	.25210	.16580
9	CHROMIUM..	.00000	5.65640	4.70680	1.08640	1.38400
10	COBALT....	1.84800	7.98000	8.05000	4.91000	11.43000
11	COPPER....	.00000	.00000	.00000	.00000	11.08800
12	GALLIUM...	.07200	.00000	.00000	.00000	70.58005
13	GOLD......	.00000	.04774	.04419	.03054	.40810
14	IRON......	62.25606	181.10004	164.57498	220.35007	.00000
15	LANTHANUM.	46.07902	.64680	.24780	.00000	.00000
16	LEAD......	2.74522	.55093	.28491	.31514	5660.4589
17	MANGANESE.	496.52856	145.80002	.00000	.00000	.00000
18	MERCURY...	.00000	.07150	.06910	.04800	1.79990
19	NICKEL....	.00000	.00000	.00000	.00000	7.98000
20	POTASSIUM.	3267.7285	705.54821	579.59814	518.73095	185.99728
21	RUBIDIUM..	.85150	2.39440	1.98414	1.51256	3.70840
22	SELENIUM..	.00060	.01364	.01294	.00964	.11080
23	SILVER....	.00000	.02640	.00000	.00000	.00000
24	STRONTIUM.	1.09292	30.30443	23.91481	12.36200	4.83980
25	TIN.......	.20130	.65094	.40812	.78546	.24510
26	TITANIUM..	13.19318	34.12920	24.70100	21.53560	17.78030
27	VANADIUM..	.00000	2.86131	2.44416	1.69882	4.12741
28	YTTRIUM...	.15611	1.22590	1.01762	.69208	15.75466
29	ZINC......	.00000	.00000	.00000	.00000	13.07300
30	ZIRCONIUM.	.59280	7.73300	6.32200	3.69900	.76800
	RB/SR/Y/ZR	8/10/ 1/ 5	1/10/ 0/ 3	1/10/ 0/ 3	1/10/ 1/ 3	2/ 3/10/

Early Accomplishments

Compositional patterns of glass and metallic art objects made in various manufacturing centers and time periods have been established by analyzing the various parts of over 6000 identifiable objects in the Winterthur and other museum collections. By comparing x-ray spectra of questioned objects with those in the Winterthur files, it has been possible to confirm unequivocally the authenticity of many historically important art objects and to present convincing evidence that many objects had incorrect attributions or were outright fakes.

Early Analysis of Graphics

In 1973, a few attempts were made to analyze paper in the forms of documents, prints, and watercolors. In spite of the low signal levels obtained at that time, definite reproducible spectral patterns were found for papers from specific mills made over several decades. This provided encouragement to optimize the strength of the excitation radioactive sources and to acquire a more sophisticated computer to improve the baseline correction techniques and the signal to noise ratio.

It was at this time that Winterthur's paper conservator, Anne Clapp, while examining an etching print, Franklin's Apotheosis after Fragonard, found it to be of such pristine condition that she requested an analytical examination to confirm its authenticity. The ink, which had a brownish-green cast, was found to contain copper and arsenic in about the proportions of Paris green, $Cu(C_2H_3O_2)_2 \cdot 3Cu(AsO_2)_2$, a very poisonous pigment and insecticide. While this revelation did not establish immediately the authenticity of the print, it did suggest that the poisonous pigment might have indeed protected the print from insect attack for 150 years.

A request to identify the colorants in another lithograph disclosed the presence of zinc in all the colors. Since zinc is not an element

Table IV. Amies Colored Papers; Typical Printout, Five Paper Samples

A.L. #	910.1.1	910.2.1	910.3.1	910.7.1	891.7B
SEQ. #	#A1432	#A1433	#A1434	#A1438	#A1449
TEST DATE	221,1979	221,1979	221,1979	221,1979	227,1979
TEST TIME	12:33	12:53	13:11	14:33	10: 4
ACCESSION #	76.166.81A	76.166.82	76.166.81B	76.166.40	76.166.36A
OWNER	WNTHR	WNTHR	WNTHR	WNTHR	WNTHR
OBJECT	PINK FOLD	BLUE FOLDE	YELLOW FOL	WHITE FOLD	LEGAL,HOLI
DESC'N	SHEET	D SHEET	DED SHEET	ED SHEET	NGSHEAD
PART	X	X	X	X	X
MAKER	AMIES	AMIES	AMIES "A"	AMIES	AMIES
DATE	C1820	C1820	C1820	/?	1817
PROV'NCE	PHLA	PHLA	PHLA	PHLA	PHLA
ELEMENT	MUG/CM2	MUG/CM2	MUG/CM2	MUG/CM2	MUG/CM2
1 ANTIMONY..	.06600	1.98000	.00000	.85800	.85800
2 ARSENIC...	.00000	.00000	7.85335	23.82172	113.29443
3 BARIUM....	.00000	.00000	.00000	.00000	.00000
4 BISMUTH..	.00000	.00000	.00000	5.40170	10.41500
5 CADMIUM...	.00000	.00000	.00000	.00000	.00000
6 CALCIUM...	10.22200	6.97400	8.38600	12.68201	19.11900
7 CERIUM....	.00000	.00000	.00000	.00000	.21000
8 CESIUM....	.53000	.66500	.58500	.57000	1.33500
9 CHROMIUM..	.00000	.77800	58.75201	5.34000	.00000
10 COBALT....	.00000	.00000	.00000	53.54400	21.33000
11 COPPER....	7.13440	10.51681	.84000	9.16440	2.70480
12 GALLIUM...	5.76000	6.42000	24.95001	6.26000	8.28000
13 MERCURY 2.	6.32970	6.27480	.00000	9.43245	8.66400
14 IRON......	6.88000	22.33599	5.98400	5.31200	13.13700
15 LANTHANUM.	.05600	.04000	.05800	.03800	.02400
16 LEAD......	.17160	2.11750	318.53369	.00000	.00000
17 MANGANESE.	.37500	3.45000	.00000	3.45000	6.15000
18 MERCURY...	4.55760	3.43245	.00000	.00000	.00000
19 NICKEL....	.87210	.00000	3.37110	.00000	10.50090
20 POTASSIUM.	22.41360	24.75121	27.48480	63.50402	54.92399
21 RUBIDIUM..	1.85077	1.73105	.00000	3.13051	3.57377
22 SELENIUM..	.55200	.55500	1.50200	.78500	1.03200
23 SILVER....	.00000	.00000	.00000	.00000	.00000
24 STRONTIUM.	2.47800	2.34360	3.85560	2.79720	3.43140
25 TIN.......	.00000	.00000	.00000	.00000	.00000
26 TITANIUM..	1.28217	1.34379	1.57763	1.85255	1.62108
27 VANADIUM..	1.06363	.98307	1.42254	1.15580	1.30639
28 YTTRIUM...	6.82140	6.67760	16.09009	7.92190	10.27910
29 ZINC......	.00000	.00000	.00000	.10800	1.24800
30 ZIRCONIUM.	3.11700	2.94300	3.70200	3.17700	4.56000
RB/SR/Y/ZR	3/ 4/10/ 5	3/ 4/10/ 4	0/ 2/10/ 2	4/ 4/10/ 4	3/ 3/10/

commonly found in colored inks, a check of the background of the print revealed the presence of zinc uniformly distributed over the surface. This zinc must have been picked up by contact with a zinc lithograph plate. Subsequent examination of other prints disclosed some to have been made from zinc plates and some from copper plates. Lithographs free of zinc and copper are presumed to be made on stone and to predate those containing copper or zinc. A re-examination of the Franklin print revealed neither copper nor zinc, thereby confirming its authenticity.

A large group of watercolor paintings made by Pennsylvania Germans in the early nineteenth century was compared with cakes from paint boxes of the period by Janice Carlson and John Krill of Winterthur (3), revealing the brand of colors used by some of the artists and dispelling the myth that these primitive artists made their own colors.

These findings were reviewed by the conservation staffs at The Library of Congress, the National Archives, and The Folger Shakespeare Library. They subsequently supplied samples of problem papers and leather bindings to determine if a correlation could be established between concentrations of elements found and the physical state of the papers and bindings. They especially were interested in the transition elements that are known to induce deterioration reactions in paper. The Winterthur laboratory was urged to prepare and "prove" a set of analytical reference standards and to seek financial support to examine large groups of papers to determine if correlations could be established between impurity types and levels with the physical condition of problem papers.

Study Objectives

This chapter is a progress report on the findings of trace elements in selected groups of papers supplied by the above institutions to demonstrate the capabilities of Winterthur's analytical equipment and to provide a basis for speculating as to the origin of those elements. That is, to determine which elements were: chemically a part of the original fiber; added by the papermaker; suspended or dissolved in the processing water; picked up from the processing equipment; or added by the user of the paper; and also to determine on which side of two-sided printings (such as currency) do the various elements reside.

Analysis Procedure

Three radioactive sources were used successively to cover the fluorescence range of 0–40 keV, producing a continuous spectrum with minimum backscatter from the sources. Figure 1 shows the spectrum of the tentative paper standard that has twenty-six elements at the 20-μg/cm^2 level.

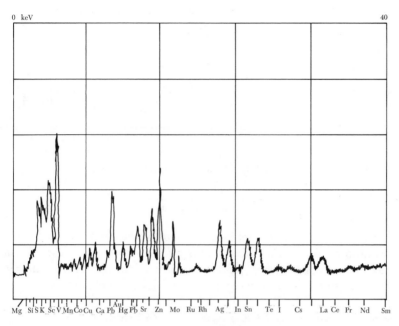

0 keV   40

Mg Si S K Sc V Mn Co Cu Ga Pb Hg Pb Sr Zn Mo Ru Rh Ag In Sn Te I Cs La Ce Pr Nd Sm

Figure 1. Spectrum of revised paper reference standard 967.68.5; 26 elements at 20 μg/cm² density level; vertical scale, 2,000 pulse counts full scale; excitation schedule according to Table V.

A reference standard was prepared for setting into the computer the normalizing factor, channel location, exponential factor, and baseline correction factor for each element listed on Table I. The standard was prepared by micropipetting 0.1% solutions of the various elements in Fisher's Certified Atomic Absorption Standards to a strip of du Pont's Nomex high-temperature, spun-bonded, nylon paper having a 5 cm² defined area. The strip, outlined by nitrocellulose laquer, was supported on a 35-mm film slide mount. A few drops of dilute Triton 100X wetting agent were added to the Nomex to provide a uniform distribution of the solutions. The Nomex slide mount assembly was rotated for 15 min at 100 rpm under a heat lamp to evaporate the water.

The instrument response was determined, after which additional elements were added successively and analyzed, and adjustments made to compensate for interferences caused by peak overlap and nonlinear count versus concentration relationships.

The element densities are reported as micrograms per square centimeter and basis weights of the papers are in grams per square decimeter. A microgram per square centimeter is equal to 0.7 oz/acre, or 44,000 ft².

Table V. Radiation Excitation Schedule

Strength	Source	Range (keV)	Time (s)	Elements Determined
300 mCi	Fe 55	0–6	100	K, Ca, Ti, V
30 mCi	Cd 109	6–18	300	Cr, Mn, Fe, Co, Ni, Cu, Zn, As, Rb, Sr, Y, Zr, Pb, Hg, Bi
200 mCi	Am 241	18–40	100	Ag, Cd, Sn, Ba, La, Cs, Ce

Weight percentage of element in paper $=$ wt $\%$ $=$

$$\frac{0.01 \times \text{element density}}{\text{basis weight}}$$

The actual correlation between elemental concentrations and state of deterioration will be the subject of future studies under the National Science Foundation award that was granted to Winterthur after the symposium presentation of the paper from which this chapter was written.

Elements Found in Early European and American Paper

A group of early European and American papers covering the period 1770 to 1900, supplied by the National Archives conservation laboratory (Table VI), and a group of papers made by Thomas Amies of Philadelphia, 1770–1840, and now in the Winterthur Library, were analyzed in this study. Thomas Gravell determined the dates of the papers from their watermarks according to his recently published book (4).

A group of modern U.S. Federal Reserve notes was analyzed to demonstrate the feasibility of determining which elements are in the black ink, which are in the green inks, and which are in the paper.

Table VI. National Archives Test Samples

Number	Description	Provenance	Date
1	W/M GR Crown—Made for England	Holland	1760
2	W/M GR Crown—Customs Journal	Holland	1778
3	W/M J. Honig—From Christiansted, St. Croix	Holland	1770
4	W/M "Propatia"	Holland	c.1770
5	U.S. District Court Book, Montgomery, Alabama	USA	1836
6	W/M "Economy Linen Ledger"	USA	1900
7	W/M FG Crown—Ledger	England	1770
8	Cambden's Britannia—Pages 65 & 75	England	1637
9	Bluish French—Pages 67 & 75—Ref. Lebwohl Letter of October 31, 1977	France	1815

The principal elements found in the Amies' and the National Archives' papers are plotted in Figure 2 with vertical scales selected to accommodate the maximum concentrations found for each element. Also, the Amies' data are tabulated in Table VII. The measured pH values of the National Archives' papers are on the top right of Figure 2.

The plot (on the right of Figure 2) of relative abundance of the elements in the earth's crust (5) serves as a guide to the probability of of some elements to have originated in the sediment, in solutions in the processing water, or in fillers and sizings deliberately added. High concentrations of low abundance elements are presumed to have been added deliberately by the papermaker or -processor.

The rare earths and lanthanide series of elements, which are normally determined, were omitted from this plot in the interest of simplification.

Starting at the bottom and working up (Figure 2):

1. *Calcium* in the form of the carbonate averaged about 9 μg/cm^2 for all but the white 1770 Holland paper (watermarked GR Crown), which contained 25 μg/cm^2. The source of the calcium may be from the lime used to disintegrate the rags, the lime used in the preparation of the gelatin size, a natural element in the cellulose, a whitening agent, or a sediment in the processing water (6). It is interesting to note that the pH pattern followed the calcium pattern very closely in the National Archives' samples.

2. *Potassium* at the 25-μg/cm^2 level is added mostly with the potassium alum sizing. Note that two American-made papers of 1900 have a low potassium content, indicating that aluminum sulphate sizing probably was used. The high potassium values associated with the bismuth peaks are unaccounted for.

3. *Barium* appeared only in Holland 1770 paper watermarked J. Honig. This paper has a splotchy appearance for reasons not yet determined. The absence of zinc and the early date preclude lithopone white pigments, so it probably is there as barium sulphate. Photographic papers and the United States currency use large quantities of barium sulphate.

4. *Bismuth* was used by Amies in white papers in 1820 and papers watermarked "Law" or "Legal." The low natural abundance of bismuth indicates that bismuth was added deliberately by the papermaker as bismuth white, a poisonous pigment.

5. *Arsenic* appeared with cobalt as an impurity in smalt (cobalt aluminate), the blue glass pigment or bluing used for disguising the yellowish paper color attributable to iron and other impurities. Chambers' 1783 Encyclopedia describes the smalt-making process in detail, pointing out the great trade secret of some early smalt producers,

namely, re-adding the arsenic sublimed from the smaltite ($CoAs_2$) during the roasting process, which produced a dramatic improvement in the pigment qualities (7). Arsenic found in the absence of cobalt was possibly there as a pesticide.

6. *Iron* dissolved in water is precipitated at pH 7 and deposited about 8 $\mu g/cm^2$ in the paper, producing an objectionable yellowish color. The three blue 1820 Amies papers had 25 $\mu g/cm^2$ of iron, probably Prussian blue, $Fe_4(Fe[CN]_6)_3$ (8).

7. *Cobalt.* See *Arsenic* above.

8. *Copper* appeared generally distributed at about 2 $\mu g/cm^2$, probably from the processing water or equipment. Copper was the blue colorant in the French papers, perhaps Blue Verditer, $2CuCO_3 \cdot Cu(OH)_2$ (8). Copper was present at the 10-$\mu g/cm^2$ level in Amies' pink, blue, cream, and white papers, but was absent in his yellow paper.

9. *Zinc* at 1$\mu g/cm^2$ levels appeared in all papers but the GR Crown watermarked 1770 Holland papers, which were at 12 $\mu g/cm^2$, possibly as white zinc oxide.

10. *Manganese* appeared randomly at the 0–5-$\mu g/cm^2$ level in a pattern similar to, but lower than, that of iron, indicating that it probably was present in the processing water.

11. *Nickel* appeared generally at the 1-$\mu g/cm^2$ level in the Holland-made papers and at the 3-$\mu g/cm^2$ level in the pink Amies' papers. It is likely that mercury, whose concentrations are questionable and not plotted here, actually is responsible for the pink color.

12. *Chromium* appeared randomly at 0–4 $\mu g/cm^2$. The Amies yellow paper had 54 $\mu g/cm^2$ together with a 325-$\mu g/cm^2$ lead level, which is within 40% of the stoichiometric ratio of lead chromate, the same pigment used in U.S. currency.

13. *Lead* was found frequently at the 0–10 $\mu g/cm^2$ level in many old papers, possibly picked up from processing equipment. The wt % of the 325 $\mu g/cm^2$ of lead as the chromate, $PbCrO_4$ (8), found in the Amies yellow paper, basis weight 0.92 g/dm^2, is $325/0.92 \times .01 = 3.5\%$.

14. *Antimony* appeared randomly at the 0–2-$\mu g/cm^2$ level.

15. Other elements found but not plotted were: titanium, cerium, cesium, gallium, mercury, rubidium, strontium, vanadium, yttrium, and zirconium.

16. Elements sought but not detected were: cadmium, lanthanum, selenium, and silver.

Analysis of Elements in United States Currency

Objectives. The analysis by x-ray fluorescence of the inks and the paper of United States currency offered an opportunity to evaluate the new computer program for analyzing paper objects and printed docu-

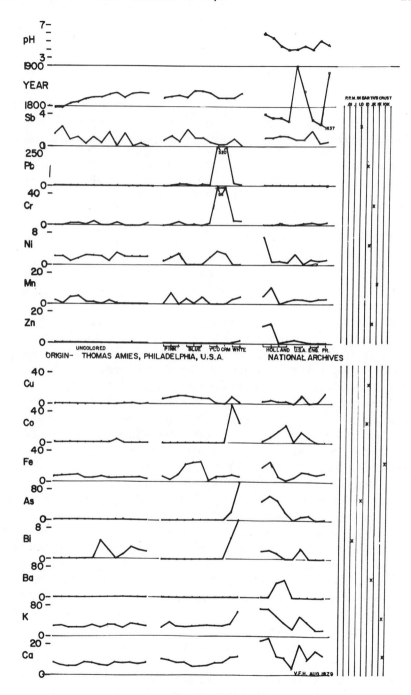

Figure 2. Trace elements in paper (μg/cm²)

Table VII.   Amies

		Element Concentration ($\mu g/cm^2$)				
Color	Year	As	Bi	Ca	Cr	Co
Colored Samples						
Pink	1823–1834	0	0	8.9	2.2	0
Blue	c.1820	1	0	6.5	0	0
Yellow	c.1820	0	0	8.4	56	0
Cream	c.1820	0	0	7.3	2	0.6
White	c.1820	24	5.4	1	5.3	54
White "Law"	1832	130	10	13.7	4.9	27
Uncolored Samples (10 Samples)						
Plain	1790–1840					
$\overline{x}$		0.89	0.8	7.7	0.95	0
s.d.		±0.9	±1	±1	±1.6	

ments, since close control was maintained on the materials used. Furthermore, extremes in concentrations of various elements used in the paper base and in the inks, and the minor elements present adventitiously, provided a rigorous test for the new baseline compensation techniques being evaluated for the paper analysis program.

Since the excitation x-rays are energetic enough to penetrate most papers, it was important to develop techniques to distinguish which side of a document having printing on both sides is being measured. Part of this program was aimed at demonstrating several alternate methods for determining the side containing the various elements observed.

An opportunity also existed with these materials to provide techniques for determining small amounts of certain elements that appear within the spectral envelopes of other elements present in high concentrations. For example, lead has been found to be present in such high concentrations in currency that it introduces uncertainties as to the presence of observed elements such as arsenic, mercury, bismuth, and rubidium, which appear at or near the ubiquitous lead peaks. There are also extremely strong iron peaks appearing at or near important trace elements such as manganese, nickel, cobalt, and copper, which require further study to avoid serious error.

A frustrating feature of x-ray fluorescence measurement is the radiationless energy transfer from higher Z (atomic number) elements to lower Z contiguous elements or multiple scattering, making the former appear to be at a lower concentration and the latter to be at a higher concentration than they actually are. Compensation for these factors will receive careful study to avoid serious analysis error.

Papers 1790–1844

Element Concentration ($\mu g/cm^2$)						Thick-ness (μm)	Basis Wt (g/dm^2)
Cu	Fe	Pb	Mn	K	Ni		
8.2	6	2	2.2	30	2.1	127	0.87
7.5	26	3.5	4	25	0.2	125	0.77
0	6.5	320	0	27	3.1	102	0.92
6.4	2.5	0	0	28	1.8	100	0.70
9	8.3	2	4.3	31	0	75	0.73
1.8	58	0	3.5	64	0	128	0.95
0.6 ±0.7	6.9 ±0.8	0	1.3 ±1.9	26.8 ±4	0		

Measurement Procedures. An area of high ink density, as judged by eye, was marked on each side of the note, placed over the sample port, and measured according to the Table V schedule. The black portrait side of the bill was designated as "front" and the green side as "back" in the tabulations. These measurements, which represent an integrated average of a 15-mm-diameter area, are plotted in Figure 3.

The measured areas then were rubbed vigorously with a narrow strip of cotton gauze to determine which elements might be rubbed off during normal usage of the note (Figure 4). The rubbed areas then were remeasured and tabulated as "rubbed." Material collected on the gauze was measured and tabulated as "rubbing," and is reported in Figure 5.

A used $1 note placed in a pants pocket was laundered in a clothes washer with Duz laundry detergent to determine how much of the various elements were removed (Figure 5). This laundered note was analyzed, rubbed with gauze, reanalyzed, and the deposits on the gauze analyzed and reported in Figure 5.

Other elements, including copper and arsenic, were observed near the green Treasury Department and the black Federal Reserve Bank Seals on the front of the notes. These areas were measured carefully, rubbed, remeasured, and recorded.

Results. The data tabulated by the computer (Tables VIII–XII) are plotted in Figures 3, 4, and 5. Most of the measured data are reproducible to within about 10% of the measured values on duplicate measures if the sample is repositioned within 1 mm.

Some minor elements displayed may be fictitious because of improper baseline compensation. Information on the questionable elements as well

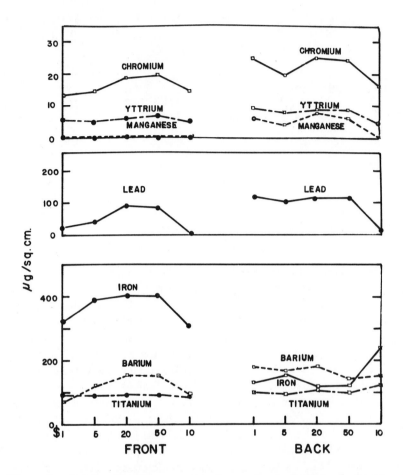

Figure 3.   Origin of x-rays emanating from paper printed on both sides.

X-rays emanating from elements in inks printed on currency will be more intense on the side they are printed on than those transmitted through the paper. Furthermore, x-rays from low atomic numbered elements will be absorbed more strongly than those from heavier elements. These features provide clues as to the location of elements on paper printed on both sides, viz: chromium, barium, lead, manganese, and yttrium are mostly in the green ink; titanium is in the paper and in the green ink; most of the iron is in the black ink; and the absence of lead observed in three 1969 issues of $10 notes was confirmed by the Director of the Bureau of Engraving and Printing who stated that attempts made to eliminate toxic lead from currency failed because of technical difficulties in printing at high speeds.

as the major elements was requested from the Secretary of the Treasury (9). A confirmation of most of the findings of this study was received from the Director of the Bureau of Printing and Engraving (*10*).

Elements Sought in Study and Their Role in Currency.

1. *Antimony* appeared in all notes at a low level and was rubbed off both front and back, indicating its presence in the inks. If it was not added deliberately, it might have been present as an impurity in lead. Antimony frequently is alloyed with lead to increase its strength and to improve the electrical properties of lead plates in storage batteries and often is present in reclaimed lead.

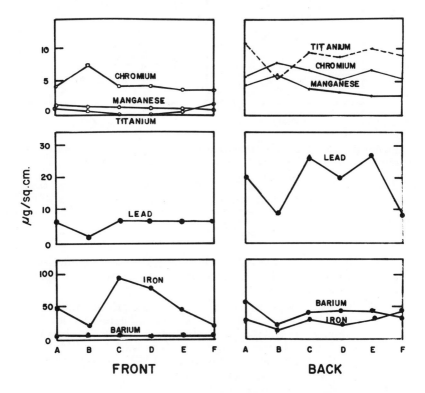

Figure 4.   Elements removed from Federal Reserve Notes by rubbing with cotton gauze.

The fugitive nature of the inks on Federal Feserve Notes is illustrated by rubbing them with cotton gauze and analyzing the inks picked up on the gauze: The low values picked up from the "Old $1 Note" indicate that over half the ink has been rubbed off previously by handling the note. The high exposure to lead, chromium, and bismuth of the citizenry handling currency was called to the attention of the Department of the Treasury. The removal of titanium from the back indicates that it is a component of the green ink as well as an ingredient of the paper (Refer to Figure 3).

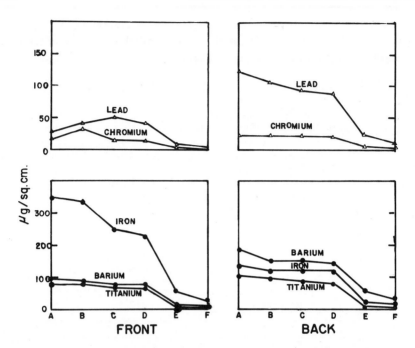

*Figure 5.   Elements on or removed from new $1 note: (A) elements ob-
served on new 1977 note; (B) elements remaining after rubbing "A" with
cotton gauze; (C) elements remaining after laundering "B" with Duz
detergent; (D) elements remaining after rubbing "C" with new gauze;
(E) elements deposited on gauze after rubbing "A"; (F) elements deposited
on gauze after rubbing "D".*

2. *Arsenic* appeared only on the Federal Reserve Bank Seal.
   Seals on $5, $10, and $50 denominations were not anal-
   yzed.

3. *Barium* was present in high concentrations on the green
   side of all denominations and might be present as the
   sulphate or as lithopone, which is a mixture of barium
   sulphate and zinc sulphide. Barium was rubbed readily
   off the green but not the black side, indicating that it
   was definitely a part of the green ink.

4. *Bismuth*—none was found.

5. *Cadmium* appeared in small amounts in all determinations
   and may be a baseline defect.

6. *Calcium* was found in substantial amounts on the fronts
   of $1 and $5 notes and especially on the green Treasury
   Department Seal on the $10 notes (Table XV).

7. *Cerium* and 8. *Cesium.* These two rare earth elements
   were found in low concentrations in barium and clays and
   probably are present as trace impurities.

9. *Chromium* appeared in highest concentration on the green side as barium or lead chromate (yellow).

10. *Cobalt*—none was found.

11. *Copper* appeared in the $10 notes signed by George Shultz, John Connally, and David Kennedy in 1969, apparently as a substitute for the use of lead chromate in these notes. The copper may be present as the basic carbonate (malachite), which is green and insoluble. The color was still clear on notes made about nine years ago, raising the question of why the Treasury returned to the use of lead in 1977 $10 notes. The reply from the Director of Printing and Engraving was (*10*): "The 1969 series of $10 Federal Reserve notes that you analyzed and found to have a low concentration of lead was a part of a reformulation attempt."

12. *Gallium*, which is a rare metal of the aluminum group, may well be a baseline defect.

13. *Gold*—none was found.

14. *Iron* was present in large amounts on both sides of all notes. It was rubbed off readily and large quantities could be removed by laundering. It may be present as Prussian blue in the green ink and sulphate in the black ink.

15. *Lanthanum*, present in trace amounts, is probably an impurity in its contiguous element, barium.

16. *Lead.* The presence of large quantities of lead, which was readily rubbed off or laundered off, was a big surprise in view of the strict Federal regulations prohibiting its use in paints and decorated objects that might be sucked or chewed by children. The lead content of $10 notes issued by John Connally, William Simon, and David Kennedy indicated that they must have recognized the lead hazard, since their issues contained only one-fifth to one-tenth the lead content of the other denominations analyzed in this study. The response from the Bureau of Engraving was (*10*): "The formulation of lead-free green ink continues to hold a high priority in our ink development program."

17. *Manganese* was found in all green inks on the back of notes except for the $10 issue. It was found on the Treasury Department Seal and the Federal Reserve Bank Seal of the $10 issue.

18. *Bromine* was found in the green Treasury Department Seal of the $10 issue only.

19. *Nickel*—none was found.

20. *Potassium* was found on both sides of all notes. Its concentration was not reduced significantly by laundering, indicating that it was in the form of a water-insoluble compound such as orthoclase-based clay filler in the paper.

Table VIII.   Elements Seen from Front (Black Side) of New Notes:
No. A 1085, $1; No. A 1094, $5; No. A 1090, $10,
No. A 1092, $20; No. A 1102, $50

		750.15.1F	750.18.2F	750.18.3F	750.18.4F	750.18.5F
	A.L. #					
	SEQ. #	#A1085	#A1094	#A1090	#A1092	#A1102
	TEST DATE	258,1978	259,1978	259,1978	259,1978	259,1978
	TEST TIME	13: 1	12:28	11:16	11:51	14:21
	ACCESSION #	A17193029A	C17968609A	C61040893A	C01109918A	B48857929A
	OWNER	VFH	VFH	VFH	VFH	VFH
	OBJECT	$1 FEDRES	$5 FEDRES	$10 FEDRES	$20FED RES	$50FEDRES
	DESC'N	NOTE	NOTE	NOTE	NOTE	NOTE
	PART	FRONT	FRONT	FRONT	FRONT	FRONT
	MAKER	BLUMENTHAL	BLUMENTHAL	J.CONNALLY	BLUMENTHAL	WM.SIMON
	DATE	1977	1977	1969	1977	1974
	PROV'NCE	PHLA	PHLA	PHLA	PHLA	NEW YORK
	ELEMENT	*MUG/CM2	*MUG/CM2	*MUG/CM2	*MUG/CM2	*MUG/CM2
1	ANTIMONY..	3.50900	3.43200	4.90600	4.95000	3.74000
2	ARSENIC...	.00000	.00000	.00000	.00000	.00000
3	BARIUM....	75.06728	117.81650	94.12521	151.86093	156.68634
4	BISMUTH..	.00000	.00000	.00000	.00000	.00000
5	CADMIUM...	3.67640	3.15280	4.79920	3.16680	3.61760
6	CALCIUM...	4.67390	22.48324	4.95880	7.07630	7.01855
7	CERIUM....	1.03400	1.58300	3.17900	1.39600	1.75300
8	CESIUM....	2.05000	2.83500	3.52500	3.65000	4.04500
9	CHROMIUM..	13.61201	15.29200	14.41601	18.91600	18.68800
10	COBALT....	.00000	.00000	.00000	.00000	.00000
11	COPPER....	.86800	1.09200	3.38800	.00000	.00000
12	GALLIUM...	5.12000	1.93200	1.80800	2.83200	2.70800
13	GOLD......	.00000	.17000	.00000	.09000	.00000
14	IRON......	343.82617	390.08099	306.44360	428.17370	407.43207
15	LANTHANUM.	.58580	.38580	.84760	.29200	.26210
16	LEAD......	26.56200	41.36303	8.41700	92.52997	88.67299
17	MANGANESE.	.00000	.00000	.00000	.00000	.00000
18	BROMINE	.86448	2.30928	3.75504	.61056	.64368
19	NICKEL....	.00000	.00000	.00000	.00000	.00000
20	POTASSIUM.	13.63200	18.90720	14.97361	15.07201	14.92080
21	RUBIDIUM..	.00000	1.55595	2.05296	1.25340	1.18189
22	SELENIUM..	.37400	.38000	.38300	.46900	.50000
23	SILVER....	3.37050	.28000	.00000	.43750	.93625
24	STRONTIUM.	3.55100	4.52620	5.09860	6.43420	6.04200
25	TIN.......	5.81760	6.72120	7.45920	6.10200	6.22800
26	TITANIUM..	89.92905	91.84575	95.51175	97.43428	95.53664
27	VANADIUM..	.00000	.00000	.00000	.00000	.00000
28	YTTRIUM...	4.95520	5.12870	4.52660	6.43490	6.85970
29	ZINC......	5.02255	5.38135	6.33685	6.45645	5.76420
30	ZIRCONIUM.	2.63580	2.67720	3.29820	2.64960	2.69100
	RB/SR/Y/ZR	0/ 7/10/ 5	3/ 9/10/ 5	4/10/ 9/ 6	2/10/10/ 4	2/ 9/10/

*MICROGRAMS/CM^2

Table IX. Elements Seen from Back (Green Side) of New Notes:
No. A 1084, $1; No. A 1095, $5; No. A 1091, $10;
No. A 1093, $20; No. A 1103, $50

A.L. #	750.15.1B	750.18.2B	750.18.3B	750.18.4B	750.18.5B
SEQ. #	#A1084	#A1095	#A1091	#A1093	#A1103
TEST DATE	258,1978	259,1978	259,1978	259,1978	259,1978
TEST TIME	12:48	12:41	11:34	12:10	14:33
ACCESSION #	C17193029A	C17968609A	C61040893A	C01109918A	B48857929A
OWNER	VFH	VFH	VFH	VFH	VFH
OBJECT	$1 FEDRES	%	$10 FEDRES	$20FED RES	$50FED RES
DESC'N	NOTE	$5 FED RES	NOTE	NOTE	NOTE
PART	BACK		BACKGREEN	BACK	BACK
MAKER	BLUMENTHAL	BLUMENTHAL	J.CONNALLY	BLUMENTHAL	WM.SIMON
DATE	1977	1977	1969	1977	1974
PROV'NCE	PHLA	PHLA	PHLA	PHLA	NEW YORK
ELEMENT	*MUG/CM2	*MUG/CM2	*MUG/CM2	*MUG/CM2	*MUG/CM2
1 ANTIMONY..	3.53100	3.49800	3.91600	4.23500	4.36700
2 ARSENIC...	.00000	.00000	.00000	.00000	.00000
3 BARIUM....	184.29330	169.06253	157.41443	185.79101	141.56491
4 BISMUTH...	.00000	.00000	.00000	.00000	.00000
5 CADMIUM...	3.19480	3.32360	3.28440	3.29280	3.18640
6 CALCIUM...	5.25756	13.54970	5.59251	6.24932	6.01909
7 CERIUM....	1.09400	1.17300	1.42300	1.25100	1.30100
8 CESIUM....	4.74000	3.90500	4.10500	4.60500	3.70500
9 CHROMIUM..	24.27200	19.10799	16.61200	24.49600	23.30800
10 COBALT....	.00000	.00000	.00000	.00000	.00000
11 COPPER....	.00000	.00000	1.35200	.00000	.00000
12 GALLIUM...	8.72000	3.06400	1.57200	3.17600	3.44000
13 GOLD......	.00000	.01000	.00000	.01000	.09000
14 IRON......	134.92551	159.62622	241.97351	123.75688	122.09126
15 LANTHANUM.	.15290	.25590	.31050	.24960	.39830
16 LEAD......	121.03012	106.78000	14.11701	118.52203	117.99000
17 MANGANESE.	6.44796	4.18896	.00000	8.08182	6.05826
18 BROMINE	.00000	.65568	3.22560	.00000	.00000
19 NICKEL....	.00000	.00000	.00000	.00000	.00000
20 POTASSIUM.	15.29280	16.99920	16.20481	16.31520	16.01280
21 RUBIDIUM..	.00000	1.11699	1.79006	1.31098	1.01150
22 SELENIUM..	.55500	.54700	.37200	.53200	.50400
23 SILVER....	2.73350	.00000	.00000	.23625	.00000
24 STRONTIUM.	7.52601	7.58960	5.49080	7.83340	7.55780
25 TIN.......	5.85000	6.16680	6.08040	6.28200	6.28560
26 TITANIUM..	101.11046	98.77055	122.43072	109.27359	104.55298
27 VANADIUM..	.00000	.00000	.00000	.00000	.00000
28 YTTRIUM...	8.97750	7.78970	4.16650	8.27700	8.56740
29 ZINC......	5.03035	6.06255	4.49670	5.70245	5.36055
30 ZIRCONIUM.	3.27980	2.99920	2.72320	3.09580	2.96240
RB/SR/Y/ZR	0/ 8/10/ 4	1/10/10/ 4	3/10/ 8/ 5	2/ 9/10/ 4	1/ 9/10/

*MICROGRAMS/CM^2

Table X.   Pick-up on Gauze by Rubbing Front of Notes: No. A 1088, $1; No. A 1106, $5; No. A 1108, $10; No. A 1110, $20; No. A 1112, $50

A.L. #	750.17.1F	750.20.2F	760.20.3F	750.20.4F	750.20.5F
SEQ. #	#A1088	#A1106	#A1108	#A1110	#A1112
TEST DATE	253,1978	259,1978	259,1978	259,1978	259,1978
TEST TIME	13:48	15:26	15:52	16:16	16:40
ACCESSION #	NONE	//	/	/	/
OWNER	VFH	//	/	/	/
OBJECT	RUBBING	GAUZE RUB-	GAUZE RUBB	GAUZE RUB-	GAUZE RUB-
DESC'N	GAUZE	BING	-ING $10	BING $20	BING $50
PART	FRONT	FRONT$5	FRONT	FRONT	FRONT
MAKER	//	//	/	/	/
DATE	1978	1978	/	/	/
PROV'NCE	//	//	/	/	/
ELEMENT	*MUG/CM2	*MUG/CM2	*MUG/CM2	*MUG/CM2	*MUG/CM2
1 ANTIMONY..	1.60600	1.49600	1.98000	1.81500	2.01300
2 ARSENIC...	.00000	.00000	.00000	.00000	.00000
3 BARIUM....	4.65400	3.59840	3.38520	3.57240	3.52040
4 BISMUTH..	.00000	.00000	.00000	.00000	.00000
5 CADMIUM...	1.19840	1.49800	1.37480	1.17890	1.60440
6 CALCIUM...	1.06876	5.22599	1.16039	1.37060	1.45761
7 CERIUM....	.50000	.51300	.64900	.34800	.47300
8 CESIUM....	.56000	.46500	.40500	.60000	.45500
9 CHROMIUM..	4.41200	4.61600	3.84800	4.44400	3.72000
10 COBALT....	.00000	.00000	1.16467	.00000	.00000
11 COPPER....	1.26400	.92000	1.13600	.74400	.60400
12 GALLIUM...	1.96000	.78000	.85600	.80400	.78400
13 GOLD......	.00000	.00000	.00000	.00000	.00000
14 IRON......	51.35477	101.77354	22.95799	82.47893	46.38110
15 LANTHANUM.	.29030	.34230	.30120	.23650	.36460
16 LEAD......	6.87800	7.06800	6.51700	6.46000	6.59300
17 MANGANESE.	.78480	.00000	2.42442	.00000	.44208
18 BROMINE	.95112	1.50864	1.17984	1.22400	1.34928
19 NICKEL....	.00000	.00000	.02746	.00000	.00000
20 POTASSIUM.	10.60080	12.52081	11.73360	10.96561	11.10960
21 RUBIDIUM..	.00000	.78092	.74434	.69620	.65915
22 SELENIUM..	.18100	.16900	.17800	.16000	.16000
23 SILVER....	2.09300	1.15500	1.29500	1.43500	1.06750
24 STRONTIUM.	1.77020	1.63240	1.60060	1.26140	1.50520
25 TIN.......	2.60280	2.61720	3.06000	2.37240	2.63160
26 TITANIUM..	1.01760	10.79360	.95360	1.22830	1.14624
27 VANADIUM..	.67625	.00000	.57175	.58430	.59057
28 YTTRIUM...	1.83130	1.44310	1.83110	1.63000	1.77370
29 ZINC......	2.40500	2.24770	2.32180	2.14630	1.82845
30 ZIRCONIUM.	1.01660	1.02580	1.01200	.89700	.95220
RB/SR/Y/ZR	0/10/10/ 6	5/10/ 9/ 6	4/ 9/10/ 6	4/ 8/10/ 6	4/ 8/10/

*MICROGRAMS/CM^2

Table XI. Pick-up on Gauze After Rubbing Back of Notes: No. A 1089, $1; No. A 1107, $5; No. A 1109, $10; No. A 1111, $20; No. A 1113, $50

A.L. #	750.17.1B	750.20.2B	750.20.3B	750.20.4B	750.20.5B
SEQ. #	#A1089	#A1107	#A1109	#A1111	#A1113
TEST DATE	258,1978	259,1978	259,1978	259,1978	259,1978
TEST TIME	14: 5	15:40	16: 4	16:28	16:52
ACCESSION #	C17193029A	//	/	/	//
OWNER	VFH	//	/	/	/
OBJECT	$1 GAUZE	GAUZE RUB-	GAUZE RUB-	GAUZE RUB-	GAUZE RUB-
DESC'N	RUBBING	BING $5	BING $10	BING $20	BING $50
PART	BACKGREEN	BACK	BACK	BACK	BACK
MAKER	//	/	/	/	/
DATE	1978	1978	//	/	/
PROV'NCE	//	/	//	/	/

	ELEMENT	*MUG/CM2	*MUG/CM2	*MUG/CM2	*MUG/CM2	*MUG/CM2
1	ANTIMONY..	1.87000	2.35400	1.73800	2.05700	1.92500
2	ARSENIC...	.00000	.00000	.00000	.00000	.00000
3	BARIUM....	57.81881	36.82642	34.57479	43.74760	43.44084
4	BISMUTH..	.00000	.00000	.00000	.00000	.00000
5	CADMIUM...	1.26560	1.30480	1.26840	1.55680	1.39720
6	CALCIUM...	1.65396	1.66320	1.40294	1.45838	1.79025
7	CERIUM....	.67600	.55800	.61100	.47200	.65600
8	CESIUM....	1.38000	.98000	.96500	1.36000	1.08000
9	CHROMIUM..	5.72400	6.60000	5.38400	5.14800	6.88000
10	COBALT....	1.26786	.00000	.36873	.83640	.00000
11	COPPER....	.00000	.00000	.58800	.36400	.00000
12	GALLIUM...	2.47000	1.12800	.90800	.88400	1.14400
13	GOLD......	.00000	.00000	.00000	.00000	.32000
14	IRON......	19.24915	28.05816	35.04032	19.12561	28.42155
15	LANTHANUM.	.13730	.23640	.23940	.13570	.16880
16	LEAD......	20.91899	26.50499	8.24600	20.46301	27.58801
17	MANGANESE.	4.60836	4.03110	2.79198	3.21840	2.90268
18	**BROMINE**	.00000	.77808	1.46784	.94944	1.25328
19	NICKEL....	.22925	.00000	.00000	.19392	.00000
20	POTASSIUM.	11.26800	12.06240	12.23040	12.39840	11.87280
21	RUBIDIUM..	.00000	.74293	.66764	.67000	.68275
22	SELENIUM..	.18400	.20700	.21200	.18400	.20500
23	SILVER....	1.65200	.97125	.91000	1.37375	1.02375
24	STRONTIUM.	2.51220	3.06340	2.69240	2.06700	2.71360
25	TIN.......	3.29400	2.84040	2.66400	2.99880	3.39120
26	TITANIUM..	12.36736	9.03552	7.79264	8.65408	10.03968
27	VANADIUM..	3.11780	2.21585	1.80420	2.19915	2.46577
28	YTTRIUM...	2.41350	2.52320	1.73360	2.12510	2.74870
29	ZINC......	1.74655	2.36730	2.25485	2.12225	2.14565
30	ZIRCONIUM.	.87860	1.15920	.93380	.97520	1.02580
	RB/SR/Y/ZR	0/10/10/ 3	2/10/ 8/ 4	2/10/ 6/ 3	3/10/10/ 5	2/10/10/

*MICROGRAMS/CM^2

Table XII. Measurements on Front of $1 Notes: No. A 1085, New Note; No. A 1086, Same After Rubbing With Gauze; No. A 1088, Pick-up on Gauze Rubbing; No. A 1114, Used Note Laundered with Duz; No. A 1118, Pick-up on Gauze Rubbing of Laundered Note

	750.15.1F	750.16.1F	750.17.1F	750.21F	750.23.1F
A.L. #	#A1085	#A1086	#A1088	#A1114	#A1118
SEQ. #	258,1978	258,1978	258,1978	261,1978	261,1978
TEST DATE	13: 1	13:20	13:48	8: 9	9:27
TEST TIME	A17193029A	A17193029A	NONE	C85509530B	/
ACCESSION #	VFH	VFH	VFH	VFH	/
OWNER	$1 FEDRES	$1 FEDNOTE	RUBBING	$1 FEDSNOTE	RUBBING $1
OBJECT	NOTE	RUBBED	GAUZE	LAUNDERED	RUB&SCRUB
DESC'N	FRONT	FRONT	FRONT	FRONT	FRONT $1
PART	BLUMENTHAL	BLUMENTHAL	//	GEO.SHULTZ	/
MAKER	1977	1977	1978	1969	/
DATE	PHLA	PHLA	//	PHLA	/
PROV'NCE					
ELEMENT	*MUG/CM2	*MUG/CM2	*MUG/CM2	*MUG/CM2	*MUG/CM2

	ELEMENT					
1	ANTIMONY..	3.50900	2.10100	1.60600	4.69700	3.56400
2	ARSENIC...	.00000	.00000	.00000	.00000	.00000
3	BARIUM....	75.06728	74.96324	4.65400	69.73204	7.64920
4	BISMUTH..	.00000	.00000	.00000	.00000	.00000
5	CADMIUM...	3.67640	1.36920	1.19840	3.64000	3.36560
6	CALCIUM...	4.67390	4.53684	1.06876	9.94455	1.36675
7	CERIUM....	1.03400	.78900	.50000	1.26000	1.66400
8	CESIUM....	2.05000	2.02500	.56000	2.43000	.84000
9	CHROMIUM..	13.61201	40.70800	4.41200	14.89600	7.82400
10	COBALT....	.00000	.00000	.00000	.00000	4.87220
11	COPPER....	.86800	.00000	1.26400	3.36800	2.85200
12	GALLIUM...	5.12000	3.54000	1.96000	2.42800	1.65200
13	GOLD......	.00000	.00000	.00000	.47000	.50000
14	IRON......	343.82617	334.52789	51.35477	249.40640	18.51077
15	LANTHANUM.	.58580	.08950	.29030	.74180	.76730
16	LEAD......	26.56200	37.84801	6.87800	52.47834	1.90000
17	MANGANESE.	.00000	.00000	.78480	.00000	7.36920
18	BROMINE	.86448	.00000	.95112	3.34416	4.68816
19	NICKEL....	.00000	.00000	.00000	.00000	2.42496
20	POTASSIUM.	13.63200	13.86721	10.60080	16.76161	11.30160
21	RUBIDIUM..	.00000	.00000	.00000	2.21746	1.92246
22	SELENIUM..	.37400	.22600	.18100	.49200	.37900
23	SILVER....	3.37050	1.93900	2.09300	.43750	.00000
24	STRONTIUM.	3.55100	2.65000	1.77020	5.84060	4.05980
25	TIN.......	5.81760	3.29040	2.60280	7.38000	6.01920
26	TITANIUM..	89.92905	85.18397	1.01760	75.10207	.97664
27	VANADIUM..	.00000	.00000	.67625	.00000	.56445
28	YTTRIUM...	4.95520	3.70380	1.83130	6.61140	4.71890
29	ZINC......	5.02255	2.74495	2.40500	7.73891	4.95755
30	ZIRCONIUM.	2.63580	1.33860	1.01660	3.68920	3.03140
	RB/SR/Y/ZR	0/ 7/10/ 5	0/ 7/10/ 4	0/10/10/ 6	3/ 9/10/ 6	4/ 9/10/

*MICROGRAMS/CM^2

Table XIII.   Measurements on the Back of $1 Notes: No. A 1084, New Note; No. A 1087, Same After Rubbing with Gauze; No. A 1089, Pick-up on Gauze; No. A 1115, After Laundering Used $1 Note with Duz; No. A 1117, After Gauze Rubbing of Laundered Note

A.L. #	750.15.1B	750.16.1B	750.17.1B	750.21.1B	750.22.1B
SEQ. #	#A1084	#A1087	#A1089	#A1115	#A1117
TEST DATE	258,1978	258,1978	258,1978	261,1978	261,1978
TEST TIME	12:48	13:34	14: 5	8:23	9: 2
ACCESSION #	C17193029A	A17193029A	C17193029A	C85509530B	C85509530B
OWNER	VFH	VFH	VFH	VFH	VFH
OBJECT	$1 FEDRES	$1 FEDNOTE	$1 GAUZE	$1 FEDNOTE	$1 FEDNOTE
DESC'N	NOTE	RUBBED	RUBBING	LAUNDERED	RUB&SCRUBB
PART	BACK	BACK	BACKGREEN	BACK	BACK
MAKER	BLUMENTHAL	BLUMENTHAL	//	GEO.SHULTZ	GEO.SHULTZ
DATE	1977	1977	1978	1969	1969
PROV'NCE	PHLA	PHLA	//	PHLA	PHLA

	ELEMENT	*MUG/CM2	*MUG/CM2	*MUG/CM2	*MUG/CM2	*MUG/CM2
1	ANTIMONY..	3.53100	4.02600	1.87000	4.13600	4.91700
2	ARSENIC...	.00000	.00000	.00000	.00000	.00000
3	BARIUM....	184.29330	147.34210	57.81881	150.33206	135.16357
4	BISMUTH..	.00000	.00000	.00000	.00000	.00000
5	CADMIUM...	3.19480	3.74920	1.26560	3.73520	4.15240
6	CALCIUM...	5.25756	5.11973	1.65396	8.77646	7.78855
7	CERIUM....	1.09400	1.32500	.67600	1.85500	1.51200
8	CESIUM....	4.74000	3.24500	1.38000	4.33500	4.00000
9	CHROMIUM..	24.27200	21.54002	5.72400	21.19600	20.30801
10	COBALT....	.00000	.00000	1.26786	.00000	.00000
11	COPPER....	.00000	.00000	.00000	.00000	.00000
12	GALLIUM...	8.72000	7.25000	2.47000	2.93600	2.83200
13	GOLD......	.00000	.00000	.00000	.00000	.20000
14	IRON......	134.92551	118.01775	19.24915	119.54715	115.16049
15	LANTHANUM.	.15290	.20740	.13730	.39370	.58010
16	LEAD......	121.03012	106.53313	20.91899	92.75804	89.03403
17	MANGANESE.	6.44796	7.17930	4.60836	7.23924	6.19704
18	BROMINE	.00000	.00000	.00000	1.38672	1.52640
19	NICKEL....	.00000	.00000	.22925	.00000	.00000
20	POTASSIUM.	15.29280	15.23521	11.26800	17.30400	16.05360
21	RUBIDIUM..	.00000	.00000	.00000	1.52385	1.47264
22	SELENIUM..	.55500	.51500	.18400	.56100	.52400
23	SILVER....	2.73350	3.33900	1.65200	.29750	.00000
24	STRONTIUM.	7.52601	6.66741	2.51220	7.56841	7.32460
25	TIN.......	5.85000	6.42240	3.29400	6.06240	7.47720
26	TITANIUM..	101.11046	96.75465	12.36736	85.16415	74.76677
27	VANADIUM..	.00000	.00000	3.11780	.00000	.00000
28	YTTRIUM...	8.97750	7.29020	2.41300	8.43130	7.43100
29	ZINC......	5.03035	5.26370	1.74655	6.39145	6.48570
30	ZIRCONIUM.	3.27980	3.07740	.87860	3.74900	3.17400
	RB/SR/Y/ZR	0/ 8/10/ 4	0/ 9/10/ 4	0/10/10/ 3	2/ 9/10/ 4	2/10/10/

*MICROGRAMS/CM^2

Table XIV. Weight Percent of Principal Elements Found in U.S. Currency[a]

Element	Front	Back	Paper
Barium	0.03	1.4–1.9	—
Chromium	0.01	1	—
Copper	0.01	0.01 (0.05 in 1969 $10 notes)	—
Iron	3.0–4.3	1.2–2.4	—
Lead	0.00	0.14–1.2 (0.08 in 1969 $10 note)	—
Manganese	0.00	0.05 (0.25 in 1969 $10 note)	—
Titanium	0.00	0.1	1.0
Yttrium	0.04–0.05	0.05–0.08	—

[a] As measured from the front and from the back.

21. *Rubidium*, which is generally found in all clays, was probably in the filler in the paper.

22. *Selenium* was seen only in trace amounts.

23. *Silver* found in trace amounts in a few determinations is probably a baseline defect.

24. *Strontium*, like rubidium, is found in clay fillers used in the paper.

25. *Tin* is probably a baseline defect.

26. *Titanium*, which was present in large amounts in all denominations, is a white opacifier in the paper and an ingredient in the green ink, since it rubbed off the green side only.

27. *Vanadium*—none was found.

28. *Yttrium*, a rare earth of the lowest abundance in the earth's crust, was the highest of the four rare earths found in the notes. It might have been added as a tracer element for identifying counterfeit notes.

29. *Zinc* may be present with barium sulphate if lithopone was used as a paper opacifier. It might have been picked up from zinc lithographic plates if they were used.

Summary

A series of scouting experiments were made to determine if new and useful information could be derived from the presence or absence of key elements that are known to affect the stability and durability of paper.

Elements present in papers made by various makers at various times have been identified.

The feasibility of identifying which elements are in the paper and which are in the printing inks employed has been demonstrated.

Table XV. Seals on Front Side of $10 Federal Reserve Note: No. A 1313, Green Department of Treasury Seal; No. 3 1315, Gauze Rubbing from Same; No. 1314, Black Federal Reserve Bank Seal; No. A 1316, Rubbing from Same

A.L. #	750.XY.1	750.XW.1.3	750.XW.1.2	750.XW.1.4
SEQ. #	#A1313	#A1315	#A1314	#A1316
TEST DATE	275,1978	275,1978	275,1978	275,1978
TEST TIME	15:43	16:26	16: 5	16:45
ACCESSION #	C61040893A	C61040893A	C61040893A	C61040893A
OWNER	VFH	VFH	VFH	VFH$10
OBJECT	$10 TREAS	RUBBINGTRES	$10 FEDRES	RUBBING FED
DESC'N	DEPT. SEAL	DEPTSEAL	FEDRESSEAL	RESBANKSEAL
PART	FRONTGREEN	FRONTRIGHT	FRONT LEFT	FRONT LEFT
MAKER	J.CONNALLY	/	J.CONNALLY	/
DATE	1969	/	1969	/
PROV'NCE	PHLA	/	PHLA	/
ELEMENT	*MUG/CM2	*MUG/CM2	*MUG/CM2	*MUG/CM2

	ELEMENT	*MUG/CM2	*MUG/CM2	*MUG/CM2	*MUG/CM2
1	ANTIMONY..	3.45400	1.25400	2.79400	1.61700
2	ARSENIC...	.00000	.00000	.00000	.00000
3	BARIUM....	83.39999	2.15600	43.93199	3.12800
4	BISMUTH..	.00000	.00000	.00000	.00000
5	CADMIUM...	5.27040	1.80480	4.48320	2.19360
6	CALCIUM...	30.77689	1.86571	6.62046	1.45607
7	CERIUM....	1.05000	.29100	1.25700	.21800
8	CESIUM....	2.39000	.32500	1.59500	.35000
9	CHROMIUM..	18.59400	5.59000	16.12300	4.89000
10	COBALT....	.00000	2.96163	.18387	2.35575
11	COPPER....	5.42400	1.34000	2.24400	.90800
12	GALLIUM...	1.56400	.68000	1.32400	.72800
13	GOLD......	.00000	.00000	.00000	.00000
14	IRON......	153.94797	7.49256	53.62103	6.64056
15	LANTHANUM.	.50200	.27000	.65120	.28480
16	LEAD......	15.10500	5.52000	7.62750	6.16500
17	MANGANESE.	8.08570	5.95385	12.89365	6.95625
18	BROMINE...	31.31679	3.35812	5.10600	1.99272
19	NICKEL....	.00000	1.60680	.00000	2.13000
20	POTASSIUM.	27.83283	5.60640	13.49040	5.25840
21	RUBIDIUM..	4.15680	.77832	1.53000	.74592
22	SELENIUM..	.44600	.12800	.28300	.16200
23	SILVER....	3.10270	1.49040	2.24710	2.57830
24	STRONTIUM.	5.07000	1.41000	3.74000	1.26000
25	TIN.......	5.42080	2.21760	5.22240	2.26560
26	TITANIUM..	110.96770	.76544	115.46893	1.11488
27	VANADIUM..	.00000	1.40440	.00000	1.35930
28	YTTRIUM...	3.78300	1.65120	3.52500	1.36720
29	ZINC......	6.54080	1.85360	5.85840	2.99920
30	ZIRCONIUM.	5.64000	2.10000	5.14000	1.89000
	RB/SR/Y/ZR	7/ 9/ 7/10	4/ 7/ 8/10	3/ 7/ 7/10	4/ 7/ 7/10

*MICROGRAMS/CM^2

Acknowledgments

This study was funded in part by a grant from the National Museum Act and by The Henry Francis du Pont Winterthur Museum. A recent grant from the National Science Foundation will support additional work that will be under the guidance of the conservation laboratories of The Library of Congress, the National Archives, The Folger Shakespeare Library, and the Winterthur Museum.

Literature Cited

1. Hanson, V. F. *Appl. Spectrosc.* **1973,** *27* (5), 309–334.
2. Hanson, V. F. "X-Ray Spectrometry"; Marcel Dekker: 1978; Chapter 15.
3. Carlson, J. H.; Krill, J. *J. Am. Inst. Conserv.* **1978,** *18,* 19–32.
4. Gravell, T. "Catalogue of American Watermarks, 1690–1835"; Garland: New York, 1979.
5. "Handbook of Chemistry and Physics," 44th ed.; The Chemical Rubber Publishing Company: 1963; p. 3487.
6. *"Encyclopedia and Dictionary of Arts and Sciences";* Philadelphia: 1978; Vol. 13.
7. "Chambers Encyclopedia"; London: 1783.
8. Gettens, R. J. "Painting Materials, A Short Encyclopaedia"; Dover Publications: New York, 1966.
9. Letter to W. M. Blumenthal, Secretary of the Department of the Treasury, October 27, 1978.
10. Letter from Seymour Berry, Director, Bureau of Engraving and Printing, November 16, 1978.

RECEIVED October 23, 1979.

The Crystallinity of Cellulosic Fibers

Dependence on History and Influence on Properties

RAJAI H. ATALLA

Department of Chemistry, Institute of Paper Chemistry, P.O. Box 1039, Appleton, WI 54912

Celluloses are similar to other linear polymeric materials in that they can possess one-dimensional order within an individual chain as well as three-dimensional order within an aggregate of chains. Increments in the levels of order occur during the isolation of native celluloses and also as a result of exposure to conditions that promote molecular mobility, such as elevated temperatures and immersion in plasticizing fluids. These increments generally result in embrittlement of the cellulosic materials. Similar effects are expected to occur upon aging of cellulosic textiles and papers over extended periods, and may be accelerated by hydrolytic cleavage of cellulosic chains. The implications of these effects for conservation practices, both with respect to recovery of function as well as in the assessment of deterioration, are reviewed.

Crystallinity long has been recognized as one of the characteristics of native cellulosic fibers. Indeed, native cellulose was observed to diffract x-rays, in the manner characteristic of three-dimensionally ordered molecular systems, before the hypothesis of polymeric structure had been proposed by Staudinger ([1, 2]).

Over the years, many efforts have been made to characterize the nature of order in native cellulose. Although significant progress has been made, a number of questions remain open. One of the complications is that cellulose in the native state is part of biological tissue. Thus, although it can be highly ordered, the ordering is homogeneous over

0065-2393/81/0193-0169$05.00/0

submicroscopic domains only. Furthermore, these domains are organized relative to each other, at a higher level, in diverse ways according to the biological species from which the cellulose is isolated. In this respect, native celluloses are fundamentally different from synthetic semicrystalline polymers, or even regenerated celluloses that, although heterogeneous at the submicroscopic level, are generally homogeneous at a higher level.

The complexity of ordering in native celluloses has prevented the development of quantitative measures of the degree of order that could be applied uniformly to the celluloses from different biological sources. This, in turn, has limited the exploration of relationships between molecular order and macroscopic properties in general, and papermaking properties in particular.

In the systematization of information on papermaking properties, the difficulty of characterizing molecular order in the native fibers generally has been circumvented by focusing on qualitative variables such as the native source and/or method of isolation as the bases for property correlation. Such characterization of native celluloses, in terms of source and pulping procedure, would be quite adequate if not for the dynamic nature of order in semicrystalline polymers. Thus, depending on conditions and the degree of molecular mobility, an ordering that can be described as a slow crystallization continues at a barely perceptible rate. Though this type of crystallization has been recognized and characterized in many synthetic semicrystalline polymers, it generally has been ignored in cellulose.

As part of continuing studies of polymorphic variations in cellulose, we have focused some attention on factors that lead to variations in crystallinity, and some effects of these variations on papermaking properties. Some of our findings, when adjusted for time-scale, suggest that crystallization processes may be an important factor in the aging of cellulosic fibers in both paper and textiles. This chapter represents an effort to interpret our results in this light and to develop suggestions for avenues that might be pursued in search of improved conservation procedures.

Molecular Order in Cellulose

Crystallinity in polymeric materials represents an ordering at the molecular level that is, by its nature, different from ordering in crystals of nonpolymeric species. Thus, in polymers, crystallization implies an intramolecular ordering as well as regularity in three dimensions. This difference is an important one in characterizing order in polymeric systems, particularly in instances when the molecules are inherently rigid and, hence, tend to remain in a relatively extended conformation.

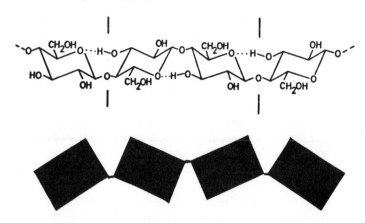

Figure 1. (Top) Structure of cellulose molecule, (bottom) model of structure

The ordering of cellulose can be depicted in two dimensions if the anhydroglucose units are represented as rectangular blocks connected at diagonally alternating corners as shown in Figure 1. If a chain made up of a large number of such blocks is considered, it suggests that a chain of cellulose could assume a wide range of configurations, from an extremely disordered one, to a perfectly straight form. In fact, cellulose is a rather stiff molecule; a more accurate representation of what prevails in most celluloses is a partially disordered chain.

It is clear that the degree of order in a segment of a chain can vary. For example, one can have a number of short ordered regions (Figure 2A), or fewer longer regions (Figure 2B), or perhaps ultimately, the segment can be one long, ordered region (Figure 2C). The order in one dimension is one type of variation in order that is of concern. Indeed, sometimes the concept of a one-dimensional crystal is used to describe the ordered regions of such a chain.

Figure 2.   Degrees of order in cellulose chain

The next step up on the scale of structure is an aggregate of chains that, of course, is what occurs in the native fiber. When an aggregate of chains is considered, the relationship of the chains to each other adds a new dimension to the possible ordering. One can then envision a sequence in which the order slowly increases from one configuration to the next (Figure 3). It is this kind of ordering or crystallization that we believe takes place in cellulose fibers as they age or as they are exposed to accelerated aging procedures. A moment's contemplation of this sequence suggests that the final configuration is bound to be more brittle than some of the earlier ones, because much of the flexibility has been removed.

An alternate description of the inherent differences between the properties of the structures at the top and the bottom of Figure 3, is to indicate

Figure 3.   Sequence of structures with increasing order

that the more ordered structure at the bottom has less freedom to absorb
the energy of mechanical deformation in an elastic mode. The structure
at the top has greater freedom to accommodate displacement by changes
in the linkages between the blocks. These are symbolic of the possibility
of torsion of the glycosidic linkage, as well as internal tortions in the anhydroglucose ring, when the chains are free to move independently of
each other.

Paper Properties and Ordering

The possibility of ordering in native celluloses used in papermaking,
and the significance of such ordering to the paper properties were
explored in an experiment designed to simulate the physical environment
during a typical commercial pulping operation (3).

The basic experiment that demonstrated the effects of molecular
ordering is a rather simple one. Southern pine chips were delignified
using the acid chlorite process at 60°C, then extracted with caustic
solutions to remove the hemicelluloses. The pulp was then divided into
two batches. One was used as a control; the other was immersed in
distilled water inside stainless steel vessels and heated through the
temperature cycle of a typical kraft cook. During this cycle, the pulp
was held at 170°C for approximately 2 h. The two batches of pulp were
then used to make handsheets, and their papermaking properties were
compared.

All of the papermaking properties showed deterioration as a result
of the exposure to the temperatures of the kraft cycle. The tensile
strength was reduced by 20%, the burst properties declined by 30%,
and the tear properties, by approximately 45%. A test of the absorbency
of the fibers indicated that the water retention characteristic of the fibers
had declined to 60% of its original value after the heat treatment. All
of the changes observed as a result of the exposure to elevated temperatures reflect an increase in the level of crystallinity of the pulp fibers.

The measure of crystallinity used to monitor the changes in molecular
order was the width at half-height of the 002 peak in the x-ray diffracto-
grams of pellets pressed from these pulps. A comparison of the diffracto-
grams of the low-temperature pulp and the pulp treated at elevated
temperatures showed a significant change in the direction of increased
order, that is, a reduction in the width at half-height of the 002 peaks.
The possibility of chemical degradation during the exposure to elevated
temperatures in water was investigated, and although a small amount of
chemical degradation did occur, it was not sufficient to account for the
magnitude of the observed changes in properties.

The results of the experiment outlined above clearly indicate that isolation processes involving exposure to elevated temperature alter the basic structure of the cellulosic fibers. One must conclude that isolated celluloses differ in physical structure from the native celluloses in the unperturbed biological structures. The influence of isolation procedures on properties long have been recognized in correlations of papermaking properties with pulping procedures, but they usually have been interpreted only in terms of differences in the chemical structure of the fibers. It is clear from the above studies that the physical changes must be considered as well, since it has been demonstrated that fibers differing only with respect to physical structure can have significantly different papermaking properties. It follows that similar effects from other circumstances also would influence the macroscopic properties of objects fabricated from cellulosic fibers.

To assess the importance of these effects in the behavior of various cellulosic materials exposed to different environments, an investigation of several aspects of crystallization processes in cellulosics was undertaken (4). A number of factors were investigated; those of interest in this context were temperature, chemical environment, and the degree of polymerization.

As anticipated, it was observed that elevated temperatures enhance molecular mobility and accelerate the ordering process. But the effect of temperature was, to a large extent, dependent on the availability of an environment or medium that facilitates molecular mobility. Thus, exposure of a low-temperature pulp to elevated temperatures, of the order of 150°C, in an inert atmosphere (N_2) resulted in little change in the x-ray diffractogram of the fibers, while exposure to the same temperature cycle while the pulp was immersed in glycerol resulted in significant increases in crystallinity (5).

In later studies, the effectiveness of glycerol in promoting molecular motion was compared with that of dimethylsulfoxide and water. It was found that, although all three promote ordering in cellulose, water was definitely the most effective.

Perhaps the most significant observation, in this context, was with regard to the effect of molecular weight or degree of polymerization (DP). The susceptibility of cellulosic samples to the ordering influence of elevated temperatures and immersion in mobilizing media increased as the DP decreased. Clearly, molecules of lower DP have fewer constraints hindering realignment and crystallization. Some of the observations were made on amorphous cellulose regenerated from an anhydrous solvent system under anhydrous conditions. Samples of DP greater than 1000 were unaffected by exposure to water at room temperature, while samples of DP below 100 would begin to crystallize upon exposure to the prevailing moisture content in the laboratory atmosphere.

Implications for Conservation

The series of observations outlined above have a number of implications for any program directed at preserving the quality of cellulosic materials. These can be categorized broadly as relating to three types of objectives: (1) prevention of further deterioration, (2) recovery of some of the properties already lost through aging, and (3) the interpretation of accelerated testing procedures.

The prevention of further deterioration requires arresting the chain scission reaction caused by acid or enzymatic hydrolysis of the glycosidic linkages. The reduction in DP through chain scission has a dual character to its negative effect upon properties. In addition to the inherent reduction in the tensile properties of the fibers, the lower DP enhances the opportunity for crystallization with resulting embrittlement.

Recovery of properties already lost through aging would require efforts to modify molecular order along two lines. The first would involve a decrystallizing treatment that can reduce the dimensions of the brittle domains and increase the capacity of fibers to respond to deformation in an elastic mode. Although a number of approaches to decrystallization of cellulosic materials are available, most are unsuited for conservation applications. This approach might be pursued in search of suitable methods.

Yet another approach to recovery of lost properties could be based on cross-linking. The primary objective here would be to extend the domain spanned by covalently linked molecular entities to counteract the reduction resulting from the chain-scission reaction. Cross-linking, however, is a rather complex process, particularly for native fibers; if carried too far it could result in embrittlement, further compounding the effects of age.

An optimum procedure would combine the decrystallization and cross-linking to recover properties lost through aging. However, the feasibility of such an approach for restoration of paper properties is dependent on the development of vapor-phase processes to accomplish the desired effect. Such processes would permit application to cellulosic objects without mechanical disruption. For cellulosic materials that are not dependent on hydrogen bonding for their mechanical integrity, such as cellulosic textiles, application of the decrystallizing and/or cross-linking procedures in the liquid phase may be feasible.

Finally, the effect of ordering processes must be considered in the interpretation of results from accelerated aging tests. The activation energies for the chain-scission reaction and for molecular ordering are likely to be quite different. Furthermore, enhancement of the ordering process through the reduction in DP caused by chain scission is likely to manifest itself as an autocatalytic effect wherein the rate of decay of properties may appear to increase with time. The dependence of aging processes on temperature is thus expected to be quite complex. The coupling of the effects of temperature and DP no doubt is compounded further by the influence of moisture content. Thus, comparisons of aging tests carried out in environments that differ in moisture content are complicated by differences in the effects of moisture on chain scission and molecular mobility.

In summary, the ordering or crystallization process in cellulosic materials has a complex influence on properties and aging. A number of implications of these phenomena have been outlined, and some suggestions for avenues worthy of further exploration have been put forth. Consideration of these matters should enter into the planning of programs that search for new and improved methods of preservation and restoration of objects made of cellulosic materials.

Literature Cited

1. Purves, C. B. In "Cellulose and Cellulose Derivatives," 2nd ed.; Ott, E.; Spurlin, H. M.; Graflin, M. W., Eds.; Interscience: New York, 1954; p. 29.
2. Howsman, J. A.; Sisson, W. A. In "Cellulose and Cellulose Derivatives," 2nd ed.; Ott, E.; Spurlin, H. M.; Graflin, M. W., Eds.; Interscience: New York, 1954; p. 231.
3. Atalla, R. H.; Whitmore, H. *Polym. Lett.* **1978**, *16*, 601.
4. Ellis, J.; Atalla, R. H., unpublished data.
5. Atalla, R. H.; Nagel, S. C., unpublished data.

RECEIVED December 4, 1979.

The Application of Several Empirical Equations to Describe the Change of Properties of Paper on Accelerated Aging

G. D. MENDENHALL[1]

Battelle, Columbus Laboratories, 505 King Avenue, Columbus, OH 43201

G. B. KELLY and J. C. WILLIAMS

The Library of Congress, Washington, DC 20540

Several empirical and semiempirical equations were applied to folding endurance and reflectance data from Kraft paper samples aged at 70–100°C. For both properties, better fits to the data were obtained with a plot of the logarithm of the property versus the square root of aging time rather than the aging time itself. Several schemes with consecutive, competitive, or reversible reactions also were considered, and from them equations were derived that also could describe the change of properties of paper with time.

This chapter is a report of the results of conventional testing procedures carried out on a series of kraft paper samples at the Library of Congress. The chemiluminescence emission from the paper samples was measured concurrently in a study at Battelle's Columbus Laboratories, and the results of that study have been presented elsewhere (1). In summary, the chemiluminescence maxima from the papers in humid or dry atmospheres adhered fairly well to a conventional Arrhenius expression from 25° to 100°C, which suggested a continuity in the oxidative mechanism over this temperature range, at least in the initial stages of aging.

The results of the conventional tests were more puzzling, because extrapolation of the apparent first-order rate constants for loss of folding and reflectance properties gave lifetimes at room temperature in reverse

---

[1] Current address: Department of Chemistry and Chemical Engineering, Michigan Technological University, Houghton, MI 49931.

order to the rankings obtained at the temperature of the accelerated aging experiments. The limited temperature range of the study precluded any statistical confidence in this extrapolation, however, and we have instead made use of the data to study some alternate equations to describe the change in properties of the samples with time. In particular, we have tested some equations that reproduce the curvature noted in semilogarithmic plots of the data, including ones derived from schemes with several steps.

Experimental—Accelerated Aging Tests

Samples of the papers, prepared as described in the previous publication (1), were aged under two conditions: one set in a forced circulation oven (Blue M, Powermatic 60) at 80°, 90°, and 100°C with ambient air intake to give less than 2% relative humidity in the oven and one set in a forced circulation humid oven (Blue M, Powermatic 60 Humid Flo) at 70°, 80°, and 90°C and 50% relative humidity. Test specimens were removed from both ovens at various intervals, conditioned as specified in TAPPI method T402, and tested for brightness (TAPPI method T452) and MIT folding endurance at 0.5 kg load (TAPPI method T5111). In each case, ten specimens of each sample were tested and the results averaged and compared with the controls similarly conditioned and tested at the start of the tests (zero aging time). One specimen from each of the samples was tested also for pH and acidity at each aging period using the pulp procedure described previously (2).

Computer Programs

Simple linear regression analysis of the data was carried out initially with advanced pocket calculators and with a utility program supplied with a HP9815A programmable calculator. The routine was modified for use with Arrhenius rate expressions. The constants to fit Equation 11, below, were selected initially with an iterative program written for the HP9815A. Later calculations were carried out with a nonlinear, iterative program (SPSS Subprogram Nonlinear, Manual No. 433, August, 1977, Northwestern University). Since the data had to be punched onto computer cards for this program, we then checked the regression analyses with the same data cards and another program (SPSS Regression, Manual No. 414, Northwestern University, June, 1976) by adding the appropriate compute statements. The SPSS and Gear programs were executed in a CDC Cyber multiframe system at Battelle Laboratories. A HP9815A or HP33E calculator was preferred for carrying out the linear regression programs for the Arrhenius expressions, however, because of the greater convenience in obtaining extrapolated values of the rate constants.

Since most of the rate constants can be derived easily, only the averaged, original data are reproduced here (Table I) together with selected parameters where appropriate for discussion. The use of the

Table I. Accelerated Aging of Washed Kraft Paper

100°C Dry Oven
90°C 50% Relative Humidity Oven

Days Oven	Fold MD	Fold CD	Bright-ness	pH	meq/kg
0	1651 ± 227	1584 ± 335	74.9	6.9	3
	1651 ± 227	1584 ± 335	74.9	6.9	1
3	1429 ± 215	1057 ± 143	73.3	6.3	5
	1400 ± 172	940 ± 247	72.1	6.6	2
6	1375 ± 314	896 ± 195	72.1	6.6	4
	1155 ± 298	945 ± 243	70.9	6.4	4
12	1119 ± 215	869 ± 130	72.5	6.6	2
	822 ± 290	1003 ± 275	69.3	6.3	4
24	896 ± 125	600 ± 139	71.9	6.8	2
	597 ± 146	630 ± 159	66.2	6.1	5
36	701 ± 162	709 ± 116	71.1	6.2	5
	507 ± 79	485 ± 98	65.4	6.2	6

90°C Dry Oven
80°C 50% Relative Humidity Oven

Days Oven	Fold MD	Fold CD	Bright-ness	pH	meq/kg
0	1651 ± 227	1584 ± 335	74.9	6.9	1
	1651 ± 227	1584 ± 335	74.9	6.9	1
6	1428 ± 227	995 ± 253	74.1	6.6	2
	1334 ± 259	1040 ± 213	73.1	6.4	4
12	1211 ± 180	1017 ± 299	73.5	6.7	2
	1176 ± 125	962 ± 158	72.5	6.5	3
24	1101 ± 271	852 ± 290	73.0	6.3	6
	1092 ± 124	701 ± 297	71.5	6.6	2
36	1099 ± 258	928 ± 215	73.4	6.3	4
	917 ± 133	826 ± 111	69.4	6.4	4
48	907 ± 166	803 ± 238	71.3	6.4	4
	883 ± 122	645 ± 144	68.5	6.6	3

80°C Dry Oven
70°C 50% Relative Humidity Oven

Days Oven	Fold MD	Fold CD	Bright-ness	pH	meq/kg
0	1651 ± 227	1584 ± 335	74.9	6.9	1
	1651 ± 227	1584 ± 335	74.9	6.9	1
12	1288 ± 202	965 ± 252	73.7	6.7	2
	1155 ± 254	965 ± 272	72.6	6.8	1
24	1258 ± 204	1101 ± 256	73.5	6.5	4
	1110 ± 126	978 ± 255	72.9	6.5	4
38	1137 ± 169	839 ± 202	73.9	6.5	3
	849 ± 264	908 ± 284	72.8	6.5	2
48	713 ± 231	559 ± 234	73.3	6.4	3
	815 ± 336	585 ± 218	72.3	6.5	4
96	908 ± 181	688 ± 232	72.4	6.2	8
	952 ± 131	450 ± 86	70.6	6.2	8
179	635 ± 155	603 ± 156	69.3	6.2	5

average values, rather than the ten individual measurements, in calculating rate constants improved the coefficient of determination for loss
of folding endurance in one case (washed paper, 100°C, dry oven,
machine direction) from 0.73 to 0.96. The rate constants selected by the
computer were within 2% of each other for the two procedures, so it was
assumed that the use of average values did not affect significantly the
outcome of the other computations, although this conclusion is not
statistically rigorous. Values of folding endurance were divided by their
respective initial values for machine and cross direction and entered
together for the calculations with the SPSS programs. Otherwise, the
actual values of the properties were entered.

Results and Discussion

After examination of the four properties given in Table I, we selected
folding endurance and reflectance for detailed evaluation. For most
testing conditions, the precision in the pH measurements and neutraliza-
tion equivalents listed in the table is not high compared with the overall
change in these properties during aging. The folding endurances showed
the greatest changes with aging, although there are numerous instances
where the values do not decrease smoothly with time. The reflectance
(brightness) measurements decreased smoothly with accelerated aging
in nearly all cases, although the relative magnitude of the changes were
less than for the folding endurance.

Following Browning and Wink (2), we analyzed the loss of folding
endurance and reflectance according to Equations 1 and 2.

$$\ln (P_o/P) = kt \tag{1}$$

$$\ln (P_o/P) = kt^{1/2} \tag{2}$$

In these equations P is a material property, t is the time of aging, and k
is the effective rate constant for the process.

The introduction of $t^{1/2}$ in Equation 2 in effect corrected for positive
curvature in plots of the logarithm of the property versus time according
to Equation 1. A more general way to correct for this curvature is to
write Equations 1 and 2 in the form of Equation 3, where n is the exponential term in t.

$$\ln (P_o/P) = kt^n \tag{3a}$$

In a linearized form, Equation 3a becomes Equation 3b.

$$\ln t = \frac{1}{n} \ln\ln (P_o/P) - \frac{1}{n} \ln k \tag{3b}$$

The curvature also can be corrected by addition of a quadratic term, Equation 4.

$$\ln (P_o/P) = k_1 t - k_2 t^2 \tag{4}$$

Equation 4 also can be rewritten in a form suitable for regression analysis, Equation 5.

$$t^{-1} \ln (P_o/P) = k_2 - k_2 t \tag{5}$$

Finally, the upward curvature may result from a reconstitution step superposed on an effective first-order degradation process. This possibility was discussed by Browning and Wink (2) and is consistent with the initial increase in wet breaking strength observed by Graminski et al. (3), on accelerated aging of paper. In the latter example, it is possible that the rate of the reconstitution process initially exceeds that of the degradation process. If the degradation and reconstitution mechanism proceed consecutively, we can represent the process in the simplest

Scheme 1

$$P \xrightarrow{k_1} X \tag{6}$$

$$X \xrightarrow{k_2} P' \tag{7}$$

way as depicted in Equations 6 and 7, where the properties of the paper are proportional to $P + P'$. The appropriate first-order equations and

$$\frac{dP}{dt} = - k_1 P \tag{8}$$

$$\frac{dX}{dt} = k_1 P - k_2 X \tag{9}$$

$$\frac{dP'}{dt} = k_2 X \tag{10}$$

$$\frac{P_o}{P + P'} = (k_2 - k_1) [k_2 - k_1 (1 - e^{-k_2 t})]^{-1} \tag{11}$$

their solution are shown in Equations 8–11, where P_o is proportional to the initial concentration of reactive groups.

In addition to the usual, statistical criteria for goodness of fit, an even more fundamental requirement for a suitable function is that the constants uniformly increase or decrease with the temperature of aging.

Table II. Regularity and F Values for Equations to Describe Change and Folding Endurance of Paper

		Folding Endurance		Reflectance	
Equation	$F(t)$	Dry Oven	Humid Oven	Dry Oven	Humid Oven
1	kt	$k : 18+$	$39+$	$13+$	$70+$
2	$kt^{1/2}$	$k : 34+$	$73+$	$22+$	$210+$
5	$k_1 t + k_2 t^2$	$k : 5+$	$9+$	$6+$	$7+$
		$k : \quad +$	$+$	$+$	$+$
11	(exp)	$k : \quad +$	$+$	$+$	$+$
		$k : \quad -$	$-$	$-$	$+$

Table II contains the average F-statistic for the rate constants derived at each of the three oven temperatures for Equations 1, 2, 5, and 11, together with a $(+)$ if the constants changed regularly with temperature and $(-)$ if they did not. The F-statistic was not computed for the nonlinear program applied to Equation 11. Equations 1 and 5 were satisfactory on the basis of uniform change of the constants. The quadratic expression was not satisfactory because the term in t^2 dominates at long times, resulting in predicted values of P that increase at an increasing rate with time. Scheme 1 as expressed by Equation 11 is deficient in a similar way because it predicts that the properties of the paper eventually return to their original values.

We next sought to improve upon the results of Equations 1 and 2 by determining optimal values of n for Equation 3. This was carried out by regression analysis with Equation 3b, and the results appear in Table III. With one exception, the optimal ns all fall between 0.5 and 1.0. The overall mean n for both properties in Table IV was 0.68 ± 0.18, with the optimal n for reflectance closer to 0.5, and the optimal n for folding endurance closer to 1.0.

Table III. Values of n for Best Fit of Folding Endurance and Reflectance to Equation $\ln (F_o/F) = kt^n$

$^\circ C$ Dry Oven	Folding Endurance	Reflectance
80	1.00	0.66
90	0.82	0.74
100	0.86	0.37
Mean	0.89 ± 0.09	0.59 ± 0.19
Humid Oven		
70	0.51	0.51
80	0.68	0.66
90	0.75	0.54
Mean	0.65 ± 0.12	0.57 ± 0.08

Table IV. Optimized Rate Constants Corresponding to Equation 15
to Describe the Loss of Folding Endurance (MD),
90°C, Humid Oven[a]

	Temperature (°C)		
	70	*80*	*90*
k_{12}	0.03732	0.0352	0.0660
k_{13}	0.0478	0.0410	0.0255
k_{14}	0.00449	0.000150	0.000293

[a] Rate constants in days⁻¹.

We were also able to obtain excellent fits to the data in a selected case (machine direction folding endurance, 80°C, humid oven) with an equation based on the scheme shown in Equations 12–14.

Scheme 2

$$P \xrightarrow{k_{12}} X \tag{12}$$

$$X \xrightarrow{k_{13}} P' \quad (P' \text{ equivalent to } P) \tag{13}$$

$$X \xrightarrow{k_{14}} Y \tag{14}$$

The equations associated with this system are relatively complicated, but fortunately, they can be derived from solutions given by Frost and Pearson (4) with neglect on the back reaction leading from Y to X. The equation is:

$$P + P' = P_0 \left[\frac{\lambda_3}{k_{13}} \left(\frac{\lambda_2 - k_{13}}{\lambda_2 - \lambda_3} \right) e^{-\lambda_2 t} - \frac{\lambda_2}{k_{13}} \left(\frac{\lambda_3 - k_{13}}{\lambda_2 - \lambda_3} \right) e^{-\lambda_3 t} \right] \tag{15}$$

In this equation, λ_2 and λ_3 are defined as follows:

$$\lambda_2 = \frac{1}{2} [k_{12} + k_{13} + k_{14} + ((k_{12} + k_{13} + k_{14})^2 - 4 k_{12} k_{13})^{1/2}]$$

$$\lambda_3 = \frac{1}{2} [k_{12} + k_{13} + k_{14} - ((k_{12} + k_{13} + k_{14})^2 - 4 k_{12} k_{13})^{1/2}]$$

We attempted unsuccessfully to use the nonlinear computer program to solve for the k_{13}, λ_2, and λ_3 that best fit the data according to Equation 15. We then resorted to the use of the Gear program (5), which gave values of P, X, and Y as a function of time and the three rate constants:

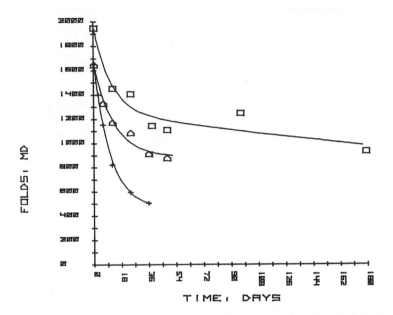

Figure 1. Computer curves for loss of folding endurance (washed Kraft, MD) with rate constants of Table IV. The curves pass through the data for (□) 70°C, (○) 80°C, and (+) 90°C. The data for the curve at 70°C has been displaced upward by 300 units for clarity.

k_{12}, k_{13}, and k_{14}. A reasonably good fit was obtained by trial-and-error selection of ks, and we were gratified to find that the constants were optimized quickly when the nonlinear program was reapplied to the data with values of λ_2 and λ_3 calculated from values that we had selected. The optimized values of k_{12} and k_{14} were then derived from the optimized k_{13}, λ_2, and λ_3 by algebraic manipulation. The ks so obtained are tabulated for three temperatures in Table IV, and plots of the calculated values of folds versus time, obtained with optimized ks and the Gear program, appear in Figure 1.

The fits of the curves to the data are seen to display the rapid initial drop followed by the slower decline in endurance that is responsible for the curvature in the semilogarithmic plots. Scheme 2 can also potentially explain an initial increase in a measured property on aging by postulating that an initial concentration of intermediate X is present such that, with appropriate rate constants, the conversion of X into P' will be faster than the transformation of P into X. A third feature of the above scheme is that when k_{12} and k_{13} greatly exceed k_{14}, the property P will quickly reach a quasiequilibrium value of $(k_{12}/k_{13})P_0$ and then decay by first-order kinetics. When $k_{12} >> k_{13}$, the kinetics will be first-order from the beginning, so that in limiting cases the conventional Equation 1 is obtained.

The optimized rate constants in Table IV unfortunately do not change regularly with temperature. This result is not surprising in view of the imprecision of the data, and the fact that the loss of folding endurance at 70° and 80°C are inexplicably almost coincidental. However, we could select a "consistent fit" of rate constants that obeyed Equation 1 and described the data fairly well (Figure 2).

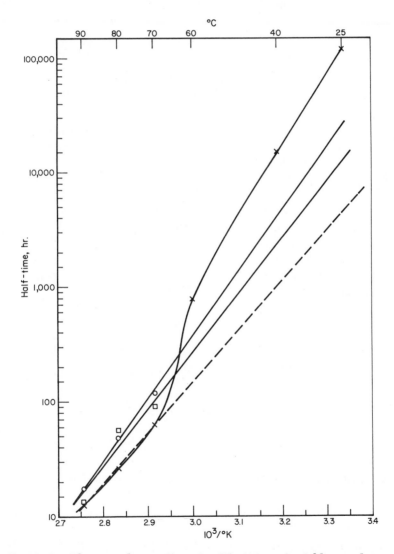

Figure 2. Plot according to Equation 17 of times for folding endurance (MD) to reach a value of 826: (○) values calculated with linear regression and Equation 1; (□) Equation 2; (×) Equation 15 with $\ln k_{12}$ (days^{-1}) = 15.680 − 6,686/T_{abs}, $\ln k_{13} = 1.8124 − 1,935/T_{abs}$, and $\ln k_{14} = 13.5692 − 7,890/T_{abs}$.

Browning and Wink (2) analyzed some of their oven-aging data by plotting the log of halftimes vs. $1/T$ and extrapolating the line drawn through the points to room temperature. The general validity of this approach for any system described by an equation of the form of Equation 3 can be seen by expanding as follows:

$$\ln (P_o/P) = kt^n = Ae^{-E/RT}t^n \tag{16}$$

$$\ln t_{1/2} = \frac{1}{n}(\ln\ln 2 - \ln A) - \frac{E}{nRT} \tag{17}$$

Thus, a plot of the logarithm of the halftimes (or any fractional time) vs. $1/T_{abs}$ will give a linear relation with a slope of E/nR. Plots of the logarithms of the times for folding endurance to decrease by half vs. $1/T_{abs}$ for one set of data appear in Figure 2. Also shown in Figure 2 are the halftimes obtained with the Gear program and selected rate parameters corresponding to Scheme 2. A linear relationship in a plot of this type is not predicted except under some limiting cases discussed above.

We should also note that Arney et al. (7), have shown recently that the loss of some properties of paper could be represented as the sum of two pseudo first-order processes, one oxygen independent and one linearly dependent on the oxygen concentration. The model corresponding to this result would then be Equation 18, which is equivalent to the conventional Equation 1

$$\ln (P_2/P_t) = k_1t + k_2t \tag{18}$$

with $k_{obs} = k_1 + k_2$. On the other hand, we may justify an alternate, Equation 19, by noting that the two processes involved may not have the same preexponential factors.

$$P_t = P_1e^{-k_1t} + P_2e^{-k_2t} \tag{19}$$

With the normalizing condition that $P_1 + P_2 = P_0$, we have an expression with three independent parameters, which has the attractive feature that with appropriate choice of constants, we can duplicate upward curvature in semilogarithmic plots of data.

Equation 19 was applied to the folding endurance and reflectance data through manual selection of rate constants that roughly fit the experimental values, and then by optimizing the selections for the data at a given temperature with the nonlinear program. The results were very similar to the application of Equation 15, that is, in most cases, a good fit to the data was obtained at a single temperature, but the rate

Table V.   Calculated Brightness for Washed Kraft Paper, 70°C, 50% Relative Humidity, According to Equations 2 and 19

Time (Days)	Equation 19[a]	Equation 2[b]	Observed
0	74.9	74.9	74.9
12	73.9	73.4	72.6
24	72.9	72.8	72.9
38	72.0	72.3	72.9
48	71.4	72.0	72.3
96	69.1	70.8	70.6
179	66.9	69.3	69.3
$\Sigma(\text{Calc-Obs})^2$	11.3	1.1	—

[a] Calculated with $\ln k_1$ (days^{-1}) $= 59.892\text{-}25{,}014.2/T_{abs}$, $\ln k_2$ (days^{-1}) $= 32.405\text{-}12{,}720.8/T_{abs}$, $P_1 = 65.0$, $P_2 = 9.9$.
[b] Calculated with $\ln k_2$ (days^{-1}) $= 21.034\text{-}8{,}897.4/T_{abs}$.

constants did not vary regularly with temperature, and the computation time required to obtain a best fit to the data was often excessive. In Table V, we present one set of calculations on reflectance properties in a humid atmosphere according to Equation 19 together with those from Equation 2. There is a general agreement between the results from the two equations, although the fit to Equation 2 is better.

Discussion

The foregoing treatment of the data was carried out without the dry certainty of statistical rigor, but with the conviction that multiple processes do occur in paper (7) whose detailed kinetic treatment will yield complex equations analogous to those tested in this study. A number of workers have observed enhanced rates of oxidation (8) and hydrolysis (9, 10, 11, 12) of cellulose-based materials in the early stages of reaction, implying the existence of differential susceptibility of chemical bonds or morphological areas of the polymer to degradation (12). A similar feature may be responsible for the curvature in the semilogarithmic plots in our data. This curvature would result in a better fit of Equation 2, which is supported by the high F-values in Table II associated with this equation. In addition, Tongren (13) has derived an expression relating the ratio of absorption coefficient to the scattering coefficient to the square root of aging time (Equation 20). Although the experimentally measured

$$K/S = (K/S)_o - k_{20}t^{1/2} \tag{20}$$

property is not exactly the same, the fit of Equation 2 to our reflectance data can be shown to be consistent with Tongren's equation by noting the approximation for $P_o \simeq P$ shown in Equation 21 or 22. Since the

$$\ln (P_0/P) \cong 1 - \frac{P_0}{P} = kt^{1/2} \tag{21}$$

$$P = P_0 - Pk_{22}t^{1/2} \simeq P_0 - P_{\text{avg}}k_{22}t^{1/2} \tag{22}$$

changes in reflectance were small, Equation 22 is approximately of the same form as Equation 20, since the term Pk_{22} is nearly constant.

Acknowledgment

The authors thank Dr. Bruce Buxton and Mr. Jim Tauschek for assistance with the computer programs. The work at Battelle was supported in part under Contract No. DAAG29-78-C-0001 with the U.S. Army Research organization.

Literature Cited

1. Kelly, G. B.; William, J. C.; Mendenhall, G. D.; Ogle, C. A. "Durability of Macromolecular Materials," *Adv. Chem. Ser.* **1979**, *95*, 117.
2. Browning, B. L.; Wink, W. A. *Tappi* **1968**, *51* (4), 156.
3. Graminski, E. L.; Parks, E. J.; Toth, E. E. "Durability of Macromolecular Materials," *Adv. Chem. Ser.* **1979**, *95*, 341.
4. Frost, A. A.; Pearson, R. G. "Kinetics and Mechanism," 2nd ed.; John Wiley & Sons: New York, 1965; p. 175.
5. Gear, C. W. *Commun. Assoc. Comput. Mach.* **1971**, *14*, 176.
6. Gray, G. G. *Tappi* **1969**, *52* (2), 325.
7. Arney, J. S.; Jacobs, A. J.; Newman, R. *Tappi* **1979**, *62*, 89.
8. Hernadi, S. *Sven. Paperstidn.* **1976**, *13*, 418.
9. Saeman, J. F. *Ind. Eng. Chem.* **1945**, *37*, 43.
10. Harris, J. F. *J. Appl. Polym. Sci. Appl. Polym. Symp.* **1975**, *28*, 131.
11. Daruwalla, E. H.; Narsian, M. G. *Tappi* **1966**, *49*, 106.
12. Sharples, A. In "Cellulose and Cellulose Derivatives," In "High Polymers 5," part 5, 2nd ed.; Bikales, N. M.; Segal, L., Eds.; Wiley–Interscience: New York, 1971.
13. Tongen, J. C. *Pap. Trade J.* **1938**, Aug. 25, 34.

RECEIVED October 23, 1979.

A Kinetic Study of the Influence of Acidity on the Accelerated Aging of Paper

J. S. ARNEY and A. H. CHAPDELAINE

Carnegie–Mellon Institute of Research, 4400 Fifth Avenue,
Pittsburgh, PA 15213

The influence of acidity on the rates of yellowing and of tensile strength loss of a newsprint and a 100% cotton rag paper were examined at 90°C, 100% RH, under both an atmosphere of air and an atmosphere of nitrogen. From a kinetic analysis of the data, an empirical rate law was derived expressing the total rate of degradation as the sum of an atmospheric oxidation process and an oxygen-independent process, both of which were found to depend linearly on the concentration of acidity in the paper. The relative importance of the two processes appeared to be insensitive to changes in the acid content of the papers below pH 5. The results suggest that the influence of acidity on the rate of natural paper degradation would be the same regardless of which degradation process predominates at room temperature.

Acidity has long been recognized as a major factor contributing to the deterioration of cellulose-containing materials. In an effort to combat the harmful influence of acidity, researchers have developed a variety of deacidification techniques capable of decreasing the acid content of most paper-containing objects that are found in museums and libraries. These techniques often are used by conservators in the care of books and works of art on paper (1). Nevertheless, the nature of the chemical processes that cause papers to yellow and to lose strength remains somewhat obscure, and the role of acidity in these processes also is not well understood.

A recently published study concerned with the influence of oxygen on paper aging concluded that the total rate of degradation may be expressed as the sum of two general types of degradation processes: an

0065-2393/81/0193-0189$05.00/0
© 1981 American Chemical Society

atmospheric oxidation process and an oxygen-independent process (2). The relative importance of these two processes was found to depend on the moisture content of the paper, the type of paper, the temperature of the accelerated aging experiment, and the property monitored in determining the rate of degradation (2, 3). One might also expect the acid content of the paper to influence the ratio of the two processes. However, the influence of acidity on this ratio is difficult to predict.

If one were to assume that a hydrolytic reaction controls the rate of the oxygen-independent process (4, 5), then acidity would be expected to accelerate the process and perhaps increase its relative contribution to the total rate of degradation. However, the atmospheric oxidation process may also be pH dependent. Cellulose oxidations are known to be either accelerated or retarded by an increase in acidity. The particular influence depends on the oxidizing agent and mechanism involved (6). Without an understanding of the mechanism of the atmospheric oxidation process observed during the accelerated aging of paper, it is not possible to predict whether acidity will accelerate or retard the process. Moreover, with little evidence to suggest which of the two types of degradation processes predominates at room temperature, it is difficult to predict the overall influence of acidity, and thus of deacidification, on the room temperature aging of paper.

In this chapter, empirical rate constants were determined by following the loss of tensile strength and the decrease in diffuse reflectance of a rag and a newsprint paper buffered over a range of pH values. From the results of these experiments, the influence of acidity on both the atmospheric oxidation process and the oxygen-independent process was determined. Before describing the results of these experiments, the methodology employed to obtain the empirical rate constants will be discussed.

The Kinetic Analysis of Complex Properties

There is a practical difference between exploring the chemical kinetics of a reaction and exploring "property kinetics": the rate of change in a useful property of a complex material such as paper. The discipline of chemical kinetics has a sound theoretical foundation directly related to the mechanism of chemical reactions. Property kinetic studies, on the other hand, are empirical and are difficult to relate to chemical mechanisms. The difficulty arises because a complex property, such as tensile strength or brightness, cannot be related easily to the chemical composition of the material under study. Nevertheless, empirical rate constants can be obtained, and these rate constants can be related to chemical processes occurring within the paper.

Most property kinetic studies reported in the literature are conducted by analogy with the methodology of chemical kinetics. A physical property, P, observed to change monotonically with time is assumed to obey a differential expression similar to a rate law in chemical kinetics. Equation 1 is a general expression of this kind where k is a constant and

$$\frac{dP}{dt} = k \, f(P) \tag{1}$$

$f(P)$ is some integrable function of the property. If $f(P)$ were known, integration would yield a linear equation (Equation 2). However, unlike

$$F(P) \equiv \int \frac{dP}{f(P)} = kt \tag{2}$$

a rate law in chemical kinetics, Equation 1 has no a priori mechanistic significance and generally is not known. Thus, integration is not possible, and one must search empirically for some function, $F(P)$, that will linearize the experimental data (P vs. t). The slope may then be used as a measure of the empirical rate constant, k.

Several examples of this line–slope approach to property kinetics have been reported in the literature. For example, Browning and Wink (7) and Gray (8, 9), in Arrhenius studies of paper degradation, found that a logarithmic function would linearize most folding endurance data [$F(P) = \log(P_o/P)$]. The analogy with chemical kinetics occasionally is carried farther, and folding endurance has been said to obey first-order kinetics, [$f(P) = P$], although the term has no mechanistic significance in a property kinetic study. Any other function that will linearize the experimental data also can be used to obtain rate constants, and there is no theoretical or mechanistic restriction to the selection of such a function. Thus, choosing a linearizing function can be a somewhat subjective process, and it often is tempting to use a simple function in a regression analysis and to assume that the standard deviation of such a regression reflects only the experimental error of the measurement.

An alternative technique for obtaining kinetic information that does not require knowledge of the linearizing function $F(P)$ has been suggested by Frank (10) and by Sizmann and Frank (11). If two identical papers are allowed to degrade under two different conditions such that identical changes in the property, P, occur, then Equation 2 may be written as Equation 3, where the subscripts, 1 and 2, refer to the degra-

$$\frac{k_2}{k_1} = \frac{t_1}{t_2} \tag{3}$$

dation under conditions 1 and 2. If condition 1 is selected arbitrarily as a standard for comparison, then the ratio t_1/t_2 is simply a relative rate constant, k_r, equal to k in Equation 1 divided by the value of k under the standard condition.

The time–ratio technique eliminates the necessity of linearizing the experimental data. Nevertheless, the nature of the function $F(P)$ must still be considered in any kinetic study, as pointed out by Gray (9). If the mathematical form of $F(P)$ is not the same under conditions 1 and 2, discussed above, then the property, P, will not cancel out in the determination of the time–ratio, as shown in Equation 4. This problem is of

$$\frac{k_1 \, F_2(P)}{k_2 \, F_1(P)} = \frac{t_2}{t_1} \tag{4}$$

concern whether the time–ratio technique or the line–slope technique is used. However, application of the line–slope technique involves the assumption that the empirical kinetic order is the same under the two conditions compared. On the other hand, application of the time–ratio technique allows a convenient test of the similarity of the empirical kinetic orders. If the value of t_2/t_1 is independent of the degree of degradation, then $F_1(P)$ and $F_2(P)$ are of the same form and Equation 3 is valid.

A Test of the Invariance of F(P) with pH

In exploring the influence of acidity on the rate of degradation of the rag and newsprint papers, it was necessary, as pointed out above, to establish that the mathematical form of $F(P)$ in Equation 2, is invariant with pH. To test this, a newsprint paper with a cold extraction pH of 4.5 was subjected to accelerated degradation at 90°C and 100% relative humidity. Samples of the newsprint that had been buffered at pH 7.9 (*see* Experimental section) were subjected to the same accelerated aging conditions. As shown in Figure 1, the percentage change in tensile strength appears to be related linearly to time. Thus, one might simply assume that $F(P)$ is invariant with changes in acidity and perform linear regressions as shown in Figure 1. In this way, a rate of $k_r = 10.7 \pm 2$ was found for the acidic paper relative to the buffered paper. Thus, the acidic paper seems to degrade by a factor of about ten times faster than the buffered paper.

The value of k_r also can be estimated using the time–ratio technique. As shown in Figure 2, a line can be drawn through the pH 7.9 data using a French curve. Though not as elegant as a computer regression analysis, the French curve technique is at least no more subjective than arbitrarily constraining the data to a straight line. No line was drawn through the

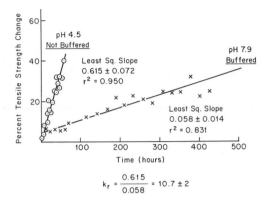

Figure 1. *Percent change in tensile strength vs. time at 90°C, 100% RH, for (⊙) not buffered and for (×) buffered newsprint. The relative rate of degradation, k_r, is estimated as the ratio of the slopes.*

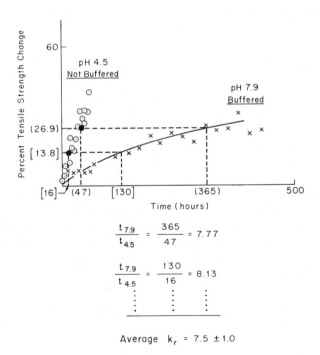

Figure 2. *Percentage change in tensile strength vs. time at 90°C, 100% RH, for (⊙) not-buffered and for (×) buffered newsprint. The relative rate of degradation, k_r, is estimated as the average time–ratio.*

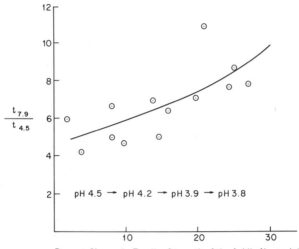

*Figure 3.   Individual values of the time–ratios obtained from Figure 2 vs.
the percentage change in tensile strength*

pH 4.5 data, but relative rates were estimated by determining a time
ratio, as illustrated in Figure 2, for each of the pH 4.5 data points up to
about a 27% change in tensile strength. These individual time–ratios
can be averaged to obtain an estimated relative rate of $k_r = 7.5 \pm 1.0$.
However, if the individual values of the time–ratios are plotted as a
function of the degree of degradation used in each determination, as
shown in Figure 3, then it is evident that the error limit on the average
value of k_r reflects more than experimental uncertainty. Certainly the
trend in Figure 3 will depend somewhat on the particular line one draws
through the data points in Figure 2. Nevertheless, the time–ratio treatment strongly, if not unequivocally, indicates that significant kinetic dissimilarities may be expected in comparing the buffered to the not-buffered
paper. The possibility of such dissimilarities in the mathematical form of
$F(P)$ might be overlooked by arbitrarily constraining the data to a linear
function, as in Figure 1.

It is not difficult to guess why the time–ratios in Figure 3 increase as
degradation proceeds. The cold extraction pH of the acidic paper was
found to decrease during the degradation process, reaching pH 3.8 by
the end of the experiment. The pH of the buffered paper remained
constant. Therefore, it seems probable that the increased value of the
time–ratio as degradation occurred is a manifestation of an autocatalytic
process. Similar results were obtained in the comparison of samples of a
buffered and a not-buffered rag paper. Thus, the autocatalysis process

is not limited to groundwood papers. Furthermore, it was found that the time–ratios did not vary with the degree of degradation if buffered papers were compared with buffered papers of a different pH. This not only supports the autocatalytic hypothesis for the not-buffered papers, but also demonstrates that $F(P)$ is invariant with pH for the buffered papers. Thus, the mathematic restriction suggested by Gray (9) is met, and a kinetic evaluation of the influence of acidity on these papers is feasible.

Rate Versus Acidity

The newsprint and rag papers were buffered (*see* Experimental section) at a series of acidities and were subjected to accelerated degradation at 90°C in sealed tubes containing atmospheres of air at 100% relative humidity. Time–ratios, or relative rate constants, were determined as described above by comparison with papers buffered at pH 4.00 (cold extraction). Both the change in tensile strength and the change in reflectance at 500 nm were monitored. As expected, both the rag and the newsprint papers lost strength and yellowed more rapidly at the higher acidities. Figure 4 illustrates the results obtained for the rag paper.

Although pH is a convenient measure of acidity in paper, it is not the same as the concentration of acid in the paper. In a heterogenous material such as paper, the molar concentration of hydrogen ions is not an easily defined quantity (12). Nevertheless, since the buffer system [maleic acid/Ca(OH)$_2$] in the paper is the primary factor controlling the acid content of the paper, one might expect the cold extraction pH to reflect an effective acid concentration. This effective acid concentration can be expressed as shown in Equation 5. Values of [H$^+$] were calculated from

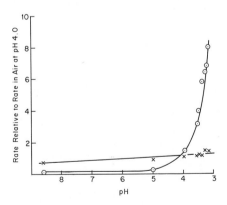

Figure 4.   Relative rate of (⊙) tensile strength change and (×) yellowing vs. cold extraction pH for rag paper degradation at 90°C, 100% RH, in an air atmosphere

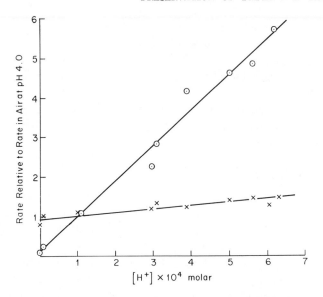

Figure 5.   Relative rate of (⊙) tensile strength change and (×) yellowing vs. relative acid concentration for rag paper degradation at 90°C, 100% RH, in an air atmosphere

$$[H^+] = 10^{-pH} \qquad (5)$$

the cold extraction pH of the samples, and the experimental values of the relative rate constants were found to vary linearly with this estimate of effective acid concentration. Figures 5 and 6 show the results for the rag and the newsprint papers.

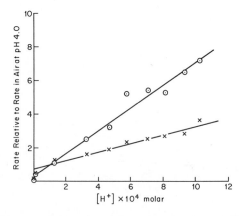

Figure 6.   Relative rate of (⊙) tensile strength change and (×) yellowing vs. relative acid concentration for newsprint paper degradation at 90°C, 100% RH, in an air atmosphere

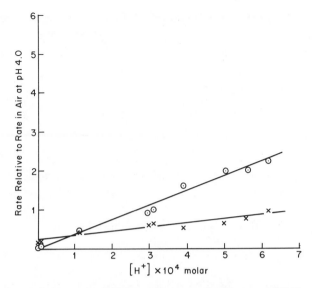

Figure 7. Relative rate of (⊙) tensile strength change and (×) yellowing vs. relative acid concentration for rag paper degradation at 90°C, 100% RH, in a nitrogen atmosphere

The above experiments also were conducted on buffered rag and newsprint papers sealed under nitrogen atmospheres. As before, relative rates were determined at 90°C and 100% relative humidity by comparison with the data taken on the papers at pH 4.00 exposed in an atmosphere of air. At every pH, the rate under nitrogen was slower than the rate in air, as shown in Figures 7 and 8. Moreover, in the absence of oxygen, as

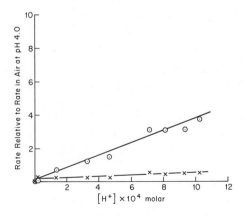

Figure 8. Relative rate of (⊙) tensile strength change and (×) yellowing vs. relative acid concentration for newsprint paper degradation at 90°C, 100% RH, in a nitrogen atmosphere

Table I.   Experimental Values of the Rate Constants in
of Degradation at pH 4.0

Paper	Property	$k_{\alpha 1}$	$k_{\alpha 2}$
Newsprint	tensile strength	0.68 ± 0.09	$[0.32 \pm 0.60]$
Newsprint	reflectance	0.26 ± 0.05	0.74 ± 0.29
Rag paper	tensile strength	0.89 ± 0.11	$[0.11 \pm 0.42]$
Rag paper	reflectance	0.09 ± 0.05	0.91 ± 0.21

[a] Numbers in brackets are $= 0$ within experimental error.

well as in air, the rates of degradation appear to decrease linearly with [H⁺]. Thus, Equations 6 and 7 may be written to describe the results of

$$\text{Rate in air:} \quad k_T = k_{\alpha 1}[\text{H}^+] + k_{\alpha 2} \tag{6}$$

$$\text{Rate in N}_2: \quad k_b = k_{b1}[\text{H}^+] + k_{b2} \tag{7}$$

these experiments. In these equations, k_T and k_b are the rate constants in Equation 1 determined in air and in nitrogen relative to the rate of degradation in air at pH 4.00. The slopes ($k_{\alpha 1}$ and k_{b1}) and the intercepts ($k_{\alpha 2}$ and k_{b2}) were determined from linear regressions of the data in Figures 5–8. Expressing the acid concentrations relative to the acid concentration at pH 4 ($[\text{H}^+] \equiv 1.00$), the linear regressions yield the ocnstants shown in Table I. Thus, the constants in Table I are empirical rate constants expressed relative to the total rate, $k_T = 1.00$, in air at pH 4.00.

The difference between the rate of degradation in air and the rate in nitrogen ($k_a = k_T - k_b$) is a measure of the rate of the atmospheric oxidation process. As shown in Equation 8, the rate of this atmospheric

$$\text{Atmospheric Oxidation:} \quad k_a = k_{a1}[\text{H}^+] + k_{a2} \tag{8}$$

oxidation also varies linearly with [H⁺], where $k_{a1} = k_{\alpha 1} - k_{b1}$ and $k_{a2} = k_{\alpha 2} - k_{b2}$. Values of k_{a1} and k_{a2} are shown in Table I.

In an earlier investigation, the rate of the atmospheric oxidation process was found to vary linearly with the oxygen concentration in the atmosphere surrounding the paper (2). Thus, Equation 9 may be written

$$k_T = k_{a1}[\text{O}_2][\text{H}^+] + k_{a2}[\text{O}_2] + k_{b1}[\text{H}^+] + k_{b2} \tag{9}$$

to summarize the observed influence of oxygen and acidity on the rate of degradation of the rag and newsprint papers at 90°C, 100% relative humidity. In this expression, $[\text{O}_2]$ is the concentration of oxygen relative to the concentration of oxygen in an atmosphere of air, and $[\text{H}^+]$ is the acidity function, $10^{-\text{pH}}$, relative to the value of $[\text{H}^+]$ at pH 4.00. Using this

Equations 6, 7, and 8 Determined Relative to the Rate in an Atmosphere of Air[a]

k_{b1}	k_{b2}	k_{a1}	k_{a2}
0.36 ± 0.05	$[0.17 \pm 0.28]$	0.32 ± 0.09	$[0.15 \pm 0.57]$
0.03 ± 0.025	0.21 ± 0.16	0.23 ± 0.06	0.53 ± 0.37
0.38 ± 0.05	$[0.0 \pm 0.2]$	0.51 ± 0.14	$[0.11 \pm 0.53]$
0.11 ± 0.02	0.21 ± 0.10	$[-0.02 \pm 0.05]$	0.70 ± 0.20

equation, relative rates of degradation at any pH under any concentration of oxygen can be estimated from the constants in Table I.

Relating Property Kinetics to Chemical Kinetics

Equation 9 is an empirically derived expression of the property kinetic rate law for yellowing and tensile strength loss in the rag and newsprint papers. Intuitively, one would suspect that a similar kinetic expression might describe the chemical processes occurring within the paper and that the constants on the right of Equation 9 reflect chemical kinetic rate constants. In the absence of an analytical expression relating the observed property, P, to the chemical concentrations undergoing change in the paper, it is not possible to derive a unique relationship between the empirical rate constant, k in Equation 1, and the chemical rate constants governing the chemical reactions in the paper. However, the general nature of such a relationship can be derived.

If the property, P, monitored in a property kinetic experiment, is a function of chemical concentrations, C_i, in the paper, then a total differential of P with respect to time can be written (*see* Equations 10 and 11).

$$P = P(C_1 \ldots C_n) \tag{10}$$

$$\frac{dP}{dt} = \sum_{i=0}^{n} \frac{\partial P}{\partial C_i} \cdot \frac{dC_i}{dt} \tag{11}$$

Strictly speaking, the concentration terms may represent amounts of particular groupings within the paper, such as amorphous cellulose, as well as discrete chemical species. The total derivatives on the right of Equation 11 are the kinetic expressions for the chemical (and perhaps morphological) changes occurring in the paper. In Equation 12, k_i is a chemical

$$\frac{dC_i}{dt} = k_i \, g(C_1 \ldots C_n) \tag{12}$$

rate constant, and $g(C_1 \ldots C_n)$ is a generalized expression of the chemical reaction order. Combining Equations 1, 11, and 12, the linear expression shown in Equation 13 is obtained. Thus, the empirical constant, k,

$$k = \sum_{i=0}^{n} a_i k_i \qquad (13)$$

$$a_i \equiv \frac{\partial P}{\partial C_i} \cdot \frac{g(C_1 \ldots C_n)}{f(P)} \qquad (14)$$

is a linear combination of chemical rate constants, k_i. The coefficients, a_i, are functions of the concentration terms, C_1–C_n.

In principle, if values of a_i could be determined n times throughout an accelerated aging experiment in which the empirical rate constant, k, is determined, then n simultaneous equations could be solved to yield the chemical rate constants, k_i. However, in practice this is not feasible, and Equation 13 is of little analytical value. Nevertheless, our assumption that the property kinetic constant, k, is related linearly to chemical rate constants is verified. Thus, the apparent linearity of the empirical rate constant, k_T in Equation 9, with respect to oxygen and acidity suggests the occurrence of chemical processes that are first order in oxygen and acidity.

Experimental

Both papers used in this study were manufactured commercially. The newsprint was a typical groundwood sheet, and the rag paper was made from 100% cotton linters. The data in Table II show the properties of the two papers prior to accelerated degradation.

Control of Acidity. The acidities of the paper samples were controlled with buffers containing various formal ratios of maleic acid to calcium hydroxide. A series of aqueous solutions of $1.3 \times 10^{-2}F$ Ca(OH)$_2$ was prepared. Maleic acid was added to each solution to achieve formal ratios ranging from zero to five. Paper samples, demineralized in dilute

Table II. Properties of the Unaged Rag Paper and Newsprint

Paper	Pulp	pH[a]	Reflectance[b] (%)	Tensile Strength (kN/m)
Newsprint	groundwood	4.5	62.3	1.92
Rag paper	100% cotton linters	6.0	95.5	10.8

[a] TAPPI cold extraction procedure.
[b] At 500 nm as described in text.

HCl, were soaked in the solutions, blotted with Whatman's #1 paper, and air dried to produce papers over the pH range shown in Figure 4. Atomic absorption studies of the buffered papers indicated that the pick-up of calcium was independent of acidity below pH 7 and increased slightly above pH 7. Average pick-ups of 19 ± 8 mg Ca per gram of rag paper and 42 ± 12 mg Ca per gram of newsprint were found. The pH values of the buffered papers remained the same throughout accelerated aging.

Sample Preparation. All paper samples were cut to 80 mm in the machine direction and 12.5 ± 0.3 mm in the cross direction. Samples were aged at 90.0 ± 0.1°C in sealed glass tubes measuring 17 mm in diameter and 130 mm in length. A relative humidity of 100% was maintained in each tube by including a milliliter of water in the base of each tube. The paper samples were held above the water by a glass pedestal. Air or nitrogen, passed through Ascarite and calcium chloride, was introduced into the tubes by evacuating to 0.1 torr, blending up to atmospheric pressure, and then sealing the tube with a torch.

Measurements. Tensile strengths were determined in the machine direction using an Instron tester with a 1.00 in. gauge length and a ram speed of 0.20 in./min. Yellowing was measured by following the change in diffuse reflectance of the paper samples at 500 nm with a Kollmorgan model D-1 integrating sphere spectrophotometer. A white tile of 86% reflectance relative to $BaSO_4$ was used as the reflectance standard. Acidity was determined by the Tappi cold extraction procedure, and atomic absorptions were performed by the Characterization Center, Carnegie–Mellon Institute of Research.

Data Analysis. Ten paper samples were sealed in each of the sample tubes to allow replicate determinations of tensile strength and reflectance. Rate constants at each pH were estimated by averaging at least three determinations for sample tubes exposed for different periods of time at 90°C. Thus, the data points shown in Figures 5–8 are averages.

Linear regressions of rate vs. $[H^+]$ were performed in the usual way. Rather than attempting an analysis of the error propagation in going from the physical measurements (tensile and reflectance) to average values of the rate constants, the data points shown in Figures 5–8 were treated as individual determinations, and only the number of degrees of freedom appropriate for the number of data points shown in each of the figures was assumed. Error limits of the slopes (k_{a1} and k_{b1}) and intercepts (k_{a2} and k_{b2}) were calculated as 95% confidence intervals from the standard deviation of the residuals in the regressions. Confidence intervals for k_{a1} and k_{a2} were calculated using a standard deviation estimated as the root-mean-square of the standard deviations of k_{a1} and k_{b1}, and of k_{a2} and k_{b2}, respectively.

Discussion and Conclusions

In the experiments described above, accelerated degradation occurred at 90°C in an atmosphere maintained at 100% relative humidity. Under this condition, both the oxygen-independent and the atmospheric oxidation processes contributed about equally to the degradation of the rag and newsprint papers. The 100% relative humidity condition allowed an examination of the influence of acidity on both processes, but whether or not the chemistry of natural aging is reproduced under this condition of accelerated degradation has not been determined. Thus, the results of these, and other, accelerated aging studies are best understood in terms of the behavior of processes that might contribute significantly to the natural aging of paper. For example, the observation that both the atmospheric oxidation and the oxygen-independent processes are pH dependent allows confidence in the prediction that natural aging will be similarly dependent on pH, regardless of which of the two processes plays the major role in room temperature degradation. In the following discussion, the conclusions regarding the aging of paper should be understood in the same perspective.

Empirical Interpretation of Results. Deacidification has become a widely practiced technique for inhibiting the degradation of papers of artistic and historical value. The justification for deacidifying such papers is based on numerous published reports that describe slowdowns in the accelerated degradation of neutralized papers. The results of the experiments described above further support deacidification as an effective means for inhibiting the aging process. However, the assumption that deacidification slows the aging of paper by decreasing the rate of hydrolysis of cellulose and other carbohydrates in the paper may be an oversimplification. The atmospheric oxidation process, which may play a significant role in natural aging, also is inhibited by a decrease in acidity.

In an earlier report (2), a ratio, i, was defined as the rate of degradation in nitrogen divided by the rate in air. This ratio represents the rela-

$$i = \frac{k_b}{k_T} \tag{15}$$

tive contribution of the oxygen-independent process to the total rate of degradation in air. Similarly, the relative contribution of the atmospheric oxidation process may be expressed as the fraction $j = 1 - i$. Our previous studies (2, 3) demonstrated that i is dependent on moisture, temperature, and the composition of the paper, and it was speculated that i may be a function of other variables. The relationship between i and acidity can be written (Equation 16) by combining Equations 6, 7, 8, and 15.

$$i = \frac{k_{b1}[H^+] + k_{b2}}{k_{a1}[H^+] + k_{a2} + k_{b1}[H^+] + k_{b2}} \tag{16}$$

This expression suggests that the relative importance of the atmospheric oxidation process may either increase, decrease, or remain unchanged as pH changes, depending on the relative values of the four rate constants in Equation 9. For example, by following the loss of tensile strength in the rag paper, it was found that k_{a2} and k_{b2} are essentially zero for both the newsprint and the rag paper between pH 3 and pH 5 (*see* Table I). Thus, the relative importance of atmospheric oxidation appears to be constant over this range of acidity.

Mechanistic Interpretation of Results. The kinetic experiments we performed have made possible an expansion of the empirical rate constant, k in Equation 1, as shown in Equation 9. However, Equation 9 is only an empirical approximation of the linear expression suggested by Equation 13, and the terms "atmospheric oxidation" and "oxygen-independent" describe experimental manifestations only. It is possible that these processes are the sum of other subprocesses and that Equation 9 might be expanded further.

Kinetic experiments, sensitive only to the slowest steps in a chemical sequence, are generally not mechanistically definitive. For example, Scheme 1 shows a mechanism that might account for the acid-sensitive oxidation suggested by k_{a1}. In this mechanism, the cellulose polymer is

Scheme 1

$$\text{Cellulose} + \text{H}_3\text{O}^+ \underset{k_{-1} \text{ (fast)}}{\overset{k_1}{\rightleftharpoons}} \text{cell}^{(+)}\text{—H}$$

$$\text{Cell}^{(+)}\text{—H} \overset{k_2[\text{O}_2]}{\underset{\text{(slow)}}{\rightarrow}} \text{oxycell}^{(+)}\text{—H}$$

$$\text{Oxycell}^{(+)}\text{—H} + \text{H}_2\text{O} \overset{k_3}{\underset{\text{(fast)}}{\rightarrow}} \text{fragments}$$

tendered slowly by an oxidation reaction, but the actual fall-apart of the polymer occurs during a rapid hydrolysis following the oxidation (*13*). Such a mechanism would manifest itself as an acid-sensitive atmospheric oxidation, $k[\text{H}^+][\text{O}_2]$. Whether or not Scheme 1 represents a mechanism that occurs during the accelerated degradation of the rag and newsprint papers cannot be determined on the basis of the kinetic results alone, and numerous other mechanistic schemes might also be written. Nevertheless, any chemical mechanism that is proposed to account for the degradation of the papers must agree with the empirical rate law of Equation 9.

Acknowledgment

This work was carried out at the Center on the Materials of the Artist and Conservator with matching grants from the National Endowment for the Arts and the Andrew W. Mellon Foundation.

Literature Cited

1. Clapp, A. F. "Curatorial Care of Works of Art on Paper," 3rd ed.; Inter-museum Conservation Association: Oberlin, Ohio, 1978; pp. 17–28.
2. Arney, J. S.; Jacobs, A. J. *Tappi* 1979, *62*(7), 89.
3. Arney, J. S.; Jacobs, A. J. *Tappi* 1980, *63*(1), 75.
4. Smith, R. D. *Libr. Q.* 1969, *39*, 153.
5. Smith, R. D. In "Design of a Liquified Gas Mass Deacidification System for Paper and Books," *Adv. Chem. Ser.* 1977, *164*, 149.
6. McBurney, L. F. "Degradation of Cellulose," *High Polym.* 1954, *5*, 142.
7. Browning, B. L.; Wink, W. A. *Tappi* 1968, *51*(4), 156.
8. Gray, G. G. *Tappi* 1969, *52*(2), 325.
9. Gray, G. G. In "Determination and Significance of Activation Energy in Permanence Tests," *Adv. Chem. Ser.* 1977, *164*, 286.
10. Frank, A. *Chem. Ztg. Chem. Appar.* 1962, *86*, 174.
11. Sizmann, R.; Frank A. *Chem. Ztg. Chem. Appar.* 1963, *87*, 347.
12. Browning, B. L. "Analysis of Paper"; Marcel Dekker: New York, 1977; pp. 169–177.
13. Graminski, E. L.; Parks, E. J.; Toth, E. E. In "The Effects of Temperature and Moisture on the Accelerated Aging of Paper," *ACS Symp. Ser.* 1979, *95*, 341.

RECEIVED October 23, 1979.

The Effect of Humectant and Wet Strength Resin on the Folding Endurance of Alkalized Paper

JOHN C. WILLIAMS

Preservation Office, Library of Congress, 10 First Street, SE, JAB G-1008, Washington, DC 20540

Paper may be deacidified to make it more permanent. Since the paper often has become brittle before it is treated, methods are needed for increasing folding endurance that may be applied in conjunction with deacidification. In this study, the effects of sorbitol and Hercules Kymene 557H on the folding endurance of three papers alkalized with magnesium carbonate are explored. A synergistic action of the reagents is apparent.

Deacidification plus the incorporation of an alkaline reserve greatly extends the life of acid paper. However, the treatment does not restore the pliability and folding endurance that have been lost. There is a need for a method that will regenerate these properties. This should be ultimately a mass method and should preferably be carried out in conjunction with one of the mass deacidification treatments presently being developed.

Review

Paper derives its principal properties from the cellulose fiber of which it is made. In comparison with many other fibers, cellulose fibers are not highly pliable or fatigue resistant. They are partly crystalline and partly amorphous and both portions are rather rigid when dry. The amorphous regions are relatively open, however, and they absorb moisture of humidity, which acts to flexibilize the fiber and the paper it forms.

Research of the last fifty years indicates that acid hydrolysis takes place in the open, amorphous regions of the cellulose fiber. Amorphous cellulose chains, once cut, proceed to crystallize. The water-holding power of the fiber drops and the fiber becomes brittle. Surprisingly, the fiber-to-fiber bond in the paper is affected less seriously as this occurs. On accelerated aging, papers even develop a certain amount of wet strength, indicating an improvement in the bond. Also, folding endurance of an acid paper given accelerated aging will drop off rapidly at a time when tensile has not yet started down, and tensile depends directly on fiber-to-fiber bond. New paper shows a fringe of fibers when it is torn; the fibers are stronger than the bonds. Old paper torn does not show the fiber fringe. The bonds are stronger than the fibers.

Hopefully, future research will be able to reverse the embrittlement of the cellulose fibers. Perhaps the cut ends of the cellulose chain can be decrystallized, and with the amorphous regions thus restored, the ends of the chains can be bonded chemically; but this has yet to be done.

Until appropriate methods can be worked out for rearranging the cellulose molecule and restoring the flexibility of the fiber, it is of interest to learn what can be accomplished by impregnating the paper with plasticizers to take full advantage of whatever flexibility is left in the fiber.

Some previous work is shown in Table I; R. D. Smith (1) impregnated the paper in a book with acrylic resin and ethyl hydroxyl–ethyl cellulose solutions to increase fold. Salz and Skrivanek (2) patented solutions of polyvinyl butyral and formal for the purpose; these materials have been supplied under the name of Regnal. Baer, Indictor, and Joel (3) compared the folding endurance of papers impregnated with Regnal,

Table I.   Increasing Folding

Paper	Fold	Treatment
Book	7.9 MD 2.8 CD	acrylic/ethyl hydroxyethyl cellulose 3–5%
Buffered sulfite	14 MD (1.5 lbs. 65% r.h., 21.1°C	in 5% Du Pont Elvamide 8016
Bond	231 MD (0.7 kg)	1% Na salt of CMC/20% glycerol
Bond	346 MD (0.7 kg)	1% Na CMC/0.25% Kymene 557
Foldur Kraft	1112 MD 1071 CD	in 5% Du Pont Elvamide 8061, pick-up 8.5%
		in 2% Kymene, 2 h, 100°C
		in sorbitol solution, 21% pick-up

with polyvinyl alcohols, and with the Du Pont polyamide Elvamide 8061. Raff and co-workers (*4, 5*) treated papers with dilute solutions of the sodium salt of carboxymethyl cellulose (CMC) as alkaline agent and binder combined. When 20% glycerol was added to the 1% CMC solution, a surprising increase was observed. Fold went from 231 to 1622. Polyethylene oxide, as the humectant, gave less spectacular results, but the improved properties were retained to a greater extent on acclerated aging. Hercules Kymene 557, a wet strength resin for paper, was added to the solution on the basis that it would keep the treated sheet from becoming sticky at high humidities. Kymene was found to act as a plasticizer. The polyethylene oxide was therefore dropped from the formula.

Hercules Kymene 557 is the cationic, water-soluble, wet strength resin, which conservators know because of its use in the manufacture of calcium carbonate filled P/D paper. In its synthesis, a condensation polymer of adipic acid and diethylene triamine is reacted with epichlorohydrin to introduce reactive epoxy groups. The behavior of Kymene in dispersed fiber has been investigated by Bates (*6, 7*).

Bates noted that cationic sites in the resins are formed by conversion of the secondary amine groups to quaternary nitrogen by alkylation with the epichlorohydrin. On addition of the resin to a fiber slurry, ion exchange reactions occur that bind the resin firmly to the fiber through surface carboxyl groups. However, his work indicated that the resin

Endurance of Paper by Impregnation

New Fold	Reference
32.3 MD 9.1 CD	Smith (*1*)
171 MD	Baer, Indictor, and Joel (*3*)
1622 MD	Raff, Herrick, and Adams (*4*)
491 MD	Raff, Ziegler, and Adams (*5*)
1936 MD 2084 CD	Library of Congress (unpublished)
1309 MD 1632 CD	Library of Congress (unpublished)
6674 MD 4216 CD	Library of Congress (unpublished)

molecule is too large to penetrate the 35–40-Å diameter capillaries of the interior of the cellulose fiber.

Kymene 557 reacts with amino groups, self reacts, reacts with thiohydril groups, and, to a minor extent, reacts with carboxyl groups. It is considered relatively inert to hydroxyl groups. The resin is more active on the acid than on the alkaline side. After aging, Kymene loses some of its humectant properties.

The present investigation is a continuation of the work initiated by the Raff group with Kymene 557 and humectants. Insight on the effect of binder and humectants in paper can be gained by considering a beater curve. As paper fiber is beaten, bonding increases in the formed sheet. Physical properties of the sheet change as beating proceeds, as shown in Figure 1. Tearing strength comes to a peak early in the beat and then drops rapidly as the result of the rigidity, which is increasing as more fiber-to-fiber bonds are formed. Folding endurance comes to a peak later, but then falls off for much the same reason.

The folding endurance curve is shown alone in Figure 2.

We do not know where a given piece of paper will be on the beating curve. If we assume a paper to be at A, addition of a bonding agent, or beating, will bring folding endurance along the curve towards B. If the papers started at B, addition of a bonding agent should, by the curve, lower folding endurance. As the fiber ages and degrades so that the curve B′ is followed, the possibility of improving folding endurance by adding binder becomes nonexistent.

Thus researchers in this field badly need a standard paper, or at least to know where the paper they are working with falls on the beater curve to properly rate the effect of a resin addition.

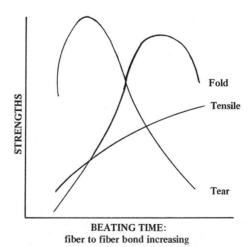

Figure 1. Generalized curves showing the effect of beating on paper properties

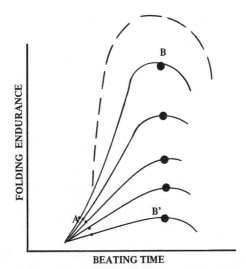

Figure 2.   The effect of beating on folding endurance of paper, with paper embrittlement on aging indicated

The curve of Figure 2 has been drawn for a given relative humidity. The folding endurance of new paper is increased by raising humidity. Crook and Bennett (8) have given curves for the change of folding endurance of new paper with humidity. A kraft paper with a fold of two hundred at 30% relative humidity has nine hundred folds at 80% relative humidity and six hundred at 90% relative humidity. The drop at the highest humidity indicates that the cellulose fiber-to-fiber bond is weakening. This effect obviously can be minimized by incorporating a wet strength resin.

By impregnating a paper with a humectant, the increase in fold can be brought down to more usual humidities. This is indicated by the broken line in Figure 2. The same reasons for using the wet strength resin exist: to preserve the fiber-to-fiber bond and to keep the sheet from becoming sticky. (There is also the possibility that a wet strength resin will keep a humectant such as sorbitol from crystallizing.)

The effect of impregnating Foldur Kraft with Kymene, with sorbitol, and with Kymene and sorbitol together is shown in Table II. The synergistic action of the two reagents on folding endurance is readily apparent.

Experimental

Further work was carried out with Foldur Kraft. However, the presence of the unusual effect was also demonstrated with GPO JCPA-60, which is the paper used in printing the *Library of Congress Information Bulletin* and Allied Superior book paper. Properties of the papers are given in Table III and the results when the papers were impregnated with Kymene and sorbitol in Table V.

Table II. Synergistic Effect of Kymene and Sorbitol on Fold

Paper	Fold 0.5 kg	Treatment	New Fold
Foldur Kraft	1112 MD 1071 CD	in 2% Kymene, 2 h, 100°C	1309 MD 1632 CD
		in sorbitol, 21% pick-up	6674 MD 4216 CD
		in 20 Kymene–80 sorbi- tol, 20% pick-up	13195 MD 7928 CD

The paper was taken from large rolls and cut into 8″ × 11″ sheets, grain long. The paper was washed two hours in Washington tap water at pH 7.5, air dried, soaked a half hour in magnesium bicarbonate solution (eight grams magnesium carbonate per liter), air dried and then oven dried.

The alkalized paper was soaked in the Kymene/sorbitol solutions for one hour, hung to drain, air dried flat on plastic screen, and then oven dried at 100°C for two hours. Kymene has a pH of 4.6–4.9. To avoid having the Kymene/sorbitol solutions reacidify the paper, they were brought to pH 7 with dilute sodium hydroxide before use.

The cured sheets were conditioned at 23°C and 50% relative humidity. MIT folding endurance was run on 1.5-cm wide strips at 0.5 kg load. Tensile was taken on the same width strip. Eight strips were run machine direction and eight cross direction . As mentioned by Raff et al. (4, 5), standard deviation and coefficient of variation were increased greatly in the treated plasticized paper; for example untreated Foldur Kraft gave:

$$MD\ 1112 \pm 173 \qquad CV = 15\%$$
$$CD\ 1071 \pm 231 \qquad CV = 21.5\%$$

while impregnated (30%) Foldur Kraft gave:

$$MD\ 43262 \pm 14021 \qquad CV = 32.4\%$$
$$CD\ 41448 \pm 19229 \qquad CV = 46.4\%$$

Curves were plotted from MD/CD averages. TAPPI brightness was read with the Photovolt Meter #670. Sheets were aged in Blue M circulating air ovens at 100°C.

Results

Foldur Kraft was dipped in 15% Kymene/sorbitol solutions made up in differing ratios. Pick-up was somewhat variable, but was around 25%, based on the final weight. The folding data is given in Table IV and plotted in Figure 3. The ratio 20 Kymene to 80 sorbitol was selected to work with.

Table III. Paper Properties

		Foldur Kraft	GPO JCPA-60	Allied Superior Book Paper
Basic weight 24 × 38 500 sheets		70 lb	50 lb	52 lb
Thickness		0.006″	0.0041″	0.0035″
Tensile 15-mm strip	MD	10.2 kg	5.7 kg	6.0 kg
	CD	5.3 kg	4.0 kg	3.0 kg
Brightness		74	78	77
pH (cold slurry)		4.8–5.1	6.1	6.2
Titration		24 meq/kg	8.0 meq/kg	10.0 meq/kg
Fiber		softwood bleached kraft	softwood bleached kraft	softwood bleached kraft
Filler (%)		8	13	25
Fold 0.5 kg	MD	1112 ± 173	704	1734 ± 221
	CD	1071 ± 231	477	980 ± 238
Fold (washed)	MD	1389 ± 203	797 ± 214	2148 ± 396
	CD	1245 ± 261	508 ± 118	1031 ± 222

The 20 Kymene/80 sorbitol solution was made up at 20% solids according to the following formula, and was used to dip the various papers. As shown in Table V, all were improved.

Wet (grams)		Dry (grams)
200	Kymene 557	20
114.3	Sorbitol	80
100	Ethanol	
85.7	Water/Alkali	
500		100
	pH 7	

A curve of folding endurance against percent impregnation with the 20 Kymene/80 sorbitol solution is shown in Figure 4. Data is in Table VI. The paper is considered usable up to about 30% pick-up. At 33% impregnation, folding endurance had gone to 49,000. The value at 60,000 (slashed point) was obtained using 40 glycerol/40 sorbitol/20 Kymene as the impregnant.

In Figure 5 and Table VII, the logarithms of folding endurances of Foldur Kraft aged in the 100°C dry oven are shown (bottom line, Figure 5) and after impregnation with the 20 Kymene/80 sorbitol solution (top line, Figure 5). Improvement in folding endurance falls off rapidly as the paper degrades. This is disappointing and negates the usefulness of the treatment because it is the very weak paper that must be improved.

Table IV. Washed Alkalized ($MgCO_3$) Foldur Kraft Dipped
in Various Ratios of Neutralized Kymene/Sorbitol

K/S Ratio	Time in 100°C Oven	Bright-ness	Thick-ness (inches)	MD	CD	% Im-preg-nation
100S	2 h	69.4	0.0078	6674	4216	21.5
	3 days	68		5038	3673	21.5
	6 days	65		3679	1986	19.8
90S/10K	2 h	69	0.0083	22114	29381	27.7
	3 days	59.7		16010	17987	27.7
	6 days	55.0		17717	10289	27.7
80S/20K	2 h	68	0.0084	24530	22960	29.2
	3 days	55.5		15798	15489	29.2
	6 days	50.2		20456	13030	29.2
70S/30K	2 h	67.2		31798	46579	31.7
	3 days	50.7		13972	5791	31.7
	6 days	39.0		9451	11598	31.7

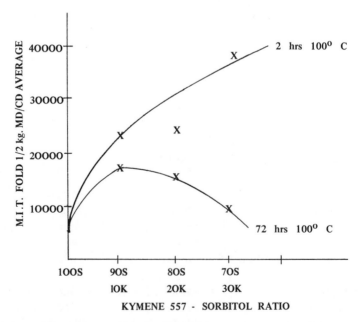

Figure 3.   The effect of the Kymene–sorbitol ratio on folding endurance;
after oven aging

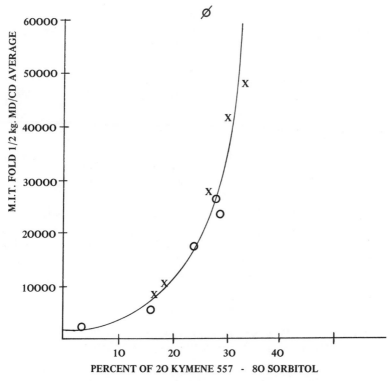

Figure 4.   The increase of folding endurance with higher impregnations

Table V.   Fold Improvement in Three Papers

	% Pick-up 20K/80S	Bright-ness	Thick-ness (inches)	Fold 0.5 kg MD	Fold 0.5 kg CD	Tensile kg MD	Tensile kg CD
Foldur Kraft							
control	0	74	0.0064	1112 ±173	1071 ±231	10.2	5.3
impregnated	30	68	0.0086	43262 ±14021	41448 ±19229	7.3	6.9
JCPA-60							
control	0	77	0.0042	704	477	5.7	4.0
impregnated	30	69	0.0058	21826	15196	5.8	4.5
Allied Superior							
control	0	78	0.0036	1735	980	6.0	3.0
impregnated	25	70	0.0052	39450	16250	5.8	4.5

Table VI. MgCO₃ Alkalized Foldur Kraft Impregnated with 20 Kymene 557–80 Sorbitol Solution, pH 5

Treat-ment (%)	Bright-ness	Thickness (in.)	Fold 0.5 kg		pH
			MD	CD	
0	74	0.0060	1338	1265	5.0
18	72	0.0077	7247	10435	5.1
20	70	0.0078	13195	7928	5.1
27	69	0.0083	24986	31926	5.1
30	68		43262	41448	5.1
33	68	0.0085	49390	48830	4.9

Kymene 557 Brought to pH 7 with Dilute NaOH Before Use

8	73	0.0070	2767	1732	8.6
17	72	0.0075	5448	6376	8.1
24	71	0.0082	19163	16549	7.4
29	68	0.0084	24530	22960	9.4

Table VII. Foldur Kraft pH 4.9 Aged in 100°C Dry Oven, Washed and Alkalized with MgCO₃

Aging Time (days)	% Kymene Sorbitol	Thick-ness (inches)	Bright-ness	Fold 0.5 kg	
				MD	CD
0	0	0.0066	74	1317	1232
3	0	0.0070	70	470	502
3.9	0	0.0064	70	362	281
5.9	0	0.0064	70	133	183
7.6	0	0.0064	71	36	93
9	0	0.0064	70	17	48
15	0	0.0064	68	2	3
15¾	0	0.0064	68	4	9

Dipped in 20% Solution, 20 Kymene 557–80 Sorbitol, Cured 2 Hours

0	30	0.0082	69	30529	16288	alk.
3	25.2	0.0080	69.6	1865	2471	acid
3.9	30.0	0.0081	67.8	1232	1060	alk.
5.9	29.1	0.0080	67.0	231	250	alk.
7.6	28.6	0.0080	66.4	92	161	alk.
7.6	31.4	0.0082	64.7	57	233	acid
9.0	27.3	0.0079	66.3	69	137	acid
15	28.8	0.0075	65.0	4.2	10.4	acid
15¾	28.8	0.0078	65.2	5.6	12.7	alk.

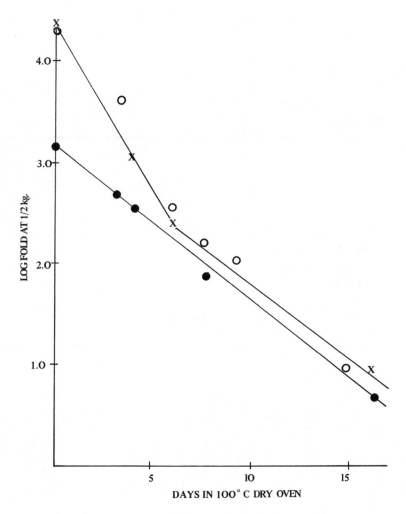

Figure 5.   The increase in folding endurance obtained with Kymene–sorbitol drops off rapidly as the paper is preaged

Observations and Conclusions

Impregiating paper with a humectant, sorbitol or glycerol, in combination with a wet strength resin with humectant properties, Kymene 557, has produced an unusually large increase in the folding endurance of new paper. The humectant action pliabilizes fiber while the wet strength resin keeps the humidified fiber-to-fiber bond intact. As the Kymene completes its cure and loses its hydrophilic character, the synergistic effect drops away.

As acid paper ages, the amorphous regions of the cellulose fiber that are plasticized by water and/or humectant tend to disappear. The sorbitol/Kymene treatment becomes ineffective with degraded paper. This suggests that somewhat the same effect would be observed between new and degraded papers when humidified. Adrian Sclawy of the Library of Congress Preservation Research and Testing Office, carried out the experiments on humidification which are reported in Chapter 16 of this volume.

The experiments reported have indicated that the methods will not rejuvenate degraded paper. On the other hand, they may make new paper more useful, and there are methods for keeping new paper from degrading. There are also procedures to prevent a thermosetting resin such as Kymene from crosslinking or losing its hydrophilicity. Including urea or amino acids in the formulation has given some success along these lines. Kymene 557 also could be reformulated to reduce the thermosetting character.

Literature Cited

1. Smith, R. D. "New Approaches to Preservation," *Libr. Q.* **1970**, *40*, 165.
2. Salz, K.; Skrivanek, L. U. S. Patent #3 698 925.
3. Baer, N. S.; Indictor, N.; Joel, A. "The Aging Behavior of Impregnated Agent—Paper Systems as Used in Paper Conservation," *Restaurator* **1972**, *2*, 5–23.
4. Raff, R. A. V.; Herrick, I. W.; Adams, M. K. "Archives Document Preservation," *Northwest Sci.* **1966**, *40*, 1–24.
5. Raff, R. A. V.; Ziegler, R. D.; Adams, M. F. "Archives Document Preservation II," *Northwest Sci.* **1967**, *41*, 184–195.
6. Bates, N. A. "Polyamide—Epichlorohydrin Wet-Strength Resin I—Retention by Pulp," *Tappi* **1969**, *52*, 1157–1161.
7. Bates, N. A. "Polyamide—Epichlorohydrin Wet-Strength Resin II—A Study of the Mechanism of Wet-Strength Development in Paper," *Tappi* **1969**, *52*, 1162–1168.
8. Crook, D. M.; Bennett, W. E. "The Effect of Humidity and Temperature on the Physical Properties of Paper," *Br. Pap. Board Makers Res. Assoc.* **1962**, (Feb.).

RECEIVED October 23, 1979.

The Effects of Varying Relative Humidity Conditions on the Folding Endurance of Aged Paper Samples

ADRIAN C. SCLAWY

Preservation Office, Library of Congress, 10 First Street, SE, TJB G-1008, Washington, DC 20540

The MIT folding endurance testing machine was used to show the effects of varying relative humidity conditions in the range of 20% to 80% on aged and unaged paper samples. The aged and unaged samples showed significant improvement of folding endurance test results when the paper was initially of a good quality. One set of Foldur Kraft paper samples was deacidified by washing in a solution of magnesium bicarbonate. The results show that the deacidification process improved the folding endurance test values.

Libraries today are filled with brittle books. Many volumes are in such bad condition that they cannot be circulated, and some can hardly be consulted. Deacidification slows the rate of degradation but does little or nothing in the way of restoring vanished physical properties.

Crook and Bennett (*1*) showed that great increases in folding endurance were obtained by humidifying new paper. The objective of this work is to learn if raising ambient humidity will restore enough pliability and fold that brittle books may again become useful. This is of particular interest with regard to deacidified papers.

Barrow (*2*) classified papers according to their folding endurance strength as follows: 1) high strength, 1000 or more folds; 2) moderate strength, 300–1000 folds; 3) low strength, 10–300 folds; 4) weak strength, 2–10 folds; 5) unusable, 1.0–0.1 fold; and 6) brittle, 0.1–0.01 fold.

Experimental

In this experiment, four types of papers were subjected to accelerated aging. The papers, Foldur Kraft, newsprint, JCPA-60 (Government Printing Office property No. 16929), and Allied Superior were placed in a

Table I.   Specifications of the Papers Used in the Experiment

Paper Sample	Pulp Composition	pH	Internal Size
Newsprint	80% ground wood, 20% bleached sulfite	5.1	unknown
Foldur Kraft[a]	90% southern pine, 10% hardwood	4.9–5.0	0.5% rosin 3.0% titanium
JCPA-60	30% bleached southern Kraft, 70% bleached hardwood Kraft	6.5	13 parts clay
Allied Superior	90% softwood bleached Kraft, 5% hardwood bleached Kraft	6.1	unknown

[a] After magnesium bicarbonate washing, the pH of the Foldur Kraft paper was 9.2 with a 1.69 alkaline reserve value.

constant humidity oven at 50% relative humidity and 90°C temperature. The specifications of the papers used in the experiment are shown in Table 1. The papers were aged at time intervals of seven, fourteen, and twenty-one days. One set of each type of paper was left unaged as a control group.

Two different sets of Foldur Kraft papers were used. One set was prewet with a solution of 1:1 denatured alcohol to distilled water and then treated with a wash of 10 g/L (1%) magnesium bicarbonate solution for thirty minutes. The other set of Foldur Kraft papers was left untreated.

After the paper samples were removed from the humid oven, they were placed in a drying oven at 100°C for one hour to remove all moisture. The samples were transferred immediately from the dry oven to specifically labeled, widemouthed, airtight containers for storage until folding endurance tests could be conducted.

Relative humidity conditions ranging from 20% to 80% with 10% increments were produced in a controlled atmosphere glove box. The temperature was held constant at 78°F throughout the experiment. Various saturated chemical solutions were used to maintain the relative humidity conditions in the glove box.

The folding endurance testing values of the paper samples were determined by using an MIT folding endurance tester. The tests were conducted at a tension of ½ kg with an angle setting of 135°. The tests were performed in the machine direction of the paper only. The ten best trials were used per sample; fifteen trials per sample were conducted, the five lowest values were dropped. The paper samples were conditioned in each relative humidity range for a period of forty-eight hours prior to conducting the folding endurance tests that were performed under the specific humidity conditions in the glove box.

Results and Discussion

1. The data in Table II show that the Foldur Kraft paper that was treated with a magnesium bicarbonate solution con-

Table II. Comparison of Aged Foldur Kraft Paper Treated with Magnesium Bicarbonate Solution with Aged Untreated Foldur Kraft Paper Under Various Relative Humidity Conditions, Average Number of Folds (MIT 1/2 kg Tension)

% RH	*Control* Treated	Un- treated	*7 Days* Treated	Un- treated	*14 Days* Treated	Un- treated	*21 Days* Treated	Un- treated
20	1291.1	973.2	430.7	1.0	413.9	1.0	307.5	0.6
30	1623.3	1052.8	523.9	1.0	457.9	0.0	416.5	0.0
40	1855.5	1122.6	832.2	1.5	907.2	0.6	820.1	0.4
50	1975.4	1203.2	1114.5	1.6	1064.9	0.5	838.5	1.3
60	4006.1	1447.1	3195.6	10.0	2374.2	0.9	1635.5	0.4
70	8412.6	1529.3	7510.6	15.0	6479.8	1.0	2274.4	0.1
80	10,521.9	1663.5	9666.4	16.9	8530.5	1.0	2592.9	0.4

sistently showed higher folding endurance test values than the untreated Foldur Kraft paper at the corresponding relative humidity ranges.

Table III is an analysis of the data in Table II. Values are expressed as the number of times that the folding endurance increased or decreased from 20% to 80% relative humidity.

2. The data in Table IV show that the folding endurance values for the control group of newsprint paper were never improved enough by exposure to the varying relative humidity conditions to reclassify them into a higher strength group than the low strength category.

There were not any significant changes in folding endurance test values by exposing the aged newsprint samples to higher relative humidity conditions. All of the aged newsprint paper samples could be placed in either the weak or unusable categories.

3. The data in Table V show that the control group for JCPA-60 paper had low strength folding endurance test values at 20% and 30% relative humidities. At 40% relative humid-

Table III. Number of Times Folding Endurance Increased for Foldur Kraft Paper Samples for the Relative Humidity Range of 20% to 80%

Control Treated	Un- treated	*7 Days* Treated	Un- treated	*14 Days* Treated	Un- treated	*21 Days* Treated	Un- treated
8.15	1.71	22.4	16.9	20.6	1.0	8.43	−0.67

Table IV.   Average Number of Folds (MIT 1/2 kg Tension) for
Aged Newsprint Paper Samples Subjected to
Varying Humidity Conditions

% RH	Control	7 Days	14 Days	21 Days
20	12.8	1.8	0.4	0.0
30	22.6	1.0	0.7	0.4
40	37.1	1.2	0.2	0.2
50	48.2	2.0	0.6	0.8
60	52.3	1.9	1.0	0.0
70	53.7	2.5	1.6	0.0
80	58.1	3.1	1.8	0.0

ity, there was a significant enough change in folding endurance test values to reclassify the paper into the moderate
strength category. At 70% and 80% relative humidities,
there was a slight decline in folding endurance but the
paper still maintained a moderate strength.

The folding endurance test values for the JCPA-60
paper aged seven days at 20%–50% relative humidities
show that the paper falls into the low strength category.
At 60% relative humidity, the paper is raised to the moderate strength category, and at 70%–80% relative humidities,
folding endurance declines and the paper is again categorized as low strength.

The data for the JCPA-60 paper aged fourteen and
twenty-one days show that for the 20%–80% relative
humidity range, the paper was of low strength. However,
the highest folding endurance values were between 50%
and 60% relative humidity.

All of the JCPA-60 papers showed an increase in folding endurance testing values up to 60% relative humidity.
A slight decline occurred for all JCPA-60 samples at 70%–
80% relative humidities.

Table V.   Average Number of Folds (MIT 1/2 kg Tension) for
Aged JCPA-60 Paper Samples Subjected to
Varying Humidity Conditions

% RH	Control	7 Days	14 Days	21 Days
20	278.2	261.4	93.8	62.8
30	294.1	282.8	129.5	66.4
40	356.2	291.6	148.3	80.3
50	550.6	293.5	249.0	136.4
60	631.3	376.4	254.2	137.9
70	582.2	222.3	137.8	96.0
80	495.8	177.7	123.8	85.9

4. The data in Table VI shows that the Allied Superior paper improved in folding endurance test values as the relative humidity was increased. This occurred in all instances except for the paper that was aged seven days and tested at 30% relative humidity.

The control group of Allied Superior paper was categorized as high strength at 20% relative humidity, and at 80% relative humidity, the folding endurance test values had increased 9.56 times.

The Allied Superior paper aged seven days at 20% relative humidity was categorized as moderate strength. At 50% relative humidity, the folding endurance had more than doubled and the paper could be reclassified as high strength.

The Allied Superior paper samples aged fourteen and twenty-one days at 20% relative humidity were classified as low strength papers. At 40% relative humidity, both groups were reclassified by the folding endurance test values. The paper sample aged fourteen days achieved high strength classification. The paper sample aged twenty-one days was reclassified as high strength at 80% relative humidity.

Table VI.   Average Number of Folds (MIT 1/2 kg Tension) for Aged Allied Superior Samples Subjected to Varying Humidity Conditions

% RH	Control	7 Days	14 Days	21 Days
20	1215.2	534.3	177.8	172.2
30	1229.2	515.5	273.9	250.6
40	1758.6	913.8	354.1	305.9
50	2516.3	1207.3	356.4	418.1
60	5012.1	2487.9	945.4	727.3
70	9504.2	4592.4	1317.2	914.3
80	11,627.0	6707.8	1502.9	1007.4

Conclusions

The results of this experiment show that folding endurance values for certain types of paper, both aged and unaged, can be improved by exposing them to atmospheres of increasing relative humidities. The use of magnesium bicarbonate solution as a deacidifying agent with Foldur Kraft paper increased the folding endurance of the paper when it was exposed to increasing relative humidity conditions.

Literature Cited

1. Crook, D. M.; Bennett, W. E. "The Effect of Humidity and Temperature on the Physical Properties of Paper," *Br. Pap. Board Ind. Res. Assoc.*, **1962**, 3.21.
2. W. J. Barrow Research Laboratory "Test Data of Naturally Aged Papers" Permanence/Durability of the Book 1964, Vol. 2, 41.

RECEIVED October 23, 1979.

17

Methods for Enhancing Ultraviolet and Radiation Grafting of Monomers to Cellulose and Derivatives to Improve Properties of Value to Conservation

NEIL P. DAVIS, JOHN L. GARNETT[1], and MERVIN A. LONG—Department of Chemistry, The University of New South Wales, Kensington, New South Wales 2033 Australia

GEOFFREY MAJOR—Art Gallery of New South Wales, Sydney, New South Wales 2000 Australia

KENNETH J. NICOL—CSIRO, Division of Food Research, North Ryde, New South Wales 2113 Australia

UV is shown to be a useful initiator for grafting styrene, methyl methacrylate, and ethyl acrylate to cellulose to incorporate improvement in the properties of value in the conservation of aged paper. To overcome homopolymerization, which severely limits the use of the last two monomers, a styrene comonomer procedure has been developed. The inclusion of organic acids in the grafting solution is shown to enhance grafting, thus reducing the total irradiation time that the cellulose is in contact with the solvent monomer solution. Analogous grafting to cellulose derivatives (i.e., the acetate) is shown to occur in the presence of ionizing radiation and to be accelerated by the presence of mineral acid. A mechanism for acid effects in both UV and gamma ray grafting procedures is proposed. Extrapolation of the present simultaneous irradiation method to more versatile, solvent free, rapid cure UV and electron beam processes for paper preservation is shown to be valid.

Copolymerization of monomers is a convenient, useful, one-step method for modifying the properties of polymers such as cellulose. Radiation

[1] Author to whom correspondence should be addressed.

possesses advantages as an initiator for such reactions, both UV (*1–7*) and ionizing radiation sources (*8–14*) being of complementary value. With cellulose, the technique is particularly attractive for improving the properties of wet and dry strength and brittleness, both of which are valuable in preservation studies of relevance to this volume. For this purpose, the simultaneous irradiation method (*13, 14, 15*) of grafting is to be preferred to the alternative of pre-irradiation (*16*). The latter procedure involves considerably greater bond rupture and chain cleavage during copolymerization (*17*) and for many aged substrates, which may already be partially degraded, any further decomposition is to be avoided if possible.

The properties capable of being incorporated into a trunk polymer depend markedly on the structure of the monomer being grafted. Thus, copolymerization of styrene to cellulose improves both wet and dry strength (*18*) while grafting of the acrylates renders the resulting paper more flexible (*18*). To achieve these improvements with styrene and the acrylates, incorporation of up to 30% of monomer usually is required (*18*). Radiation copolymerization of the acrylates to cellulose and other trunk polymers is complicated by the presence of a relatively high level of homopolymerization, which competes with grafting. Such homopolymerization is detrimental since monomer is continually being removed from the grafting solution, significantly reducing the copolymerization efficiency. Further, at high add-on (>50%), homopolymerization can be so severe as to preclude removal and purification of copolymer from the reaction mixture at the completion of the irradiation.

If the ionizing radiation technique is to be used for preservation studies, access to relatively large cobalt-60 or electron beam installations is necessary. For many research workers in the preservation field, this requirement may present logistics problems. In this respect, UV as an initiator for grafting possesses an advantage (*14*), since small scale laboratory UV facilities can be utilized without the hazards of ionizing radiation. However, with UV (especially using the simultaneous grafting method), competing homopolymerization presents an additional, unique problem not applicable to ionizing radiation systems. As homopolymerization occurs, turbidity may appear in the reaction solution, terminating the copolymerization at an early stage. Acrylates particularly are prone to such problems (*7*). A styrene comonomer technique has been developed to overcome this difficulty (*19, 20*). Even under these comonomer conditions, irradiation times could be sufficiently long for traces of homopolymer to be formed and cause turbidity in the reaction solution. Thus, any procedure for enhancing the grafting yield and hence reducing the irradiation time for copolymerization would be of value.

In this chapter, we report for the first time the use of organic acids for increasing the UV grafting yield of acrylates to cellulose using the styrene comonomer technique. Ethyl acrylate and methyl methacrylate are used as representative acrylate monomers . This comonomer procedure has the added advantage for preservation work that both styrene and the acrylate can be grafted simultaneously to incorporate into cellulose the properties representative of each monomer without using two consecutive grafting reactions to achieve this result. A mechanistic study of the fundamental aspects of the role of acid in these reactions is included, particularly possible differences between initiation by UV and ionizing radiation. For these studies, the effect of acetylating cellulose has been examined and preliminary results of a mineral acid effect for radiation grafting of styrene to cellulose acetate reported for the first time.

In terms of paper conservation, this work is of value since it is an attempt to determine: (i) if UV and EB grafting times for cellulose copolymerization can be shortened significantly by the inclusion of appropriate additives and (ii) if such a process is capable of incorporating into cellulose properties required for preservation, particularly wet and dry strength and flexibility. These studies also should indicate the feasibility of extrapolating data from the present solvent grafting systems to processes based on solvent-free, rapid-cure UV and electron beam (EB) which are the ideal polymerization conditions for preservation applications.

Experimental

Both UV and ionizing radiation grafting procedures were modifications of previously reported methods (7, 13). Monomers were purchased from Monsanto Chemicals (Australia) Limited and Polysciences Incorporated. Inhibitor was removed prior to reaction by passing the monomer down a column of activated alumina (13). All solvents were AR grade and used without further purification.

UV Procedure. Samples of cellulose (Whatman No. 41 filter paper, 5 × 4 cm) were extracted in hot appropriate solvents for 72 h prior to grafting. After 24 h preconditioning at 21°C and 65% RH, the cellulose strips were immersed completely in the monomer solution (25 mL) containing photosensitizer and held in lightly stoppered pyrex tubes. All tubes, held in a rotating rack, were irradiated at distances of 24 cm from a Phillips 90-W, high pressure, mercury vapor lamp fitted with a quartz envelope. Actinometry was performed with uranyl nitrate–oxalic acid. After irradiation, the cellulose strips were washed in the appropriate solvents and then extracted in the same solvent in a Soxhlet for 72 h to remove homopolymer. The percentage graft was the percentage increase in weight of the cellulose strip.

Homopolymerization was determined by the following modification of the Kline procedure (21). The grafting solution from the irradiation was poured into methanol (200 mL) to precipitate homopolymer and the sample tube rinsed with methanol (50 mL). Homopolymer that adhered to the polymer film and to the tube was dissolved carefully in dioxane (20 mL) and the dioxane solution added to the methanol in a beaker, together with the benzene washings from the extraction of the original film. The beaker was heated on a steam bath with frequent stirring until all polymer coagulated, the mixture cooled, filtered through a tared sintered glass crucible, washed three times with methanol (100 mL), and the crucible dried to constant weight at 60°C. The percentage homopolymer was calculated from the weight of homopolymer divided by the weight of monomer in solution. The grafting efficiency was the ratio of graft to graft plus homopolymer.

Gamma Ray Method. Cellulose acetate (powder, acetic acid content by weight, 58%) was recrystallized from an acetone solution of the polymer by the addition of 10 volumes of water; the acetate was removed by filtration and dried under vacuum. Cellulose acetate was cast into films (20 cm × 20 cm × 0.09 mm) by application of a solution in acetone (20% w/v) to glass plates using a TLC layer applicator. The films were dried at room temperature for 2 h, peeled from the plates, and cut into strips (1.5 × 4.5 cm). The strips were then dried under vacuum for 48 h.

For the grafting reactions, solutions were prepared in glass sample tubes (7.5 × 1.6 cm); solvent, sulfuric acid (to 0.2M), and monomer were added to give a total volume of 8 mL and preweighed cellulose acetate strips then were immersed completely in the solutions. Irradiations were performed in air in the spent Fuel Element Facility at the Australian Atomic Energy Commission to total doses of 2.0×10^5 rads or 1.0×10^6 rads, both at a dose rate of 1.84×10^5 rads/h. After irradiation, the grafted cellulose acetate strips were removed immediately from the monomer solutions and extracted with xylene for 24 h in a Soxhlet. The strips then were dried under vacuum for 24 h at room temperature and weighed.

Results and Discussion

Acid Effects in UV Grafting of Styrene. Since styrene is the basic monomer used in the comonomer grafting techniques to be discussed, the UV copolymerization properties of this monomer, particularly in the

Table I. UV Grafting of Styrene in Methanol to Cellulose in Presence of Organic Acids and Anhydrides (1%) [a]

					Graft % in		
Styrene (%v/v)	No Acid	Formic	Acetic [b]	Propanoic	Acetic Anhydride	Propanoic Anhydride
9	—	11	5	6	8	8
19	13	7	10 (1)	19	13	9
29	—	13	15 (1)	19	16	13
39	28	21	8 (2)	21	20	16
49	—	22	19 (2)	29	30	19
59	34	34	31 (6)	37	39	28
69	—	59	48 (7)	55	58	50
79	53	79	60 (7)	73	72	84
89	64	123	105 (17)	113	94	104

[a] In presence of uranyl nitrate (1% w/v) and irradiated for 24 h at 24 cm from 90-W high pressure UV lamp.
[b] Data in brackets, grafting without sensitizer.

presence of acid, need to be considered initially. Relevant data showing
the UV grafting of styrene in methanol to cellulose are shown in Table I,
part of which is reproduced from earlier preliminary studies (5, 22)
where uranyl nitrate was shown to be an efficient sensitizer for the reaction. Inclusion of any of the three organic acids studied enhances the
grafting appreciably, especially at the highest monomer concentrations
examined. Even the acid anhydrides, used for the first time as additives,
are almost as effective as the free acids for increasing grafting yields.
Presumably, the anhydrides are hydrolyzed readily by the residual water
in the cellulose during the course of the grafting reaction to yield the
corresponding acids, which cause the enhanced copolymerization. Consistent with previous preliminary UV grafting studies involving styrene
(5, 22), there is no Trommsdorff peak in the reaction at low monomer
concentrations, even with the anhydrides as additives.

Acid Effects in UV Comonomer Grafting of Methyl Methacrylate.
The UV grafting of methyl methacrylate dissolved in methanol to cellulose is complicated by the degree to which competing homopolymerization occurs. The problem most often encountered is the solidification

Table II.   Effect of Uranyl Nitrate Concentration in UV Grafting of
Methyl Methacrylate (30% v/v) in Methanol to Cellulose[a]

Irradiation Time (h)	Uranyl Nitrate (% w/v)	Graft (%)
1	1	29
2	1	196
3	0.5	161
3	1	296
3	3	305
3	5	58
3	7	84
3	10	36

[a] Irradiated for 24 h at 24 cm from 90-W high pressure UV lamp. Temperature of
irradiation, 50°C.

of the contents of the reaction vessel to a glassy mass, from which the
cellulose samples are difficult to extract. Under the typical conditions
used in these experiments, namely irradiation for 24 h at 24 cm from a
90-W lamp with uranyl nitrate (1% w/v) as sensitizer, all solutions containing more than 30% methyl methacrylate solidified. Thus, the studies
reported in Tables II–IV were designed to optimize methyl methacrylate
grafting conditions and also to restrict homopolymerization to manage-
able levels.

Table III.   Homopolymer Formation During UV Grafting of Methyl Methacrylate (30% v/v) in Methanol to Cellulose[a]

Irradiation Time (h)	Graft (%)	Homopolymer (%)
0.5	6	2
1.0	11	4
1.5	19	6
2.0	29	8
2.5	40	10
3.0	69	12

[a] In presence of uranyl nitrate (1% w/v) and irradiated for 24 h at 24 cm from 90-W high pressure UV lamp. Temperature of irradiation, 25°C.

These results (Table II) show that copolymerization reaches a maximum at 1%–3% uranyl nitrate. Above this concentration, homopolymer formation is severe and turbidity in the monomer solution occurs early in the grafting process. Copolymerization is much faster at 50°C than at 25°C, as is homopolymer formation (Tables II, III). To avoid the problems associated with rapid homopolymerization when uranyl nitrate is used, other sensitizers, including an organic (such as benzoin ethyl ether), were examined. The data in Table IV demonstrate that the grafting of methyl methacrylate is very low with this sensitizer, consistent with our previously reported data for copolymerization of styrene (7). There also appears to be a slight decrease in graft with increasing monomer concentration, reflecting the effect of progressive reduction in swelling of the cellulose under these conditions. Subsequent copolymerization reactions were carried out with uranyl nitrate as sensitizer at 1% concentration. Homopolymer yield increases linearly with time (Table III) at short conversions ($\simeq$ 3 h at 25°C); however, the homopolymer effect is markedly solvent dependent, since, if homopolymer is insoluble in the

Table IV.   Effect of Formic Acid on UV Grafting of Methyl Methacrylate (MMA) in Methanol to Cellulose Using BEE (1%) as Sensitizer[a]

MMA (% v/v)	Graft (%)	Graft (Formic acid)[b] (%)
40	8	6
50	10	5
60	5	10
70	5	6
80	3	4
90	2	2

[a] In presence of benzoin ethyl ether (BEE, 1%) and irradiated for 24 h at 24 cm from 90-W high pressure UV lamp.
[b] Formic acid (1% w/v) in solution.

grafting solution, turbidity becomes evident at the early stages of the reaction and grafting is terminated. Inclusion of formic acid in the reaction solution leads to marginal enhancement in copolymerization only at the 60% methyl methacrylate concentration, whereas with styrene, much larger increases in grafting yield in the presence of organic acids are observed (Table I).

From the data reported in Tables II–IV, it is apparent that the essential limitation in grafting methyl methacrylate, under the present conditions, is the degree to which competing homopolymerization occurs. In practice, the yields, especially above 50%, can be erratic and irreproducible because of this problem. The difficulty can be overcome if a styrene comonomer procedure is used (Table V), leading to high, re-

Table V. UV Grafting of Methyl Methacrylate (MMA) in Methanol to Cellulose Using Styrene Comonomer Procedure[a]

Styrene (% v/v)	MMA (% v/v)	Graft (%)
20	60	109
30	50	112
40	40	79
45	45	153
50	30	85
60	20	90
70	10	81

[a] In the presence of uranyl nitrate (1% w/v) and irradiated for 24 h at 24 cm from 90-W high pressure UV lamp.

producible grafting yields, low homopolymer formation, and good sample recovery. In preliminary experiments (23), the copolymerization yield with styrene–methyl methacrylate mixtures was found to reach a maximum at 80%–90% total monomer concentration by volume, similar to the styrene grafting alone. Thus, high total monomer concentrations (>50%) were used only for the experiments reported in Tables V and VI. As the styrene concentration in the comonomer mixture is increased, at constant total comonomer, the copolymerization yield decreases. More importantly, when formic acid (1%) is added to the reaction mixture (Table VI), high levels of graft (≃400%) are achieved readily with this additive under the same experimental conditions. This is the first report of enhancement with organic acids in UV grafting to cellulose using the comonomer procedure. A copolymerization yield of 388% was obtained with a 59% total comonomer mixture containing only 14.5% styrene and 1% formic acid. As a consequence of the styrene results (Table I), it would be predicted that any of the other organic acids previously used with the UV grafting of this monomer would be applicable to the comonomer procedure. From analogous styrene comonomer grafting experiments carried out with wool (19, 20) and polypropylene (23) as trunk polymers using two different methods of initiation, namely mineral acid and ionizing radiation from a cobalt-60 source, it is found that at low styrene concentrations in the comonomer mixture, the resulting copolymer possesses the properties essentially of the second monomer. As the proportion of styrene is increased in the comonomer mixture, copolymerization compositions are achieved where the properties of both styrene and the second monomer can be incorporated simultaneously into the cellulose. Preliminary studies on the properties of the present UV–methyl methacrylate system are consistent with these conclusions (18). The results with wool and polypropylene were checked carefully with two different techniques: a unique tritium labelling procedure and infrared spectroscopic analysis of the grafted copolymers (18, 20, 23).

Table VI. Effect of Formic Acid in UV Grafting of Methyl
Methacrylate (MMA) in Methanol to Cellulose Using
Styrene Comonomer Procedure[a]

Styrene (% v/v)	MMA (% v/v)	Graft (%)
17.5	52.5	339
14.5	44.5	388

[a] In presence of uranyl nitrate (1% w/v) and formic acid (1% w/v) and irradiated for 24 h at 24 cm from 90-W high pressure UV lamp.

Acid Effects in UV Comonomer Grafting of Ethyl Acetate. The ability to incorporate ethyl acrylate into trunk polymers is important since this monomer is known to impart significant flexibility to the resulting copolymer. Extensive work with wool (19, 20, 24), cellulose (13), and the polyolefins (25), especially with copolymerization initiated by ionizing radiation, has confirmed this conclusion. Although ethyl acrylate is not as reactive as methyl methacrylate in the current UV grafting work, it is more difficult to graft, because it readily homopolymerizes in many solvents. This leads to turbidity in the solution and very erratic and irreproducible copolymerization. Because the grafting reaction is slower than with methyl methacrylate, the turbidity effect becomes more of a problem with ethyl acrylate; thus, it is extremely difficult, a priori, to define UV conditions where a specific percentage of graft may be achieved.

The use of a styrene comonomer procedure overcomes the problems (Table VII) and leads to reproducible, uniform copolymerization. Samples from these reaction mixtures can be extracted easily from the vessel at the completion of the irradiation, even for the materials where the

Table VII. UV Grafting of Ethyl Acrylate (EA) in Methanol to Cellulose Using Styrene Comonomer Technique[a]

Styrene (% v/v)	EA (% v/v)	Graft (%)
10	30	47
12.5	37.5	44
15	45	56
17.5	52.5	55
20	60	77
22.5	67.5	125

[a] In presence of uranyl nitrate (1% w/v) and irradiated for 24 h at 24 cm from 90-W high pressure UV lamp.

graft is over 100%. The amount of copolymer achieved for ethyl acrylate by this procedure is still lower than that obtained with methyl methacrylate. Moreover, addition of formic acid (1%, Table VIII) leads to the predicted increase in grafting yield as expected from the preceding methyl methacrylate data; however, the actual level of copolymer is still considerably lower than for comparable methyl methacrylate systems.

Acid Effects in Gamma Ray Grafting to Cellulose Acetate. Of fundamental importance to general acid effects in UV and ionizing radiation grafting to cellulose, is a study of analogous reactions with cellulose that has been acetylated. The possible use of acid additives to reduce irradiation times in cellulose acetate copolymerization has not previously been investigated, although extensive radiation grafting using the simultaneous (*15, 17*) and pre-irradiation (*17*) techniques has been reported. The experiments in this section thus involve gamma irradiation initiation with acid additives to show that ionizing radiation can be a viable alternative to UV for these studies.

Table VIII. Effect of Formic Acid in UV Grafting of Ethyl Acrylate (EA) in Methanol to Cellulose Using Styrene Comonomer Technique[a]

Styrene (% v/v)	EA (% v/v)	Graft (%)
10	10	28
15	15	44
20	20	53
25	25	66
30	30	71
35	35	91
40	40	113
45	45	200

[a] In presence of uranyl nitrate (1% w/v) and irradiated for 24 h at 24 cm from 90-W high pressure UV lamp.

Table IX. Gamma Ray Grafting of Styrene to Cellulose Acetate at Low Dose in Alcohols[a]

Styrene (% v/v)	Methanol	Ethanol	n-Propanol	n-Butanol
20	20.9	16.6	15.5	6.4
30	24.5	30.1	25.9	8.6
40	25.0	41.6	34.6	12.5
60	19.0	42.7	40.5	22.8
80	27.5	44.4	41.4	10.4

[a] Irradiation at dose rate of 1.84×10^5 rads/h to a total dose of 2.0×10^5 rads.

The data in Table IX show that styrene in methanol is grafted readily to cellulose acetate when a gamma ray dose rate of 1.84×10^5 rads/h is used to a total dose of 2.0×10^5 rads. Copolymerization is marginally highest in ethanol and gradually decreases to n-butanol. A Trommsdorff effect is observed only in n-butanol (at 60% monomer concentration), the results with the other three alcohols being consistent with that observed previously with unacetylated cellulose at the dose and dose-rate used. As with cellulose (13), the data show the dose and dose-rate dependence for the appearance of the Trommsdorff peak. Addition of $2.0 \times 10^{-1}M$ H_2SO_4 leads to slight increases in grafting yields for the first three alcohols studied (Table X) at certain monomer concentrations. In methanol, addition of acid leads to the observation of a Trommsdorff peak in grafting at 30% monomer concentration.

Table X. Effect of Acid on Gamma Ray Grafting of Styrene to Cellulose Acetate at Low Dose in Alcohols[a]

Graft (%) in $2.0 \times 10^{-1}M$ H_2SO_4 in

Styrene (% v/v)	Methanol	Ethanol	n-Propanol	n-Butanol
20	22.7	17.6	13.8	3.2
30	28.2	31.2	22.0	7.6
40	20.9	36.2	31.2	8.9
60	19.9	49.9	45.8	19.6
80	17.3	45.6	49.5	9.7

[a] Irradiation at dose rate of 1.84×10^5 rads/h to a total dose of 2.0×10^5 rads.

When the total radiation dose is increased to 1.0×10^6 rads (Table XI) at the same dose rate as previously, significant gel peaks appear at 20%–40% monomer concentrations in all nonacidified alcohol solutions. Addition of acid leads to an enhancement in these Trommsdorff peaks for the first three alcohols studied. When dimethyl formamide is used as solvent at 2.0×10^5 rads, a Trommsdorff peak is observed at 60% styrene concentration, the intensity of this peak being increased by the inclusion of H_2SO_4 ($2.0 \times 10^{-1}M$). In the chlorinated methanes, the order of copolymerization reactivity is $CH_2Cl_2 > CHCl_3 > CCl_4$, indicating the beneficial effect of hydrogen atoms in the solvent molecule and, thus, the

Table XI. **Effect of Acid on Gamma Ray Grafting of Styrene Cellulose Acetate at High Dose in Alcohols[a]**

Graft % in

Styrene (% v/v)	Methanol[b]		Ethanol[b]		n-Propanol[b]		n-Butanol[b]	
20	126.6	—	69.9	—	45.5	—	24.5	—
30	58.2	74.7	158.0	209.5	75.4	95.1	28.0	24.4
40	35.3	—	69.1	—	85.0	—	82.7	—
60	25.3	23.0	37.0	35.3	47.5	59.3	62.2	31.6
80	27.4	—	32.2	—	40.4	—	35.1	—

[a] Irradiation at dose rate of 1.84×10^5 rads/h to a total dose of 1.0×10^6 rads.
[b] Second column in $2.0 \times 10^{-1}M$ H_2SO_4.

possible role of hydrogen atoms as radiolytic intermediates in the grafting process (*13*). In the simple aromatic hydrocarbons, no grafting is observed under the radiation conditions used, presumably reflecting the relatively poor swelling properties of these solvents on the cellulose acetate (Table **XII**).

Table XII. **Effect of Acid on Gamma Ray Grafting of Styrene to Cellulose Acetate in Miscellaneous Solvents[a]**

Graft % in

Styrene (% v/v)	DMF[b]		Methylene Chloride	Chloroform	Carbon Tetrachloride	Benzene	Toluene	p-Xylene
20	8.3	8.0	3.3	0	0	0	0	0
30	—	—	5.6	5.5	0	0	0	0
40	14.2	10.0	6.6	10.4	0	0	0	0
60	20.1	22.0	20.1	25.7	0	0	0	0
80	0	3.0	26.8	3.8	0	0	0	0

[a] Irradiation at dose rate of 1.84×10^5 rads/h to total dose of 2.0×10^5 rads.
[b] Second column in $2.0 \times 10^{-1}M$ H_2SO_4.

Mechanism of Acid Effect in Cellulose UV Comonomer Grafting Procedure. In the earlier work (*7*) involving the UV grafting of monomers to cellulose, it was shown that radical sites, where copolymerization can occur, are formed in cellulose either by the direct action of UV on the trunk polymer or as a consequence of the presence of sensitizer. With uranyl nitrate, this sensitizer absorbs UV, then creates grafting sites in the trunk polymer by two predominant processes: intermolecular hydrogen atom abstraction and energy transfer. Using methanol as solvent, intermolecular hydrogen abstraction can lead to styrene grafting in several ways. In solvent methanol, radicals can be formed according to Equations 1 and 2.

$$UO_2{}^{2+} + h\nu \rightarrow (UO_2{}^{2+})^* \tag{1}$$

$$(UO_2{}^{2+})^* + CH_3OH \rightarrow CH_3O\cdot + H^+ + UO_2{}^+ \tag{2}$$

These solvent radicals then can yield grafting sites in cellulose by hydrogen abstraction (Equation 3, CeH = cellulose).

$$CH_3O\cdot + CeH \rightarrow CH_3OH + Ce\cdot \tag{3}$$

In a similar manner, sensitizer can diffuse into the alcohol-preswollen cellulose and either directly abstract hydrogen atoms (Equations 1 and 4) or rupture bonds as shown in Equation 5 to form additional copolymerization sites.

$$(UO_2{}^{2+})^* + CeH \rightarrow UO_2{}^+ + H^+ + Ce\cdot \tag{4}$$

Direct action of UV on cellulose also can lead to radical site formation, although the yields are relatively small. In terms of this model, small solvent molecules such as methanol, which can wet and swell cellulose and also readily diffuse into the trunk polymer, are attractive for UV grafting. In addition to radical processes in copolymerization, energy transfer involving species such as $(UO_2{}^{2+})^*$ has been proposed (7) as being involved in the grafting mechanism; however, contributions from these species are considered to be minimal. Once radicals have been formed in both grafting solution and trunk polymer, it is suggested that the final steps in the copolymerization reaction occur via the charge-transfer concepts already discussed in detail elsewhere (7, 13) and briefly summarized in Equations 6–9. Using styrene as representative monomer, initial π-complex formation occurs between styrene and the radical sites in cellulose (Equation 6). From this intermediate charge-transfer complex, specific grafting mechanisms can be proposed (Equations 7–9).

$$2\overset{\cdot}{P} + \bigcirc\!\!-CH=CH_2 \longrightarrow \bigcirc\!\!-CH{-}CH_2 \qquad (6)$$

$$\bigcirc\!\!-CH=CH_2 + \overset{\cdot}{P} \longrightarrow \bigcirc\!\!-CH=CH_2 \qquad (7)$$

$$\bigcirc\!\!-CH=CH_2 \longrightarrow \left[\; \right] \longrightarrow \bigcirc \qquad (8)$$

$$\bigcirc\!\!-CH{=}CH_2 \longrightarrow \bigcirc\!\!-\overset{\cdot}{C}H{-}\overset{\cdot}{C}H_2 \xrightarrow[\substack{R=M \text{ or } R=H \\ \text{grafting if } R=M}]{+ R} \bigcirc\!\!-\overset{H}{\underset{\overset{\cdot}{P}}{C}}{-}CH_2R \qquad (9)$$

The significance of radical formation in the trunk polymer in UV grafting is apparent when the effect of temperature on the copolymerization reaction is studied (Tables II and III). The increase in rate with increasing temperature parallels analogous data obtained using ionizing radiation intitiation (*26*). In the latter system, the increased graft at the higher temperature was attributed to the greater mobility of the trapped radicals. A similar explanation can be advanced to explain the present UV results, although the magnitude of the effect should be less for UV grafting since this type of radiation does not penetrate the backbone polymer as does gamma radiation. Thus, the concentration of trapped radicals formed by direct irradiation will be lower in the UV system. Free radicals may be generated within the substrate by excited photosensitized molecules, but this is limited by the degree to which substrate is swollen and therefore accessible to those molecules.

In this respect, the use of organic sensitizers, such as benzoin ethyl ether, in radical formation in this work is interesting. This sensitizer exhibited poor grafting efficiency when compared with uranyl nitrate; however, benzoin ethyl ether is very effective for initiating UV grafting to synthetic trunk polymers such as the polyolefins (*27*). It, thus, appears that sensitizers such as UO_2^{2+}, which can complex readily with the hydroxyl groups of the cellulose, are more effective than the less polar organic equivalents for the cellulose system.

The addition of organic acids or anhydrides to the grafting solution enhances the yields, especially above 50% monomer concentration. If the data in Table I are graphed (Figure 1), the percentage graft curves for the three carboxylic acids converge and become virtually parallel.

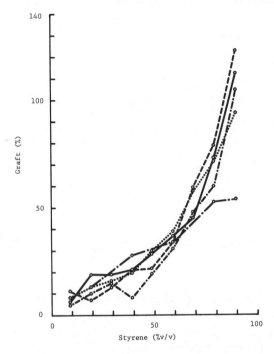

Figure 1. Grafting of styrene in methanol to cellulose with uranyl nitrate (1%) for 24 h at 24 cm from 90-W lamp using the following additives (1%): (– – –) formic acid; (——) propanoic acid; (– · – ·) acetic acid; (· · ·) acetic anhydride; (— · —) no additive

The similarity in the shape of these curves indicates that the grafting mechanism is the same for all acids studied. Additional experiments (23) show that very little (≈3%) copolymer is formed in the absence of UV when cellulose is stored in the presence of acid, with or without photosensitizer. Acid addition to the solvent without photosensitizer also can initiate grafting to cellulose upon irradiation (Table I); however, under these conditions, grafting is only appreciable at 90% monomer concentration and is only a fraction of that produced by a combination of photosensitizer and acid. Thus, acid appears to be acting in consort with light to improve the yield of copolymer. The fact that organic acids alone (Table I) can sensitize these grafting reactions, although much less efficiently than uranyl nitrate, suggests that their enhancement effect is attributable to a synergistic action involving direct absorption of UV. Preliminary experiments (23) also show that mineral acids can achieve a similar effect; thus, acid enhancement in grafting appears to be a general phenomenon.

The mineral acid results also suggest the simultaneous participation of further mechanisms in general acid enhancement grafting with cellulose, particularly possible inducement of physical changes in the cellulose itself. For example, the presence of acid is known to have a catalytic effect on the hydroysis of cellulose leading to the breaking of chains and the creation of further grafting sites during hydrolysis; the cellulose chains also are known to uncoil (*28*) allowing better access of monomer to copolymerization sites. The intermediate complex in this hydrolysis reaction is considered to be the protonated glycosidic bond (*29*). Irradiation of the system causes excitation of this complex and subsequent rupture of this bond (Equation 10).

$$
\underset{H}{\overset{H}{\big\rangle}} \kern-0.3em \overset{O}{\underset{+}{\big|}} \kern-0.3em K \longrightarrow \left[\underset{H}{\overset{H}{\big\rangle}} \kern-0.3em \overset{O}{\underset{+}{\big|}} \kern-0.3em K \right]^{*} \longrightarrow \big\rangle \kern-0.3em \overset{O}{\big|} + \ K + H^{\cdot} \tag{10}
$$

It is also known that chemical and physical abnormalities in the cellulose molecule can produce weak bonds (*30, 31*); thus, structural abnormalities may set up strain at localized points. At such positions, the rate constants for hydrolysis may be increased by as much as 10,000 (*31*). In the presence of acid, these properties would be enhanced and would assist UV grafting. Such a mechanism may even be the predominant process by which acid accelerates UV grafting.

The preceding discussion relates to the effect of acid on the grafting of a single monomer, like styrene. In the comonomer procedure, simultaneous grafting of styrene and a second monomer (e.g., ethyl acrylate) must be considered. From analogous studies with grafting to wool and the polyolefins (*32*), evidence is accumulating in these comonomer reactions to show that the monomer other than styrene (i.e., ethyl acrylate) initially is absorbed more strongly at the grafting site, presumably as a π-olefin type complex (Equation 11). A donor–acceptor interaction in-

$$
CH_2{=}CH{-}\underset{O}{\overset{\|}{C}}{-}O{-}C_2H_5 + \dot{P} \rightarrow CH_2{=}CH{-}\underset{\dot{P}}{\overset{\downarrow}{\big|}} \quad \underset{O}{\overset{\|}{C}}{-}C_2H_5 \tag{11}
$$

volving the carbonyl group may also assist this adsorption process. In this context, styrene may act as a carrier. That is, styrene and ethyl acrylate form a primary complex that migrates to a grafting site where the ethyl acrylate is adsorbed preferentially and grafts. Data to support this mechanism originates from analogous grafting studies with wool and polyolefin systems (*20, 32*) where the composition of the graft copolymer has been analyzed. When the mixed monomer grafting solution contains relatively low percentages of styrene (10%–20%), higher percentages of the second, more polar monomer are incorporated into the graft copolymer than predicted by the copolymerization equation (*33*). For example, in grafting ethyl acrylate to wool using the styrene comonomer procedure, with monomer mixtures containing 90% ethyl acrylate, 97% of the 9.4% graft is ethyl acrylate (*20, 23*). Preliminary experiments with grafting to cellulose by the present procedures indicate that similar trends in reactivity would be expected (*23*). The acid enhancement effect for the comonomer system, mechanistically, also would be similar to that already proposed for analogous acid effects in grafting with solutions containing only one monomer species (*19, 32, 34, 35*).

Mechanism of Acid Effect in Cellulose Acetate Grafting. This work is of significance to the mechanism of the preceding UV cellulose system, since the cellulose acetate grafting reactions were carried out with ionizing radiation initiation, and mineral acids are known to accelerate grafting to styrene using these sources with cellulose, whereas organic acids are not as effective under these radiation conditions (*36*). Cellulose acetate is also more soluble in organic solvents than cellulose; thus, its copolymerization behavior may resemble more closely that of the synthetic trunk polymers than of cellulose itself (*17, 37*).

Mechanistically, the grafting characteristics of cellulose acetate are similar to cellulose, especially when mineral acid is included in the grafting solution with ionizing radiation initiation. The data suggest that radiolytically produced hydrogen atoms may influence the reaction pathway. Thus, with the chlorinated hydrocarbon solvents (Table XII), the presence of protons in these solvent molecules is necessary to achieve any grafting under the conditions of irradiation used. Addition of acid to the low molecular weight alcohols (i) induces a gel peak (Table X) or (ii) enhances the intensity of the Trommsdorff effect if it is already present (Table XI). The results clearly demonstrate that additional grafting pathways exist for ionizing radiation systems when compared with the corresponding UV processes, reflecting the ionic nature of the radiation in the former system. With ionizing radiation, a pool of secondary electrons and ions exist as intermediates in the reaction. In the presence of acid, these secondary electrons can interact with the protonated solvent species shown in Equation 12 to produce additional hydrogen atoms capable of initiating further grafting. As proposed previously for radiation copolymerization to cellulose (*32*), the polyolefins (*35*), and PVC (*34*), acid also may affect the stability of the intermediate charge-transfer complex in the grafting process leading to changes in the ultimate reaction pathway for the copolymerization.

$$CH_3OH_2^+ + e \rightarrow CH_3OH + H\cdot \qquad (12)$$

Significance of Present Grafting Studies in Conservation.   In terms of preservation of cellulosic art treasures, this work demonstrates that UV and ionizing radiation sources can be used to copolymerize the relevant monomers to cellulose and derivatives to incorporate the properties necessary for paper conservation purposes. In practical terms, the actual technique used for these experiments, namely the simultaneous irradiation procedure, is only of limited value for paper preservation work since the process is time consuming and requires solvent to achieve maximum efficiency in copolymerization. The ultimate stage in the development of these processes for this current application is to remove solvent and convert the procedure to sensitized UV or EB rapid-cure methodology, where polymerization is achieved in less than one second. Preliminary experiments by the present authors (38, 39) show that this extrapolation is valid and there is every indication that the monomer grafting techniques reported in these studies can be converted into analogous solvent free, rapid-cure, UV and EB systems to incorporate the necessary preservation properties into aged cellulosics. Most importantly, the UV and gamma radiation work reported in this chapter has been necessary to show that radiation techniques under ideal conditions are capable of incorporating the appropriate properties into paper for conservation purposes. Thus, there is the incentive to develop the process further to the point where simple, cheap, efficient, laboratory scale UV lamps can be used for such treatments without the complications of processing in the presence of solvents. Ionizing radiation EB sources can be used for the same objective; however, such facilities are expensive and technically more complex. Recourse to the EB procedure would appear to be necessary only if residual sensitizer in copolymerized polymer from the analogous UV process were a problem in the conservation of the final product. In this respect, reversibility of the polymerized monomer also may be a determining factor in the choice of radiation initiator used for a particular preservation problem (38, 39).

Acknowledgments

The authors thank the Australian Institute of Nuclear Science and Engineering and the Australian Atomic Energy Commission for the irradiations. They are also grateful to the Australian Research Grants Committee for continued support. One of them (N.P.D.) wishes to thank Sidney Cooke Chemicals Pty. Ltd. for the award of a Fellowship.

Literature Cited

1. Geacintov, N.; Stannett, V.; Abrahamson, E. W. *Makromol. Chem.* **1960**, *36*, 52.
2. Oster, G.; Yang, N. L. *Chem. Rev.* **1968**, *68*, 125.
3. Kubota, H.; Murata, T.; Ogiwara, T. *J. Polym. Sci.* **1973**, *11*, 485.

4. Arthur, J. C., Jr. *Polym. Preprints* **1975**, *16*, 419.
5. Davis, N. P.; Garnett, J. L.; Urquhart, R. G. *J. Polym. Sci.* **1976**, *55*, 287.
6. Tazuke, S.; Kimura, H. *Polym. Lett.* **1978**, *16*, 497.
7. Davis, N. P.; Garnett, J. L. "Modified Cellulosics"; Rowell, R. M.; Young, R. A., Eds.; Academic Press: New York, 1978; p. 197.
8. Krassig, H. A.; Stannett, V. T. *Adv. Polym. Sci.* **1965**, *4*, 111.
9. Moore, P. W. *Rev. Pure Appl. Chem.* **1970**, *20*, 139.
10. Arthur, J. C., Jr. In "Properties of Graft and Block Copolymers of Fibrous Cellulose," *Adv. Chem. Ser.* **1971**, *99*, 321.
11. Guthrie, J. T.; Haq, Z. *Polymer* **1974**, *15*, 133.
12. Nakamura, Y.; Schimada, M. In "Cellulose Chemistry and Technology," *ACS Symp. Ser.* 1977, *48*, 298.
13. Garnett, J. L. In "Cellulose Chemistry and Technology," *ACS Symp. Ser.* 1977, *48*, 334.
14. Garnett, J. L. *Proc. 2nd Inter. Meet. Radiat. Process., Miami Beach, 1978*, in press.
15. Chapiro, A. "Radiation Chemistry of Polymeric Systems"; Interscience: New York, 1962.
16. Dilli, S.; Garnett, J. L. *Aust. J. Chem.* **1971**, *24*, 981.
17. Wellons, J. D.; Stannett, V. T. *J. Polym. Sci. Part A* **1965**, *3*, 847.
18. Garnett, J. L.; Levot, R., unpublished data.
19. Garnett, J. L.; Kenyon, R. S. *Polym. Lett.* **1977**, *15*, 421.
20. Garnett, J. L.; Leeder, J. D. In "Textile and Paper Chemistry and Technology," *ACS Symp. Ser.* 1977, *49*, 197.
21. Kline, G. M. "Analytical Chemistry of Polymers"; Interscience: New York, 1966; Part 1.
22. Davis, N. P.; Garnett, J. L.; Urquhart, R. G. *Polym. Lett.* **1976**, *14*, 537.
23. Ang, C. H.; Davis, N. P.; Garnett, J. L., unpublished data.
24. Williams, J. L.; Stannett, V. T. *Polym. Lett.* **1970**, *8*, 711.
25. Garnett, J. L.; Yen, N. T., unpublished data.
26. Dilli, S.; Garnett, J. L.; Martin, E. C.; Phuoc, D. H. *J. Polym. Sci. Part C* **1972**, *37*, 57.
27. Garnett, J. L.; Levot, R. In "Polymeric Materials and Pharmaceuticals for Biomedical Use," *ACS Symp. Ser.*, in press.
28. Vitol, Y. V.; Odintsov, P. N. *Vysokomol. Soedin. Ser. B,* **1969**, *11*(2), 83.
29. Sharples, A., "High Polymers"; Bikales, N.; Segal, L., Eds.; Interscience: New York, 1971; Vol. 5, p. 991.
30. Ranby, B. G.; Marchessauer, R. H. *Sven. Papperstidn.* **1959**, *62*, 230.
31. Sharples, A. *J. Polym. Sci.* **1954**, *14*, 95.
32. Ang, C. H.; Davids, E. L.; Garnett, J. L.; Schwarz, T. "Photoinitiated Grafting and Curing Processes for Cellulosic, Paper and Textile Products," presented at the *176th Natl. Meet. Am. Chem. Soc., Miami Beach, FL, Sept., 1978.*
33. Odian, G.; Rossi, A.; Ratchek, E.; Acker, T. *J. Polym. Sci.* **1961**, *54*, 511.
34. Barker, H.; Garnett, J. L.; Levot, R.; Long, M. A. *J. Macromol. Sci. Chem.* **1978**, *A 12*, 261.
35. Garnett, J. L.; Yen, N. T. *Aust. J. Chem.* **1979**, *32*, 585.
36. Garnett, J. L.; Phuoc, D. H.; Airey, P. L.; Sangster, D. F. *Aust. J. Chem.* **1976**, *29*, 1459.
37. Bentvelzen, J. M.; Kimura-Yeh, F.; Hopfenberg, H. B.; Stannett, V. *J. Appl. Polym. Sci.* **1973**, *17*, 809.
38. Garnett, J. L.; Major, G. *Paper Conserv. News* **1979**, *10*, 2.
39. Garnett, J. L.; Major, G. *Inst. Conserv. Cultural Material Bull.* **1979**, *S*(2), 49.

RECEIVED October 23, 1979.

18

The Impact of Increasing Paper Consumption and Resource Limitations on Alkaline Papermaking

R. W. HAGEMEYER

J. M. Huber Corporation, 6855 Jimmy Carter Blvd., NW, Building V, Suite 2300, Norcross, GA 30071

Despite moderation from historical growth rates, world demand for paper is expected to more than double within the next twenty-one years. Forecasts place consumption in the year 2000 at between 350 and 450 million metric tons. Under static conditions, this volume would relate to a corresponding increase in the various elements required to produce it. Conditions will be far from static with significant changes forecast in the cost of fiber, water, energy, chemicals, machinery, and capital. During the period, fiber and energy are expected to double in real cost, while the price of water for a grass-roots location is forecast to triple. These factors will create an increasing economic incentive to utilize systems that conserve the various inputs. Alkaline papermaking with its potential savings in fiber, energy, water, and chemicals is a practical and proved option. A significant additional benefit is the accompanying improvement in paper permanence.

A century ago, the rapid rise in printing paper consumption was creating a growing shortage of the traditional rag and linen papermaking fibers. This situation prompted the development of alternate materials and procedures for book paper production. Unfortunately, in the process, an undesirable side effect crept in; namely, there was a reduction in the permanence of high-quality book paper. The significance of this deficiency was not recognized widely until about 1950 when the

0065-2393/81/0193-0241$05.00/0
© 1981 American Chemical Society

Library of Congress and others started having problems with paper fragility in many of their so-called permanent reference books. Subsequent investigations determined the reduced permanence resulted from a combination of two factors, the use of wood as a source of cellulose fiber coupled with acid papermaking and sizing systems.

Today, the forecast of increased paper consumption and a continued tightening in the fiber supply are again prompting some substantive changes in papermaking procedures. Fortunately, for those interested in paper durability, a desirable side effect for high quality book papers will be a return to the permanence levels of a century ago. The underlying technical factor is a move to neutral and alkaline papermaking systems both to conserve fiber and to achieve water, energy, and chemical savings. For brevity, since the two processes are similar, subsequent reference to alkaline systems will include neutral systems as well.

In this chapter, the outlook for paper consumption to the year 2000 will be reviewed. Even the most conservative projections indicate the volume will more than double from present levels. The more optimistic forecasts project a tripling in consumption. Recognizing the finite limitations of the earth's resources, finding adequate quantities of the various raw materials needed to meet this doubling or tripling in demand poses a significant challenge.

Following the general law of supply and demand, most raw material prices are expected to escalate at a rate exceeding that of general inflation. Specific projections for fiber, water, energy, and chemicals will be discussed. Concurrent with the increase for raw materials, the real price of paper will rise to recover the higher raw material costs. There will be a steadily increasing incentive to conserve materials and thus minimize the escalation in paper prices. Failure to achieve this could result in paper pricing itself out of some of its present markets.

One practical method for conserving fiber, water, and energy is to make paper under neutral or alkaline conditions. A few papermills have already made the conversion from acid systems and many more are expected to follow.

Some of the advantages to be gained and problems to be overcome will be cited. Making the change from acid to alkaline systems is not as simple as it might seem. In spite of the problems, as the economic incentives continue to grow, there will be a corresponding growth in the number of conversions.

Paper Consumption Outlook

As mentioned previously, the consumption of paper and paperboard is expected to more than double and possibly triple within the next twenty-one years. The sharp drop in volume accompanying the 1975 recession has caused a reassessment of the projected growth rate. Most forecasters agree that the rate at which volume escalates will moderate from the 1960–1975 average of five percent annually. All agree that total consumption will continue to grow, but there is considerable disagreement on the rate at which it will grow.

To illustrate the divergence of opinion, as well as the departure from the prerecession trend line, four forecasts are compared. The reference forecast is "Outlook for Pulp and Paper Consumption, Production and Trade to 1985," published by the Food and Agriculture Organization of the United Nations (FAO) Secretariat in 1972 (*1*). Five years later, FAO published "World Paper and Paperboard Consumption Outlook," by an Industry Working Party (IWP) (*2*), and "Demand, Supply and Trade in Pulp and Paper: Trends and Prospects to 1990" (*3*). Finally, a composite forecast (CF) was prepared by compiling information from several sources outside the paper industry. While the composite has the disadvantage of being prepared from a disjointed set of figures, this is offset partially by the benefit of an external viewpoint.

The three FAO forecasts are very comprehensive in scope with a corresponding amount of documentation. Projections by the Secretariat are built on historical trends with modifications for expected changes in population, income, literacy, and price. The Industry Working Party forecast is much more subjective and reflects the collective opinion of ten industry specialists and ninety-eight operating executives worldwide. This forecast includes both subjective and mathematical predictions.

An important factor to remember when comparing these forecasts is the business environment under which they were made. The reference forecast was prepared during 1971, when world paper demand had been expanding at five percent annually for more than a decade. By contrast, the forecasts published in 1977 were prepared in the wake of the strong cyclical disturbance caused by the 1975 recession. In the case of the composite forecast, most of the projections were made in 1978. All the forecasts have been extrapolated to 2000 using the prevailing growth rate for the last five-year period.

Looking first at the differences in the percentage growth, using 1975 volume as the index point, the expected increases are shown in Table I.

Table I. **World Paper and Paperboard Consumption**
(1975 = 100)

		1980	*1985*	*1990*	*2000*
FAO	1972	146	183	231	373
IWP	1977	126	152	180	253
FAO	1977	127	156	196	316
CF	1978	126	159	195	297

All the post-recession projections anticipate slower growth with the reduction ranging between fifteen and twenty-seven percent. However, even the most conservative forecast indicates consumption will more than double during the next twenty-one years. The actual tonnages represented in these percentages are shown in Table II.

Table II. World Paper and Paperboard Consumption in Millions of Tons (Metric)

		1980	*1985*	*1990*	*2000*
FAO	1972	207	260	328	530
IWP	1977	180	216	256	360
FAO	1977	182	223	280	452
CF	1978	179	227	278	422

These figures are for total consumption worldwide. The expected volumes for specific types of paper and for the various geographic regions are presented in the FAO reports. The outlook for the printing and writing grades, which include book papers, is somewhat better than the average. All of these projections call for a substantial expansion in production capacity as well as a corresponding increase in raw material demands. Recognizing the finite limitations of the earth's resources and the present demands thereon, procuring adequate quantities of suitable raw materials at an affordable cost could be the determinant of future growth in paper volume.

Raw Material Outlook

The following projections for key papermaking raw materials were developed by the Future Technical Needs and Trends (TNT) Committee of the Technical Association of the Pulp and Paper Industry (TAPPI) (4). Periodically, the Committee prepares long-range forecasts covering important papermaking and related activities. This serves the dual purpose of pointing out areas wherein new technology will be needed and providing the lead time for its orderly development. From a recent review of the raw materials outlook, it appears there should be adequate quantities available but at a substantial increase in their "real" cost. The expected price escalation is shown in Table III.

These are average figures and may vary significantly depending upon regional situations. For example, the cost of water from local surface sources should not increase much in real dollars. On the other hand, where mining, desalination, or lengthy transport is involved, the cost will be markedly higher than from what is presently a very low base. The accelerated increase in the final ten years reflects the nearing of supply limits.

Table III.   Raw Material Price Index

	1977	1980	1990	2000	%/Year
Fiber	100	109	140	190	2.8
Water	100	120	180	300	4.9
Energy	100	110	140	200	3.1
Chemicals	100	105	120	140	1.5

Regarding specific materials, fiber is a renewable resource, thus the total supply can be regulated. Unfortunately, most methods for increasing its availability, such as the harvesting of remote areas and more intensive timber management, add to its total cost. Further restrictions on the removal of timber from public lands and, in some regions, the probable allocation of a substantial acreage of arable land for agricultural use are factors that could further limit supply.

On the demand side, by the year 2000, the paper industry's fiber requirement is expected to more than double. Structural wood products will continue to expand, but at a somewhat slower rate. Many sources predict a substantial increase in the volume of wood used as fuel for domestic and commercial purposes. Total demand will force the utilization of some more expensive timber sources, thus adding to the average cost. The indicated increase in the real price of fiber reflects these developments.

The earth's total water resource is a constant quantity, but water quality and availability in arable regions are diminishing. Industries and municipalities are being forced to conserve water, yet total demand will continue to grow. Methods to increase supply in shortage areas include mining of ground water, transport of surface waters, and desalination. Despite the substantial additional cost, these measures will become increasingly commonplace in the years ahead.

The projected increases in the price of energy is not only because of the cost of oil, but also because of investment costs for conversion of existing and new coal-burning facilities as well as a marked increase in the price of natural gas. After 1990, a world oil shortage will generate further increases. The cost of electric power will rise in line with added fuel and investment costs.

Three factors are responsible for the forecast increase in chemical prices. Energy intensive materials, such as chlorine and caustic soda, will have a corresponding increase in cost. Mining and recovery expenses for natural minerals will increase with the need to utilize more remote deposits. Capital costs for additional and replacement facilities will continue to rise faster than the forecast rate of inflation. This is especially true for grass-roots plants in remote areas, which entail the additional costs of the supporting infrastructure.

Economies Through Alkaline Papermaking

In addition to its study of the paper consumption and raw materials outlook, the TNT Committee considered other external factors that could alter future paper operations. Two significant predictions were: (1) Competitive factors will limit any cost-saving adjustments in paper quality and could even force higher standards; and (2) Barring a major technological breakthrough, the real cost of paper will increase (4).

Faced with the prospect of these external developments, the TNT Committee compiled a list of internal process changes that could help offset the negative factors. Actions germane to this presentation included: (1) Substantial reduction in water consumption per unit of output with further closing of white water systems; and (2) Fiber extension through lighter weights, more recycle, alkaline sizing, and increased use of fillers (4).

Both of these recommendations strongly favor the move to alkaline papermaking systems. In the case of acid papermaking using rosin–alum size, some of the alumina and most of the sulfate ions remain in the white water. With recirculation, a gradual build-up occurs with the maximum level increasing as the system is closed. Eventually, the high concentration causes scale and corrosion problems that limit recirculation levels. Mills that have converted to alkaline sizing have been able to reduce water consumption by more than fifty percent. At the same time, the need for make-up water is reduced by a corresponding amount with an accompanying saving in the energy required to heat this water to process temperatures. Finally, effluent volume is reduced, plus it is already in the optimum pH range for clarification and treatment. Total savings in water and related costs can exceed fifteen dollars per ton of paper produced.

Regarding the second recommendation, the cost of fiber represents twenty to twenty-five percent of the total cost of the finished paper. Thus, methods for reducing the fiber content without a compensating loss in quality or increase in manufacturing cost are of prime interest to the papermaker. Forming the web under alkaline conditions produces increased and stronger fiber bonding. Tensile and burst values from twenty to forty percent higher are common.

This increase in strength can be capitalized on in several ways. One approach is to reduce fiber refining and get a sheet that is faster draining and easier to dry. This provides energy savings, a higher production rate, and the commensurate reduction in costs. An alternative approach is to make a lighter weight sheet of equal strength.

A third option, which is probably the one most commonly practiced, is to reduce the fiber content by seven to ten percent and substitute an equivalent weight of filler. With fiber being more expensive than filler, this provides an obvious cost saving and usually results in a sheet with improved optical and printing properties. Also, under alkaline conditions, lower cost calcium carbonate can be used as a replacement for more expensive paper fillers. The combined savings are illustrated in the following simplified calculation for an actual conversion.

A Midwest papermill had previously run eight percent filler in a fifty-pound high-quality offset grade. On converting to alkaline size, two major changes were made. The filler level was increased to sixteen percent and less expensive fillers were used. The primary raw material costs were as follows:

Acid System

Fiber furnish	1840 lb @ $0.17/lb	$312.80
Titanium dioxide	40 lb @ $0.48/lb	19.20
TiO$_2$ extender	80 lb @ $0.17/lb	13.60
#1 Clay	40 lb @ $0.05/lb	2.00
Cost per ton		$347.60

Alkaline System

Fiber furnish	1680 lb @ $0.17/lb	$285.60
Calcium carbonate	200 lb @ $0.07/lb	14.00
#1 Clay	120 lb @ $0.05/lb	6.00
Cost per ton		$305.60
Savings in primary raw materials		$ 42.00

Other chemical and production costs were essentially a standoff. The finished sheet met all specifications and, when printed, gave superior press performance. If the reduced water costs mentioned previously are added in, the combined savings amount to fifty-seven dollars per ton or roughly ten percent of the cost of the finished paper. In addition, this paper has much better permanence. If the real cost of the fiber rises as forecast, the incentive to save fiber by going alkaline will increase by a corresponding amount.

Conversion Problems

With the many savings and advantages indicated, it would seem that the paper industry should be engaged in an all-out effort to make the conversion to an alkaline system. Several mills already have converted to alkaline and many more are studying the possibilities. Unfortunately, there are a number of auxiliary changes that must be made and each, in turn, represents an individual problem. Papermills that try to make a partial conversion of switch back and forth from one system to the other make the situation even more difficult. Without going into detail, the most common problems seem to be dirt from acid deposits that now become soluble, causing spots and breaks, different microorganisms that require a change in the slimicide/fungicide combination, and a fiber furnish that appears and reacts differently during refining, forming, pressing, and drying. Probably the most crucial change involves the machine tender who can no longer use alum as the cure-all for any operating problems.

Converting to alkaline requires a total commitment at all levels from top management on down. It takes considerable time, learning, and reorientation to make the changeover. During this period, operating efficiencies drop and unsaleable production rises. It is a complex and expensive undertaking, but it pays dividends in the long run. As the economic incentives increase, there will be more conversions.

Summary

During the next twenty-one years, paper consumption is conservatively forecast to more than double. Optimistic projections indicate the volume may triple. Forecasts place world annual consumption in the year 2000 at between 350 and 450 million metric tons. Recognizing the finite limitations of the earth's resources, finding adequate quantities of the necessary papermaking raw materials represents a significant challenge. As demand approaches supply limits, raw material prices are expected to rise in constant dollars. By the year 2000, the index price for key papermaking materials is forecast to be fiber, 190; water, 300; energy, 200; and chemicals, 140.

With this outlook for raw material prices, the paper industry must develop ways to conserve these materials and thus minimize the offsetting escalation in paper prices. Failure to accomplish this could result in paper pricing itself out of some markets.

Alkaline papermaking provides several opportunities for conserving papermaking raw materials and thus should become more prevalent in the years ahead. Making the conversion from an acid to an alkaline system includes many problems, but they are solvable and the ultimate savings warrants the effort. The strength and optical properties are similar for paper made by either system, but the permanence properties of the alkaline sheet are substantially better.

Literature Cited

1. "Outlook for Pulp and Paper Consumption, Production and Trade to 1985," *Food Agr. Organ. U.N.* **1972**, (Mar.).

2. Industry Working Party "FAO World Pulp and Paper Consumption Outlook: Phase I World Outlook for Paper and Paperboard; Phase II World Outlook for Regional Self-Sufficiency and Fiber Furnish," *Food Agri. Organ. U.N.* **1977**, (May).
3. "Demand, Supply and Trade in Pulp and Paper: Trends and Prospects to 1990," *Food Agri. Organ. U.N.* **1977**, (June).
4. "Future Technical Needs and Trends in the Paper Industry—III," *Tech. Assoc. Pulp Paper Ind.* **1979**, (Mar.).

RECEIVED October 23, 1979.

TEXTILES

Textile Conservation for Period Room Settings in Museums and Historic Houses

MARGARET FIKIORIS

The Henry Francis du Pont Winterthur Museum, Winterthur, DE 19735

The first section of this chapter is a survey of the variety of problems encountered in a museum that displays textiles in a historic period room setting and the solutions available in the past and now. First to be considered is the problem of light, both direct sunlight and artificial lighting, and the various means of controlling light in the museum rooms and in the conservation laboratories. Other important environmental factors such as temperature and relative humidity are also reviewed. Special consideration is given to the problems of abrasion to rugs and upholstery, acidity of wood and paper supports, and acts of general carelessness, which can cause serious damage to historic textiles. The second section of the chapter surveys the storage of textiles and rugs at Winterthur. The final section discusses cleaning of textiles and rugs in the textile conservation laboratory at the Louise du Pont Crowinshield Research Building at Winterthur.

The Henry Francis du Pont Winterthur Museum is located six miles north of Wilmington, Delaware. It offers visitors an opportunity to see an outstanding collection of American decorative arts displayed in more than 195 room settings spanning the time period from 1640 until 1840. The room displays encompass six style periods—the Seventeenth Century, William and Mary, Queen Anne, Chippendale, Federal, and Empire. Textiles and rugs play an important role in the room displays, covering windows, chairs, sofas, beds, tables, and floors (Figure 1). They provide accent to the walls with framed needlework pictures and samplers and to the tables with embroidered pocketbooks, pin cushions, and hand-held fire screens. It is to their care that textile conservation at Winterthur

0065-2393/81/0193-0253$05.50/0

Figure 1. View of the Marlboro Room from Patuxent Manor, 1744, Lower Marlboro Maryland, displaying Queen Anne and Chippendale furniture from the middle colonies and the south.

is directed. The first section of this chapter surveys the variety of problems encountered in a museum that displays textiles in a historic period room setting and the possible solutions available in the past and now.

The foremost concern in any display of historic textiles is the problem of light. Historic fabrics are extremely sensitive to light damage. Exposure to light, whether by direct sunlight or by an artificial light source causes dyes to fade and natural fibers to lose their strength. Both forms of deterioration are linked to the effect of UV radiation; however, visible light is also responsible for fading even the most stable of textile dyes. The intensity of the lighting and the length of exposure determine the rate of deterioration. Damage from exposure to light is accelerated if the atmosphere is either damp or overheated or if there is the presence of dust or soot in the environment.

Light damage to collections in historic houses and museums is increasing in the recent decades. With the availability of air conditioning to maintain an artificial climate balance, there is little need to seal off the sunlight entering a room. This phenomenon is coupled with the increase in the number of historic private houses that are being converted into public museums with an emphasis on visibility and easy accessibility.

The owners of the great houses in the eighteenth and nineteenth centuries were well aware of damage caused by sunlight as recorded by

Susanna Whatman, Mistress of Turkey Court in Kent, England. After her marriage in 1776, she wrote detailed instructions to her staff, now published in *The Housekeeping Book of Susanna Whatman* (*1*) 1776–1880. She wrote to the housemaid, "The sun comes into the Library very early. The window on that side of the bow must have the blind let down" (*1*). Concerning her own dressing room she warned "The sun must always be kept out, or it will spoil the carpet, chairs, and mahogany cabinet" (*1*). Exterior and interior window shutters and Venetian blinds were used by the eighteenth century householder to seal out the sun, while allowing air circulation. Trade cards from the second half of the eighteenth century advertised stylish examples of painted Venetian blinds available in many colors. Winterthur has a fine example of late eighteenth century narrow-slatted (1¼ ") dark green Venetian blinds that were used in the house of John Imlay, a Philadelphia merchant who retired to Allentown, New Jersey, around 1790 (Figure 2). Present day museum administrators need to return to the eighteenth and nineteenth century sensitivity to the problem of light and its certain damage to textiles and rugs, wallpaper, prints, and furniture and close their shutters and lower their blinds. Ironically, the energy crisis and rising utility costs may speed this process.

From 1951 until 1976 when separate morning and afternoon tours were given in the main Museum at Winterthur, opaque window shades were used to darken totally those rooms not on tour. These shades were pulled by cords located at either end of the rod pocket and were concealed from view. The museum maintenance staff had to walk across

The Henry Francis du Pont
Winterthur Museum

Figure 2.   Example of a ca. 1790 narrow-slatted green Venetian blind used in the house of John Imlay, Allentown, New Jersey

rugs and reach behind the curtains to pull the shades, which over the years caused some damage from abrasion to these textiles. The pulling of the shades was discontinued in 1977 with the doubling of the Museum tours so that all rooms were on view from 10:00 A.M. until 3:30 P.M. There is now evidence of accelerated fading in the collection and the shades again need to be pulled for protection against the late afternoon and early morning sun when the rooms are not on tour.

Closing historic window curtains to block the sun is not a viable solution. Curtains hanging at the windows are especially damaged by direct sunlight, as illustrated by this curtain set of an English copperplate print of exotic flowers dating from 1775–1785 that hung for many years in a dormer window of a historic house (Plate I). The intense blue of the print is barely visible and there are numerous losses in the cotton ground. The curtain set had both an interlining of a modern blackout material and a cotton outer lining. However, under such strong sunlight conditions a blackout lining gave only a false sense of security.

Winterthur has tried several other modern window covering techniques to prevent light damage to its collection. In the mid 1960s, ⅛″ Pittsburgh Plate Glass Pennvernon Graylite storm windows were installed on the exterior of each window of the period rooms. This tinted glass causes the windows to appear dark when viewed from a distance with the individual window mullions obscured; however, inside the museum, the visitor is seldom aware of the tinted storm windows because the historic window frames, glass, and mullions are clearly in view. While the Graylite Plate Glass greatly cuts back on light by allowing only a 31% transmittance of visible light, it does not appreciably screen out all harmful UV wavelengths.

Two possible solutions to the UV problem are found in the contemporary Louise du Pont Crowinshield Research Building, constructed in 1969. The Paper Conservation Laboratory and the Maps & Prints Study Collection have interior window inserts of UV absorbing plexiglass that eliminate almost all of the UV radiation from the daylight entering the rooms. Sheets of Rohm & Haas Plexiglas UF-3, available in ⅛″ and ¼″ thicknesses, can be cut to fit inside existing window openings. The Research Building has ⅛″ Plexiglas UF-3 panels mounted into wooden frames, painted to match the existing trim, which are held in place with wing bolts for easy removal for cleaning. These sheets of Plexiglas UF-3, which are lightly tinted, give a slight yellowish color to the window insert.

The interior surfaces of the skylight windows of the Technical Library in the Research Building are covered with 3M Scotchtint Solar Control Film, attached at the top and bottom by rods. This screening material is made of a flexible polyester film of 15/1000″ total thickness and is aluminum vapor coated. The color selected was smoke (grey black) and,

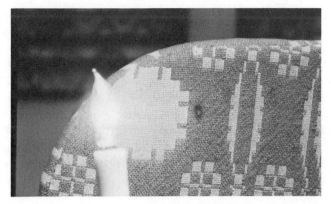

Figure 3.   Example of a scorch mark resulting from the artificial candle bulb

according to the manufacturer, it reflects 75% of solar heat, 82% of solar glare, and 99% of UV radiation. The 3M Solar Control films generally are applied directly to window glass, but the wire-glass in the skylights at Winterthur prevented this. These reflective solar control films are available in varying metallic colors: smoke, silver, bronze, and gold; and are compatible with the broad glass expanses of modern architecture. However, reflective glass surfaces are not a part of the seventeenth through nineteenth century architectural vocabulary, and such a design factor should be considered in the modification of window glass of a historic building.

The fading of fabrics can be accelerated by artificial lighting within the period rooms. At Winterthur, the individual lighting fixtures are wired to use 7½-watt incandescent candle bulbs with a candelabra base and candle flare. The bulbs lower the light intensity considerably in the rooms and give a more authentic atmosphere to the museum tours. The candle flame bulbs present their own problem, because if placed too close to an object such as a curtain or an upholstered easy chair, the fabric may become badly scorched (Figure 3) from the heat generated. From a random sampling in the collection, it was found that light fixtures with a single candle bulb need to be placed 14″–16″ from museum objects to maintain a light level of five foot candles. A greater distance is required for lighting devices with two or more bulbs.

In textile research and reproduction work, one must be alert to the changes in textiles caused by overexposure to light. The light-sensitive yellow in green leaves in a French "Indienne" block print from the late eighteenth century (Plate 2) has vanished, leaving the originally green leaves blue in color. Also, examples of the same fabric can appear quite different as a result of their surrounding environment and use as seen in the faded and unfaded examples of the copperplate print by Francis Nixon, 1765–1775 (Plate 3). Compare the three examples of a resist-dyed cotton print from Rouen, France dating from the late eighteenth century (Plate 4). The soiled and faded slipcover in the background of the illustration gives a false impression that the eighteenth-century preference was for muted, pastel colors. In reality, the color schemes of that century could be extremely vibrant and even gaudy, especially in the first half of the century. An unexposed seam, when opened, can give a good indication of original color as seen in the example of a blue resist-dyed cotton, "Roosters and Pomegranates," dating from the third quarter of the eighteenth century (Plate 5). Therefore, it is critical to search for original color in unexposed seam and hem areas of bedspreads and curtains, on the reverse of framed textiles and lined rugs, and in tucked away areas such as under the flaps of needlework pocketbooks, in between pleats and gathers of garments, and along the tacking edge of upholstery.

Another important environmental factor for any museum or historic house is that of relative humidity. The entire museum at Winterthur is air conditioned with the temperature maintained at 68°–72° F and the relative humidity at 50% ± 5%. With the need to conserve fuel, the offices and work areas are set at 66° F ± 2° in the winter and 78° F ± 2° in the summer. Should the relative humidity drop below 40%, there is the danger of embrittlement of the textiles; if the relative humidity rises over 70%, there is the danger of mold growth. Textiles, especially those of vegetable fibers, are susceptible to attack by molds that flourish in dark humid places with little or no ventilation. In the early stages of mold growth, there may be a musty smell before any visible sign of deterioration appears. In the late stages of mold damage, staining occurs, which weakens the fibers and badly discolors the historic textile. This discoloration can be of greenish, yellowish, or grey–brown spots that are irregular and speckled in appearance. Wet cleaning alone cannot remove this staining. Bleaching may be the only effective method of removing the staining, but this will further degrade the weakened cellulose and cannot be used on printed or dyed fabrics.

A needlework or textile displayed in a tightly sealed, standard wood molding frame may be damaged by mold growth from within, especially if the textile is in direct contact with the glass where moisture condensation occurs. Framed textiles and needlework pieces should be mounted on an acid-free support with an acid-free mat placed under the rabbet of the frame to keep the textile from touching the glass. This air space serves to protect the framed textile from the possibility of condensation and its possible result in mold growth.

Museums and historic houses without an air-conditioned environment lend themselves to tragic accidents resulting from open windows and doors. Curtains, rugs, and upholstery can be destroyed needlessly by rain water containing atmospheric pollutants. Plate 6 shows a late eighteenth-century floral silk stripe material, used on an upholstered sofa, that was damaged irreversibly by rain water. The tide line of bleeding dyes and soil moving across the fabric left a permanent area of discoloration and degradation of the silk. Open windows and doors with improper screening also can give access to textile pests, which feed on collection objects and may leave excreta on the decorative surfaces.

The official "open door policy" with the goal of increased attendance presents other problems and challenges to public institutions. How can museums and historical societies charged with the preservation of the past balance the growing need for public participation in educational functions and maintain the stability of their collections? How can visitor numbers be increased in a historic house structure with limited space accommodation and often difficult access? Unsupervised crowds increase the possibility of theft, vandalism, and handling of objects.

One method to control museum visitor traffic is to have a physical barrier between the guests and the display. In the Washington Wing at Winterthur, where unreserved tours are offered, there are various barrier systems: ropes, wooden handrails, and drywall dividers, which are placed more than an arm's length from the object. Guests can look into the room or pass along one wall but they cannot enter the display area. With these restraints, groups as large as ten may be accommodated with a guide, and there is no minimum age limit. The guests may carry coats, jackets, handbags, and cameras on the tour; however, photography is not permitted in the collection.

On the reserved tours of the main museum, which lasts two hours, guests actually enter the period rooms escorted by trained guides. With four guests to a group, the guide is responsible for the tour and for the safety of the collection (Figure 4). There is a minimum age limit of twelve. The guests are asked to leave their coats and jackets in the entrance cloak room. Sweaters and jackets must be worn and may not be carried over the arm. All purses, tote bags, and cameras are placed in lockers before entering the period rooms.

In the main museum, the guests are instructed not to touch any museum objects and to walk only on the modern rug runners that cover the historic rugs in the collection. This routing keeps the guests together and away from the many decorative art objects on open display. The runners also protect the carpets underneath. These runners, woven with an uncut loop wool pile, were available until the mid 1970s from Hardwick and Magee Manufacturing Company. They were ordered in a neutral sandbark color without a rosin backing. A binding was applied to the edges to prevent raveling. The present museum runners are 28″

The Henry Francis du Pont Winterthur Museum

*Figure 4.   A Winterthur guide with four guests on a reserved tour of the
main museum*

wide but they are soon to be changed to 36″ or 40″ wide to accommodate
visitors in wheel chairs. Since these runners are no longer available
Bigelow–Sanford, Incorporated has offered to provide a museum rug
runner if there is sufficient need.

The practice of placing a lesser rug on top of a more valuable rug is
quite common in American life. The painting of Henry Sargent "The
Dinner Party" (1821–1823) at the Museum of Fine Arts, Boston, shows the
use of a green baize rug or crumb cloth placed under the dining room
table to protect against spillage. Placing protective scatter rugs over
larger rugs was a common practice in the nineteenth century. Thus, the
twentieth-century museum rug runner is a continuation of this tradition.

It often has been asked if abrasion occurs on historic rugs with the
traffic of guests, guides, and staff walking on top of the runners. The
problem of abrasion is reduced greatly but not eliminated. However,
without protection, fine pile or embroidered surfaces will be destroyed
completely if constantly walked on, as is illustrated by this example of
an English needlework carpet with the wool embroidery completely worn

away, exposing the canvas beneath (Figure 5). Traffic patterns over the years result in severe damage down the center of a rug located in an entrance hall or across a rug if there is a window or telephone to be reached (Plate 7). In some instances, the rotation of a rug may slow down this wear. It is better to locate important rugs away from general traffic, although this becomes difficult in a historic house or museum with narrow halls and exhibition areas using room size carpets.

The problem of abrasion does not need to be confined to the floor, as witnessed by the worn areas of nineteenth century wool and cotton American double-cloth coverlets that have been tucked in religiously by well intending housekeepers, or by the threadbare remains of once-elegant upholstered chairs that have received a great deal of wear and abuse over the centuries.

A common practice of the eighteenth century was to place protective cloth covers, "cases," over expensive upholstery to shield them from dirt, light, and wear. These covers were often plain weave linen or cotton woven in a stripe or check as illustrated in the print of the month of "January" by Robert Dighton d. 1784 (Figure 6). These slipcovers were generally loose fitting. However, until recently, twentieth-century collectors and curators made their eighteenth-century-styled slipcovers appear as actual upholstery, fitted tightly to the chair and held under a great deal of tension (Figure 7). Considerable damage occurs to the upholstery underneath as a result of changing of tight clipcovers (Plate 8). Museums are now returning to the looser slipcovers, which will again save both layers of fabric.

Another problem associated with upholstered furniture is the use of iron upholstery tacks, which will rust and thereby cause large holes in the upholstery fabric (Plate 9). Modern upholsters find that the use of the magnetic tacking hammer hastens production and, therefore, continue

The Henry Francis du Pont
Winterthur Museum

Figure 5.   Detail of loss of the wool embroidered surface of an English needlework carpet through abrasion from traffic

*Figure 6.   Print of the month of "January" by Robert Dighton d.1784
showing a loose fitting slipcover*

to use upholstery tacks with high iron content. Commonly used are blued
and sterilized upholstery tacks that are coated to prevent infection if
accidentally swallowed. Often, upholsterers hold the tacks in their mouth
while working, which begins the corrosion process. Corrosion of the
tacks is accelerated by high humidity and the presence of acids in the
wood. Brass, copper, and bronze tacks also present a corrosion problem.
The substitution of stainless steel tacks, if available, or anodized aluminum tacks may reduce the problem of tack corrosion in upholstery work.
If decorative exterior tacks are required, they should be of anodized
aluminum and not electroplated iron. They can be obtained in any color
simulating the brass or bronze used originally.

The problem of wood in direct contact with historic fabrics is a
pervasive one throughout a historic house museum. Textiles often are
displayed or stored against wood with its problem of acidity. In a number

Plate 1. Detail of sunlight damage to a curtain set of an English copper-plate print dating from 1775–1785

Plate 2. Detail of a French "Indienne" block print from the late eighteenth century showing light damage

Plate 3. Two details (one faded) of an English copperplate by Francis Nixon, 1765–1775

Plate 4. Three examples of the same resist-dyed print from Rouen, France dated from the late eighteenth century showing the results of poor environmental conditions

Plate 5.   Detail of an exposed seam of a blue resist pattern of "Roosters and Pomegranates" dating from the third quarter of the eighteenth century

Plate 6.   Example of water damage to a late eighteenth century floral stripe silk material

Plate 7.   Detail of a rolled rug showing the loss of pile down the center through abrasion from constant traffic

Plate 8.   Example of the damage resulting from abrasion through the changing of slipcovers

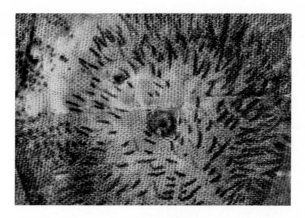

Plate 9.   Damage to upholstery fabric through the use of iron tacks

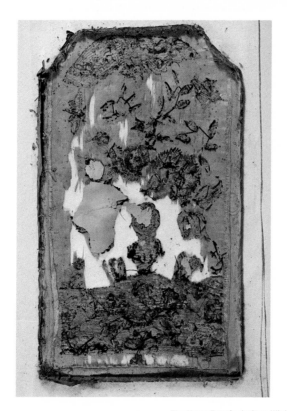

Plate 10.   Example of a poor mount destroying the fabric it supports; a 1738 framed English silk embroidery

Plate 11.   Example of light damaged silk tassel trim exposing the wooden spool cores

Plate 12.   Example of the danger of home laundering; the canvas of a mid nineteenth century Berlin Wool Work parrot disintegrated

of rooms at Winterthur, lengths of linen homespun are displayed folded on wooden shelves in large schranks as seen in an example from the Kershner Parlor (Figure 8).

A common occurrence found with historic household linens and clothing is dark areas of discoloration where the cloth has been in direct contact with wood. A good example of a shelf mark and surface dust deposit is shown in Figure 9. This man's linen shirt from the nineteenth century had been neatly folded and stored on a wooden shelf. Here, the dark staining was removed by wet cleaning. However many historic tablecloths, napkins, towels, sheets and pillowcases often have a dark gridwork of fold marks that cannot be remedied by wet cleaning only. Bleaching is difficult because of the degradation of the fibers and the presence of polychrome embroidered monograms or ink signatures.

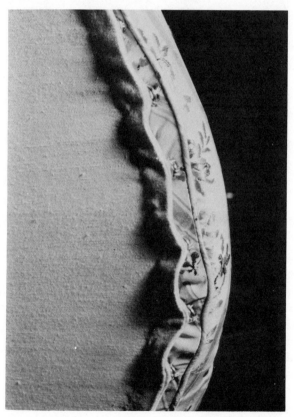

The Henry Francis du Pont Winterthur Museum

Figure 7.   An example of the tension placed on a historic fabric when the slipcover is designed to look like upholstery

The Henry Francis du Pont Winterthur Museum

*Figure 8.   View of lengths of homespun stored in a large schrank in the
Kershner Parlor*

For the storing of textiles on new wooden shelving or drawers, a
coating of a polyurethane varnish may be applied to seal the wood.
Sufficient time, up to a month, should be allowed for the coating to dry.
The shelves then can be lined with acid-free, buffered papers purchased
from archival paper supply firms. These papers liners can be cut to fit the
contour of any object and so need not to be noticeable in a display.

Framed needlework in the eighteenth and nineteenth centuries
generally were mounted directly onto wooden stretchers or boards that
were often covered with paper or fabric. Over the years, these materials
can destroy the textile that they are supporting because of the acidity
in the wood and in the paper. A good example of a poor support and
its result is the 1738 framed floral silk embroidery shown in Plate 10,
where there are great losses in the silk background. External environmental factors (light, heat, and humidity) can accelerate this destruction.

At Winterthur, framed needlework pictures and samplers on harmful supports are remounted on acid-free mounts held in place by stitches and not by nails. This mounting procedure for framed historic textiles was devised by Wanda Guthrie in the early 1960s (2).

The combination of the acidity of the wooden spool supports and the damage by sunlight can destroy elegantly adorned silk curtain tassels and braid trim of the late eighteenth and nineteenth centuries (Plate 11). These trims are extremely difficult to duplicate in their extravagance, fine workmanship, and attention to detail.

Curators, collectors, and conservators need to be on constant guard against acidic tissue paper that has discolored with age. Textiles stored with highly acid tissue papers also will become discolored with time. There are acid-free and alkaline-buffered tissue papers commercially available through archival paper and supply firms. In the last several years, paper companies have become aware of the needs of historic textiles and costume departments in museums, historical societies, and universities and are placing into production acid-free rolling tubes, tissue paper, and storage boxes for costumes and accessories.

The Henry Francis du Pont Winterthur Museum

Figure 9. Example of surface dust and shelf mark staining on a nineteenth-century man's linen shirt that was folded neatly on a wooden shelf

Unsuitable cloth lining materials also can do extensive damage to historic fabrics. It was common in the 1940s and 1950s for Winterthur's curtains to be lined with a plain weave linen. With fluctuation of temperature and humidity, these linen linings moved considerably and caused pockets of sagging of the lining at the bottom of the curtains. Winterthur now uses closely woven cotton linings for curtains and washed unbleached muslin for sampler mounts.

Museums are often the recipients of textile disasters. Unknowing, untrained people can cause great damage to historic textiles when attempting cleaning at home. Many tragic results are brought into Winterthur's Diagnostic Art Conservation Clinic, which is open to the public. Inheritors of nineteenth-century quilts and coverlets think nothing of putting their heirlooms through the "gentle cycle" in a home washing machine and wonder why only shreds remain. Purchasers of nineteenth-century needlework will wash them gently in a bath tub with a cold water detergent and then are surprised to see that the canvas has disintegrated, as in the case of this Berlin wool work parrot from 1850s (Plate 12).

Unanticipated accidents can occur if museum staff members and volunteers use ink near historic textiles, costumes, and rugs. There should be no ink used in the collection, in storage, or in the workrooms. Writing with ink for insurance forms or any legal document should take place away from textile objects. Pencils should be used for all catalog work sheets, condition reports, and conservation treatment records. A supply of pencils should be on hand to give to students and visitors. Other common rules for textile safety in a work space are to have a clean, uncluttered, padded work table, a nearby water supply for conscientious washing of hands, and a policy of no food or smoking in areas with textiles. There also should be large trays, sturdy mat boards, and other smooth, clean, flat supports easily available for transporting textiles from one area to another. Historic textiles need to be supported at all times.

Guides should use clean, white, cotton gloves while giving special subject tours on textiles and should try to avoid all unnecessary touching of objects. Clean cotton gloves should be worn by custodial staff when moving upholstered furniture. However, in dressing a bed or hanging curtains, cotton gloves may become awkward for working with snaps and hooks. Then great attention should be paid to general cleanliness and numerous hand washings. Clean, close-fitting smocks or garments should be worn for work with textiles in the collection. Personal jewelry, whether for male or female, should not be worn when working with historic textiles. There is a great risk of snagging, tearing, and abrasion.

Outside the museum, general carelessness can cause extensive harm to textiles and costumes before they reach the museum. Antique dealers and shop owners often use sticky glue-on labels to list lot number and sale price. Once the labels are removed, the label marks remain. The adhesive darkens the textile underneath and becomes embedded in the fibers. The use of Scotch Tape or any adhesive tape for patching small tears or breaks in a fabric has the same result. Modern framers are continuing to glue needlework and printed textiles to cardboard. Moreover, dealers, collectors, small historical societies, and museums fall into the practice of using plastic drycleaning bags to cover their costume collections. These plastic bags, though a convenience, need to be discarded because of the eventual degradation of the film. Other serious drawbacks are their static electrical property, which attracts and holds dust and the constant problem of condensation and its resulting mold growth if there is great fluctuation of humidity and temperature. At Winterthur, washed muslin or cotton and polyester sheets are used for dust covers in storage and in work areas.

The Storage of Textiles at Winterthur

Winterthur has eight large textile and rug storage rooms to accommodate those objects that are not on view in the period rooms. Many are alternated sets held for seasonal changes. Still others are kept for the study for visiting scholars, graduate students in the Winterthur Program in Early American Culture and the Winterthur/University of Delaware Program in the Conservation of Artistic and Historic Objects, and participants in Special Subject Tours on needlework and textiles. The rooms are described in detail in Reference 3.

The curtains are stored in two storerooms, constructed in 1948 and 1957 (Figure 10). They are stored on curtain racks attached to a sliding carriage with permanent curtain rings. The carriages are raised and lowered by means of ropes and pulleys and are locked in place to boating cleats. The curtain racks may be pulled out into the room to have the curtains changed. When a curtain set is taken off or placed back on the rack, a white mattress pad is spread out on the floor, and the curtain carefully placed onto it. The curtain can be transferred onto a special cart that fits the museum elevator and passes easily over the museum runners.

The outside walls of the curtain storage rooms have been furred out with two-by-fours covered with plywood and painted. This false wall has a 4″ spacing behind to prevent condensation. Box valances are held in place on the walls with L-shaped brackets; flat valances are attached by means of snaps or Velcro tape. There are no windows in the storage rooms and the rooms are kept in total darkness.

Bedspread storage (Figure 11) is a long, low ceilinged room accommodating over 183 spreads. The bedspreads are stored on long, varnished wooden poles suspended from standard aluminum curtain tracks. Bedspread storage was designed in 1962 and completed in 1967. The original

The Henry Francis du Pont Winterthur Museum

Figure 10.   Overall view of curtain storage

pole length was 9′ 3½″, and each bedspread could be moved fully out
into the room. In 1969, to double the storage, the nine-foot poles were
cut back to 6′11″ and a second bank of 5′7″ poles were added to the
existing tracks. One or the other can be pulled into the center of the
room. Now the bedspreads have to be folded to fit the shorter poles,
which causes abrasion problems when the spreads are being pulled out
or being placed back in again. Ideally, both sets of poles should be long
enough to accommodate the full width of the spreads, and there should
be adequate space in the center of the room to pull out either bank
completely. Most bedspreads range in width from 8′–10′; however, there
are some bedspreads in the Winterthur collection that measure over
12′ wide.

The space between the tracks measures 5″, which is adequate for lighter spreads, but a 6″ spacing is generally better. However, there should be up to an 8″ spacing between the tracks for heavy quilted pieces and large bed rugs. Although the poles are varnished, there should be an additional barrier between the bedspread and the wood. Under consideration are a covering of acid-free paper tube or a sleeve of polyethylene tubing. The polyethylene sleeve may cause the problem of a static build up with the spreads being taken on and off.

General Textile Storage houses rolled textiles in movable storage cabinets. These units were based on a design by Virginia Harvey (4). Winterthur's carts measure 6′6½″ outside height, 6′5″ outside width, 24¼″ outside depth. There are twenty-two shelf supports to a cabinet with an average of three poles to a shelf. There are a total of sixty-four poles to a cabinet. Each shelf support has holes drilled every 1½″ to accommodate adjustable pegs. Thus, the poles can be arranged to give an adequate spacing between the rows of rolled textiles suspended on them.

The rolling of textiles takes place elsewhere and is described in Reference 5. As mentioned earlier, the major archival paper suppliers are now producing 10′ acid-free rolling tubes for textiles in 3″-, 4½″-, and 6″-diameter sizes. This eliminates the problem of using regular mailing tubes for a support. Also, the museum slipcover changes are stored in recently available acid-free boxes for textiles, and costumes; these storage boxes measure 40″ × 18″ × 6″.

The Henry Francis du Pont Winterthur Museum

Figure 11.   View of bedspread storage

Figure 12.   View of rug storage

The rugs at Winterthur are stored rolled on heavy gauge aluminum tubes protected by muslin sleeves (Figure 12). The tubes are 4¼″ in diameter and vary in length from 5′ to 16′7″. They are suspended from industrial, cadmium-plated, welded steel chains attached to steel trolleys and tracks used in factory assembly line production. The combined weight of the rugs, tubes, chains, and tracks is carried by the steel beams of the roof rafters. Each rug is placed on alternate sides of the chain with an 8″ to 12″ spacing between each tube. The rugs are generally rolled pile side in and in the direction of the pile. Most embroidered rugs are rolled with the embroidered surface out. This also applies to most of the lined rugs so that any buckling will occur in the lining. However, the best rule for rolling rugs and textiles is to consider each one individually.

The Cleaning of Textiles and Rugs

The cleaning and mounting of textile objects takes place in two large rooms on the fourth floor of the Louise du Pont Crowinshield Research Building constructed in 1969. The Sewing Room is a large L-shaped room and houses four large padded work tables constructed on wheels to be arranged easily for different projects. The overall dimensions of the tables are 10′ × 6′ and 12′ × 6′ and the height of each is 31″. The table dimensions were determined by the sizes of Winterthur's window curtains and bedspreads. The table tops are covered with cotton mattress pads and cotton sheets, which can be easily removed and laundered.

Before wet cleaning a textile or rug, a condition report is filled out for each object and record photographs are taken. The textile is measured, the fiber content identified, and the construction of the weave recorded. The nature of the support is documented. This heading covers various categories ranging from historic wooden frames for needlework samplers to historic or modern lining materials with support hardware such as rings, hooks, rods, and Velcro. The condition of the external edge is described with a general contour sketch added when amplification is needed. The interior condition is discussed with a description of missing areas, tears, and areas of abrasion with loss or warp and/or weft. The next heading is that of surface disfigurement where fading, soiling, stains, marks, and accretions are noted. Then all previous repairs are described and located. Because textiles present such varied problems, general headings are used on the condition form rather than a detailed line by line check list, which may not always be applicable.

The textile or rug is then vacuumed carefully through a flexible fiberglass screen with an upholstery brush attachment to a vacuum that has adjustable suction. The edges of the screen are bound with cotton twill tape to prevent snagging. Vacuuming a textile or rug in this manner protects the piece from direct suction and possible abrasion. Also, the vacuuming should follow the predominate element of the weave. Two people should work together if the object is especially fragile. One can hold and adjust the screen while the other vacuums. The textile or rug should be vacuumed on both sides beginning with the side with the largest amount of loose surface dirt.

After vacuuming, the dyes are tested first with distilled water and a detergent solution; in this instance, with a 1%–2% solution of Orvus, a neutral synthetic anionic detergent. Each color is tested with an eye dropper and blotting paper (Figure 13). The blotting paper is placed

The Henry Francis du Pont Winterthur Museum

Figure 13.   Testing of the dyes with distilled water and a detergent solution

underneath and on top of each test area and then gently pressed to see if any dye appears on the test paper. Repair areas are also checked carefully for dye bleeding.

If the dyes prove to be fast, the textile or rug may be wet cleaned. The cleaning process takes place in a large adjacent room that is connected by double doors. The object to be cleaned is placed in a large stainless steel wash table that measures 13' long by 6' wide and 6" deep. The length of the wash table was determined by the average curtain panel at Winterthur. The width was designed so that two people can reach to the center for sponging and blotting. If the textile or rug is in strong condition, it may be placed directly in the sink for wet cleaning. However, fragile textiles are sandwiched between polypropylene screening with additional protective fine nets used when needed.

The first step in the wet cleaning process is the clear rinse to remove loose surface soil. Rinsing is accomplished by moving a hose attached to a perforated 1" stainless steel pipe across the width of the wash table. The pipe is mounted on two 17½" × 17½" × ¼" Teflon square supports that hold the pipe 8" above the textile being rinsed. The pipe can be moved easily up and down the length of the sink. The rinse water with the loose soil is drained quickly from the table as clean water comes in through the hose. There are three sunken drains at the end of the table located in a 3" deep trough, which is 12" wide. These drains empty into a large drain box located below the sink, which then empties into a floor drain. The drain trough has an ⅛" mesh stainless steel screen cover to protect the textile or rug in the sink from the suction of the draining water.

After the first clear rinse is finished and much of the loose surface soil removed, the sink is filled, and the detergent is added. Generally 2–4 fluid ounces of Orvus detergent is added to 75–100 gallons of water with a water temperature determined by the nature of the fibers. The detergent solution is sponged carefully into the rug or textile (Figure 14). The length and number of the detergent baths is determined by the amount of the soil to be removed. Rinsing is a long process, employing a combination of long soaking baths and shorter hose rinses. Rinsing varies in time according to the object and generally takes several hours.

After the final rinse, the table is tilted to be drained, and the textile or rug is blotted with cotton mattress pads to remove excess moisture. The pads are placed underneath of and on top of the textile object. If the object is in a strong condition, it often is rolled between pads to further extract the water (Figure 15). After blotting with mattress pads, the textile or rug is placed on a stretched polypropylene screen in a large drying cabinet on a specially constructed cart that houses four 4' × 9' expanded metal shelves (Figure 16). If the textile or rug is too large for the shelf units, the piece can be draped over four 10' metal poles

The Henry Francis du Pont Winterthur Museum

Figure 14.   The detergent bath

The Henry Francis du Pont Winterthur Museum

Figure 15.   Blotting between cotton mattress pads

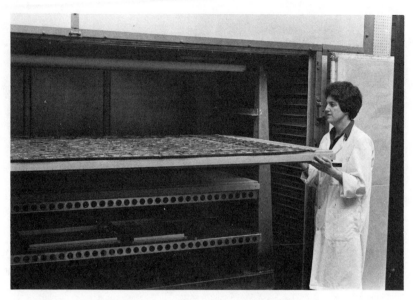

The Henry Francis du Pont Winterthur Museum

Figure 16.   The drying cabinet

covered with muslin sleeves, suspended across the top of the cart. The air inside the cabinet is heated by steam generator and is circulated across the surface of the textile. The cabinet is heated to 90°–110° F depending on the fiber content of the textile object. Unheated air can be circulated when possible shrinkage may occur. There is an auxiliary thermostatic, bell-type alarm system separate from the temperature control unit. It will sound an alarm should the drying cabinet exceed 130° F. After the textiles and rugs are cleaned, they are reassembled and returned to exhibition or storage.

One final aspect of Winterthur's textile conservation program is the construction of new reproduction sets, which present to the public an authentic view of eighteenth- and nineteenth-century designs for windows and bed treatments that demand an abundance of yardage. With the use of reproductions, Winterthur's historic fabric collection can be preserved for study and for the future.

Literature Cited

1. "The Housekeeping of Susanna Whatman"; Balston, Thomas, Ed.; Geoffrey Bles: London, 1956; pp. 19, 22.
2. Fikioris, M. A. *Museum News* **1976**, 55(2), 8–9.
3. Fikioris, M. A. *Museum News* **1973**, 52(3), 34–41.
4. Harvey, V. *Museum News* **1963**, 42(3), 28–33.
5. Fikioris, M. A. *Museum News* **1976**, 55(1), 13–18.

RECEIVED March 31, 1980.

Color Conservation Problems of an Early Twentieth Century Historic Dress

E. D. ADAMS WILSON

228 County Road 203, Space #98, Durango, CO 81301

Possible causes of both underarm splotches and darkening and yellowing of fabric in a silk historic dress (ca. 1906–1908) were determined by finding out what constituted the fabric colorant and how the color of the original fabric remnant reacted to tests simulating conditions the garment possibly encountered in wear and in use. Results from x-ray analysis and fabric color responses to test conditions suggest that the light orange fabric color was produced by a pink aluminum-mordanted dye topped with a yellow acid dye. Splotching in underarm region appears to be caused by a disassociation of the two dyestuffs. The light orange fabric tended to become pinker and lighter under most test conditions. The darkening and yellowing effect of the dress fabric was duplicated in only one test situation, that simulating a pretreating method used earlier in this century.

A particular early twentieth century dress (ca. 1906–1908) in Colorado State University's Historic Textile and Costume Collection evidenced some specific types of color damage. Since this garment was being restored as part of a Master's thesis project, the conservation problems posed by the discolorations were investigated. This chapter centers on the specific testing done to understand the reasons for the color problems. Preliminary and subsidiary historical investigations and the resultant restoration processes are reported elsewhere (1).

The dress was in a disassembled state when donated, such that the bodice and skirt portions were no longer attached and the once totally enclosed waistline seam allowance was exposed. A piece of what is believed to be a remnant of the original fabric from which the dress was made was also included in the donation. A visual comparison of the

0065-2393/81/0193-0275$05.00/0

used silk voile fabric in the dress and the unused remnant indicated that the dress is darker and more yellow in color. The now-exposed seam allowance seemed to be the same light orange color as the remnant, and, thus, this color is believed to represent closely the original color of the dress. The particular hues found in both dress and remnant were classified according to the Munsell color system, a tristimulus color coding method, to clarify vague and nonspecific verbal descriptions of color. These color specifications are recorded in Table I.

Besides the total-garment discoloration, another type of color damage was apparent in the underarm portion of the dress bodice. Perspiration is a known color contaminant, but the discoloration in this garment was unusual, in that there were distinct yellow and pink regions within the stained area. Munsell notations for the particular hues represented in these regions are listed in Table I.

Rice has remarked that conservation of historic textile artifacts includes a restoration of their colors (2). Certainly, if possible, from a restoration standpoint, it would be advantageous to minimize the total-garment and underarm color alterations so that the dress is color-wise, as well as structurally, as it was originally. Werner notes that preventative treatment in conservation and restoration involves first a diagnosis—an understanding of what caused the deterioration (3). These discolorations could evidence specific reactions of the fabric colorant to some unknown factor(s), which forewarn that certain precautions must be taken in conservation to prevent further dramatic discolorations.

Although specific to one case, the investigation of this specific item could be of more general benefit in the field of conservation of textile items. Diagnosing the discolorations of the silk voile dress could alert conservationists to possible eventual color problems with other susceptible silk garments either dyed similarly or subjected to similar environmental factors in use or in care and could help explain causes for similar color changes that may have occurred already in other garments. The total-

Table I. Fabric and Stain Color Descriptions Using Munsell Color Classification

	Color Description		
Color Source	Hue	Value	Intensity
Dress fabric			
all-over	10 YR	7	4
bodice seam	10 YR	8	4
Remnant fabric	7.5 YR	7	4
Bodice underarm stains			
yellow areas	5 Y	8.5	10
pink areas	7.5 R	7	4

garment color change of the dress may have gone unnoticed if the dress had not been disassembled, exposing the lighter lower bodice seam, and if the unused remnant had not been retained and included in the donation. It is therefore possible that similar color changes have occurred in other early twentieth century garments or fabrics that were either dyed in the same way as the study dress and/or subjected to similar treatments or environmental conditions, but that these changes thus far have been undetected.

Related Research

Color changes have been encountered on other historic textiles. It is not unknown for historic colorants to shift in hue with age. Stromberg has recounted that certain green shades on old textiles have become bluer, certain purples redder, and certain blues grayer with time (4). Giles reports that fading commonly is accompanied by a change in color, and that soluble-dye produced colors commonly turn redder (5). "Negative fades" (i.e., a darkening of fabric color) can also occur with certain dyes in response to external stimuli, such as heat (6). Some natural dyes reportedly became darker before fading when exposed to light in one study (7). Dyeing manuals and texts dating from early in this century also reiterate that some dyes characteristically changed color with age (8–12).

Previous research has also indicated that certain dyestuffs can react to particular external conditions and thus produce color changes. An overview of related research articles indicate that factors influencing color changes involve internal characteristics of the substrate and dye molecules in combination and external forces, such as light, humidity, heat, atmospheric contaminants, or other foreign substances introduced in wear and in cleaning processes (4, 6, 13, 14, 15).

Objectives

Rice has suggested that in order to conserve historic colorants, it is necessary to know what constitutes the color, what chemicals affect it and how, and what factors cause it to fade or change (16). The specific objectives of this investigation were two-fold; to discover dye types and characteristics in the voile fabric; to discover if and how the fabric color changes in response to selected conditions it could have encountered in its wear life. This information could indicate possible factors to explain the types of discolorations on the dress. Experimental procedures and results for both objectives followed separate courses and therefore will be discussed separately. Results from the investigation of the first objective in part determined testing procedures for the second.

The fortuitous availability of a considerable amount of the fabric in the remnant enabled some extensive testing, which under circumstances ordinarily encountered by the conservationist—not desiring to destroy or damage the item itself—would not be possible.

Procedures to Discover Dye Type

Colorfastness Tests. Several authors writing about the dye technology in use early in this century have catalogued dyestuffs and dyeing methods used on silk fabrics, and their characteristic reactions to certain conditions, especially to light, to washing, and to perspiration (8–12). Certain present-day writers have stressed that particular classes of dyes have characteristic reactions to these various media. Corbman has charted the behavioral characteristics of each dye class (17). A fabric's unknown colorant can be determined by evaluating its reaction to various media and comparing its behavior with those of known dyes within the various classes.

For this portion of the study, specimens cut from the unused fabric were subjected to separate tests, following methods specified by the American Association of Textile Chemists and Colorists (A.A.T.C.C.), to determine its reaction to washing, drycleaning, light, perspiration, and crocking, as well as the fabric's tendency to transfer color to other fibers in solutions.

COLORFASTNESS TO WASHING. Following the A.A.T.C.C. Test 61–1975 IIA, one specimen was basted to a multifiber test fabric and placed in launderometer according to specifications. A biodegradable, low-sudsing, concentrated laundry detergent (manufactured by Sears, Roebuck, and Company) was used. This product contained sodium metasilicate and ethoxylated acids. The machine was operated as described at 49°C. After washing, the contents of the launderometer can were poured into a glass beaker and observed. The fabric had become a bright pink color and the wash water was bright yellow. The specimen was rinsed and soured as directed and excess moisture was blotted between paper toweling and dried.

COLORFASTNESS TO DRYCLEANING. One fabric sample was drycleaned using perchloroethylene, following procedure specified by A.A.T.C.C. Test 132–1976. Specimen was enclosed in a 8.8-cm square cotton bag and submitted to treatment.

COLORFASTNESS TO PERSPIRATION. Two specimens of the dress fabric were basted to separate squares of multifiber test fabric squares, according to A.A.T.C.C. Test Method 15–1975. One was immersed in an acid solution and the other in an alkaline solution for 20 min each. After wetting, the specimens were blotted between paper toweling to absorb

moisture. The fabric weight was not measured at this point. The specimens were treated in the A.A.T.C.C. Perspirometer and dried according
to the test specifications.

COLORFASTNESS TO CROCKING. Five specimens of the historic fabric
were tested for crocking color transference when wet and five specimens
were tested dry, using the Rotary Vertical Crockmeter as specified in
the A.A.T.C.C. Method 116–1977. In wetted specimens, the excess moisture was blotted between paper towels.

COLORFASTNESS TO LIGHT. Specimens were exposed to continuous
light provided by the carbon arc lamp of a Weatherometer for various
periods of time, ranging from 30 min to 40 h. It was necessary to evaluate
the color change at more frequent intervals than those suggested in the
test method 16A–1977, because studies have indicated silks sometimes
lose color within an hour of exposure (7).

EVALUATION OF SPECIMENS. For the colorfastness tests to washing
and to perspiration, the staining of the multifiber test strips included in
the tests was evaluated using the Gray Scale for Staining. For the crocking test, the white crockmeter cloth was evaluated as well. All staining
results are listed in Table II.

For every colorfastness test conducted, the color change of tested
specimen was evaluated by comparing it with the remnant fabric color
using the Gray Scale for Color Change. In addition, the color of the
resulting specimen for each test was analyzed and assigned a Munsell
color number. Results are in Table III.

All of these evaluations were made in the MacBeth SpectraLight
chamber, with daylight illumination. Because of the voile fabric sheer-
ness, two layers of fabric were evaluated.

Table II. Transfer of Color from Fabric to Multifiber Test Strip in
Colorfastness to Washing and Colorfastness to Perspiration Tests
(Evaluated Using Gray Scale for Staining)

| | *Perspiration* | | *Washing* |
Fiber[a]	*Acid Solution*	*Alkaline Solution*	*Detergent Solution*
Acetate	4[b]	4–5	3
Cotton	4	3–4	4–5
Nylon	2	3	2–3
Silk	3	3–4	3–4
Viscose	4–5	3–4	4–5
Wool	2–3	4	3–4

[a] In multifiber test strip.
[b] Represent Class on a 1 to 5 scale. Highest number indicates less color change
on fiber and therefore less color transfer from fabric dyes. Lower number indicates
greater color change and consequently greater color transfer.

Table III.   Color Change in Tested Specimens Using Gray Scale for Color Change

Test	Color Change Class[a]	Color Description	
		Verbal	Munsell
Washing[b]	2–3 redder	pink	5 R 7/2
Drycleaning	4–5 duller	light orange	7.5 YR 7/4
Crocking[c]			
dry	4–5	light orange	7.5 YR 7/4
wet	5	light orange	7.5 YR 7/4
Perspiration			
acid	3–4 redder	pink	7.5 R 7/4–6/4
alkaline	2–3	streaked with pink	7.5 YR 7/4 and 5 R 7/2
Light–carbon arc			
0.5 h	5	light orange	7.5 YR 7/4
1 h	4–5 redder	light orange	7.5 YR 7/4
2 h	4 redder	light orange	7.5 YR 7/4
4 h	4 redder	light orange	5 YR 7/2–7/4
8 h	3–4 redder	pink	2.5 YR 7/2
12 h	3 redder	pink	2.5 YR 8/2
16 h	2–3 redder	pink	2.5 YR 8/2
20 h	2 redder	pink	2.5 YR 8/4
40 h	1–2 redder	pink	2.5 YR 9/4

[a] On a 1 to 5 scale. Higher number indicates less color change.
[b] Wash water was observed to be a bright yellow color.
[c] Evaluated by absence of color on crockmeter cloth.

Dyestuff Recognition Tests for Historic Fabrics. Methods have been developed specifically for identifying general dye classifications on historic textile artifacts. Procedures outlined by Rice (14) were followed in this portion of the study.

Five 3.5 cm squares of the remnant fabric were treated to different chemicals. Specimens 1, 2, and 3 were wetted using 4 drops of a single solution, applied by use of an eyedropper to the center of each square. Specimens 4 and 5 were wetted similarly with 4 drops of one solution, followed by 4 drops of a second solution.

The first specimen was wetted with distilled water (pH approximately 5–6), the second with a 2% acetic acid solution, and the third with a 2% ammonium hydroxide solution. The fourth square was treated initially with a 2% acetic acid solution blotted after 1 min and then followed by a 2% ammonium hydroxide solution and blotted again after 1 min. The final specimen was treated similarly, first with a 2% ammonium hydroxide solution, followed by a 2% acetic acid solution.

EVALUATION. About 1 min after each specimen was wetted in the manner described above, it was blotted with a white crockmeter cloth square. Any color transference on the blotter was noted and evaluated using the Gray Scale for Staining. The resulting color of the fully dried specimen was evaluated and assigned a Munsell color number. Evaluations were done in the MacBeth SpectraLight chamber under daylight illumination. The voile fabric was folded so that 2 layers of material could be evaluated. Results of this test series may be found in Table IV.

X-ray Analysis with Electron Microscope. Knowing what elements are present in the voile fabric could conceivably help isolate the dyestuff used as the colorant on this material. Also, since the washing test changed the color so dramatically and since the color of the wash water suggested that some substance had been removed from the fabric, the tested specimen could show a removal of certain elements, which might contribute to knowledge about the dyeing of this fabric.

A spot analysis, using a Kevex-ray unit on a scanning electron microscope was performed on a piece of the fabric remnant and a piece of the washing test specimen. These specimens were mounted on a copper stud and had a thin deposition layer of carbon deposited over them. The following results were obtained from the technician who devised and performed the tests.

FABRIC REMNANT. Analysis of the fabric remnant showed that significant amounts of aluminum and sulfur were present.

WASHED SPECIMEN. X-ray analysis indicated that aluminum was slightly lower in this specimen, as compared with the fabric remnant. Sulfur was virtually absent. Sodium and silicon were reportedly present in significant amounts, but since the detergent used in the washing test contained these elements, it is believed that the detergent residue accounts for the presence of these elements.

Results and Discussion of Dye Type Investigation

The color test results indicate that probably two dyes are present in the historic dress fabric. There seems to be a pink dyestuff and a yellow dyestuff that together yield the light orange color of the yardage. In the washing test, for example, the historic fabric became pink, while the

Table IV. Fabric Response to Recognition Tests for Historic Colorants

	Trans-ference of Color to Blotter[a]	Color Evaluation	
Wetting Solution		Color Change[b]	Munsell Designation
Distilled water (pH 5–6)	5	4–5 duller	7.5 YR 7/4
2% CH_3COOH	5	4–5 brighter	7.5 YR 7/4
2% NH_4OH	3	3–4 redder	7.5 YR 7/4
2% CH_3COOH + 2% NH_4OH	4	4 redder	7.5 YR 7/4
2% NH_4OH + 2% CH_3COOH	4–5	3–4 redder	7.5 YR 7/4

[a] Evaluated using Gray Scale for staining.
[b] Evaluated using Gray Scale for color change.

wash water was observed to take on a vivid yellow color and yielded a bright yellow powder precipitate. In the lightfastness test, the yellow color component seemed to be completely removed from fabric samples subjected to the 20-h as well as 40-h exposure, and was decreased dramatically after only 4 h, leaving the fabric predominantly pink in color.

Perspiration tests similarly indicated the presence of two dyestuffs. In the alkali solution, the yellow color seemed to be removed almost completely, leaving a pink-colored fabric. In the acidic solution, the yellow dye migrated to the wool, silk, and nylon sections of the multifiber test strips, staining these fibers a bright yellow shade. The pink color seemed to bleed minimally; a small amount of color was transferred in the alkali solution tests, but generally this pink color remained comparatively very fast.

The wide variation in behaviors of the pink and yellow colors suggests that two distinct classes of dyes have been used to render the dress fabric color. An examination of the separate properties of the two dyestuffs will give an indication of their respective dye classes.

Yellow Dyestuff. The yellow-producing dyestuff is suspected to be an acid dye, primarily because its behavior responses to the A.A.T.C.C. tests parallel those typical of this class of dyes, as outlined by Corbman (17). The poor washfastness, tendency to bleed easily, and fair perspiration fastness exhibited by this yellow component are distinctly like those of the acid dyes. The historic textile, moreover, demonstrates the acid dye's typically excellent resistance to crocking. This yellow color was transferred to wool, silk, and nylon—all of which have an affinity for acid dyes.

Rice's historic dyestuff recognition test results corroborated with those of A.A.T.C.C. Colorfastness tests. The absence of color transfer in acetic acid, but the ready transfer of yellow color in ammonium hydroxide indicates a yellow acid dye is present. Less yellow was transferred when the fabric first moistened with ammonium hydroxide is rewetted with acetic acid.

X-ray analysis of the washed specimen from which the yellow color leached out showed some slight diminishing of aluminum and virtually no sulfur, whereas sulfur was present in the remnant fabric. Although it is possible that sulfur was in some way connected with the yellow dyestuff molecule, it may also be that a sulfur-containing acid was used to affix the yellow dyestuff on the cloth. Acid dyes are so-named because they are set with acids, and sulfuric acid commonly was used at this time to serve this function (8–12).

Pink Dyestuff. The superior fastness of the pink dye to all of the testing conditions indicates that it is probably a mordanted dye type. It does not demonstrate the same characteristics that are associated with either acid dyes or basic dyestuffs. Pink color intensity seems to be retained after washing, and there is no evidence of any pink color leaching into the wash water or staining fibers in the multifiber test strip. The good fastness of the pink dye to the perspiration tests and its resistance to transferring color further strengthens the hypothesis that it is of the mordant class.

None of the pink color was transferred to the blotter cloth in the historic dyestuff recognition tests. Rice says these results suggest a mordanted dyestuff produced the pink color (*14*).

The x-ray analysis tests help substantiate the dyestuff type as well. The significant amounts of aluminum in the remnant and the washed fabric suggest that aluminum may have been a component of the mordanting substance. Dyeing manuals dating from this time period indicate that aluminum-containing compounds were used to assist dyeing of certain dyestuffs (*8, 9, 10*).

Summary.   It is believed that the historic silk fabric was dyed in a two-stage process, using two distinctly different dyestuffs. There appears to be a mordanted pink-colored dye that has been topped with a brilliant yellow acid dye. This combination produced the light orange shade of the historic fabric.

This combination of colorant types also helps explain the peculiar staining of the underarm portions of the silk historic garment. Pink-colored regions may be viewed as areas from which the yellow dye migrated in the presence of alkaline substances in the perspiration, and the yellow regions as areas to which this bleeding acid dye was transferred.

Procedures to Test Fabric Color Response to Selected Conditions

Tested specimens in the preceding test series exhibited certain color changes in response to the isolated conditions, yet none of the conditions tested produced a specimen that became darker or yellower in hue. In instances where some sort of color change did occur, the opposite reaction occurred—fabric became redder, corroborating with Giles' report that certain dyes redden upon losing color (*5*).

This second series of tests was designed to include the effect of more factors in investigating the color response of the silk voile fabric and, where possible, to duplicate more closely conditions the fabric probably would have encountered in use and in cleaning during its wear life. In addition, x-ray analysis of the used fabric in the dress was conducted and compared with that of the remnant to see if there is a measurable elemental difference that might be traced to some external source. The analysis of the washed specimen in the preceding test series indicated that certain chemicals left in cleaning could be left as residues on the fabric. Any residues left on the used fabric in the voile dress might be detected with the Kevex-ray unit on the scanning electron microscope.

X-ray Analysis. Elemental analysis of the dress fabric mounted and analyzed as described in earlier tests, indicated that although the aluminum content was about as high as that of the remnant, the sulfur content was increased, and significant amounts of potassium were present, which were not evident in the remnant.

Colorfastness to Acids and Alkalis. In wear, the garment probably would have come in contact with atmospheric contaminants and with dust. A.A.T.C.C. Test Method 6–1975, Colorfastness to Acids and Alkalis, is designed to test a fabric's color reaction to acid fumes, applied alkaline or acid sizings, alkaline cleansing agents, and alkaline street dirt. All of these factors have been noted earlier as possible contributors to color change.

The specimens were subjected to separate tests for reaction to the chemicals specified in the testing procedure. Since a 4-L bell jar specified for the ammonium hydroxide fume test was not available, a glass globe with a slightly smaller capacity was substituted. The degree of color change as compared with the original remnant fabric was evaluated following procedures described for other colorfastness tests. Munsell color designations were assigned to each tested specimen after drying. Results are recorded in Table V.

Colorfastness to Daylight. Colorfastness to daylight tests indicate how fabric would react to outdoor exposure in a glass cabinet. This method exposes the fabric not only to naturally produced lighting, but to air contaminants and to airborne particles, helping to test the combined effects of light, humidity, and atmospheric contaminants on the fabric color.

One set of specimens was exposed only during the hours between nine and three o'clock, standard time. These nine fabric samples were exposed at 2-h intervals during three successive days, so that the first specimen was exposed 18 h and the ninth, 2 h.

Table V. Color Change of Specimens in Colorfastness
to Acids and Alkalis Test

Chemical	Color Change[a]	Munsell Color Description
Acids		
35% HCl	4–5	7.5 YR 7/4
56% CH$_3$COOH	4–5 duller	7.5 YR 7/4
Alkalis		
28% NH$_3$ (solution)	3 redder	5 YR 7/2
28% NH$_3$ (fumes)	4–5 redder, brighter	7.5 YR 7/4
10% Na$_2$CO$_3$	2–3 brighter	7.5 YR 8/4
Ca(OH)$_2$ (paste)	2	5 YR 8/2

[a] Using Gray Scale for color change.

Table VI. Color Reaction in Specimen Exposed to Daylight Between 9:00 and 3:00 Standard Time

Time Exposed (h)	Color Change[a]	Munsell Color Description
2	4–5 redder	7.5 YR 7/4
4	4–5 duller	7.5 YR 7/4
6	4 duller	7.5 YR 7/4
8	3–4 duller	7.5 YR 7/4
10	3–4 redder	7.5 YR 7/4
12	3 redder	5 YR 7/2
14	3 duller	5 YR 7/2
16	3 duller	5 YR 7/2
18	3 duller	5 YR 7/2

[a] Evaluated using Gray Scale for color change.

In a second test, six specimens were exposed in the glass-enclosed cabinet from 9:00 A.M. one morning to 9:00 A.M. the next. One specimen was added each day, so that the first specimen had been exposed six complete days and the last specimen, one day. This test allowed more exposure to environmental substances, temperature extremes, and light.

The degree of color change as compared with the original fabric and the Munsell color of the tested specimens were evaluated in the MacBeth SpectraLight, following previously explained procedures. Results are recorded in Tables VI and VII.

Color Reaction to Historic Cleaning Procedures. Another set of colorfastness tests was adapted primarily to simulate conditions under which the dress may have been cleaned. X-ray analysis indicated the presence of potassium and the higher levels of sulfur on the dress, as compared with the unused remnant. In the earlier X-ray analysis, the Kevex-ray detected some detergent residues on the washed specimen. It is possible that the elements detected on the dress could be residues from cleaning processes used earlier in this century, which might have been used to care for this dress.

Table VII. Color Reaction in Specimens Exposed in Outdoor Cabinet 24 Hours per Day

Time Exposed (days)	Color Change[a]	Munsell Color Description
1	4–5 duller	7.5 YR 7/4
2	4 duller	7.5 YR 7/4
3	4 duller	7.5 YR 7/2
4	3–4 duller	7.5 YR 7/2
5	3–4 redder	7.5 YR 8/2–7/2
6	3 redder	7.5 YR 8/2

[a] Evaluated using Gray Scale for color change.

A subsidiary investigation of cleaning techniques used earlier in this century on silk garments similar to the study garment was conducted to see what kinds of products and procedures were used. The information from that study has been detailed by Adams (1) and was used to draw up the tests in this particular portion of the colorant investigation. This study indicated that potassium- and sulfur-containing compounds frequently were used to clean and pretreat silk fabrics, that cleaning methods frequently produced color changes on silk garments, and that if wet-cleaned, silk garments probably would have been hand-washed carefully and quickly with a mild soap and lukewarm water, rinsed with water of the same temperature, and may have been given a special bluing rinse or a gum arabic rinse. The study also indicated that fabrics sometimes were pretreated to improve fastness qualities of notoriously fugitive dyes before cleaning.

On the basis of the information from that investigation, fabric specimens were subjected to pretreating and cleaning procedures simulating techniques and formulas used earlier in the century. Formulas specifically containing potassium and sulfur were selected especially.

REACTION TO PRETREATING. One particular method of "setting" fugitive colors on fabrics reported by Adams (1) was of particular interest because it involved compounds containing potassium and sulfur, both elements detected in the dress fabric x-ray analysis. As reported in that study, similar sorts of solutions were used by dyers and cleaners to increase the dye resistance to light and washing.

This laundry method was found in an early twentieth century text (18), and the procedure was followed for the test in this study. Chemicals used and their proportions are listed in Table VIII.

Six fabric specimens were basted to cotton squares (5 cm) and were placed in a beaker containing 500 mL of this solution at room temperature (20°C). As directed in the old textile text, the beaker and its contents were warmed for 10 min. After 5 min, the temperature was measured at 32°C and after 10 min, at 47°C. These squares were rinsed twice individually in 100 mL of distilled water at 20°C, then blotted and allowed to air dry.

The color of one of these squares was evaluated to determine color change and given a Munsell color designation. This result is recorded in Table IX. The other squares were reserved for further testing

Table VIII. Pretreating Formula

Distilled Water (mL)	Potassium Dichromate (g)	Copper(II) Sulfate (g)	Vinegar (mL)
950	2.2	3.4	2.2

Table IX.   Color Reaction to Historic Pretreating and Cleaning Procedures

Method	Color Change[a]	Munsell Color Designation
Pretreating	3–4 yellower	10 YR 7/4
Washing		
basic method		
yellow soap	2–3 redder	5 YR 7/2
white soap	2–3 redder	5 YR 7/2
bluing rinse		
yellow soap	2–3 redder	5 YR 7/2
white soap	2–3 redder	5 YR 7/2
gum arabic rinse		
yellow soap	2–3 redder	5 YR 7/2
white soap	2–3 redder	5 YR 7/2
pretreated		
yellow soap	2–3 redder	5 YR 7/2
white soap	2–3 redder	5 YR 7/2–6/2

[a] Evaluated using Gray Scale for color change.

REACTION TO HISTORIC WASHING METHODS.   A.A.T.C.C. Test Method 61–1962 IA was adapted to simulate historic cleaning methods. A 0.5% soap solution was substituted for the 0.5% detergent solution. Two kinds of soap were used, since, as reported in another study, both were available earlier in this century (*1*).

Fabric specimens (5-cm square) were basted to cotton squares and placed individually in wash cans containing 200 mL of soap solution. Steel balls were not added, since silk garments seem to have been washed rapidly and with considerably more care than other garments. Water temperature was warmed to 41.5°C. The Launderometer was operated only 4 min, again because silk garments were subjected to less stress than the average garment. A summarization of the method used is recounted in Table X.

After washing, specimens were rinsed twice for 1 min each in distilled water at 41.5°C. One set of specimens was given a third rinse in gum arabic water and one set was given a third rinse in a bluing

Table X.   Simulated Historic Cleaning Method

Cleaning					Rinsing	
Solution			Procedure		Rinsing	
Temperature (°C)	Volume (mL)	Amount of Soap (%)	Number of Steel Balls	Time Agitated (min)	Temperature (°C)	Volume (mL)
41.5	200	0.5	0	4	41.5	100

solution. The final set of specimens had been pretreated using the solution and procedure described earlier and were washed, rinsed twice in distilled water and dried, as were the first set of specimens.

All the specimens were dried according to test directions with an iron, as this is how silk garments were cared for at that time. The iron temperature was set on the "silk" setting, measured at 140°C.

These specimens were evaluated for color change and assigned a Munsell color designation, following procedures outlined in previous tests. Results are recorded in Table IX, along with those of the pretreating test.

Results and Discussion of Color Responses

Most of the test conditions produced specimens that became lighter in value and redder in hue, agreeing with Gile's report on the behavior of soluble dyes (5). Sunlight tests, acid and alkali tests, and laundering tests produced specimens with pinker colors, as the tabular information indicates. However, the pretreatment used to "set" the colorant on this fabric, and, as reported in Adams' review (1), conceivably used by commercial dyers and cleaners to "fix" colors that tended to be fugitive, produced almost the exact same color as that of the used fabric in the dress. The Munsell color number of both fabrics are the same, although a visual comparison does show a slight difference in color. This method of pretreating, as has been noted, was selected in this study primarily because its chemical components coincided with what the x-ray analysis indicated was different between the dress and the voile fabrics. When followed with washing treatments, the pretreated specimens did not seem to retain their original color significantly better than nonpretreated specimens. Of course, a less concentrated soap solution may not produce as dramatic a color shift and could have been used to clean this fabric in the dress. Just as likely, the dress could have been sent to a professional cleaner who had access to both the dye-setting technique simulated in this study and to dry cleaning methods, which Adams reports were used early in this century (1).

This series of tests indicates that a color change similar to that seen on the dress fabric is reproducible. The only method by which it was produced in this study was with a pretreating solution that contained sulfur and potassium, both elements shown in the x-ray analysis to be increased in the dress fabric.

Conclusions

This study indicates that the color of the voile fabric was produced by two distinct dyestuffs—an aluminum-mordanted dyestuff producing the pink color topped with a yellow acid dye. The fugitive nature of the yellow acid dye explains the peculiar color splotching in the underarm regions of the dress where the acid dye bled in contact with the alkali of the perspiration.

When specimens of the unused fabric remnant were subjected to conditions that an historical investigation and x-ray analysis indicated it conceivably could have come in contact with in wear and in cleaning, the fabric tended to become lighter and redder in color—the yellow-producing dye component contributing less to the color. However, when subjected to a pretreating solution composed of elements specifically isolated by the x-ray analysis as being present in the used fabric to a greater extent than in the unused fabric, the specimen became both yellower and darker and assumed the color of the used dress fabric.

It is likely that similar color changes could be evidenced on other garments treated in the same way. Sources, as reported in one study (*1*), suggest that professionally-cleaned goods and some home-cleaned goods may have been treated similarly. As mentioned earlier, the color change is a total-garment color change and would have been undetected if the remnant were not retained and if the dress had not been disassembled.

The color change exemplified on this dress, if indeed caused by a cleaning or precleaning process, is not like any of the known and reported reversible color changes noted in the literature. Until further study is made, no attempt will be made to alter the present color, even though it does not represent the color of the original dress.

Subsequent study could use the information gained in these tests to isolate more specifically the dyestuffs used to produce the color of this fabric. In addition, more in-depth investigation needs to be done to determine if the chemicals involved in this dye-setting technique could harm the fabric in some way and to determine if these chemicals could be removed without altering the fabric, reinstating the original color.

Further studies into the possible effects historic cleaning methods had on garments could be valuable in explaining some fabric colorant behaviors presently exhibited by collected textile items of historical significance. It is recommended that the usefulness of x-ray analysis techniques to determine colorant type or residual effects of treatment be studied further. Tests similar to those conducted in this study could be done to test colorant responses to situations using a more refined color comparison method, such as the Hunter Color Difference Meter.

Literature Cited

1. Adams, E. A. "Aesthetic and Structural Restoration of an Early Twentieth Century Historic Garment," Colorado State Univ., Fort Collins, 1980.
2. Rice, J. W. *Text. Museum J.* **1962**, *1*, 47–51.

3. Werner, A. E. *Museum* **1960**, *13*, 201–207.
4. Stromberg, E. *I.C.O.M. News* **1950**, *3*, 1–4.
5. Giles, C. H. In "1964 Delft Conf. Conserv. Text.: Collect. Reprints," 2nd ed.; Internatl. Inst. Conserv.: London, 1965; 8–26.
6. Giles, C. H.; McKay, R. B. *Text. Res. J.* **1963**, *33*, 528–577.
7. Padfield, T.; Landi, S. *Stud. Conserv.* **1966**, *11*, 181–196.
8. Hummel, J. J. "The Dyeing of Textile Fabrics," New and revised ed.; Cassell: New York, 1906.
9. Von Georgievics, G. C. T. "Chemistry of Dye-Stuffs"; translated from the 2nd German ed. by Charles Salter; Scott, Greenwood, & Co.: London, 1903.
10. Pellew, C. E. "Dyes and Dyeing"; McBride, Nast, & Co.: New York, 1913.
11. Matthews, J. M. "Laboratory Manual of Dyeing and Textile Chemistry," 1st ed.; John Wiley & Sons: New York, 1909.
12. Fraps, G. S. "Principles of Dyeing"; Macmillan: New York, 1903.
13. Van Beek, H. C. A.; Heertjes, P. M. *Stud. Conserv.* **1966**, *2*, 123–132.
14. Rice, J. W. In "Textile Conservation"; Leene, J., Ed.; Butterworths: London, 1972; 32–72.
15. Nogid, I.; Zornova, A. In "1964 Delft Conf. Conserv. Text.: Collect. Reprints," 2nd ed.; Internl. Inst. Conserv.: London, 1965; 121–125.
16. Rice, J. W. *Text. Museum J. 1*, 55–61.
17. Corbman, Bernard P. "Textiles: Fiber to Fabric," 5th ed.; McGraw–Hill: New York; p. 230–235.
18. Woolman, M. S.; McGowan, E. B. "Textiles: A Handbook for the Student and Consumer"; The Macmillan Co.: New York, 1913; 338–339.

RECEIVED December 4, 1979.

Dye Analysis of a Group of Late Intermediate Period Textiles from Ica, Peru

M. E. GEISS–MOONEY[1] and H. L. NEEDLES

Division of Textiles and Clothing, University of California, Davis, CA 95616

This chapter reports the analysis and identification of the natural dyestuffs used on a group of Late Intermediate Period, epoch 3B textiles from one grave lot (Site Z, grave 4, Hacienda Galagarza) in Ica, Peru. With no written records from the Peruvians themselves, dye analysis can provide information on the technology and ethnobotany of the culture that created the textiles. This information also can be used in conjunction with other research to prolong the life of the textiles. Thin layer chromatography and UV/vis spectroscopy were used since these analytic techniques can utilize the small samples necessary when sampling from historic textiles. Comparisons were made between the archaelogical samples and standards dyed with known dyestuffs. In general, the textiles from this grave site have reds that match the date for cochineal (carminic acid) and blues and greens that match indigo (indigotin). Whites, yellows, and browns were found to be the natural colors of the cotton and camelid fibers.

Dye analysis, especially in conjunction with other research, can provide much information for those entrusted with historic textiles. Information regarding the effects of pesticides, conservation procedures, storage environments, and exhibition conditions on fibers and dyes will allow curators and conservators to make decisions in the best interest of the preservation of the textiles. In the past, dye analysis of historic textiles has not always been successful, attributable to a great extent to the small sample sizes afforded. Refinements in the field of thin layer chromatography, especially in adsorbants, has made dye analysis much more

[1] Current address: P.O. Box 11002, Santa Rosa, CA 95406.

0065-2393/81/0193-0291$05.00/0

successful with sample sizes of a half-inch of fiber. This research analyzed a group of textiles excavated by Max Uhle at Galagarza, Site Z, grave 4, Peru at the turn of the century (1897–1905). The collection is dated at Late Intermediate Period, epoch 3B (A.D. 1050–1170) (1) and is housed at the R. H. Lowie Museum of Anthropology, University of California, Berkeley campus.

Experimental Procedures

First, the textiles were photographed, using 35-mm photoflood slide film and a seven-inch Kodak color separation ruler. This gives an idea of scale and color trueness in the photography. Samples of one-half to one inch were removed with scissors and tweezers, from protected areas if possible. Because of the deterioration of construction, none of the textiles were taken apart in any way. Sampling was done from different constructions and different colors as discernable to the unaided eye under fluorescent lighting. This may have led to some duplication of samples. Munsell notation was then assigned, using natural southern exposure lighting (Tables I and II) (2).

Fiber analysis was conducted using a binocular microscope and *n*-heptane as the mounting fluid for the longitudinal view. The plate method of cross sectioning with dull cellulose acetate as the packing fiber also was done. Casts were not successful as the fibers proved to be too brittle. Scanning electron microscopy was performed on a few samples with a Cambridge Stereoscan Mark IIA scope after sputtering a 200-Å layer of gold over the sample mounted on an aluminum stub. Polaroid film was used to record the images.

All samples (all colors cotton and camelid) first were washed in warm distilled water for 30 min and blotted on filter paper. When dry, the sample (except for blue- and green-colored samples) was then placed in a 25-mL round-bottom flask with four drops of 10% hydrochloric acid and heated in a warm water bath (90°C) for 20 min. Seven to ten milliliters of spectroscopic grade methanol was added and the flask then was hooked up to a micro Soxhlet apparatus. The flask was heated in a water bath for 30–45 min, the methanol collecting in the Soxhlet chamber and concentrating the solution in the flask. The sample was removed to filter paper and the two solutions to separate flasks. The extraction solution was spotted onto precoated 5 × 10 cm 10% acetylated cellulose plates (J. T. Baker), allowed to dry, and developed in

Table I.   Munsell Notation for Yellow and Brown Camelid Fibers

10 YR 6/8	7.5 YR 6/8
5 YR 5/8	5 YR 2/2

Table II.   Munsell Notation for Yellow and Brown Cotton Fibers

10 YR 8/4	7.5 YR 6/6
5 YR 4/6	2.5 YR 4/6

2.5 Y 8/4

Table III.   Munsell Notation for Red Camelid Fibers

Before Extraction	*After Extraction*
7.5 R 3/6	7.5 YR 6/8
5 R 4/10	7.5 YR 6/8

Table IV.   Munsell Notation for Blue and Green Camelid Fibers

Before Extraction	*After Extraction*
5 B 3/2	7.5 YR 5/6
10 BG 2/2	7.5 YR 5/6
2.5 BG 3/2	7.5 YR 5/6
10 G 3/2	7.5 YR 5/6
10 GY 4/2	7.5 YR 5/6

a saturated chamber with an eluent mixture of ethyl acetate–tetrahydrofuran–water (6:35:47). The elution took about 30–40 min to complete. The solvent front was marked and the plate examined under fluorescent lighting and short-wave (350 nm) UV light, marking any spots and noting colors. The plate was then sprayed with a 1% solution of 2-aminoethyldiphenyl-borate (Naturstoff reagent, Tridom Chemical) in methanol and re-examined under the previously mentioned lighting conditions. Spot colors were again noted. R_f values were calculated.

The rest of the extraction solution was then placed in a semimicro cuvet (10-mm path length) and run on a Beckman DB-G grating spectrometer between 200 cm and 800 cm^{-1}, the visible and UV range. The other methanol solution was used in the reference cuvet. The spectrum curve was recorded on a chart paper recorder. Infrared spectroscopy also was tried, dropping the extraction solution onto potassium bromide powder and drying in a hot vacuum oven before pressing into a pellet using handpress equipment (Perkin–Elmer). But the results were not definitive nor conclusive. Munsell notation was assigned to the dried extracted samples, using the same lighting conditions as before (Table III).

The blue- and green-colored samples were not affected by the methanol extraction and so were analyzed differently. After washing, the sample was placed in a small test tube with 1 mL of a solution containing 50 g of sodium hydrosulfite and 50 g of sodium hydroxide per liter of water. The test tube was warmed in water for a few minutes and then one drop of spectroscopic grade ethyl acetate was added. The test tube was shaken. If the ethyl acetate layer turns clear bright blue, indigo is present (3). The ethyl acetate layer was spotted onto 10% acetylated cellulose plates and developed in an eluent mixture of ethyl acetate–ethanol–water (2:1:1). Spot color was noted and R_f calculated. The ethyl acetate layer also was run through UV/vis spectroscopy with a reference of spectroscopic grade ethyl acetate. If the ethyl acetate layer stayed clear, the sample was run as a normal one. Munsell notation was assigned to the dried extracted samples, using the same lighting conditions as before (Table IV).

Known dyeings of natural dyes on sheep wool and synthetic equivalents of the dye constituents also were characterized by the same analytical scheme. These included cochineal, carminic acid, (H. Kohnstamm & Company), madder, alizarin (Aldrich Chemical), purpurin (J. T. Baker), Relbunium hypocarpium, pseudopurpurin (K&K–ICN Labs), brazilwood, and brazilin (J. T. Baker) for reds; indigo, indigotin (J. T. Baker), logwood, and Genipa americana for blues; Bixa orellana for oranges; Schinus molle, Baccharis genistolloides, Bidens andicola, Dicliptera hookeriana, Berberis species, curcumin (J. T. Baker), lawsone (Aldrich Chemical), and crocetin (J. T. Baker) for yellows (4, 5, 6).

Results and Conclusions

In regards to fiber analysis, it was not possible to differentiate between archaeological alpaca, llama, and possibly vicuña and so the woolen fibers were called camelid (Figure 1). The cottons had the appearance in cross section of cotton today that is unmercerized. One cotton sample proved to be very interesting as an earth pigment was used for the bright orange color (Figure 2). X-ray fluorescence analysis confirmed that the earth pigment used was cinnabar (mercury sulfide) (Figure 3). None of the other cotton samples were dyed except for one blue sample, which was dyed with indigo and used as a decorative warp stripe (Figure 4) along one selvedge of the textile 4-4873B. The camelid samples were the naturally occurring fiber colors except for the reds, blues, and greens (Figure 5). The reds were obtained from a source of carminic acid,

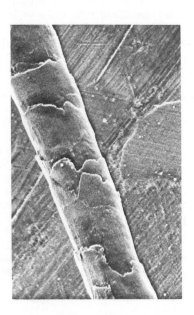

Figure 1.   Scanning electron microscopy: textile 4-4868, camelid fiber (504×)

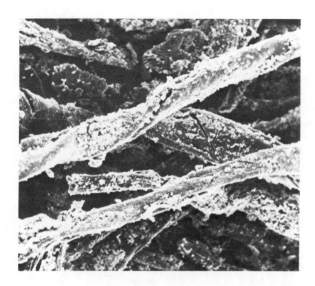

Figure 2.   Scanning electron microscopy: textile 4-4842, cotton fiber with cinnabar pigment (186×)

probably the native Dactylopius confusus (cochineal) species (*7*) (Table V and Figure 6). The blues and greens were obtained from a source containing indigotin, probably the native species of Indigofera suffruticosa (*8*) (Table VI and Figure 7).

Much dye analysis work remains to be done on historic textiles of all kinds. Recently, there has been some research including thin layer chromatography using micropolyamide plates with much success (*9, 10*). Future work could use both types of plates to increase the accuracy of identification. Thin layer chromatography is proving to be an inexpensive and simple method for the identification of dyestuffs used on historic textiles. As well as providing information used in conjunction with other research that could increase the longevity of the textiles, information on the culture and technology that created the textiles is also a welcome result.

Acknowledgments

We thank the staff of the R. H. Lowie Museum of Anthropology for their assistance in providing well-provenanced textiles. Thanks to Dr. Wilfred Ward, USDA Regional Lab, Albany, California, for the confirmatory camelid fiber analysis. Also, many thanks for the help for so long

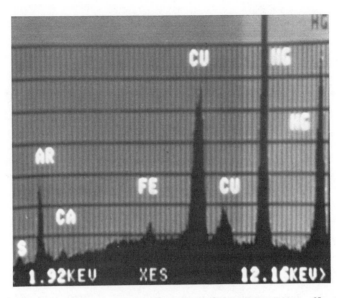

Figure 3. X-ray fluorescence analysis: textile 4-4842, cotton fiber with cinnabar pigment; 10-min scan, Cu and Ar peaks are artifacts of the instrument.

Figure 4. Textile 4-4873B, only dyed cotton fiber in grave lot

Figure 5.   Textile 4-4866, example of full range of natural and dyed camelid fibers

**Table V.   Thin Layer Chromatography of Red Knowns and Unknown
4-4866 in Methanol on 10% Acetylated Cellulose Plates**

	R_f	Spot Color (Fluorescent) Unsprayed/ Sprayed[a]	Spot Color (350 cm^{-1}) Unsprayed/ Sprayed[a]
Unknown 4-4866	0.86	pale pink/bright pink	pink/pink
Cochineal, Sn Mordant, Sheep Wool	0.86	orange/dark rose pink	bright pink/dark pink
Carminic Acid Dye Powder	0.86	orange/dark rose pink	bright pink/dark pink

[a] 1% solution of 2-aminoethyldiphenylborate in methanol.

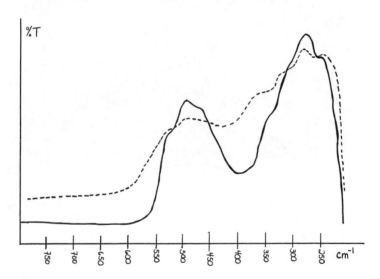

*Figure 6.   UV/vis spectroscopy: (———) known cochineal on sheep wool;
(– – –) unknown 4-4866 in methanol*

**Table VI.   Thin Layer Chromatography of Blue Knowns,
Unknowns 4-3873A(Cotton) and 4-4866(Camelid) in Ethyl
Acetate on 10% Acetylated Cellulose Plates**

	$R_f{}^a$	*Spot Color (Fluorescent)*
Unknown 4-4873A (Cotton)	0.82	pale blue
Unknown 4-4866 (Camelid)	0.82	pale blue
Indigo, Sheep Wool	0.82	pale blue
Indigotin Dye Powder	0.82	pale blue

^{a} After positive result of initial test for indigo.

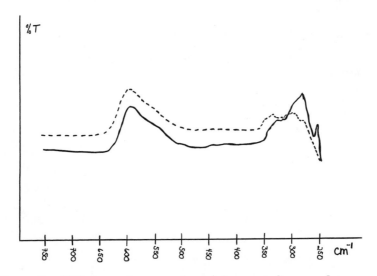

*Figure 7.   UV/vis spectroscopy: (——) known indigo on sheep wool;
(— — —) unknown 4-4866 (blue) in ethyl acetate after positive initial test for
indigo.*

by K. Alger, Textiles & Clothing, University of California, Davis. And thanks to G. Carriveau, Research Laboratory, Metropolitan Museum of Art, New York City for the confirmatory x-ray fluorescence analysis.

Literature Cited

1. Menzel, D. "The Archaeology of Ancient Peru and the Work of Max Uhle"; University of California Printing Department: Berkeley, 1977; pp. 58, 131.
2. Munsell Color Company "Munsell Book of Color"; Munsell Color Company: Baltimore, MD, 1954.
3. Hofenk-deGraaf, J. *Stud. Conserv.* **1974,** *19,* 54.
4. Autunez de Mayolo, Kay K. M.S. thesis, California Polytechnic Univ., San Luis Obispo, 1977.
5. Yacovleff, E.; Herrera, F. L. "El Mundo Vegetal de los Antiguos Peruanos," *Rev. Mus. Nac. (Lima)* **1934,** *3* (3), 243.
6. Towle, M. A. "The Ethnobotany of Pre-Columbian Peru"; Aldine Publishing: New York, 1961.
7. Brunello, F. "The Art of Dyeing in the History of Mankind"; Phoenix Dye Works: Cleveland, OH, 1973; 344.
8. MacBride, J. Francis, ed. "Flora of Peru," Field Museum of Natural History Botanical Series; Field Museum Press: Chicago, 1943; Vol. 13, Part 3, No. 1.
9. Schweppe, H. "Nachweis von Farbstoffen auf alten Textilien," *Z. Anal. Chem.* **1975,** *276,* 291.
10. Schweppe, H. "Identification of Dyes on Old Textiles," *J. Am. Inst. Conserv.* **1980,** *19* (1), 14.

RECEIVED November 27, 1979.

Protection of Light-Sensitive Blue Wool Fabric with Cellulose Acetate Films Containing Ultraviolet Stabilizers

TYRONE L. VIGO and NANCY E. WYATT

USDA Textiles and Clothing Laboratory, Knoxville, TN 37916

Cellulose acetate films containing various ultraviolet stabilizers were evaluated for their ability to protect light-sensitive fabric from color change on exposure to an artificial light source at relative humidities and temperatures simulating warm, moderately humid indoor climates. Stabilizers that absorb ultraviolet light were the most effective in protecting the wool fabrics while zinc acetate dihydrate was moderately effective; however, the mechanisms by which the zinc salt offers photochemical protection are not known. Color differences in the exposed fabrics were determined by ΔE values computed from L,a,b readings. The most effective stabilizers gave ΔE values of 0.8–0.9 relative to a 550 kJ/m^2 fabric exposure; unprotected fabric gave a ΔE value of 2.7. Cellulose acetate films containing no stabilizers offered little protection; other film thicknesses or combinations of stabilizers afforded no advantage over using one stabilizer in 8-mil-thick film.

Although the importance of environmental factors (temperature, relative humidity, airborne contaminants, and oxygen) that affect the fading of dyed textiles exposed to artificial and natural light indoors is well documented (*1, 2*), relatively little information exists on the effectiveness of UV stabilizers incorporated into plastic films to minimize or retard such fading. To obtain this information, light-sensitive blue wool fabric (AATCC L–4 standard) was exposed to light from a xenon-arc source, with and without protection by clear cellulose acetate films

0065-2393/81/0193-0301$05.00/0

containing UV stabilizers. This fabric was chosen as a prototype in this study because its fading characteristics are well known, and because results obtained with this fabric could prove useful for evaluating other light-sensitive fabrics.

Color changes in the fabrics were quantitatively determined by changes in ΔE—computed from L,a,b, tristimulus measurements by the Scofield–Hunter color difference equation (3). Unlike results reported in a previous study (4), it was demonstrated that the cellulose acetate films containing UV stabilizers did not need to be colored to minimize fading in the exposed fabric. The primary advantage of using cellulose acetate rather than other polymer substrates as the plastic film is that the true effectiveness of various stabilizers for protecting fabrics could be determined since cellulose acetate film without stabilizers offers little photochemical protection. Another advantage is that cellulose acetate films may be cast from solution in a laboratory and do not require special polymer processing equipment.

As noted in other studies (5, 6), a quantitative assessment of color change in the blue wool or other dyed fabrics is more reliable than the use of subjective visual assessments that classify fading by relationship to a grey scale standard (7) and that employ such terminology as "just appreciable fading." Results with five different stabilizers (four commercial and one experimental) at three different levels of stabilizer concentration and at three different film thicknesses were investigated. Fabric exposure times simulated those occurring with 20–100 h of noon sunlight indoors under warm, moderately humid conditions.

Experimental

Preparation of Cellulose Acetate Films. Commercial cellulose acetate powder (Eastman Cellulose Acetate 398–3) (15 wt %) and five commercial and experimental UV stabilizers (0.25–1.0 wt % cellulose acetate) were dissolved in 35% diacetone alcohol–45% acetone–5% ethanol. All solvents were reagent grade and the solvent composition used was adapted from recommendations in a technical bulletin (8). The mixture was stirred in a Waring blender to insure homogeneity, then poured into glass tubes, and centrifuged for 5 min at 2000 rpm to remove air bubbles. The solution was then poured onto ¼-in-thick plate glass and spread with a Gardner knife that has a set of adjustable micrometers, allowing films of uniform thickness to be cast. A 5-mil film required micrometer settings of 0.040 in and an 8-mil film required settings of 0.058 in. The 12-mil films were cast in multiple layers, each layer requiring micrometer settings of 0.047 in. By this procedure, cellulose acetate films of 5-, 8-, and 12-mil were obtained after the solvents had been allowed to evaporate for at least 72 h at ambient temperature. During this time, the plate glass was protected from dust by a sheer muslin cloth supported on a framework above and around the side of the glass.

Ultraviolet Stabilizers. Four commercial UV stabilizers and zinc acetate dihydrate (U.S.P. grade) were added to various films during their preparation. Two were of the hydroxybenzotriazole type, one a hydroxybenzophenone, and another a hindered-amine type (Table I).

Exposure to Wool Fabrics to Light. Blue Wool Fabric L–4 (1978 lot—a fabric dyed with two blue dyes, one fugitive, the other substantative) was used as the test fabric. This particular fabric fades approximately one unit on the grey scale (7), i.e., "just appreciable fading," when it is exposed for 20 h to an artificial light source. Samples (6.5 × 10 in) of this L–4 fabric were covered with samples of the various cellulose acetate films prepared as described above (films having different thicknesses and containing different concentrations and types of UV stabilizers), inserted into sample holders and exposed in an Atlas Weatherometer (a 2500-W xenon-arc light source) to a light intensity of 110–550 kJ/m² for approximately 20-h exposure intervals. The Weatherometer test conditions were set for 85°F and 50% relative humidity with a black panel temperature of 100°F.

Because the light intensity of a xenon-arc light source varies with the age of the lamp (9), a light monitor was attached to the light source to insure that light exposure (total radiation dose) was the same for all fabric samples. The light monitor measures and integrates the radiant energy from the xenon-arc lamp. Infrared-absorbing inner and outer filters (10) were used for all exposures. The resultant UV component of the transmitted spectrum closely resembles UV in natural sunlight except for a peak at 390 nm and an additional energy distribution at 300–320

Table I. UV Stabilizers Incorporated into Cellulose Acetate Films

UV Stabilizer Number	Chemical Structure	Trade Name
UV–1A		Cyasorb 5411[a]
UV–1B		Tinuvin 328[b]
UV–2		Cyasorb 531[a]
UV–3		Tinuvin 770[b]
UV–4	$Zn(O{-}\overset{O}{\underset{\|}{C}}{-}CH_3)_2 \cdot 2H_2O$	—

[a] Trademark of American Cyanamid.
[b] Trademark of Ciba–Geigy.
[c] Proprietary product presumed to contain a tetramethylpiperdine moiety.

nm. The UV component transmitted to the fabric was about one-third greater in intensity than for an equivalent 550 kJ/m² exposure to natural sunlight.

Ultraviolet Absorption/Transmission Curves of Plastic Films. Three 8-mil-thick cellulose acetate films containing: (a) no stabilizer, (b) 0.5% UV–1A (hydroxybenzotriazole type), and (c) 1.0% UV–4 (zinc acetate dihydrate) were inserted into a Cary 17D UV/VIS/NIR Recording Spectrophotometer and their absorption/transmission curves run in the region of 250–500 nm. The film containing no stabilizer was run against air as the standard while films containing stabilizers were run against the unstabilized film as the standard.

Testing of Fabrics for Colorfastness to Light. After each interval of exposure, fabrics protected by the films were measured for their color change by taking six L,a,b readings on the fabric with a Hunter color difference meter. By this method, the L,a,b readings were used to calculate the ΔE value, which denote the magnitude of total color difference, by the formula $\Delta E = (\Delta L^2 + \Delta a^2 + \Delta b^2)^{\frac{1}{2}}$ (3). An average ΔE for each exposed fabric was calculated with standard deviations of 0.01–0.10 for fabrics having a ΔE of 1 or less, 0.12–0.20 for fabrics having a ΔE between 1 and 2, and 0.21–0.38 for fabrics having a ΔE between 2 and 3.

Testing of Fabrics for Tensile Properties. Unexposed and exposed pieces of L–4 Blue Wool fabrics were tested in the warp and fill direction for tearing strength by ASTM Method D–1424 on an Elmendorf tester (11).

Results and Discussion

Cellulose acetate films of the same thickness (8 mil) containing five different stabilizers at three concentrations were evaluated for their effectiveness in protecting the blue wool fabrics (Table II). Unprotected wool fabric and wool fabric covered with film containing no stabilizers exposed to the xenon-arc source under comparable conditions served as primary and secondary controls. Film without any stabilizer offered little protection throughout the exposure period; after 550 kJ/m² exposure, fabric protected by such a film had a ΔE value of 2.38 and unprotected fabric had a value of 2.70.

Of the five stabilizers, the two hydroxybenzotriazole (UV–1A and UV–1B) and hydroxybenzophenone (UV–2) compounds were most effective in preventing changes in the color of wool fabric. Although these stabilizers were effective at concentrations as low as 0.25%, the best protection at this particular film thickness was achieved with 0.5% of either hydroxybenzotriazole or 1.0% hydroxybenzophenone. ΔE values after 550 kJ/m² were 0.79 for UV–1A, 0.80 for UV–1B, and 0.83 for UV–2 at these concentrations. Equal parts by weight (a total concentration of 0.5 and 1.0%) of the hydroxybenzophenone (UV–2) and one of the hydroxybenzotriazoles (UV–1A) in the film did not afford any better protection; indeed, color changes in the fabric were somewhat greater when combinations of stabilizers were used than when only one stabilizer was used. Since these hydroxybenzotriazoles and hydroxybenzophenones are known to function as photostabilizers by absorbing UV light in the 300–360 nm range, it is not surprising that they are effective for protecting the wool fabric from photofading when incorporated into the cellulose acetate films (*12*). Absorption/transmission curves of cellulose acetate film containing no stabilizer and one containing 0.5% of a hydroxybenzotriazole (UV–1A) confirmed that protection from photofading of the blue wool fabric by the hydroxybenzotriazole was through maximum absorption of UV light by the stabilized film over a wide range (the region of 250–375 nm). The film containing no stabilizer exhibited maximum absorption only in the region of 250–275 nm.

The other commercial stabilizer (UV–3), a hindered-amine type, is presumed to afford photochemical protection by functioning primarily as a free radical and/or oxygen scavenger (*13*). Thus protection should only occur in the primary substrate, the cellulose acetate film, and not in a secondary substrate such as the blue wool fabric. The results shown in Table II verified this assumption; the ΔE values obtained, irrespective of the concentration of UV–3 used in the film, were within experimental error of those observed with the unprotected fabric.

It was not possible to evaluate insoluble pigments such as zinc oxide for their effectiveness as UV stabilizers in the cellulose acetate films because the centrifugation necessary to remove air bubbles prior to film casting caused such insoluble materials to be distributed unevenly in the casting solution. Therefore, a soluble experimental stabilizer, zinc acetate dihydrate (UV–4) was chosen for this study. Although previous research (*14*) had demonstrated that it reacts readily with peroxides (i.e., it functions chemically as a peroxide scavenger), it had not been determined whether or not it also could function photochemically as a peroxide scavenger or be effective as a UV stabilizer. However, a recent patent (*15*) describing zinc acetate as an effective photostabilizer for polyurethanes created additional interest for evaluating it as a stabilizer in the cellulose acetate films for protecting the blue wool fabrics from photofading.

At concentrations of 0.25 and 0.50%, the zinc acetate behaved like the hindered-amine stabilizer—it afforded little or no photochemical protection to the wool fabric; ΔE values of 2.47 and 2.21 were observed at the above concentrations after 550 kJ/m² exposure. Thus, one could assume it functions photochemically as an oxygen/peroxide scavenger. At concentrations of 1.0%, zinc acetate did afford moderate protection to the wool fabrics (ΔE value of 1.55 after 550 kJ/m² exposure), but its absorption/transmission curve exhibited a maximum absorption only at 250–300 nm. Thus, the moderate protection afforded to the wool fabric

Table II.   Effectiveness of UV Stabilizers in 8-Mil-Thick Cellulose Light of

Stabilizer Number	Stabilizer Type	Concentration (%)[b]
UV–1A	hydroxybenzotriazole	0.25
		0.50
		1.0
UV–1B	hydroxybenzotriazole	0.25
		0.50
		1.0
UV–2	hydroxybenzophenone	0.25
		0.50
		1.0
UV–1A/UV–2	hydroxybenzotriazole/ hydroxybenzophenone	0.5
		1.0
UV–3	hindered amine	0.25
		0.50
		1.0
UV–4	zinc acetate dihydrate	0.25
		0.50
		1.0
Control (no stabilizer)	none	0.0
Control (no film) [c]	—	—

[a] Calculated from L,a,b values on a Hunter color difference meter (average of six readings on each sample); exposure in Weatherometer is listed in kilojoules per square meter (ambient dry bulb temperature, 85°F $\pm$ 3°; wet bulb temperature, 70°F $\pm$ 4°, black panel temperature 100°F; % relative humidity, 50 $\pm$ 8%). Each 110 kJ/m² corresponds to about 20 h exposure to noon sunlight conditions.

by films containing 1.0% zinc acetate was not attributable to absorption maxima above 300 nm, and indicated that additional studies are needed to determine mechanisms by which it functions as a UV stabilizer.

ΔE values and light exposure in kilojoules per square meter for the primary and secondary controls, and for fabrics covered by 8-mil films containing 0.5 and 1.0% stabilizers (extracted from data in Table II) were given a least-squares treatment to fit an exponential curve $y = ab^x$ (where $y = \Delta E$ and $x =$ exposure in kJ/m²). In curves generated for stabilizer concentrations of 0.5 and 1.0% (Figures 1 and 2), two general families of curves are observed: (a) those for treatment that effectively protect the wool fabric (i.e., the films containing hydroxybenzotriazoles

Acetate Film for Protection of Blue Wool Fabrics from Xenon-Arc Different Intensities

$$\Delta E \; Values^a$$

110 kJ/m²	220 kJ/m²	330 kJ/m²	440 kJ/m²	550 kJ/m²
0.54	0.60	0.73	0.91	1.02
0.60	0.64	0.72	0.71	0.79
0.55	0.72	0.66	0.75	1.01
0.74	0.72	0.80	0.85	1.10
0.56	0.62	0.69	0.60	0.80
0.69	0.82	0.77	0.74	0.89
0.45	0.66	0.82	1.05	1.28
0.58	0.62	0.68	0.86	1.00
0.57	0.59	0.67	0.67	0.83
0.51	0.67	0.73	0.91	1.04
0.59	0.74	0.71	0.92	0.94
0.76	1.30	1.64	2.08	2.21
0.62	1.33	1.32	2.46	2.70
0.80	1.36	1.54	2.45	2.48
0.94	1.52	1.94	2.40	2.46
0.79	1.33	1.78	2.20	2.21
0.37	0.81	1.27	1.52	1.55
0.82	1.34	1.71	2.36	2.38
0.96	1.60	2.15	2.68	2.70

[b] Based on weight of cellulose acetate powder used for casting film; when more than one stabilizer was used, equal amounts of each were incorporated into the solution.

[c] No film. Blue Wool Fabric L–4. ΔE values for primary and secondary controls (8-mil film with no stabilizers over wool fabric and wool fabric alone) are mean values based on four samples subjected to UV.

and the hydroxybenzophenone) and (b) those for treatments that do not protect the wool fabric (the unprotected control and the film without stabilizer, the hindered-amine stabilizer, and the zinc acetate dihydrate stabilizer at low concentrations). At 1.0% levels of stabilizer, the zinc acetate dihydrate curve (Figure 2) is intermediate between the two families of curves, indicating that it affords moderate protection to the wool fabric.

Correlation coefficients were very good for most of the curves (0.92 or greater) with the exception of three: UV–1B at 0.5 and 1.0% (correlation coefficients of 0.76 and 0.64, respectively) and UV–1A (correlation coefficient of 0.89). Lack of good correlation, particularly with the UV–

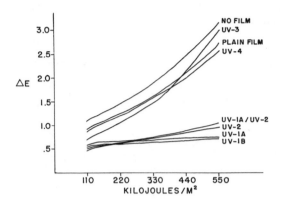

Figure 1.   Least-squares fit to exponential curve y = ab^x (y = ΔE; x = kJ/m^2) *for unprotected blue wool fabric, and for blue wool fabrics covered with cellulose acetate films (8-mil) containing no stabilizer, or one or more stabilizers at 0.5% concentration*

1B stabilizer, is attributable to reversals in ΔE observed at 220–440 kJ/m^2. However, such reversals are within the standard deviation. Thus, the exponential relationship above generally defines the color change in the blue wool fabrics as a function of light intensity × time.

To determine whether or not changes in color were accompanied by fiber damage, unexposed fabric and several fabrics exposed to the xenon-arc source for 550 kJ/m^2 (ΔE from 1 to 3) were tested for tearing strength by the Elmendorf method (*11*). Before exposure, the tearing strength of the blue wool fabric was 2040 g in the warp and 1710 g in the fill direction. For all other fabrics tested after exposure to light, the

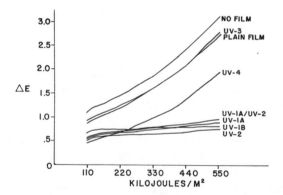

Figure 2.   Least-squares fit to exponential curve y = ab^x (y = ΔE, x = kJ/m^2) *for unprotected blue wool fabric, and for blue wool fabrics covered with cellulose acetate films (8-mil) containing no stabilizer, and one or more stabilizers at 1.0% concentration*

lowest values observed for tearing strength were 1830 g in the warp and 1490 g in the fill direction. This 10% reduction in tearing strength is not significant. Thus, even fabrics that underwent the greatest color change on exposure to the xenon-arc light suffered no perceptible loss of tensile properties.

To determine whether or not film thickness had any effect on protection of the wool fabrics, various 5- and 12-mil-thick cellulose acetate films were cast and used to cover fabrics exposed in the Weatherometer. Although it was possible to obtain films of good clarity and a minimum of surface defects at 5- and 8-mil thickness, two castings were necessary to obtain 12-mil-thick films. Attempts to prepare a 12-mil-thick film in a single cast resulted in pronounced cratering and poor clarity.

Table III shows results obtained when three UV stabilizers, alone or in combination, were used in 5- and 12-mil films for protecting the blue wool fabrics. The hindered-amine stabilizer (UV-3) was not tested because it was ineffective in 8-mil films (Table II). In 5-mil-thick films, the trends in ΔE values for the hydroxybenzotriazole (UV-1B), hydroxybenzophenone (UV-2), and the zinc acetate (UV-4) stabilizers were the same as they were when these stabilizers were incorporated into 8-mil-thick films. However, after maximum exposure time, the ΔE values were somewhat higher than those observed with 8-mil films. Similar trends were observed with films of 12-mil thickness. Only the hydroxybenzophenone (UV-2) had ΔE values less than 1.0 after 550 kJ/m^2 exposure. The relative effectiveness of a hydroxybenzotriazole (UV-1B), a hydroxybenzophenone (UV-2), and combinations of each of these stabilizers as a function of film thickness are shown in Figure 3. All films, even those containing no stabilizers, were most effective in protecting the wool fabrics from color change when they were 8-mil thick. Again, no advantage was observed in using combinations of stabilizers instead of a single stabilizer in the film.

Conclusions

1. Cellulose acetate films of 8-mil thickness containing 0.5–1.0% hydroxybenzotriazole or hydroxybenzophenone UV stabilizers were the most effective in protecting Blue Wool L-4 fabrics from undergoing color changes when exposed to a xenon-arc light source that simulated 20–100 h of noon sunlight indoors under warm, moderately humid conditions.

2. Films containing no stabilizers afforded little protection to the blue wool fabrics when they were exposed to the light source.

3. Varying film thickness or using combinations of stabilizers afforded no advantage over using one stabilizer in 8-mil-thick cellulose acetate films with regard to fabric protection.

Table III.   Effectiveness of UV Stabilizers in 5- and 12-Mil-Thick
Xenon-Arc Light of

Stabilizer Number	Stabilizer Type	Concen-tration (%)[b]	Film Thick-ness[a] (mils)
UV–1B	hydroxybenzotriazole	0.5	5
UV–2	hydroxybenzophenone	0.5	5
UV–1B/UV–2	hydroxybenzotriazole/ hydroxybenzophenone	0.5	5
UV–4	zinc acetate dihydrate	1.0	5
Control (no stabilizer)	none	0.0	5
UV–1B	hydroxybenzotriazole	0.5	12
UV–2	hydroxybenzophenone	0.5	12
UV–1B/UV–2	hydroxybenzotriazole/ hydroxybenzophenone	0.5	12
UV–2	hydroxybenzophenone	1.0	12
UV–1B/UV–2	hydroxybenzotriazole/ hydroxybenzophenone	1.0	12
Control (no stabilizer)	none	0.0	12
Control (no film)[d]	—	—	—

[a] Same conditions as Table II, footnote [a].
[b] Same conditions as Table II, footnote [b].

Cellulose Acetate Films for Protection of Blue Wool Fabric from Different Intensities

ΔE Values[a]				
110 kJ/m²	*220 kJ/m²*	*330 kJ/m²*	*440 kJ/m²*	*550 kJ/m²*
0.54	0.67	0.79	0.97	1.06
0.45	0.56	0.80	0.94	1.38
0.75	0.94	0.92	0.96	1.10
0.47	0.95	1.34	1.73	1.80
1.00	1.15	2.14	2.22	3.29
0.91	0.94	0.98	1.09	1.00
0.74	0.72	0.75	0.82	0.92
0.92	1.01	0.99	1.08	1.09
0.87	0.93	0.88	0.95	0.93
1.03	1.12	1.12	1.22	1.20
0.78	1.29	1.58	1.78	3.11
0.96	1.60	2.15	2.68	2.70

[c] 5-mil-thick film was cast at a micrometer setting of 0.040 in; 12-mil film cast in multiple layers, each layer requiring 0.047 in setting.
[d] Same controls as Table II, footnote [c].

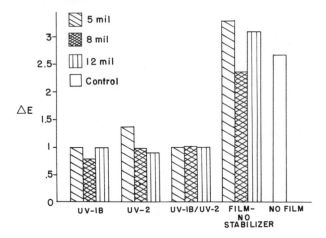

Figure 3.   Plot of ΔE after 550 kJ/m² exposure of blue wool fabric with and without cellulose acetate films of varying thickness, films contained stabilizers at 0.5% concentration

4. The hindered-amine type stabilizer was ineffective, and the zinc acetate dihydrate moderately effective, in protecting the wool fabrics. Further study is needed to determine the mechanisms by which the latter compound imparts photostabilization.

5. The relation between ΔE (color change) in the fabrics to exposure intensity (kJ/m²) generally can be described by an exponential curve ($y = ab^x$) derived from a least-square treatment.

6. The results obtained using the L-4 Blue Wool standard fabric with these films could be used to evaluate protection of other dyed textiles from photofading.

Acknowledgments

The authors thank Dorothy Carter Southerland, Department of Textiles & Clothing, University of Tennessee, Knoxville for performing parts of the experiment and Dr. James F. Kinstle, Associate Professor, Department of Chemistry, University of Tennessee, for his helpful suggestions and discussions on the preparation of plastic films. Mention of a trade name does not constitute a recommendation or endorsement of that product by the U.S. Department of Agriculture to the exclusion of other suitable products.

Literature Cited

1. Thomson, G. "Textile Conservation"; Leene, J. E., Ed.; Smithsonian Institution: Washington, DC, 1972; p. 98.
2. Kajitani, N. In "Preservation of Paper and Textiles of Historic and Artistic Value," *Adv. Chem. Ser.* **1977,** *164,* 161.

3. Hunter, R. S. "The Measurement of Appearance"; Hunter Associates Laboratory, Inc.: Fairfax, VA, 1973.
4. Garrow, C.; King, M. G.; Roxburg, C. M. *Text. Inst. Ind.* **1970**, *8*(7), 197.
5. Wood, L. A.; Shouse, P. J.; Passaglia, E. *Text. Chem. Color.* **1970**, *2*(11), 182.
6. Vaeck, S. V. *J. Soc. Dyers Color.* **1978**, *94*(7), 301.
7. *Am. Assoc. Text. Chem. Color. Tech. Man.* **1977**, *53*, 132.
8. "Eastman Cellulose Acetate for Coatings," Publication No. E-140A, Eastman Chemical Products, Kingsport, TN, June, 1976.
9. *Am. Assoc. Text. Chem. Color. Tech. Man.* **1977**, *53*, 144.
10. "Atlas Fade-ometer and Weatherometer," Bulletin No. 1300 C, Atlas Electric Devices Co., Chicago, 1978.
11. *Am. Soc. Test. Mater., Book ASTM Stand. Relat. Mater.* **1978**, *32*, 323.
12. Ranby, B.; Rabek, J. "Photodegradation, Photo-oxidation and Photostabilization of Polymers"; Wiley–Interscience: New York, 1975.
13. Patel, A. R.; Usilton, J. J. In "Stabilization and Degradation of Polymers," *Adv. Chem. Ser.* **1978**, *169*, 116.
14. Danna, G. F.; Vigo, T. L.; Welch, C. M. *Text. Res. J.* **1978**, *48*, 173.
15. Maki, H.; Takamura, Y. Jap. Pat. 78 52 598, 1976; *Chem. Abstr.* **1978**, *89*, 181078n.

RECEIVED November 19, 1979.

Reinforcing Degraded Textiles[1]

Some New Approaches to the Application of Consolidants

J. K. HUTCHINS, S. P. HERSH, P. A. TUCKER,
D. M. McELWAIN, and N. KERR

School of Textiles, North Carolina State University, Raleigh, NC 27650

Gentler physical techniques and milder chemical conditions were explored for applying potential consolidants to artificially aged cotton textiles. These included vapor phase and spray applications of acrylonitrile, vapor phase and immersion applications of dimethyldichlorosilane, free and vacuum draining of acrylic resins, microwave drying of acrylic resins, and applications of nonacidic acrylic resins. Although none of these treatments produced any notable advantages over known procedures, the last two approaches show the most potential. An exploratory study indicated that cotton cellulose fibrils or wood pulp can be used to patch highly damaged textile artifacts. The fibers were applied by passing dilute suspensions through the specimens supported on a screen. Openings and tears in deliberately damaged fabrics were repaired by the technique.

Part II of this series (1) describes studies undertaken to determine if various classes of resins and monomers are potentially useful for consolidating brittle, fragile archeological fabrics. The goal was to screen available products and select the most promising for future examination under the stringent standards imposed by museum conservation practice. That cycle of tests employed a rather severe but standard method to apply the resins and monomers to artificially degraded substrates prior to evaluating them for changes in tensile strength, tearing strength, flexibility, and hand.

[1] This chapter constitutes Part IV in a series of papers.

0065-2393/81/0193-0315$05.00/0
© 1981 American Chemical Society

In the work described here, gentler application techniques and milder chemical conditions have been examined in an effort to reduce the chances of harming the fabric substrate. Additional consolidants also have been examined. In previous experiments, the substrate was dipped into the consolidant and passed through a laboratory padder to promote even penetration and remove excess resin. The fabric was then dried in an oven. It is clear that a laboratory padder is likely to cause mechanical damage to a fragile fabric and that high temperature oven curing of the consolidant also poses a risk. Current consolidation experiments utilize consolidants that may be applied under milder physical and chemical conditions. Possible approaches included applying the monomer in the vapor phase to a pretreated substrate, spraying the consolidant onto the fabric, drying in a microwave oven to reduce migration, and draining the consolidant through the supported fabric rather than squeezing and pulling through pad rolls. Other options were to employ less acidic resins and to modify papermaking or paper conservation techniques for use with fabrics. Combinations of some of these approaches were also examined.

Once it is ascertained that a consolidant meets the original criteria of increasing tensile and tearing strength (or at least not decreasing them) while maintaining hand and flexibility and that the application process will not harm the fabric, it will be possible, and necessary, to address the questions of long term effects of treatment with the material. Only when this final characteristic is known will a consolidant be considered for use in the textile conservation laboratory.

Experimental—Resins and Monomers

Substrates. The fabric substrates consisted of a standard 80×80 count (nominal) 3.5 oz/yd^2 cotton print cloth, machine washed in a 0.1% solution of Triton X–100; this fabric exposed to 50- ,100-, or 150-Mrad doses of high energy electrons as described in Part I of this series (2); or this fabric degraded by hydrolysis in 5N HCl at room temperature for 5.5 h. These degraded model fabrics were selected because their properties were sufficiently similar to those of archeological samples and because they could be prepared readily in large quantities.

Vapor or Spraying Applications. CYANOETHYLATION. Reaction of cellulose with acrylonitrile, $CH_2=CHCN$, a vinyl monomer, was selected for study because it is known to produce several desirable changes in the properties of cellulosic fabrics and yarns. After cyanoethylation, undegraded cotton becomes more resistant to microorganism attack, heat, acid, and abrasion (3). Moisture absorption decreases and the electrical properties change. The extent of these changes varies considerably because of the many variables involved in application methods and in fabric and yarn properties.

Cyanoethylation of cotton is a reaction represented by Moncrieff (4) as:

$$\text{Cell—OH} + \text{CH}_2\text{==CHCN} \xrightarrow{\text{base}} \text{Cell—O—CH}_2\text{CH}_2\text{CN}$$

Substitution usually occurs at the primary hydroxyl group of the anhydroglucose unit in cellulose.

Four types of fabric substrates were cyanoethylated: the control, acid hydrolyzed, 50 and 100 Mrad. Fabric specimens 19 × 89 mm were sprayed with a fine mist of 2% NaOH solution using a hand spray bottle until a 100% pickup by weight was achieved. The specimens were then left to air dry until just damp. Six samples were then placed on a rack inside the sealed reaction vessel, which had inlet and outlet connections to permit the acrylonitrile vapor to flow through and around the reactive fabric. This vessel was connected to two bubble bottles containing water and acrylonitrile with which to saturate nitrogen gas as it entered the reaction vessel. The water was necessary to swell the cellulose so the acrylonitrile could penetrate. It was determined that varying nitrogen flow rates and reaction time had little effect on the percent add-on.

After treatment, the samples were raveled from 19 × 89 mm to 13 × 89 mm and evaluated for tensile strength on an Instron tensile testing machine according to ASTM method D 1682-64, ½ in raveled strip test. This test method was utilized for the vapor and spraying applications. A summary of the results averaged over three runs varying in nitrogen flow rate and exposure time is presented in Table I. None of the fabrics benefited from the treatment, and the 50-Mrad samples decreased to 54.3% of their original strength. The degraded samples lost weight because of their alkali solubility. The 100-Mrad samples were so weak they could not be removed from the reaction vessel, and their breaking strengths are therefore not recorded.

GRAFTING OF ACRYLONITRILE. The next vapor phase reaction investigated was the grafting of acrylonitrile, since this reaction has been reported to increase tensile strength and abrasion resistance as well as stiffness (5).

The fabric substrates were first impregnated with a free-radical-forming catalyst by spraying the samples with a 2% potassium persulfate solution. The samples were air dried, placed in the reaction vessel, and exposed to acrylonitrile vapor as described above. The add-on achieved was 2–5%, but unfortunately these grafting treatments do not appear to cause any significant improvement in strength. As shown in Table I, the undegraded and acid hydrolyzed samples increased slightly in strength while the 50-Mrad samples did not change. The 100-Mrad sample lost

Table I.   Summary of Results of

Monomer	Application Method
Cyanoethylation	spray with 2% NaOH, acrylonitrile vapor
Acrylonitrile graft	spray 2% $K_2S_2O_8$, acrylonitrile vapor
Silane polymerization	spray with 50% pyridine/water, $(CH_3)_2SiCl_2$ vapor
Silane polymerization	spray with 50% pyridine/water, dip in $(CH_3)_2SiCl_2$

[a] Sample could not be removed from rack for testing.

some strength. None of these changes was statistically significant, however. There was no apparent correlation between percent add-on and strength of the individual samples and, though it could not be measured because of the small sample size, stiffness did not seem to increase.

An alternative method of applying acrylonitrile was investigated. Fabric samples were sprayed with 2% $K_2S_2O_8$ as before, and then sprayed with acrylonitrile and water. Very low add-ons were obtained with negligible changes in strength. Because acrylonitrile tends to yellow, specimens were washed after treatment to remove any excess, and the loose fibers and yarns lost in the process could explain the low percent add-ons. Furthermore, different parts of the fabric had different tensile strengths. The variation may arise from uneven spraying or uneven penetration of the spray.

DIMETHYLDICHLOROSILANE. Because dimethyldichlorosilane has been polymerized to a silicone polymer on cotton fabrics to impart stain and water resistance and can be applied as a vapor, this agent was examined as a possible consolidant. This treatment also improves fabric hand, resistance to chemicals and weathering, resistance to abrasion (by reducing friction), and reduces the tensile strength loss when resin finishes are applied; all factors that should make the material a desirable and effective consolidant. The reactions involved are as follows:

$$\underset{\underset{CH_3}{|}}{\overset{\overset{CH_3}{|}}{Cl-Si-Cl}} + 2(HOH) \longrightarrow \underset{\underset{CH_3}{|}}{\overset{\overset{CH_3}{|}}{HO-Si-OH}} + 2HCl$$

Applications of Monomers to Cotton Print Cloth

Substrate	No. of Samples	Add-on (%)	Strength (% of Substrate)	
			Tensile	Tearing
undegraded	6	1.2	100.5	—
acid	6	−1.1	98.6	—
50 Mrad	3	−1.9	54.3	—
100 Mrad	—	—	0.0[a]	—
undegraded	8	11.7	104.8	—
acid	6	4.0	108.5	—
50 Mrad	9	3.2	100.0	—
100 Mrad	3	4.5	91.7	—
undegraded	3	14.2	13.0	—
acid	3	16.5	20.3	—
undegraded	3	22.4	51.4	—
50 Mrad	3	23.5	64.2	—

$$n \, HO\!-\!\underset{\underset{CH_3}{|}}{\overset{\overset{CH_3}{|}}{Si}}\!-\!OH \longrightarrow \left(-\underset{\underset{CH_3}{|}}{\overset{\overset{CH_3}{|}}{Si}}\!-\!O\!- \right)_n + n H_2O$$

To apply dimethyldichlorosilane in the vapor phase, there must be an absorbed layer of water on the fabric samples so the vapor will react with the surface water and the hydroxyl groups in the cellulose (6, 7).

The most severe problem arising from the reaction of methylchlorosilanes with hydroxyl groups is the formation of HCl gas, an acid that severely degrades cellulose. It has been suggested that the problem may be alleviated by carrying out the reaction in the presence of ammonia or other alkaline vapors. The fabric must be free of wetting agents, size, and detergents.

Two methods of application were investigated. In the first, 13 × 89 mm samples sprayed with a 50% solution of pyridine in water were suspended in a reaction vessel containing a small amount of dimethyldichlorosilane. The water was to serve as a swelling agent and the pyridine as an acid acceptor. Because the silane hydrolyzes so easily, a vapor of HCl was observed to form in the reaction vessel. Add-ons of 13–17% were obtained. However, because of the formation of HCl, breaking strengths decreased by roughly 80%, suggesting that more effective buffering techniques are necessary.

The second method of application was to dip the specimens in the silane monomer and allow them to dry at room temperature. Add-ons of up to 26% were obtained. However, the breaking strengths again decreased. They were 33–50% lower than those of the untreated substrate, a decided improvement over the breaking strengths obtained after treatment in the vapor phase, but still unsuitable for consolidation purposes.

It is also possible to apply silicone by padding on a water emulsion of methylsilicone $(CH_3(H)—Si—O—)_n$ designed to give a 1–2% pickup of the silicone at room temperature (8). If the sample is dried and heated 5 min at 160°C, a soft hand and water resistant properties should result. It is possible to add catalysts to decrease the time and temperature of curing. This approach has not been tried as yet.

Draining of Consolidants. EFFECT OF CONCENTRATION. As noted in the introduction, one objective of the studies described here is to examine techniques for applying consolidants under conditions that will reduce the physical hazards to which the fabric substrate is exposed. Since the acrylic resins examined in Part II of this series (1) have outstanding resistance to degradation from UV light and heat and normally do not yellow or stiffen under adverse conditions, some of these resins were re-examined using a much less severe application technique. Milder curing procedures also were utilized.

The application method developed is similar to that used in papermaking. However, instead of using a paper sheet mould apparatus, the fabric was sandwiched between two wire mesh screens and placed in a 89-mm diameter Buechner funnel. The resin solution or emulsion was poured over the sample and left to soak for 10 s, then a vacuum of 15 torr pressure was applied to draw the resin through the fabric and into a glass vacuum flask. The specimen was placed carefully between two sheets of blotting paper and pressed with a roller to insure penetration and to remove excess resin from the surface. For breaking strength measurements, the 76 × 89 mm treated samples were cut into six 13 × 89 mm (warp × fill) samples for testing by ASTM method D 1682-64, ½ in raveled strip method. For tearing strength measurements, a 44-mm cut was made in each specimen, and the remaining 38 mm in the filling direction was torn on an Instron tensile testing machine.

Prior to applying the acrylic resin, all fabric specimens except one replicate set were sprayed with a 2% emulsion of a polyethylene softening agent (Cyanalube TSI Special, 25% solids, from the American Cyanamid Company). This material lubricates the yarns and thereby increases the tearing strength of the resin-treated fabrics.

Three of the sample fabrics were used as substrates for the resin applications: the undegraded, acid hydrolyzed, and 50-Mrad degraded. The acrylic latex (Rhoplex HA–16, 46% solids, from the Rohm and Haas Company) was diluted with water to give 6.9%, 13.8%, and 20.7% resin concentrations. Higher concentrations were not used because the fabrics became very stiff at concentrations above 20.7%. The treating solution also contained 0.2% Triton X-100, a nonionic detergent, as a wetting agent. As expected, add-ons increased with increasing resin concentrations, and ranged from 4.5 to 12.2%. As shown in Table II, breaking strengths increased after application of the resin, although none of the increases was statistically significant. The tearing strengths decreased up to 20% after resin application, probably because the yarns could no longer slip to redistribute stress. An increase in polyethylene softener or a change in application technique might alleviate the problem. As shown in Table II, the breaking strength of the 50-Mrad fabric having 3.4% Rhoplex HA–16 applied by the conventional padding technique (1) was greater (154% of original) than that of the sample containing 4.8% applied by the draining technique (102%). The tearing strengths were comparable, however (82.3 vs. 88.0%). However, the padded sample did not contain any polyethylene softener, which probably contributed to this difference.

To assess the effect of including polyethylene in the resin bath rather than applying it by prior spraying, a solution of 20% Rhoplex HA–16, 0.2% Triton X-100, and 0.5% polyethylene (Aerotex Softener TSI Special, from the American Cyanamid Company) was applied in the manner described above. The breaking and tearing strengths of fabrics treated with this mixture were virtually identical to those having equal add-ons of polyethylene applied by spraying (Table II).

EFFECTS OF MICROWAVE DRYING. It was postulated that drying the resin-treated fabrics in a microwave oven rather than in air or in a forced draft convection oven might lead to improved properties because of reduced resin migration. To determine if microwave drying might be beneficial, a piece of each of the three test fabrics was prepared using the procedure described in the preceding paragraph, except that the fabrics were dried for three minutes in a microwave oven after the resin was applied. As shown in Table II, both tearing and breaking strengths of the 50-Mrad fabric, which was the most fragile, increased compared with that of the air dried samples. The breaking strength increased from 99.6 to 111.5% of the original and the tearing strength from 65.8 to 76.3% of the original. This promising lead should be pursued further.

GRAVITY DRAINING ON HIGHLY DEGRADED SUBSTRATES. To determine if resin applications might be useful on more highly degraded fabrics than those previously used, fabrics degraded with 150 Mrad of ionizing radiation were treated with the three concentrations of Rhoplex HA–16 used in the experiments described above. The strength of the degraded fabric was 2.3% of the original (½ in raveled strip test of warp) compared with about 25% and 15% for fabrics degraded with 50 and 100 Mrad of ionizing radiation, respectively. Because of the fragile nature of the substrate, an even gentler application method than draining under

Table II.   Summary of Results of

Resin Formulation	Application Method
Rhoplex HA-16	pad, oven dry (Ref. *1*)
Rhoplex HA-16	spray with 2% polyethylene, drain resin emulsion, air dry
Rhoplex HA-16, 0.2% Triton X-100, 0.5%, polyethylene in bath	drain, air dry drain, microwave dry drain, air dry drain, microwave dry drain, air dry drain, microwave dry soak 1 hr, drain, air dry
Rhoplex AC-22N 0.5% poly-ethylene in bath	soak, drain, air dry

a Three samples were used to measure tensile strength, 2 to measure tearing strength.

vacuum was used in this set of experiments. To ensure that the resin penetrated thoroughly, and to prevent damage from handling, each sample was immersed in the emulsion. After soaking 1 h, the fabric was removed carefully and placed on a supporting polyester screen while the excess latex was permitted to drain. The add-ons were slightly lower than those obtained with vacuum draining, but in this case no polyethylene was applied. The breaking strength of the fabric with the lowest add-on increased by 19.9%, a change that was statistically significant. At higher add-ons, the strength changes were not significant. It is probable that long soaking in this emulsion, which has a pH of 2.9, degrades the material enough to offset any improvements from consolidation. As noted below, buffering or using a higher pH resin might be helpful. At any rate, it has been demonstrated that even extremely fragile textiles can be treated by this method without causing further damage.

Applications of Resins to Cotton Print Cloth

Substrate	No. of Samples	Add-on (%)	Strength (% of Substrate) Tensile	Tearing
50 Mrad	4	3.4	154.1	82.3
100 Mrad	4	1.0	101.7	47.3
undegraded	5[a]	5.4	115.1	105.3
undegraded	5[a]	6.9	111.1	109.0
undegraded	5[a]	9.2	112.7	95.5
acid	5[a]	6.7	103.4	83.7
acid	5[a]	9.3	107.1	83.4
acid	5[a]	12.2	104.8	78.5
50 Mrad	5[a]	4.5	102.0	88.0
50 Mrad	5[a]	6.9	105.4	89.2
50 Mrad	5[a]	9.5	100.5	87.8
undegraded	2[b]	9.0	115.3	103.3
undegraded	2[b]	8.2	115.2	107.0
acid	2[b]	11.7	102.2	76.2
acid	2[b]	10.8	98.9	81.0
50 Mrad	2[b]	6.0	99.6	65.8
50 Mrad	2[b]	5.2	111.5	76.3
150 Mrad	1	4.1	119.9	—
150 Mrad	1	6.1	102.3	—
150 Mrad	1	8.6	88.6	—
undegraded	2[b]	5.0	104.8	115.2
acid	2[b]	10.8	102.8	92.1
50 Mrad	2[b]	3.9	97.8	89.5

[b] One sample was used to measure tensile strength, 1 to measure tearing strength.

APPLICATION OF RHOPLEX AC–22N. A second acrylic resin, Rhoplex AC–22N (from the Rohm and Haas Company) was examined because it has a pH of 9.8 and a desirable T_{300} value of 16°C. This temperature is the temperature at which the torsional modulus of an air-dried film is 300 kg/cm², a measure of film stiffness. A T_{300} temperature around room temperature should provide a finish that is neither too soft and gummy nor too stiff and hard at room temperature. The emulsion was applied using the Buechner funnel technique described above from a solution containing 0.1% Triton X-100 and 0.5% polyethylene softener. The fabrics were air dried because Rhoplex AC–22N, a noncrosslinking resin, requires no curing. (Rhoplex HA–16 also does not require curing, though it is a crosslinking resin). The add-ons varied widely, but all of the fabrics had a very soft hand. The breaking strengths of those fabrics (reported in Table II) are similar to those of fabrics treated with the

HA–16 acrylic, but the tearing strengths improved considerably. Nevertheless, the tearing strengths of the degraded fabrics were still less than those of fabrics that were not treated.

Experimental—Cellulose Fibrils as Consolidants

Fibrils from Cotton and Rayon. Paper pulp has been successfully for the conservation of damaged works of art on paper, and although the apparatus is different, the technique used here is similar to that used for paper sheet formation (*9, 10*). Hydrogen bonding, which plays a major role in intermolecular bonding of cellulosic fibers, long has been recognized as a source of paper sheet strength. It was hoped that highly fibrillated cotton fiber would be able to penetrate and strengthen the structure of a weak fabric by means of the reinforcement resulting from hydrogen bonding between the fibrils and the fibers in the treated specimen. The large surface area of the minute fibrils could produce great bonding strength, even though the strength of individual hydrogen bonds is weak compared with that of covalent bonds. Another interesting feature of this approach is that the consolidant would be the same type of polymer, i.e., cellulose, as the degraded fabric and hence should answer the objections of conservators reluctant to apply foreign materials to museum specimens. In addition to native cellulose from cotton fiber, regenerated cellulose (viscose rayon) also was examined as a possible source of cotton fibrils that could serve as a reinforcing agent.

Evidence indicates that dry strength adhesives increase the strength of paper by bridging the separation between fibrillated cellulose fibers (*11*). One such adhesive is carboxymethyl cellulose (CMC). In this study, CMC was evaluated as a consolidant and as an agent for bonding broken fibers and fibrils to the fabric and forming a supporting fiber sheet of appropriate strength. There can be continuous loss of fibers arising from crumbling of the yarns in a degraded textile, and it was hoped that such a backing sheet might prevent this loss (*12*). Rhoplex HA–16 also was assessed as a dry strength adhesive that might increase the adhesion of fiber fragments and fibrils to the fabrics. The substrate chosen for this cycle of experiments was the 100-Mrad degraded fabric, and the consolidants were prepared as follows:

1. Cotton Cellulose: To prepare a fibrillar or macrofibrillar suspension of native cellulosic fibrils, approximately 1% of cotton fiber was blended with water for 3 h in an ordinary blender and then filtered through a polyester screen having openings of 240 $\times$ 240 μm supported by a Buechner funnel to which a vacuum was applied. The filtrate was a cloudy suspension that contained fibrils and macrofibrils ranging in size from 100Å to several micrometers in width.

2. Regenerated Cellulose: An attempt was made to fibrillate a regenerated cellulose (1.5 denier 1-9/16 in bright Fiber 40* Rayon from Avtex Fibers Incorporated). The procedure described above was tried, but failed to fibrillate the rayon even after 10 h. Intermittent treatment of the mixture in a strong ultrasonic field did not appear helpful, and Fiber 40* rayon was not tested further.

3. Fibril and Acrylic Resin Mixture: A blend of cotton fibrils and acrylic resin was prepared by mixing a highly fibrillated but unstrained cotton with a 13.8% solution of Rhoplex HA–16 in a ratio of 50:1. The fibrils and water were mixed for 5 h to form a slurry containing approximately 0.5% fibrils and 0.29% Rhoplex HA–16.

4. CMC: The solid particles of CMC (from Hercules Incorporated) were blended with water to make a highly viscous solution with 12.5% by weight of solids.

5. Fibril and CMC Mixture: A blend of CMC and fibrils was made by mixing CMC prepared in the manner described above in the ratio of 1:50 with cotton pulp that had been beaten in a blender for 3 h.

Each of the four consolidant systems was applied using the Buechner funnel method. A sample of 100-Mrad fabric was cut to fit the 76-mm-diameter funnel, and sandwiched between two polyester screens with 240-μm openings. The top layer served to remove the large fiber fragments and the bottom layer to support the fabric. The sandwiched specimen was placed in the funnel, the consolidating mixture poured over it, and a vacuum applied to draw it through the fabric and into the glass vacuum flask leaving the consolidant in the fabric structure. The five specimens made with each consolidant were air dried and cut into 25 × 36 (warp × fill) mm samples. The tensile strengths of the specimens were then measured on an Instron tensile testing machine.

The results presented in Table III show that only the treatment with cotton fibrils (3.5% add-on) improved the tensile strength (13% increase), whereas the other treatments weakened the fabrics. Add-ons obtained with the CMC and fibril–adhesive mixtures were extremely high, ranging from 24.5 to 72.0%. The affinity between substrate and consolidant in these cases was very poor.

Patching with Wood Pulp. MATERIALS. In view of the strength increase achieved with fibrils used alone, it was thought that cotton fibrils might be used to patch as well as to strengthen fabrics. To test this hypothesis, 100-Mrad fabric samples were cut into 76-mm circles and eight 5-mm holes were punched in each, four holes spaced evenly on a circle 25 mm in diameter and four spaced evenly on a circle 51 mm in diameter. The fabric around the edges of two holes in each sample was then partially unraveled to determine if fraying the edge of the cut might improve the bonding of the fibrils collected there. To simulate

Table III. Add-on and Strength of Cotton Print Cloth Degraded by Exposure to 100 Mrad of Ionizing Radiation and Treated with Cotton Fibrils and Resins

Treatment	Number of Samples	Add-on (%)	Tensile Strength (lb)	Tensile Strength (%)
None	5	0	1.81	100.0
Cotton fibrils	5	3.5	2.05[a]	113.3
Fibrils & HA-16	5	72.0	0.70[a]	38.7
CMC	5	27.1	0.42	23.2
Fibrils & CMC	5	24.5	0.50[a]	27.6

[a] Change significant at the 95% confidence level.

tears similar to those that might be found in museum objects, other fabric disks were torn on a Mullen Bursting Strength Tester. A third group of disks was cut from a piece of 100-Mrad fabric that had been washed twice to remove extractables by immersing it in a 30°C water bath for 15 min, then draining the water. These samples were partially torn on an Instron tensile testing machine by centering the circle of fabric in 1.5 in jaws set to 1 in gauge length. The fabrics were extended at a rate of 5 in/min until the fabric tore. Ragged tears, approximately 25 mm in length, formed in the center of the fabric.

Two types of wood pulp provided the fibrils used for patching. The first was a moderately beaten wood pulp obtained from the Department of Pulp and Paper Science, North Carolina State University. The second was Cellunier P*, a cellulose provided by the ITT Rayonier Company. Portions of the pulp and Cellunier P* were dyed with 0.5% Cuprophenyl Navy Blue RL (from the Ciba–Geigy Corporation) and 0.5% tetrasodium phosphate for 30 min at 82°C to provide greater visual contrast between the fibers and the substrates. The wood pulp was diluted with distilled water to form 0.5 and 0.1% slurries. The Cellunier P* was diluted to a 0.05% slurry. Both were treated in a blender to separate lumps formed during dyeing.

APPLICATION TO FABRICS WITH HOLES. The specimens with holes punched in them were wet in distilled water, then individually placed on a coarse supporting screen (16/inch mesh) in a Buechner funnel. A vacuum of 15 torr pressure was applied, and 100 ml of slurry made from the papermaking pulp was poured over the specimen. After applying the pulp, the samples were transferred to a larger screen and air dried. The application was repeated without the initial wetting as many times as desired.

One application of the 0.5% slurry made of undyed wood pulp produced samples that were heavily and unevenly coated with fibrils. The holes in the samples were partially or completely filled, but the paper-like coating peeled easily from the substrate.

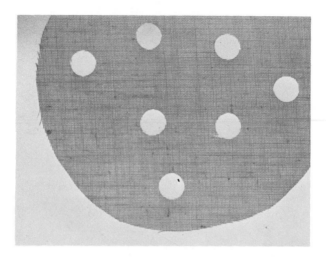

Figure 1. Fabric substrate degraded by exposure to 100 Mrad of ioniz-ing radiation showing punched holes before applying wood pulp for patching

Repeated applications (up to nine) of the 0.1% slurry of undyed wood pulp to the substrate with holes deposited a layer of fibrils in the holes. The thickness of the layer appeared to be directly proportional to the number of treatments. One to four applications partially filled the holes, and five to nine filled them completely. Typical fabrics after zero, two, four, five, and six passes of the 0.1% slurry are shown in Figures 1–5. Samples that had been treated seven to nine times, however, were

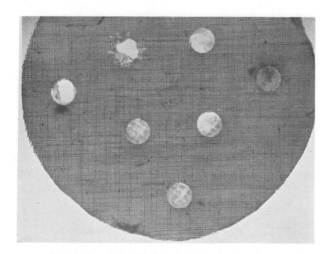

Figure 2. Fabric substrate after two applications of 0.1% slurry of mod-erately beaten wood pulp

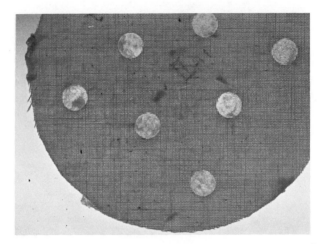

Figure 3. Fabric substrate after four applications of 0.1% slurry of moderately beaten wood pulp

rather stiff, and the layer of fibrils showed a tendency to peel from the substrate. It was observed that six applications of the 0.1% slurry yielded optimum results. Raveling of the edges around the holes had no effect on the amount of cellulose that collected in those holes.

APPLICATION TO TORN FABRICS. The samples that were burst were reinforced to varying degrees by these treatments. Qualitatively, it was observed that strengths increased with the number of treatments. Quan-

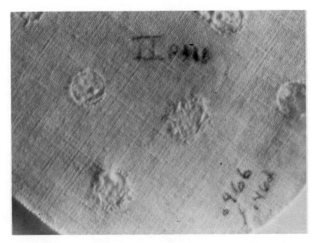

Figure 4. Fabric substrate after five applications of 0.1% slurry of moderately beaten wood pulp

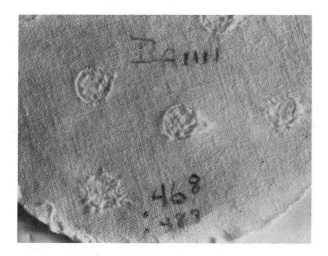

Figure 5. Fabric substrate after six applications of 0.1% slurry of moderately beaten wood pulp

titative strength measurements could not be made because the Mullen Bursting Strength Tester is not sensitive enough to measure small changes in strength. Application of the fibrils produced no significant change in weight, and it seems probable that the weight gain from the fibrils was offset by the rinsing away of degraded portions of the substrate.

To determine the quantitative effects of this consolidation procedure, fabric disks cut from the extracted degraded fabric were used as substrates. These fabrics were torn on an Instron tensile testing machine as described earlier and patched with six applications of either the 0.1% dyed wood pulp or the 0.05% dyed Cellunier P* slurry. The samples were then torn again on the Instron tester. The average breaking strengths and add-ons of the samples after six passes with slurry are reported in Table IV. A typical torn fabric and a patched fabric are shown in Figures 6 and 7.

To determine if the fabrics "repaired" with paper pulp developed the strengths that might be expected from such pulps used alone, the strengths were compared with those of light weight paper tissues. Those samples, also 76 mm in diameter, were cut from Kimberly Clark Kimwipes, a standard two-ply Kleenex, and a single ply separated from a two-ply Kleenex. They were conditioned at 70°F and 65% relative humidity for 24 h before measuring their strengths.

The data indicate that the cellulose fiber repair changes the strength from zero (after being torn on the Instron the first time) to nearly 20% of the original untorn strength. The breaking strength of the fabric to which 4% paper pulp was applied was over 1.1 lbs, which was 20% of

Table IV.   Tensile Strength of Torn Degraded Fabrics
(100 Mrad) Repaired with Wood Pulp[a]

Pulp		Num-ber of Sam-ples	Add-on (%)	Tensile Strength	
Source	Concen-tration (%)			Original (lb)	Patched[b] (lb)
Papermaker, NCSU	0.1	6	4	5.86	1.16
Cellunier P[a] (Rayonier)	0.05	6	2	5.70	1.04
Kimwipe	—	5	—	2.33	—
Kleenex, 2 ply	—	5	—	1.00	—
Kleenex, 1 ply	—	5	—	0.44	—

[a] Six applications.
[b] After patching a torn fabric having zero strength.

the original tensile strength. Applications of Cellunier P* pulp resulting
in an add-on of 2% gave about the same tensile strength. These strengths
are about equal to the two-ply Kleenex, but only about half that of the
Kimwipe. Thus, the strength imparted by the hydrogen bonded fibrils
was in the range typical of some tissues. Strengths might be further
improved by using different grade pulps, using more highly beaten pulps,
increasing the add-on, and/or adding wet strength resins to the pulp.

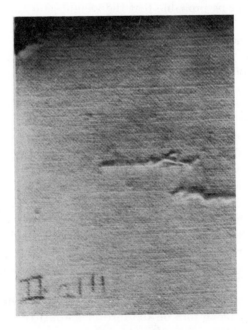

*Figure 6.   Fabric substrate degraded by exposure to 100 Mrad of ioniz-
ing radiation torn on a Mullen Bursting Strength Tester*

Figure 7. Degraded fabric substrate torn on a Mullen Bursting Strength Tester after six applications of a 0.01% slurry of moderately beaten wood pulp

Conclusions

Of all the treatments described, patching and strengthening the deteriorated fabric with fibrillated cellulose shows the greatest promise. This method is attractive because the patching material is chemically identical to the substrate, making the questions of compatibility and long term stability somewhat less worrisome. The fact that the support may be removed by immersion in water is another positive and significant feature. It is uncertain how much moisture is required to weaken the patch, so the treatment may be unsuitable for pieces stored in high or fluctuating humidity. It is, in fact, the amount of moisture that the degraded textile can withstand that will dictate whether or not the technique is useful—some fabrics cannot be subjected to the repeated wetting and drying that is necessary for the applications of the pulp. If the fabric is not harmed by immersion in water and if the small number of fibrils remaining on one side of the fabric is not objectional, the method might be considered as a means of increasing tensile strengths as well as patching.

Attempts to apply some potential consolidants by spraying or from vapors were not notably successful because of poor control and variability. Some promise was shown in the application of acrylic resins by draining rather than by padding and by drying in a microwave oven. Although these approaches were not completely successful, further efforts in the directions explored here would be justified.

Acknowledgments

This investigation was supported in part by the National Museum Act, which is administered by the Smithsonian Institution. The authors are grateful for this assistance. The authors also wish to express their gratitude to Mr. Win Chuan Chang for carrying out the experiments involving cotton fibrils.

Literature Cited

1. Berry, G. M.; Hersh, S. P.; Tucker, P. A.; Walsh, W. K. "Reinforcing Degraded Textiles, Part II: Properties of Resin-Treated, Artificially Aged Cotton Textiles," *Adv. Chem. Ser.* **1977,** *164,* 249–260.
2. Berry, G. M.; Hersh, S. P.; Tucker, P. A.; Walsh, W. K. "Reinforcing Degraded Textiles, Part I: Properties of Naturally and Artificially Aged Cotton Textiles," *Adv. Chem. Ser.* **1977,** *164,* 228–248.
3. Compton, J.; Martin, W.; Ward, B.; Barber, R. "The Cyanoethylation of Cotton," *Text. Res. J.* **1956,** *26,* 47–66.
4. Moncrieff, R. W. "Man-Made Fibers," 6th ed.; John Wiley & Sons: New York, 1975.
5. Walsh, W. K. "The Effect of Water on the Kinetics and Diffusion in Radiation Grafting of Acrylonitrile to Cellulose," Ph.D. Thesis, North Carolina State University, Raleigh, N. C., 1967.
6. Reed, C. E. "The Industrial Chemistry, Properties, and Application of Silicones"; American Society for Testing Materials: Philadelphia, 1956; 40–42.
7. Gagliardi, D. D.; Jutras, W. J., Jr.; Shippee, F. S. "Vapor Phase Reactions on Cotton Part I: General Considerations and Partial Results," *Text. Res. J.* **1966,** *36,* 168–177.
8. "LE-9300 Silicone Emulsion," Technical Bulletin F-43607A, Textile and Fiber Chemicals Division, Union Carbide Corporation, New York, Nov. 1971.
9. Keyes, K. M. "Practical Applications of Paper Pulp in the Conservation of Works of Art on Paper. Part I: A Manual Method of Application, "*AIC Prepr. 4th* (Dearborn, MI, May, 1976) 76–81.
10. Farnsworth, D. S. "Practical Applications of Paper Pulp in the Conservation of Works of Art on Paper. Part II: A Method Using Traditional Papermaking Technique," *AIC Prepr. 4th* (Dearborn, MI, May, 1976) 81–86.
11. Swanson, J. M. "Pulp and Paper Science and Technology;" Libby, C. E., Ed.; McGraw–Hill: New York, 1962; Vol. 2, Chap. 5.
12. Jedrzejewska, H. "Some New Techniques for Archaeological Textiles," in "Textile Conservation," Leene, J. E., Ed.; Smithsonian Institution: Washington, DC, 1972; Chapter 22.

RECEIVED October 23, 1979.

Assessing the Effects of Pesticidal Chemicals on Historic Textiles

S. M. SPIVAK and J. WORTH[1]

Department of Textiles and Consumer Economics, University of Maryland, College Park, MD 20742

F. E. WOOD

Department of Entomology, University of Maryland, College Park, MD 20742

In protecting textiles from insects, concern arises for the damage that the pesticidal chemical itself may cause to the textile object. A preliminary study was undertaken to assess this. Cotton and wool were each dyed with four natural dyestuffs. The dyed fabrics were exposed to pesticide-related chemicals for varying periods. Chemicals used were CCl_4 (fumigant), dichlorvos (pest strip), petroleum distillate spray (carrier), and boric acid dusting. Instrumental colorimetry was used. There was no color change from CCl_4 except for safflower-dyed wool after three years. Dichlorvos-treated samples varied, with some exhibiting a slight change. Petroleum distillate was hardly visible; most residue dissipated with no color change. Boric acid deposits were visible, but lessened after three years. Exceptions were strong color change on some wool samples. Breaking strength also was determined. Contact of the cotton by CCl_4 resulted in degradation.

M an has associated himself with textiles in many forms for thousands of years. Articles of historic and artistic value commonly have been preserved in museums and homes, but not without complications. One of these complications in particular is the attack of insects. Fibrous and

---

[1] Current address: U. S. Small Business Administration, 1240 East 9th Street, Cleveland, OH 44199.

0065-2393/81/0193-0333$05.00/0

fabric materials can be attacked by a variety of insects, for example, the carpet beetle, clothes moth, silverfish, firebrat, and cockroach.

Not all insects found in museum storage areas are necessarily damaging to textile materials, for instance, most flying moths are harmless to textiles. Alternately, insects such as termites inadvertently may damage textiles while normally feeding on other materials. Therefore, it is important for museum staff to have some familiarity with these types of insect species. In addition, pest control may be likened to the practice of medicine in that the prevention is easier than the cure. Efforts should be taken to avoid infestation of historic textiles rather than have to deal with an infestation after it has developed. An understanding of insect behavior is vital to instituting effective housekeeping and other preventative measures.

If an infestation occurs, procedures must be selected that control the insect problem without damaging the textile. Protection of the historic textile is the ultimate goal. Therefore, one must select control procedures that are proved safe and effective, or know how to find knowledgeable experts who can recommend the most appropriate control procedures.

One objective of this study is to highlight, for conservators and other museum professionals, an increasing need for attention to textile pests and their control. Rapidly changing local, state, and federal regulations, listing approved pesticides and their usage, make it imperative that museum personnel be cognizant of these dynamic changes and recent developments. This is especially important since the trend in regulation has been to restrict severely or control use of many of our proved and most effective pesticides. As a result of tightened restrictions and reduced use of pesticides, infestations are becoming more common and must be of concern to those with museum or historic textile collections. In addition, both new, exotic and older, forgotten measures of pest control have entered the available arsenal of pesticidal chemicals, and many of these are untried or unproved for safe use on historic textiles.

The major objective of this chapter is to report on preliminary laboratory investigations that simulated pesticide treatments on historic type textiles and assessed the relative safety or potential damage commensurate with their use. This experimentation will demonstrate laboratory methodology and report on color or strength changes that may ensue with pesticide treatment. It also is hoped that others will recognize the need for further related work and expanded research efforts in this fruitful and neglected area will result.

It is not the intent of this chapter to review the extensive information available on textile pests, specific insect identification, life cycle and habits, or detailed methods of control. However, reference will be made below to major works on textile pests and their control for use by the reader.

Pest Control of Museum Textiles

There is an extensive literature on insects and insect control, although little is addressed directly to museums and conservation of historic objects, specifically textiles. A detailed review of "Textile Pests and their Control," including fungicidal and microbial problems, is that by Hueck (*1*) with extensive references contained therein. The subject also receives general treatment in Plenderlith and Werner (*2*). Identification and control of insect pests in general, including textile insects, can be found by Szent–Ivany and Beecher in the UNESCO conservation work (*3,4*). Fumigation of textiles is discussed by Rice (*5*) and a treatise on mothproofing textiles is by Moncrieff (*6*), the International Wool Secretariat (*7*), or McPhee (*8*).

References in general entomology usually include insects specific to fabrics and paper, although the special concerns of museum or historic conservation, older materials and natural dyestuffs, usually are not considered. A comprehensive analysis of the complete insect-related problem, including fumigation and control of textile pests, is available in Ebeling (*9*), or in an earlier treatise by Mallis (*10*).

Experimental

Materials. In protecting textiles from the possibility of insect attack, a major concern arises for the potential damage that insecticidal chemicals may cause to the textiles. Two areas of damage that are of concern are color change and strength loss. Several chemicals that might be chosen for use in museums were tested to determine the extent of change in both color and strength from exposure to these chemicals. The chemicals chosen for experimentation were petroleum distillate, carbon tetrachloride (CCl_4), dichlorvos, and boric acid. Petroleum distillate is a light, refined oil that is a major component and carrier in many liquid or aerosol pesticide formulations. CCl_4 was tested because it represents a fumigant that can be used by museum staff in small, controlled exposures. Dichlorvos is becoming increasingly popular to museum staff and was used in the form of No-Pest Strip, in which the insecticide vaporizes at a controlled rate out of the solid strip. The active ingredient in these pest strips is 2,2-dichlorovinyl dimethyl phosphate, also known as DDVP or Vapona insecticide. Boric acid in dust form was selected because of its ready availability to the public, ease of application, and renewed interest in its long known effectiveness against roaches and beetles. Chemicals such as naphthalene and paradichlorobenzene, PDB, were not tested because of their prior widespread use by textile conservators, although long term effects are still questioned by some.

Most textiles found in historic museums are natural fibers dyed with natural dyestuffs. Therefore, in this experiment two common textiles, cotton and wool, were dyed with safflower, madder root, logwood chips, and indigo. These dyes were chosen to represent a range of colors often found in historic textiles. The cotton and wool textiles were obtained from Testfabrics (11), which permits some control over the source and prior condition of the textile fabrics used in the investigation.

The fabrics were dyed by the authors for uniformity of treatment and because naturally dyed cloth was not otherwise available. The processes used in this dyeing were those suggested by Kramer in *Natural Dyestuffs* (12). Alum was used as a mordant in all dyes except indigo where cream of tartar was used; other mordants might yield different results.

Two tests were conducted to determine the influence of the pesticidal chemicals on the fabric. On the dyed fabric samples, color change due to chemical exposure was recorded both visually and with an instrumental colorimeter. On undyed cotton and wool fabrics, change in strength was determined using a tensile tester.

Sample Preparation. CCl_4 was applied as a fumigant to fabric samples suspended near the bottom of a stainless steel dessicator. The CCl_4 liquid was placed in an open petri dish on a rack above the samples, since its vapor is heavier than air. Sufficient chemical was provided to maintain vapor equilibrium within the small, closed dessicator. Two days later, the CCl_4 was exhausted from the dessicator and it was resealed with the fabrics stored inside for four weeks, until the samples were required for testing.

The fabric samples for exposure to dichlorvos were placed in a wooden, glass-topped museum case along with one No-Pest Strip in such a manner that the strip would not touch the samples. The time of duration to the dichlorvos vapor was four weeks, after which the fabric samples were removed from the museum case for testing.

Petroleum distillate was applied to other fabric samples using a home or garden-type spray device, letting a light mist fall on the samples. Fabric samples were lightly covered with boric acid dust using a shaker device with small openings and brushing off the excess. The petroleum distillate and boric acid treated samples were then placed in separate but similar cases to the dichlorvos samples. These closed storage cases were of the type used in insect collections, and were kept covered with a dark cloth to avoid any fading from room light. After four weeks duration, the latter samples were removed from their storage cases for testing.

All samples were returned to their respective cases and stored in the dark until removal for color and strength measurement after eight weeks duration. Thereafter, samples were kept in special envelopes until 160 weeks duration and again removed for color measurement.

Measurement of Color Change. There were five replicates, each 3 in. $\times$ 3 in., of the individual treatments and control samples. These included both fabrics and the treatments comprising the four dyestuffs and four pesticide applications. The color of the dyed samples was evaluated using a Hunter Model D25M Laboratory Colorimeter. This color measurement device employs the L, a, b tristimulus value color order system. Each color is defined uniquely by its L, a, and b values. The L value represents whiteness–blackness; the a value represents redness–greenness; and the b value represents blueness–yellowness. To evaluate the effect of each pesticide on the dyed fabrics, it is necessary to calculate the color change (Δ) from the specific L, a, and b values. The components of color change are determined by ΔL, change in whiteness–blackness; Δa, change in redness–greenness; and Δb, change in blueness–yellowness. From the individual components of color change, one obtains the total color difference, ΔE, in Judd–Hunter (13) terms given by:

$$\Delta E = (\Delta L^2 + \Delta a^2 + \Delta b^2)^{\frac{1}{2}}$$

Although the individual components can tell one how a color change differs from its control, it is the total color differences, ΔE, that is most often reported and will be the focus of the following results.

There remains some question of interpretation regarding instrumentally measured color change values and how these compare with subjective perception of color change. As a recognized guide in evaluation of the data reported below, ΔE values by this method would have to be significantly greater than 1.0 unit to be visually perceived by most observers as an actual color change. In this regard, however, a visual, subjective assessment of the color change also was obtained after 160 weeks, based on the opinion of several independent observers. This is reported by use of simple, descriptive adjectives that differ from terms otherwise used in industrial color matching. The reader is directed to Hunter (13) and Billmeyer and Saltzman (14) for further discussion of the principles of color order systems, tristimulus colorimetry, and its interpretation.

Measurement of Strength Loss. The same test fabrics of 100% cotton and 100% wool were employed, although in this case undyed, to determine any potential loss in strength of the fabrics upon exposure to the four pesticides employed. Samples for the strength loss tests were prepared according to ASTM Standard Test Method D–1682–64, (15) raveled strip. Strips of the undyed fabrics were cut in the warp direction, 1½ in. × 6 in., and ravelled to 1 in. × 6 in. Ten undyed samples of cotton and wool were treated in the same manner in chemical exposure as the dyed samples used in color measurement. After four weeks, these test samples were removed from their cases and their strength measured under ambient conditions using an Instron Model 1130 Tensile Tester. The change in strength due to exposure to the chemicals was determined by comparing the mean of each set of ten exposed samples with that of an unexposed control group and the findings reported.

Results and Discussion

Color Change. Tables I through IV summarize the color change data, obtained by comparison with an untreated/unexposed control sample, for the dyed cotton and wool fabrics exposed to CCl_4, dichlorvos, petroleum distillate, and boric acid respectively. Each table reports the total color difference at 4, 8, and 160 weeks duration after initial treatment. Also reported is a visual description of the perceived color change from the untreated control after 160 weeks.

From Table I, CCl_4 samples, the cotton fabrics showed ΔE values about 1.0 or below, except for the logwood samples, which were slightly above 1.0. These changes were not readily apparent under visual inspec-

Table I.   Total Color

Cotton Fabric: Duration (Weeks)

Dye Type	4	8	160	Visual
Safflower	0.0	0.8	0.5	none
Madder root	0.5	0.7	1.1	none
Logwood	1.5	1.3	1.2	none
Indigo	0.5	1.2	0.7	none

Table II.   Total Color Difference

Cotton Fabric: Duration (Weeks)

Dye Type	4	8	160	Visual
Safflower	0.7	1.1	0.8	none
Madder root	1.0	1.3	0.6	none
Logwood	1.8	4.2	2.0	trace
Indigo	0.4	1.4	0.4	none

Table III.   Total Color Difference

Cotton Fabric: Duration (Weeks)

Dye Type	4	8	160	Visual
Safflower	2.7	1.7	0.2	none
Madder root	2.7	1.3	0.9	none
Logwood	3.0	1.3	2.5	slight
Indigo	2.3	3.3	1.3	none

Table IV.   Total Color Difference

Cotton Fabric: Duration (Weeks)

Dye Type	4	8 vac.	160	Visual
Safflower	6.2	6.7	1.6	none
Madder root	6.2	7.0	1.1	none
Logwood	4.6	6.3	1.7	slight
Indigo	6.8	6.4	0.3	none

Difference (ΔE)—CCl$_4$ Samples

Wool Fabric: Duration (Weeks)

4	8	160	Visual
0.6	0.7	3.2	noticeable
0.6	0.9	1.0	none
0.6	0.1	1.3	none
1.1	1.4	0.8	none

(ΔE)—Dichlorvos Samples

Wool Fabric: Duration (Weeks)

4	8	160	Visual
0.6	0.6	1.6	none
0.4	0.9	2.4	slight
0.4	0.9	1.3	none
0.6	1.1	1.6	none

(ΔE)—Petroleum Distillate Samples

Wool Fabric: Duration (Weeks)

4	8	160	Visual
2.5	2.4	1.7	none
3.0	2.2	1.9	none
3.0	2.3	0.7	none
2.1	1.3	0.7	none

(ΔE)—Boric Acid Samples

Wool Fabric: Duration (Weeks)

4	8 vac.	160	Visual
3.5	2.6	3.0	noticeable
4.6	7.3	2.5	slight
2.9	3.0	4.3	severe
5.4	6.2	0.7	none

tion. The woolen samples behaved similarly to the cotton over all time periods with one notable exception, the safflower at 160 weeks. In this case, a noticeable color change developed sometime between 8 and 160 weeks and this was equally recorded by the colorimeter as a sizeable ΔE of 3.2.

The dichlorvos treated samples, Table II, show varying ΔE values, representing in most cases no significant color change. However, data for the logwood dyed cotton sample indicate color change at both 8 weeks and reconfirmed at 160 weeks. The madder root dyed wool exhibited some or slight color change at 160 weeks (ΔE of 2.4) although not at the earlier times. The data for wool suggests that the color difference values may be increasing with time, although this is not the case with the cotton fabric.

Table III summarizes total color difference for the samples sprayed with petroleum distillate. The general trend for both cotton and wool fabrics with all dyestuffs is for a lessening in the apparent color change over time. At four weeks, all ΔE values are between 2.1 and 3.0 and the samples exhibited a noticeable darkening from the presence of the distillate oil. At 8 weeks, there is a tendency toward lower ΔE values, which continues thereafter. At 160 weeks, ΔE values are all below 2.0, with the exception of logwood dyed cotton, which still showed a slight color change. These findings can be explained by the nature of petroleum distillate, which is a lightweight, refined oil. After application, some of the lower molecular weight fractions may evaporate slowly while other portions of the oil will dissipate into any contiguous materials in contact with the fabrics, such as paper liners in the museum cases or paper storage envelopes. The net effect is that eventually the petroleum distillate becomes too dilute to be seen by most observers.

The boric acid dust on the samples (Table IV) was very noticeable as a light deposit, both upon application and at 4 or 8 weeks. In an effort to remove some of this residue, a laboratory vacuum was used on the samples at 8 weeks, and color change immediately following is reported in Table IV as 8 vac. These results are as severe as those reported earlier. But at 160 weeks, there is a sizeable reduction in ΔE values for all cotton samples and only logwood indicates a slight change remaining. The wool fabrics dyed with indigo and madder also showed lower ΔE values at 160 weeks, but a noticeable color change remained on most samples. The logwood dyed wool exhibited the most obvious and severe color change to boric acid (and at 160 weeks, the highest ΔE, 4.3), showing a pronounced reddish color from the otherwise brownish samples. The reduction in some of the above ΔE values for boric acid is believed to be a hygroscopic absorption of moisture by the boric acid powder, reducing the granular size and causing a more uniform but less noticeable deposit on the fabrics.

Table V. Breaking Strength of Fabrics Exposed to Chemicals

	Breaking Strength (kg)	
Treatment	Cotton	Wool
Control (untreated)	17.5 ± 1.6	14.0 ± 1.2
Petroleum distillate	20.8 ± 2.3	14.7 ± 1.1
Dichlorvos	21.2 ± 1.7	14.4 ± 1.1
CCl_4[a]	16.7 ± 6.0	14.2 ± 1.5
Boric acid	20.1 ± 2.0	15.7 ± 0.8

[a] Data do not include accidental spillage samples.

Strength Loss. The breaking strength of undyed cotton and wool fabrics exposed to each of the four pesticides, and measured after 4 weeks, are summarized in Table V. A comparison of each test value with the untreated control determines if any strength loss has occurred under our test conditions. It appears from these data that strength changes attributable to the chemical exposure were not significant at 4 weeks, that is, no strength loss occurred under these given set of conditions. The breaking strength of the test samples appears inexplicably higher in some cases than in their respective controls. However, the approximate ± range values (also shown) are sufficiently large to suggest that there are not real differences between the strength of the test samples and that of the controls. An additional set of strength samples was not available for test at 160 weeks, so that any latent or long term degradation could not be determined.

Several cotton samples, when treated with CCl_4, were contaminated inadvertently by direct spillage of the chemical. These specific samples developed stains over time and showed a marked drop in strength, with the sample breaking during the stress test at the point of staining. Those cotton samples that were not stained did not show this strength loss. It can be concluded that the presence of the CCl_4 directly on the cloth caused a strength loss, which is assumed to be through the formation of hydrochloric acid by hydrolysis. However, the same chemical used as a fumigant did not exhibit this behavior and only uncontaminated samples were reported in Table V.

Conclusions

These experiments to determine color change and strength loss through use of pesticidal chemicals were intended to illustrate that such treatments and conditions may or may not be harmful to historic textiles. No overall generalizations can be made since the findings indicate that specific effects are attributable to fiber type, dyestuff, and pesticide treatment. In most cases, no long term color changes resulted, but in selected cases, very noticeable changes remained after three years. Certain color and strength problems discussed earlier with the use of boric acid and CCl$_4$ were attributable to direct contact of the chemical with the fabric. If care is taken that contact does not occur, their possible use may be condoned for control of infestation. Petroleum distillate used alone appears safe, as determined by color and strength measurements. However, in normal use it would be combined with small quantities of other ingredients, in which case the safety is further dependent upon the ingredients added. The test samples treated with dichlorvos showed little or no change of color or strength. These results do not give unequivocal answers to the safe use of pesticidal chemicals, especially on antiquated and/or degraded materials, or for very lengthy periods. However, the experimentation illustrates how such chemicals can be tested under carefully controlled conditions and any changes in color or strength numerically assessed. Combined with prior experience, surveys and ongoing testing of pesticides by museum conservators in the field, the laboratory evaluations provide an important guide for specific recommendations of pesticide use with museum textiles.

The authors recognize several limitations of this preliminary study, along with suggestions for further work. The current research has focused only on cotton and wool textiles. Other materials such as leather, feathers, or plastic may be not necessarily amenable to similar conclusions. The general scope of the research should be expanded to include the manmade or aniline type dyes that were used increasingly in the nineteenth and early twentieth century. Likewise, there are numerous pesticides and fumigants, presently in use or suggested for use by conservators, which should be included in such controlled exposure type testing.

There are unresolved questions that could not be answered in this work, but would benefit from further study. For example, how much color change occurred in the dyed, control sample itself, independent of any pesticide exposure? Was there any dye–fabric interaction that would have resulted in a change of color with time? Is there a rigorous, uncomplicating means of accelerated aging the dyed fabrics prior to pesticide exposure? In this latter regard, most museum materials will have already "aged" fifty or one hundred years before they might be subjected to a serious pesticide regimen, e.g., for control of an infestation. Lastly, there are external factors of operator safety, plus local, state, and federal regulations, which must be considered by all researchers, conservators, or other users of pesticidal chemicals.

The best cure for insect attack is effective prevention. Careful, periodic inspection, housekeeping, and judicious use of pesticides can be valuable in preventing the need for heroic but potentially dangerous measures to the collection should a full infestation develop and strong treatment be prescribed. Awareness of the insect problem, attention to preventive maintenance, and a working relationship with a knowledgeable expert in textile/museum pest control are vital.

Literature Cited

1. Hueck, H. J. In "Textile Conservation"; Leene, J. E., Ed.; Smithsonian Institution: Washington, DC, 1972; Chap. 6, pp. 76–97.
2. Plenderleith, H. J.; Werner, A. E. A. "The Conservation of Antiquities and Works of Art," 2nd ed.; Oxford University Press: London, 1971.
3. Szent-Ivany, J. J. H. In "The Conservation of Cultural Property"; "Identification and Control of Insect Pests," UNESCO: Paris, 1968; pp. 53–70.
4. Beecher, E. R. In "The Conservation of Cultural Property"; UNESCO: Paris, 1968; pp. 251–264.
5. Rice, J. W. *Textile Museum Journal* 1969, 2(4), 31–33.
6. Moncrieff, R. W. "Mothproofing"; Leonard Hill: London, 1952.
7. International Wool Secretariat, "The Mothproofing of Wool," International Wool Secretariat, London.
8. McPhee, J. R. "The Mothproofing of Wool"; Merrow, Watford, Herts.: England, 1971.
9. Ebeling, W. "Urban Entomology"; University of California: Los Angeles, 1975.
10. Mallis, A. "Handbook of Pest Control," 3rd ed.; Mac Nair–Dorland: New York, 1960.
11. Testfabrics, P.O. Box 118, Middlesex, NJ 08846.
12. Kramer, J. "Natural Dyes: Plants and Processes"; Scribners: New York, 1972.
13. Hunter, Richard S. "The Measurement of Appearance"; Wiley–Interscience: New York, 1975, pp. 13, 140, 151.
14. Billmeyer, F. W., Jr.; Saltzman, M. "Principles of Color Technology"; Wiley-Interscience: New York, 1966.
15. "Annual Book of ASTM Standards: Part 32—Textiles"; American Society for Testing and Materials: Philadelphia, 1974 (or annually).

RECEIVED November 5, 1979.

INDEX

INDEX

A

Abrasion
  of covering fabrics 261
  of historic rugs 260–261
  resistance 317, 318
Absorption/transmission curves of
  cellulose acetate film 305
Acetic acid 280
Acetylation of groundwood 135
Acid(s)
  acceptor 319
  and alkalis, colorfastness to 284
  dyes 282
  effect(s)
    in cellulose acetate grafting .. 238
    in cellulose UV grafting ...233–238
    in gamma ray grafting to
      cellulose acetate 231–233
    in UV grafting
      of ethyl acetate 230–231
      of methyl methacrylate .227–230
      of styrene 226–227
  -free paper tube 269
  -free tissue papers 265
  paper
    extending life of 5
    upon heat aging, folding en-
      durance deterioration ... 48f
    morpholine–water vapor
      treatment of 54f
Acidity and accelerated aging of
  paper 189–204
Acidity reserve 66
Acrylonitrile 316
  grafting of 317
Actinometry 225
Adhesive(s)
  dry strength 324
  polyvinyl acetate 51
  tape 267
  water-soluble 17
Adipic acid 207
Aging
  accelerated 51–53, 87–88
  empirical equations of paper
    properties 177–188
  of paper, acidity and 189–204
  of paper, kinetic study of ..189–204
  yellowing during 88
  tests on washed Foldur Kraft
    paper 75t, 77t, 84t–85t
  tests on washed newsprint
    paper 76t, 78t, 82t–83t

Alizarin 294
Alkaline
  -buffered tissue papers 265
  earth bicarbonates 63
  extraction, chlorination and 124
  papermaking 241–249
  pulps 124
  reserve, paper 66, 78–81, 82t–85t
Alkalis, colorfastness to acids and 284
Alkalized paper 205–216
Alkyl ketene dimer sizing 47
All-rag paper 5
Alpaca, archaeological 294
Alum
  in book papers 50f
  –rosin sizing 46, 246
Aluminum-exchanged handsheets . 89
Aluminum pulp with Mg++ solu-
  tions, exchange of 103t
American Association of Textile
  Chemists and Colorists 278–279
American Library Association
  (ALA) 4
2-Aminoethyldiphenyl-borate 293
Amies papers, analyses of
            147t, 154t–155t
o-Aminophenol 135
Ammonium hydroxide 280
  fume test 284
Anhydroglucose ring 173
Antimony in currency 157
Antioxidants 135
Archival materials, conservation of 26
Archival treatments for library
  documents 13–23
Arrhenius plots 48
Arsenic 147
  in currency 158
  in paper 151–152
Association of Research Libraries
  (ARL) 5
Atomic absorption spectroscopy .. 66

B

Baccharis genistolloides 294
Barcelona, Central Library in 34, 35
Barium
  in currency 158
  hydroxide 38
  in paper 151
Barrow, William James 18, 45–46
  Research Laboratory 5
  preservation research at 45–55

Beating on folding endurance,
    effect of 209f
Bedspread storage 267–269
Belda, Sánchez 36
Bellows, metering pump 65
Benzoin ethyl ether 228, 235
Benzophenone 135
Benzoyl chloride 135
Berberis species 294
Bidens andicola 294
Binding, archival 17
Bismuth in papers 151
Bixa orellana 294
Bleaching of dyed textiles 263
Bleaching, pulp 124
Blue Verditer 152
Bond dissociation energies in paper
    constituents 126f
Bonding agent 208
Book papers 244
    impregnated with zinc carbonate 114t
Book restoration 39
Borax 88
Boric acid 335, 336
    color change by 338t–339t
Borohydride reduction of ground-
    wood 135
Boxes, acid-free 269
Brass candlesticks, analyses of ... 145t
Brazilin 294
Brazilwood 294
Breaking strength 320, 329
    of fabrics exposed to chemicals . 341t
    loss by pesticidal chemicals 341
Brightness
    and accelerated aging 180–187
    paper 115
    retention 75
    reversion 131–134
    stability and metal ions 133–134
Bromine in currency 159
Buffer system, paper 195
Burgess, Hugh 120
Burst properties 173
Bursting strength 123

                   C

Cadmium in currency 158
Calcium
    acetate 51
    bicarbonate 46, 88
    carbonate 47, 51, 123, 247
        in book papers 50f
        filter 89
    content and paper deterioration
        rate 74f
    hydroxide 46, 65, 88, 200
    in paper 151
    content 66t
Camelid 294
    fibers 297f
        blue and green 293t
        red 293t
        yellow and brown 292t

Candle bulb, scorch mark from
    artificial 257f
Carbohydrate materials, oxidation
    of paper 93t
Carbohydrates, over-oxidation of . 132
Carbon tetrachloride 335, 336
    color change by 338t–339t
Carboxyl content of hardwood
    kraft pulp 103
Carboxymethyl cellulose 207, 324
Carminic acid 294
Cataloging, centralized 8
Cation exchange 64
Cellulose
    acetate 226, 292
        films with UV stabilizers ..301–313
        grafting, acid effect in 238
            gamma ray 231–233
        lamination 18, 45
    deterioration of 63–64
    fibers 205–206
    fibrils as consolidants 324–330
    with metal ions, interactions
        of 102–104
    oxidations 190
    photodegradation 127–129
    radiation grafting of monomers
        to 233–240
    stability, metals and 88
    UV grafting of monomers to 233–240
Cellulosic fibers, crystallinity ...169–176
Center for Research Libraries 9
Central Library in Barcelona 34, 35
Cerium in currency 158
Cesium in currency 158
Chemical feeder process 64–66
Chemicals, price escalation of 245
Chemiluminescence from papers .. 177
China clay (Kaolin) 123
Chloride 245
Chlorination and alkaline extraction 124
Chromatography of blue dyes,
    thin layer 299t
Chromatography of red dyes,
    thin layer 298t
Chromium in currency 159
Chromium in paper 152
Chromophores, lignin 124, 134
Cinnabar 294
    pigment, cotton fiber with ..295f, 296f
Cleaning procedures, color reaction
    to historic 285–288
Cleaning of textiles and rugs ..270–274
Cloth lining materials 266
Cobalt in paper 151–152
Cochineal 294, 295
    on sheep wool 298f
Cold storage 16
Color
    change
        measurement of 336–337
        by pesticidal chemicals ...337–341
        in tested fabric 280t
    conservation problems 275–290
    descriptions, fabric and stain ... 276t

Color (*continued*)
difference equation, Scofield–
    Hunter 302
notation, Munsell 292–293
in pulps 123–124
reaction to historic cleaning
    procedures 285–288
reversion 131–134
stabilization 134–135
system, Munsell 276
transfer from fabric 279*t*
Colorants, historic 277
Colorfastness
to acids and alkalis 284
to daylight 284–285
to light 304
tests 278–279
Colorists, American Association
of Textile Chemists and ..278–279
Conservation
and cellulose crystallinity ...175–176
Center, New England Document 25–31
and grafting studies 239
problems, approaching 20–21
regional 25–31
in Spain, paper 33–44
Consolidants, application of ...315–332
Copolymerization, radiation 224
Copper 147
in currency 159
in paper 152
Corrosion of upholstery tacks 262
Cotton
chemical constituents of 122*t*
fiber with cinnabar pigment 295*f*–296*f*
fibers, yellow and brown 292*t*
fibrils 324–325
Council on Library Resources 5, 47
Curcumin 294
Currency, elements in U.S. 152–166
Curtain storage 267, 268*f*
Crocetin 294
Crocking, colorfastness to 279
Cross-linking, cellulosic 175
Crystallinity of cellulosic
fibers 169–176
Cyanoethylation 316–317

D

Dactylopius confusus 295
Dahl, Carl 120
Dandy roll 61
Daylight, colorfastness to 284–285
Deacidification 22, 38, 40, 46,
                        53–54, 88, 202, 205
of maps 101–102
mass 15–16
oxidizable material and paper ..93–96
process, diethyl zinc 113
Deacidifying paper, simultaneous
washing and 63–86
Decomposition, accelerated paper . 115
Decrystallization of cellulosic
materials 175

Degradation
accelerated 195
oxygen-independent paper 190
process, oxygen-independent ... 202
rate and acidity 195–199
of order in cellulose chain 171*f*
Deionized-alkaline system by
chemical feeder process 64*f*
Deionized water–alkaline system . 67
Deterioration
factors, paper 34
rate, calcium content and paper 74*f*
rate, temperature and 49*f*
Diazomethane methylation of
groundwood 135
2,2-Dichlorovinyl dimethyl
phosphate (DDVP) 335
Dichlorvos 335, 336
color change by 338*t*–339*t*
Dicliptera hookeriana 294
Diethyl zinc inhibition of paper
light sensitivity 109–117
Diethylene triamine 207
Dimethyl formamide 232
Dimethyldehydroresorcinol 135
Dimethyldichlorosilane 318–320
Disaster assistance, library 27
Discoloration
light and 125–131
of paper, photoinduced 127*f*
reactions 124–125
Dithionite 124
Document Conservation Center,
New England 25–31
Donor–acceptor interaction 237
Draining of consolidants 320–324
Drawings restoration 39–40
Dress, early twentieth century
historic 275–290
Dry strength adhesives 324
Drycleaning, colorfastness to 278
Drying cabinet, textile 272, 274*f*
Dye(s)
analysis of late intermediate
period textiles from Ica,
Peru 291–300
testing of 271*f*, 272
thin layer chromatography of
blue 299*t*
thin layer chromatography of
red 298*t*
type determination 278–281
Dyed textiles, bleaching of 263
Dyestuff
pink 282–283
recognition tests for historic
fabrics 280
yellow 282
Dylux 503 57–58

E

Ehrle, Father Franz 18
Electron microscopy 281, 292
scanning 294*f*–295*f*

Emery, Francis W. R. 18
Encapsulation, polyester film 18–19
Energy
  dispersive x-ray fluorescence .143–168
  price escalation of 245
  transfer 234
    radiationless 154
Epichlorohydrin 207
Ethyl acetate, acid effects in
  UV grafting of 230–231
Ethyl acrylate 230
  grafting to cellulose 225
Ethylzincoxycellulose group ...115–116

F

Fabric(s)
  color change in tested 280t
  color transfer from 279t
  exposed to chemicals, breaking
    strength of 341t
  patching with wood pulp ...325–330
  protection of light sensitive ..301–313
  sensitivity to light 254–258
  and stain color descriptions .. 276t
  wood in contact with historic 262–264
Fading 277
Fiber(s)
  analysis 292
  camelid
    blue and green 293t
    red 293t
    yellow and brown 292t
  content, reducing 246
  price escalation of 245
  yellow and brown cotton 292t
Fillers, mineral 123
Filter, calcium carbonate 89
Fixatives 38
Flavones 124
Fluorescence, x-ray 296f
  energy dispersive 143–168
Fold retention 67, 73
  in zinc-oxide treated papers
    exposed to light and
    humidity 116t
Folding endurance .66–74, 115, 123, 191
  and accelerated aging 180–187
  of aged paper, humidity and
                            217–222
  of book papers 52f
  deterioration of acid paper
    upon heat aging 48f
  humectant and 205–216
  of old papers 98t
  test 47
    MIT 53
  wet strength resin and 205–216
Foldur Kraft paper 72f
  aging tests on washed 75t, 77t, 84t–85t
  alkalized 212t
  folding endurance of 68t–69t
  impregnated 214t
  pH of 79f

Formic acid 229
  on UV grafting, effect
    of 228t, 230t, 231t
Framing supports 264–265
Fumigation 41
Fumigator, vacuum 26

G

Gallium in currency 159
Gallo, Alfonso 35–36
Gamma ray grafting to cellulose
  acetate, acid effects in 231–233
Genipa americana 294
Gimeno, Amalio 34–35
Glass objects, analyses of 146t
Glucose, total oxidation of 91
Glycerol 207
Glycosidic bond(s) 128, 237
Glycosidic linkages, hydrolysis of . 175
Gravity draining 321–322
Gray Scale for Staining 279, 280
Grotthus–Drapper Principle 125
Groundwood pulp 120

H

Haas, Warren J. 8–9
Hardwood kraft paper 89–90
Heat aging, folding endurance
  deterioration of acid paper
  upon 48f
Hemicellulose 122
  photodegradation of 129
n-Heptane 292
Historic
  cleaning procedures, color
    reaction to 285–288
  dress, early twentieth
    century 275–290
  houses, textile conservation
    in 253–274
  textiles, effects of pesticidal
    chemicals on 333–343
Hollander beater 16, 51
Homopolymer formation during
  UV grafting 228t
Humectant and folding
  endurance 205–216
Humidity
  and book papers impregnated
    with zinc carbonate 114t
  and folding endurance 209
    of aged paper 217–222
  and textile conservation 258
  zinc oxide and paper in 112t–113t
Hydrogen atom abstraction,
  intermolecular 234
Hydrogen iodide 111
Hydroperoxides in cellulose 128
Hydrosulfite 124
Hydroxybenzophenone 303
Hydroxybenzotriazole 303

I

Impregnated Foldur Kraft paper . 214t
Impregnation and folding
  endurance 212f, 213f, 215f
Impregnation, increasing folding
  endurance by 207t–208t
Impurities in paper, metallic 16–17
Indigo 293, 294, 340
  on sheep wool 299f
Indigofera suffruticosa 295
Indigotin 294, 295
Iodide
  protective effect of 112t–113t
  -treated paper 111
  treatment 115
Ionizing radiation 224, 238
Iron
  in currency 159
  in paper 152
  upholstery tacks 261–262

K

Kaolin (china clay) 123
Kraft paper
  accelerated aging of 179t
  bleached southern 65–86
  brightness for 187t
  folding endurance of 209
  hardwood 89–90
Kraft pulp, carboxyl content of
  hardwood 103
Kymene 557 207–208
Kymene and sorbitol, synergistic
  effect of 210t

L

Lamination 40–41
  cellulose acetate 18
Laminator, roller 45
Lanthanum in currency 159
Late intermediate period textiles
  from Ica, Peru, dye analysis
  of 291–300
Lawsone 294
Lead in currency 159
Lead in paper 152
Leaf caster 26, 39
Leaf casting 41
Library
  materials, conservation of 26
  of Congress 6–11, 14–16
  documents, archival treatments
    for 13–23
  materials, national preservation
    program for 5
  Resources, Council on 5, 26, 47
Life of paper, useful 46
Light
  -absorbing species 125
  and book papers impregnated
    with zinc carbonate 114t

Light (continued)
  colorfastness to 279, 304
  and discoloration 125–131
  fabric sensitivity to 254–258
  sensitive fabric, protection
    of 301–313
  sensitivity, diethyl zinc inhibi-
    tion of paper 109–117
Lignin 120, 122
  chromophores 124, 134
  photodegradation of 129–131
  retention of 123
Linear regression 198
  analysis 178
Lining materials, cloth 266
Lithographs 148
Lithopone 166
Llama, archaeological 294
Logwood 294, 340
Longevity, paper 16, 67
Lun, T'sai 119

M

Madder 294
  root 340
Madrid, National Library in 34
Magnesium
  bicarbonate 38, 46, 218–219
    solutions and papers 87–107
  methoxide spray 88
  silicate (talc) 123
Malachite 159
Maleic acid 200
Manganese in currency 159
Manganese in paper 152
Manuscript restoration 40
Maps, deacidification of 101–102
Mercury sulfide 294
Metals
  analysis of handsheets for 104t
  and cellulose stability 88
  ions, brightness stability and .133–134
  ions, interactions of cellulose
    with 102–104
Methanol 292
Methyl methacrylate, acid effects
  in UV grafting of 227–230
Methyl methacrylate grafting to
  cellulose 225
Methylsilicone 320
Microfilm unit, preservation 26
Microreproduction 5
Microwave drying of resin-treated
  fabrics 321
Mineral fillers 123
MIT folding endurance 210
  test 53, 66
Moisture absorption 316
Moisture in cellulose 128
Mold growth 258
Molecular mobility, cellulosic 170
Molecular order in cellulose ...170–173
Monomers as consolidants 316–324

Mordant dyes 283
Morpholine–water vapor treat-
     ment of acid paper 54f
Mulberry paper 29
Munsell color notation 292–293
Munsell color system 276
Museum textiles, pest control of .. 335
Museums, textile conservation
     in 253–274
Muslin sleeves 270

                    N

National
     Center for the Restoration of
          Books and Documents 36–42
     Library in Madrid 34
     preservation effort 1–11
New England Document Conser-
     vation Center 25–31
Newsprint 65–86
     degradation of 192
     paper 73f
     aging tests on washed 76t, 78t, 82t–83t
     folding endurance
          of 70t–71t, 219, 220f
     pH of 80f
     properties of unaged 200t
Nickel in paper 152

                    O

Opacifier, paper 166
Organic sensitizers 235
Oxidations, cellulose 190
Oxidizable material and paper
     deacidification 93–96
Oxygen
     -independent degradation
          process 202
     -independent paper degradation 190
     and paper degradation rate 198

                    P

Paper
     conservators, professional 29
     consumption 241–249
          world 243t, 244t
     deterioration factors 34
     property(ies) 211t, 218t
          and accelerated aging, empiri-
               cal equations of 177–188
          and cellulosic ordering ...173–174
          effect of beating on 208f
          kinetics 190–192
               and chemical kinetics ...199–200
     reference standard, spectrum of 149f
Paperboard consumption,
     world 243t, 244t
Papermaking 120
     alkaline 241–249
     properties of cellulose 170

Parchment restoration 42
Paris green 147
Pentosans 93
Peristaltic pump 65
Permanence/durability and pres-
     ervation research 45–55
Permanence evaluation 49
Peroxide 124
Perspiration
     colorfastness to 278–279
     stains 276
     tests 282
Pest control of museum textiles .. 335
Pesticidal chemicals on historic
     textiles, effects of 333–343
Petroleum distillate 335, 336
     color change by 338t–339t
pH
     and magnesium bicarbonate
          solution stability 90t–91t
     of paper(s)
          Foldur Kraft 79f
          newsprint 80f
          old 95–97
          and oxidizable material
               extraction 94t
          treated 76–78
     and paper degradation 192–195
Phases preservation 14–15
Phenoxy radicals 130–131
Photobleaching 130
Photodegradation
     of cellulose 127–129
     of hemicellulose 129
     of high-yield pulps 131
     of lignin 129–131
Photoinduced discoloration of
     paper 127f
Photoinduced yellowing 125
Photooxidative paper discoloration 127
Photosensitized discoloration of
     paper 127f
Pink dyestuff 282–283
Plasticizers 206
Plexiglass, UV-absorbing 256
Polyester film encapsulation 18–19
Polyethylene
     film lamination 40–41
     glycol 42
     oxide 207
     sleeve 269
     softening agent 320
Polyurethane varnish 264
Polypropylene 230
Polyvinyl acetate adhesive 51
Potassium
     in currency 159
     in paper 151
     persulfate 317
Preservation
     Office 7
     research at the Barrow
          Laboratory 45–55
     research, permanence/durability
          and 45–55

Pressure-sensitive tapes 20
Pretreating formula, fabric 286t
Prints restoration 39–40
Prussian blue 152, 159
Pseudopurpurin 294
Pulp(s)
  bleaching 124
  color in 123–124
  fibers, chemical constituents of . 122t
  photodegradation of high-yield . 131
  sulfite 134
  UV-light-induced yellowing of . 126f
Pulping operation, simulated 173
Pulping processes 121f
Purpurin 294
Pyridene 319

Q

Quinones 124, 130

R

Radiation copolymerization 224
Radiation grafting of monomers
  to cellulose 223–240
Radiationless energy transfer 154
Rag paper, properties of unaged .. 200t
Rare
  book rooms 16
  books 5
  materials 27
Raw materials, papermaking ...244–245
Rayon fibrils 324–325
de Reaurmur, Rene 120
Reduction of groundwood,
  borohydride 135
Restoration
  book 39
  of Books and Documents,
    National Center for 36–42
  drawings 39–40
  manuscript 40
  parchment 42
  prints 39–40
  seal 42
Reflectance 195
  and accelerated aging 180–187
  of old papers 100t
  standard, spectrum of paper ... 149f
Reinforcing agent 324
Reinforcing degraded textiles ..315–332
Relbunium hypocarpium 294
Research Libraries, Association
  of (ARL) 5
Research Libraries, Center for 9
Resin(s)
  as consolidants 316–324
  and folding endurance, wet
    strength 205–216
  -treated fabrics, microwave
    drying of 321
Resource limitations, paper 241–249
Rico y Sinobas, M. 34

Roller laminator 45
Rosin
  –alum sizing 246
  in book paper 52f
  sizing 123
Rubidium in currency 166
Rug(s)
  cleaning of textiles and 270–274
  runners, museum 259–260
  storage 270

S

Safflower 340
Scäffer, Jacob 120
Schinus molle 294
Scofield–Hunter color difference
  equation 302
Scorch mark from artificial
  candle bulb 257f
Seal restoration 42
Selenium in currency 166
Sheep wool, cochineal on 298f
Sheep wool, indigo on 299f
Sheet strength, paper 324
Shelf mark staining 265f
Silking 17–18
Silver in currency 166
Sizing 16
  agents 129
  alkaline 246
  alkyl ketene dimer 47
  of old papers 97–98
  rosin 123
  alum– 46, 246
Smoothness of old papers 98t
Soda, caustic 245
Soda pulp 120
Sodium borohydride 134
Sodium metasilicate 278
Softening agent, polyethylene 320
Sorbitol 209
  synergistic effect of kymene
    and 210t
Spain, paper conservation in 33–44
Spectral distribution, sunlamp 112t
Stark–Einstein Principle 125
Stiffness of old papers 98t
Storage of textiles 267–270
Strength specifications, paper 46
Strontium in currency 166
Styrene
  to cellulose, copolymerization
    of 224
  comonomer procedure 238
  grafting of
    acid effects in UV 226–227
  to cellulose acetate, gamma
    ray 232t
  with uranyl nitrate 236f
Sulfite pulp 134
Sulfur dioxide 88
Surface dust staining 265f
Swelling agent 319

T

Talc (magnesium silicate) 123
Tannins, condensed 124
Tape, adhesive 267
Tapes, pressure-sensitive 20
Tear resistance test 47
Tearing strength 208, 308–309, 320
  of old papers 98t
Temperature
  and cellulose crystallinity 174
  and deterioration rate 49f
  and oxidizable material
    extraction 96t
  on paper, effect of 47–51
Tensile
  energy absorption 102
  properties of old papers 99t
  strength 123, 173, 192, 193t,
           199, 201, 317, 325
    vs. cold extraction pH ...195f–197f
    of degraded fabrics repaired
      with wood pulp 330t
    loss measurement of 337
    time-ratios and 194f
Textile(s)
  Chemists and Colorists, Ameri-
    can Association of 278–279
  conservation in historic houses 253–274
  conservation in museums ...253–274
  effects of pesticidal chemicals
    on historic 333–343
  from Ica, Peru, dye analysis of
    late intermediate period 291–300
  reinforcing degraded 315–332
Thermomechanical pulps 121
Thin layer chromatography of
  blue dyes 299t
Thin layer chromatography of
  red dyes 298t
Tilgman, Benjamin 120
Time-ratios and tensile strength .. 194f
Tin in currency 166
Tissue
  Japanese 40
  papers, acid-free 265
  papers, alkaline-buffered 265
Titanium in currency 166
Titanium dioxide 123
Torsional modulus 323
Trace elements in paper 143–168
Trommsdorff effect 232, 238

U

Ultraviolet (UV)
  -absorbing plexiglass 256
  grafting of monomers to
    cellulose 223–240
  light, zinc oxide and paper
    in 112t–113t
  -light-induced yellowing of pulps 126f
  stabilizers, cellulose acetate
    films with 301–313
  /vis spectroscopy 298f–299f
Upholstery tacks, iron 261–262

Uranyl nitrate, grafting of styrene
  with 236f
Uranyl nitrate and UV grafting of
  methyl methacrylate 227t

V

Vacuum fumigator 26
Vacuuming a textile or rug 271
Varnish, polyurethane 264
Venetian blinds 255
Vicuna, archaeological 294
Völter, Christian 120

W

Wash table, stainless steel 272
Washing, colorfastness to 278
Washing and deacidifying paper,
  simultaneous 63–86
Water, price escalation of 245
Water retention 173
Watermarks 57–62
Watt, Charles 120
Weathering resistance 318
Wet cleaning 272–274
Wet strength resin and folding
  endurance 205–216
Wetting agent 321
Williams, Gordon 5–6
Window covering techniques 256
Window shades 255–256
Winsor, Justin 4
Wood, chemical constituents 122t
Wood in contact with historic
  fabrics 262–264
Wood, discolorations of 124
Wood pulp, fabric patching
  with 325–330
Work tables, padded 270

X

X-ray fluorescence 296f
  energy dispersive 143–168
Xenon-arc lamp 303

Y

Yellowing 199
  during accelerated aging 88
  vs. cold extraction pH 195f–197f
  determination 201
  dyestuff 282
  of modern papers 119–141
  reaction 124–125
Young, John Russell 4
Yttrium in currency 166

Z

Zinc 147–148
  acetate dihydrate 303, 305
  carbonate, book papers impreg-
    nated with 114t

Zinc (*continued*)
  in currency 166
  inhibition of paper light sensi-
    tivity, diethyl 109–117

Zinc (*continued*)
  oxide and paper in humidity 112t–113t
  oxide and paper in UV light 112t–113t
  in paper 152

The paper upon which this book is printed is 50# Decision White Opaque Smooth, 580 ppi, which is manufactured by S. D. Warren Company and distributed through Lindenmeyr Paper Corporation.

The paper was analyzed at the Research and Testing Laboratory of the Preservation Office of the Library of Congress. The following properties were determined:

pH	8.4
% calcium carbonate	5.44
TAPPI brightness	77
folding endurance, ½ kg	
MD	2683
CD	2497

Jacket design by Carol Conway.
Editing and production by Robin Giroux.

The color insert was printed by Wolk Press, Incorporated, Woodlawn, MD. The book was composed by Service Composition Company, Baltimore, MD, and printed and bound by The Maple Press Company, York, PA.